A CULTURAL HISTORY
OF WOMEN

VOLUME 1

A Cultural History of Women
General Editor: Linda Kalof

Volume 1
A Cultural History of Women in Antiquity
Edited by Janet H. Tulloch

Volume 2
A Cultural History of Women in the Middle Ages
Edited by Kim M. Phillips

Volume 3
A Cultural History of Women in the Renaissance
Edited by Karen Raber

Volume 4
A Cultural History of Women in the Age of Enlightenment
Edited by Ellen Pollak

Volume 5
A Cultural History of Women in the Age of Empire
Edited by Teresa Mangum

Volume 6
A Cultural History of Women in the Modern Age
Edited by Liz Conor

A CULTURAL HISTORY
OF WOMEN

IN ANTIQUITY

Edited by Janet H. Tulloch

Bloomsbury Academic
An imprint of Bloomsbury Publishing Plc

B L O O M S B U R Y
LONDON · OXFORD · NEW YORK · NEW DELHI · SYDNEY

Bloomsbury Academic

An imprint of Bloomsbury Publishing Plc

50 Bedford Square	1385 Broadway
London	New York
WC1B 3DP	NY 10018
UK	USA

www.bloomsbury.com

BLOOMSBURY and the Diana logo are trademarks of Bloomsbury Publishing Plc

Hardback edition first published in 2013 by Bloomsbury Academic
Paperback edition first published in 2016 by Bloomsbury Academic

British Library Cataloguing-in-Publication Data
A catalogue record for this book is available from the British Library.

ISBN: 978-08578-5097-3 (HB)
978-1-8478-8475-6 (HB set)
978-1-3500-0918-9 (PB)
978-1-3500-0984-4 (PB set)

Library of Congress Cataloging-in-Publication Data
A catalog record for this book is available from the Library of Congress.

Series: The Cultural Histories Series

Typeset by Apex CoVantage, LLC, Madison, WI, USA
Printed and bound in Great Britain

CONTENTS

SERIES PREFACE

A Cultural History of Women is a six-volume series reviewing the changing cultural construction of women and women's historical experiences throughout history. Each volume follows the same basic structure and begins with an outline account of the major ideas about women in the historical period under consideration. Next, specialists examine aspects of women's history under eight key headings: the life cycle, bodies/sexuality, religion/popular beliefs, medicine/disease, public/private, education/work, power, and artistic representation. Thus, readers can choose a synchronic or a diachronic approach to the material—a single volume can be read to obtain a thorough knowledge of women's history in a given period, or one of the eight themes can be followed through time by reading the relevant chapters of all six volumes, thus providing a thematic understanding of changes and developments over the long term. The six volumes divide the history of women as follows:

Volume 1: A Cultural History of Women in Antiquity (500 B.C.E.–1000 C.E.)
Volume 2: A Cultural History of Women in the Middle Ages (1000–1500)
Volume 3: A Cultural History of Women in the Renaissance (1400–1650)
Volume 4: A Cultural History of Women in the Age of Enlightenment (1650–1800)
Volume 5: A Cultural History of Women in the Age of Empire (1800–1920)
Volume 6: A Cultural History of Women in the Modern Age (1920–2000+)

Linda Kalof, General Editor

LIST OF ILLUSTRATIONS

CHAPTER 8

symbolism of everyday life as expressed in customs, values, and human relationships. Their interpretation of symbolism harked back to the early academic
roots of historical studies, in which terms such as *metaphor*, *representation*,
and *symbol* were taken up by nineteenth-century cultural historians—especially
Jacob Burckhardt (1818–97), Wilhelm Dilthey (1833–1911), and Johan Huizinga
(1872–1945)—to explain the mentality or "spirit of an age." Through studying
anthropological theories of culture, twentieth-century historians began to see
their own approach to the past as a "kind of retrospective ethnography."[4]

Feminist scholarship in the 1960s and beyond made a substantial contribution to the cultural turn in historical studies. From both within and outside
of the discipline, feminist theorists concerned with the lack of scholarship on
women's history began to challenge traditional historical categories (e.g., "Did
Women Have a Renaissance?")[5] and long-accepted authoritative references in
the field that excluded the lives of women. New scholarship in the discipline of
history that developed in the early 1980s was especially influenced by research
done by scholars working on women in antiquity. Sarah B. Pomeroy states that
it was her aim in *Goddesses, Whores, Wives, and Slaves: Women in Classical
Antiquity* (1975) "to write a social history of women through the centuries in
the Greek and Roman worlds" since most of the standard works in her discipline of classics did not include women.[6]

While the terms *social* and *cultural* seem to be used interchangeably in many
studies, one of the key differences between a social and a cultural history is that
social history tends to emphasize the day-to-day living and working conditions
as well as the legal status of its subject matter. Both social and cultural histories strive to be inclusive of people from all social strata in the population, a
goal that is rarely achievable due to the types of sources (discussed later on)
that have survived. A cultural history tends to emphasize imagery and literary
works as a special type of historical source in addition to documentary sources
that appear to be more objective, such as ancient histories or legal texts. This
is done in order to construct a fuller version of the historical reality of one's
subject. In this way, the historical imagination becomes more transparently a
subject of the historian's research. Attention to the historical imagination can
draw out narrative, representational, or ideological qualities in documentary
sources. While this volume contains information relating to the social history
of women, the emphasis is, as our title suggests, on cultural practices derived
from a wide array of sources.

Outside the broad field of history, feminist theorists concerned with symbolism and gender in language, including Judith Butler, Helene Cixous, Mary
Daly, Luce Irigaray, Julia Kristeva, Monique Wittig, and Mieke Bal, as well

as feminist art and film historians such as Griselda Pollock, Peggy Phelan, Linda Nochlin, and Laura Mulvey, to name only a few scholars, have contributed significantly to the growing academic discourse on gender, sexuality, and history. By the end of the twentieth century, this discourse was spilling over into most disciplines. The theories of these intellectuals contributed to the destabilization of the academic ideal of objectivity in scholarly discourse, the notion of fixed meanings in texts and visual representations, and the assumption of gender-neutral positions in ancient sources and contemporary research. Filtered through the discipline of history, their analyses of texts, art, and film raised serious questions about the historicity provided in any type of document. Further, in a series of books and essays,[7] postcolonial theorists Edward Said and Gayatri Chakravorty Spivak among others added pointed criticisms to the feminist analysis of history by calling attention to Western hegemony in scholarship, specifically drawing attention to Western historians' assumptions about the exotic "other." Feminist theorists found the term *colonizer* useful when discussing the question of whether or not women had ever had a culture of their own making, or whether women's culture making had always been directed and shaped by patriarchal interests.

WHAT IS A CULTURAL HISTORY OF WOMEN?

The title *A Cultural History of Women* implies an assumption that women—in this case those who lived in antiquity—possess a culture or cultures that can be identified as distinct from male culture, whether women are members of the same society as men or constitute a separate society. It is the view of this volume that based on sources that support the scholarly construct of "Western antiquity," the cultural divide between men and women is highly marked. However, it is unclear how much of this representation of ancient society is ideological and how much is historically reliable. According to Greek literary sources, for example, there was an understanding among male elites of women and men as belonging to separate "races" (γένη)—of males and females belonging to separate "nations" of humans who sometimes mingled in the other's sphere.[8] This idea of gendered "races" can also be found in Latin literary sources such as Virgil's *Aeneid*. Against this notion of separate races is Aristotle's (384–322 B.C.E.) perception that women are simply sexually inverted men, with the male serving as the human standard. Both ideas of male-female relatedness circulated in antiquity with each view marking the evidence for a separate women's culture in different and problematic ways.

Introduction

JANET H. TULLOCH

In this digital age, where the events of last week seem like a decade ago, younger readers might be wondering what significance the cultural history of women who lived 2,500 to 1,000 years ago has for them. Let me begin to answer that question by stating that the knowledge and documentation of women's ancient cultural history can provide a type of historical legitimacy to women's ongoing struggles for equal consideration and rights in our own time. It can be suggested, for example, that the practice of skilled midwives in ancient Greek and Roman civilizations brought a social and historical legitimacy to the North American midwife movement of the 1980s and 1990s. In another example, the evidence and practice of women who acted as priestesses in ancient Greek and Roman religions and as leaders in early Christianity and Judaism heighten the cultural legitimacy of women's ongoing struggles for sacramental authority and leadership in today's world. Many other examples could be cited. The important point is that a volume such as this one offers "a crucial set of counternarratives"[1] to the idealized representation of woman so frequently found in ancient texts and visual imagery produced by male elites. L. Stephanie Cobb writes about the rhetorical portrayal of women in early Christian texts, but Cobb's comments on the complexity of reconstructing the lives of historical women apply to the problems of researching historical women in all fields of Western ancient history, including art and archaeology. Despite these obstacles, feminist scholarship has contributed to a process whereby historical women have "come into view with greater clarity and higher levels of differentiation"[2] than the knowledge that existed even twenty-five years ago. This body of research, a portion of which can be found in this volume's bibliography, reminds all of us who live in the twenty-first century that ancient women affected, interacted with, and rejected discourses written, painted, or pronounced about them.

Many of the concerns of ancient women are ongoing in the lives of twenty-first-century women: poverty, education, work, economic independence, social relations, marriage, children, and power. Questions asked by the various authors in this volume include: Under what conditions and constraints did ancient women negotiate their lives? How different were their conditions of experience from ours? Did women have an individual identity? Economic independence from men? Legal rights? Wealth? Status? How did they communicate with one another? How did negative views of women arise? Discussion of these and other stimulating questions can be found within the chapters of this volume.

Before we turn to an introduction of the individual chapters, it is essential to understand the larger theoretical framework within which the individual essays rest. We begin with a brief discussion of the discipline of cultural history and then present our rationale for a cultural history of women in antiquity. This section is followed by a discussion of ancient sources and their problems. We then present the scope of the volume, followed by a preview of each of the eight themes explored here: the life cycle, bodies and sexuality, religion and popular beliefs, medicine and disease, public and private, education and work, power, and artistic representation. We conclude our introduction by way of offering a few remarks on "trends" or "patterns" to watch for in the 1,500 years of women's cultural history gathered and interpreted by the international group of scholars who have contributed their expertise to this volume.

WHAT IS CULTURAL HISTORY?

Cultural history (*Kulturgeschichte*) is a subfield of the academic discipline of history that had its formal beginnings in the research of male scholars working at the University of Berlin in the mid-1800s. Up until the mid-twentieth century most historical research within this discipline was focused on political history, especially military events or what some feminists of the 1970s called the "bang bang" theory of history.[3] According to Peter Burke, the "cultural turn" took place in historical scholarship sometime during the 1960s with the emerging interest among historians in anthropological theories of culture. Unlike art historians, anthropologists tended to ignore "high art" and focused more on the

It has been argued by Judith Butler and others that Western notions of es-
sentialism with regard to sexual difference are rooted in the assumptions of
Greek, male philosophical discourse on the nature of human beings. Other
scholars such as Ross Shepard Kraemer maintain that Western religions, especially the book of Genesis in the Hebrew Bible, authorized and continue
to naturalize gender difference and gender hierarchy in the West. No doubt
both sources contributed to today's discourse of sexual difference as "natural."
While the extant evidence from antiquity speaks of women as a group (i.e.,
"race"), this construct is part of the ancient historical discourse of male elites.
Readers should therefore take care not to read acceptance of sex or gender es-
sentialism into references using ancient terminology. Because the notion of a
male/female cultural divide was part of the prevailing ideology of Greek and
Roman *male* elites, we are only able to speak of a women's cultural history
in antiquity with some caution. While some fragments, like Sappho's poems,
are tempting, we do not have enough evidence from the female point of view
to know whether women in antiquity would have agreed with the notion of
separate races or how they would have interpreted such an idea. Finally, those
culture-making practices in antiquity that can be claimed by women raise the
issue of whether such practices were directed and shaped by women or by patriarchal interests. This issue is left as an open question for the reader to consider after working his/her way through the various chapters in this volume.

Recent Histories on Women in Antiquity

Since Pomeroy published her ground-breaking book *Goddesses, Whores,
Wives, and Slaves* in 1975, many excellent anthologies and monographs have
followed. Each of the themes explored in this volume—the life cycle, bodies
and sexuality, religion and popular beliefs, medicine and disease, public and
private, education and work, power, and artistic representation—represents
a substantial body of scholarship on women and antiquity that did not exist
thirty years ago. The reader will find many of these works cited in the volume's chapters and in the bibliography.[9] However, a few recent publications
in the field of women's and ancient history deserve to be highlighted here.
Indeed, some of them have been written or edited by the scholars who have
contributed to this volume. The following overview therefore is restricted to
the themes investigated in this book.

A topic frequently overlooked in scholarship on antiquity, the older adult,
especially older women, is addressed in *On Old Age: Approaching Death*

in Antiquity and the Middle Ages (2010), edited by Christian Krötzl and Katariina Mustakallio. In this volume, this topic is discussed in chapter one. The question of women's private life in antiquity and their relationship to the public/private sphere discussed in chapter five can be found more fully articulated in Kristina Milnor's *Gender, Domesticity, and the Age of Augustus: Inventing Private Life* (2005). With regard to the question of gender and agency in religious rituals, a book devoted exclusively to Greek and Roman women's rituals in the Mediterranean area, *Finding Persephone*, edited by Maryline Parca and Angeliki Tzanetou (2007), contains a number of excellent essays on a topic that is difficult to source. Carolyn Osiek and Margaret Macdonald's *A Woman's Place: House Churches in Earliest Christianity* (2006) presents the textual and visual evidence for women as leaders of house churches in ancient Christianity, with an essay on frescoes from the Roman catacombs of women presiding at funerary banquets contributed by Janet H. Tulloch. A new collection of articles on prostitution, *Prostitutes in the Ancient Mediterranean, 800 B.C.E.–200 C.E.*, edited by Madeleine M. Henry and Allison Glazebrook, a coauthor of "Bodies and Sexuality" (chapter 2), was released in 2011. Finally, Ross Shepard Kraemer's *Unreliable Witnesses: Religion, Gender, and History in the Greco-Roman Mediterranean* (2011) interrogates the intersections among ideologies of gender, religious practices, and representation of these practices through the analysis of case studies. Contrary to the views of some scholars working with ancient sources, Kraemer maintains that despite the problems with the evidence, "some aspects of women's practices . . . remain perceptible."[10]

A few important source books with information on women in antiquity have been compiled or updated in the last ten to fifteen years. These include Mary R. Lefkowitz and Maureen B. Fant's *Women's Life in Greece and Rome: A Source Book in Translation* (2005), Ross Shepard Kraemer's *Women's Religions in the Greco-Roman World: A Sourcebook* (2004), Emily Kearns's *Ancient Greek Religion: A Sourcebook* (2010), and Lynda Garland and Matthew Dillon's *Ancient Greece: Social and Historical Documents from Archaic Times to the Death of Alexander the Great* (2010). Though not specifically about women, Michael Maas's *Readings in Late Antiquity: A Sourcebook* (2010) is an important collection of later materials, including sources from the Byzantine empire. For a discussion and evaluation of the use of ancient epigraphic sources for history, see John Bodel's *Epigraphic Evidence: Ancient History from Inscriptions* (2001). It is to the subject of our sources and their problems we now turn.

ANCIENT SOURCES AND THEIR PROBLEMS

In writing a social or cultural history, scholars rely on primary sources that are made (visual and material culture) or written (literary, sacred, legal, or historical documents) or inscribed (epigraphic) by the group under study in addition to external sources contemporary with the time period that confirm the subject's historical existence. In the field of ancient studies, most extant sources about women were authored or made by elite men from the same or culturally similar societies. One view on ancient sources holds that ancient data, especially texts on women, are historically unreliable so far as reconstructing an objective history of women is the goal.[11] According to this view, what can be recovered is not "real" women but "the ways ancient authors used women to engage in rhetorical, philosophical, or theological contests."[12] A different and more accepted view holds that it is possible to recover "some aspects of women's practices"[13] from ancient sources by applying the appropriate methodology to an ancient source. According to this position, the methodology acts as a kind of archaeological field tool, filtering out the unwanted elements from the ancient source and leaving the "genuine" traces of historical women behind.

Though the use of a methodology is far more nuanced than I have described, it is important to explain why scholars find it necessary to use a methodology at all. When a researcher considers the application of a method[14] to his or her data, he or she does so because ancient sources are not neutral or self-evident in the sense that they contain biases from their own time. Understandably, ancient sources come with all sorts of opinions, attitudes, assumptions, and worldviews that ancient authors and art makers took for granted and, consciously or not, embedded in their cultural products. For example, terms used in antiquity to describe a subject, such as *superstitio*, can be a tip-off to the underlying assumption or worldview toward a particular event written about in a text. A methodology, when used properly, can render embedded worldviews that appear seamless or natural (such as a gender ideology assumed in the ancient text or image), visible to the reader. In the case of ancient studies, scholars use a variety of different methods to help unlock the internal logic of a set of data before they are analyzed. Pomeroy, for example, analyzed types of ancient classical texts with regard to their historical reliability. Surprisingly, she found that the literary genre of "comedy" from both the classical and Hellenistic periods and not legal texts, as one might expect, rated higher in historical reliability because comedy "shows ordinary people rather than heroes and heroines, and is [therefore] a more reliable source for the social historian."[15] In this volume the editorial position has been to strike a balance between the preceding two views on ancient sources, keeping in mind that the historians who contributed to this volume were aware not only of their sources' biases but also of potential "blind spots" in the application of any contemporary methodology to ancient materials.

As already hinted at, a few sources attributed to ancient women authors have survived from antiquity.[16] Something of the female voice, for example, remains in Greek and Roman poetry,[17] accounts of early Christian martyrdoms,[18] pilgrimage journals,[19] and various other genres from the classical and imperial periods (for more on this topic see chapter 6). Some early Christian apocrypha (noncanonical texts) are also attributed to female authors or compilers.[20] To what degree these sources were written by women is a matter of some debate.[21] With regard to visual and material culture, Pliny the Elder (23–79 C.E.) mentions a few Greek female painters by name,[22] but unfortunately we have no extant pottery with their signatures. However, a *caputi hydria* attributed to the Leningrad painter (460–450 B.C.E.), shown in Figure 0.1, depicts women working beside

FIGURE 0.1: Women working beside men in a painting workshop. *Caputi hydria* attributed to the Leningrad painter (460–450 B.C.E.). (Photo credit: Canali Photobank, Milan, Italy.)

men in a painting workshop. As with texts, visual imagery carries its own representational issues (see Shelby Brown's chapter on artistic representations, chapter 8). Similar to rhetoric used in texts, visual strategies can manipulate historical elements to create a new narrative or idealized portrait of the subject.

Our ability to describe the ancient social reality of women is thus limited by our sources. Further, most of our evidence relates to the lives of elites and subelites, rendering large sections of the population, the poor and the working poor, invisible. Nonetheless, until further discoveries, these are the only sources we have with which to work. We now turn to an outline of the scope of this book followed by a brief preview of the individual chapters.

THE SCOPE OF THIS BOOK

In a study of women in antiquity that attempts depth as well as breadth, one problem that immediately arises is the question of which groups of women to include. "Greek" and "Roman" women are typically the foundation of such a study, yet these terms are not so much geographic as they are cultural—their importance derives from the profound influence their rich traditions in politics, the arts, religion, and philosophy have exerted on the development of Western civilization. Given the limitations of space and the demands of a time period spanning 1,500 years, scholars in this volume were given latitude to include those geographic groups of women that were most significant to their subject matter. For example, the reader will find Egyptian princesses, a female *archisynagogos* (ruler or leader of a synagogue), and Byzantine empresses who appear in some chapters but not others. A further consideration in covering our time period was the issue of how to convey the complexity of each theme across the vicissitudes of time without minimizing the impact of these changes on the lives of women. In some chapters this challenge was met by drawing on the expertise of two scholars working in different time periods but on similar subject matter. In those chapters not authored by two scholars, the emphasis on sources within the 1,500-year time span is varied: some chapters focus on women in Greek and Roman sources and others on evidence from late antiquity (300–1000 C.E.). It has to be stated, however, that the primary emphasis of this volume is on women in Greek, Roman, and early Christian sources.

The question of periodization raises a third problem—one that includes both of the issues already mentioned. Antiquity defined as 500 B.C.E. to 1000 C.E. essentially encompasses a number of "antiquities": Greek, Roman, early Christian, Byzantine, and late antiquity. In some academic circles, anything

past 500 C.E. is considered the *early medieval* period. For most historians, accepted constructs of "antiquity" end around 200 C.E., when Rome is still stable
as the capital of an enormous empire and Constantine I has not yet arrived on
the scene to carry off the center of Western civilization to Byzantium. This is,
of course, a model of Western history based on traditional periodization—a
model still deeply ingrained in scholarly disciplines.

Recognizing the problems of periodization for historians of women's culture, Bernadette J. Brooten, in a programmatic essay published more than
twenty-five years ago, called for a shift in perspective and method that would
place women in the center of the historical frame. In her essay, "Early Christian
Women and Their Cultural Context: Issues of Method in Historical Reconstruction,"[23] Brooten called for a cognitive shift that challenged the accepted
wisdom of scholarly methods in the humanities: entrenched historical periods,
canons of art and literature, and unexamined typologies, as well as the sources
typically used in the reconstruction of historical reality. As the reader will dis-
cover in the individual chapters, some of these shifts have begun to occur. Perhaps we can think of the period 500 B.C.E.–1000 C.E., defined as "antiquity"
for this volume, in the way Brooten suggests—as a fresh reorganization of time
that places women in the center of the historical frame. As such, we suggest
that the period is flanked by two important events in the history of Western
women: the introduction of democracy in some Greek city-states, from which
citizen women were excluded even though a powerful queen sat on the throne
of Sparta,[24] and the declaration by the Council of Rome in 1059 C.E. that monastic women were to be considered as part of the laity, thus reducing female
clerical power to that of an ordinary churchgoer.

Understandably, readers might protest the bracketing of the time period for
this volume by two negative events in the cultural history of women. Surely there
were episodes in the lives of women near these dates, 500 B.C.E. and 1000 C.E.,
which we could point to that demonstrate their achievements. And there were:
the reader can find them in Lynda Garland's chronology of powerful women in
chapter 7. But when it comes to measuring the impact of events from antiquity
on women's cultural history in the West, it must be remembered that the right
to vote was not enshrined until the early twentieth century in most Western
countries and that despite women's advances in securing sacramental authority in some denominations of Judaism and Christianity, twenty-first-century
women cannot be ordained as priests in the Roman Catholic church. Nor do
they have formal power in other religions. Despite what might seem like a dark
age for women's cultural history, the scholars in this volume have approached
their individual subjects with rigor and creativity. In many cases, they have

worked with fragments and/or obscure sources to shine a light on the lives of ancient women so that they "come into view with [even] greater clarity and higher levels of differentiation." It is to a description of the individual chapters that we now turn.

In the chapter on the life cycle, Finnish scholar Katariina Mustakallio brings a social and cultural approach to what typically is perceived as a biological cycle. Her approach demonstrates that the "life cycle of a female slave was certainly different from that of a noble female citizen." She traces the life cycle of a girl from the womb to old age, including sections on female slaves, drawing our attention to peculiarities within different cultural marriage systems. Mustakallio notes that unlike in many Western societies today, there was a high regard for age. Elderly women, especially those from the various religious orders or elite families, were publicly venerated and appreciated.

Allison Glazebrook and Nicola Mellor in chapter 2 focus on gender as a social construction and sexuality as a social practice. They view female bodies as a site where gender identity and difference are performed. Within the ancient family, cultural practices of masculinity and femininity intersected with status, based on wealth and birth, linking gender to other types of identities. The authors find, however, that despite the restrictions imposed on women, "something of female autonomy and agency" in ancient cultures is revealed in "women's self-presentation and 'transgressive' desires."

Against the brand of "the infamous feminine" so frequently found in Greek, Roman, and Christian mythology, chapter 3 presents a chronological summary of what scholars know about the ritual practices of ancient women in Greek and Roman religions, early Judaism, and early Christianity. Janet H. Tulloch argues that despite the loss of the feminine divine in Western religions and the gradual suppression of female sacramental authority during 1,500 years of women's religious history, women maintained their practices of certain rites in private and forged new roles for the expression of their spiritual authority when others were closed to them. They also contributed to the advancement of the authoritative traditions in Western religions even when their involvement was not acknowledged nor welcomed by male religious elites.

In the chapter "Medicine and Disease," Steven Muir and Laurence Totelin investigate their subject from a number of different perspectives. Secular, religious, and magical data best capture the obscure and fragmented data relating to women and ancient medicine and disease. Because of their problematic sources, they use a "hermeneutic of suspicion" when analyzing the texts, especially particular cosmetic or pharmacological texts attributed to women. These scholars do not rule out the possibility of female authorship, only the probability that ancient authors with names like "Cleopatra" were authentic; that is, the texts were most likely pseudonymously written not only to lend authority to their remedies but also, one assumes, to attract a large audience.

In chapter 5, Kristina Milnor takes up the challenge of the ancient ideals that framed men's and women's activities and experience as gender-segregated spheres. Using representation theory, Milnor analyzes her sources to determine the "differences between ideology and social practice," noting the contradictions and negotiations of public/private ideologies expressed in philosophical and dramatic texts. In textual sources, gender segregation is most commonly referenced in the definition of physical space within the Greek *oikos*. According to Milnor, this model has yet to be confirmed archaeologically. Despite male rhetoric, during the Hellenistic and late Republican periods and during the early Roman Empire, our sources indicate that women became more visible in public life, especially as they moved into the management of their own businesses, properties, and finances.

One widely held assumption that Marcia Lindgren identifies in the introduction to her chapter on education and work is the positive view of slavery: "probably the most important cultural difference [between the ancient world and our own] is the institution of slavery and its unquestioned acceptance in antiquity. . . . The culture of slavery was so entrenched in the ancient world that slaves, upon being freed, purchased slaves." As unpaid labor, slaves contributed to the household economy as workers, educators, and even business representatives on behalf of their owners. However, slaves had the same legal status as property and so could be worked to death by an unjust owner with impunity. The education of freeborn children was left to individual families, or, for those who could afford it, tutors were hired. According to Lindgren, in some Hellenistic cities, private benefactors provided support for all freeborn children to receive a basic education. Except for Sparta, where education for girls was compulsory and consisted mainly of gymnastics and music, even a woman from an elite family received minimal instruction.

In chapter 7, Lynda Garland presents us with a chronology of powerful women beginning with classical Greece and ending with the imperial women of the Byzantine Empire. According to Garland, Byzantine empresses "ruled in exactly the same way as emperors: they presided over the court, appointed officials, issued decrees, settled lawsuits, received ambassadors and heads of state, fulfilled the emperor's ceremonial role, and made decisions on matters of financial and foreign policy." One way imperial women secured their power was through their display of public piety such as pilgrimages and the acquisition of holy relics. Although they could not personally lead an army, according to Garland, many empresses, like Irene, wife of Leo IV, played a role in government unprecedented in the classical world. Like their royal sisters, nonimperial women in Byzantium could hold property and administer their own estates. Some women maintained economic independence by running shops or household workshops that made clothes for sale.

Shelby Brown's chapter, "Artistic Representation: Survival of the Classical Ideal," considers how women are depicted in visual images across the 1,500 years covered by this volume. Despite the changes in location, culture, and religions, Brown argues that it is possible to identify consistently depicted attributes of women such as beauty, sexuality, and female modesty that reflect ideal physical, moral, or behavioral qualities originally found in classical art but traceable in subsequent art forms through the succeeding centuries.

CULTURAL PATTERNS ACROSS THE YEARS

Trends or patterns readers might wish to look for in the following chapters include increasing economic independence for women in the Roman and Byzantine empires, the mixed attitudes toward women and education within the Greek and Roman empires, the growing political power of imperial and noble women in the Roman and Byzantine empires, women's loss of religious authority in Western religions, the gradual acceptance of celibacy as a lifestyle choice for women, and the continued idealization of female beauty, sexuality, and modesty in artistic representations—even those of the Virgin Mary. If these trends seem contradictory or inconsistent to the reader, that is because, ultimately, they are.

CHAPTER ONE

The Life Cycle: From Birth to Old Age

KATARIINA MUSTAKALLIO

Aging and age-related behavior, as well as attitudes concerning different periods of life, have become popular topics in recent years in both the social sciences and the humanities. It is in this context that the life course approach to societies has developed. However, the concept of the life cycle is problematic. We can approach human ages from the biological, chronological, or social point of view and come to quite different conclusions. The differences between the life courses of women and men can produce different life stages in childhood, adulthood, and old age.

Even if the life course begins with birth and ends in death, it is not a description of biological aging. It is historically, socially, and culturally constructed and does not necessarily follow biological development. This is particularly true of the life course of the female members of premodern societies. We are born into the social structure and the gender system of a society. Becoming a male or a female citizen is a long cultural process that can be observed via chronological age to create social norms of male and female development and socialization. The way an individual reacts to gender and life course expectations varies according to his or her sex status, wealth, and so on. In any case, our ways of describing age, sex, or gender differences are culturally determined, yet both gender and the life course are elements of the underlying structure of a society.[1]

When we approach the life cycle of women in antiquity, we should keep in mind that the world of antiquity was geographically a very large area as well as being historically a very long period. Even if we focus on the two great centers of culture, Athens and Rome, we still have a variety of ethnic, religious, and class differences that might not always conform to the expectations that we find in textual evidence that survives from antiquity. The life cycle of a female slave was certainly different from that of a noble female citizen. Then, of course, there were differences within any social subgroup of women.[2]

Furthermore, values and attitudes concerning gender and the life span vary historically. The gender order of a society is not stable but changes continuously. This is true even within Greco-Roman antiquity.

THE LIFE SPAN IN ANCIENT AUTHORS

The common practice among Greek and Roman authors divided the life span of a human being into different periods according to the abilities connected with them. According to Marcus Terentius Varro (116–27 B.C.E.), the first part, childhood (*pueritia*), lasted from birth until the age of fifteen; then came the age of youth (*adulescentia*), which lasted from fifteen to thirty; after that a person from thirty to forty-five was *iuventus*; persons who were over forty-five were *seniors*; and old age started in the sixties (*senectus*). Of course, this model followed the life cycle of a healthy male citizen. In primary sources we do not find any references to "female adolescence."[3]

In Greece, children started their schooling at around the age of seven. Poets, according to Aristotle, usually divided the life cycle into seven-year periods. A man reached puberty around the age of fourteen, became grown up at twenty-one, and so on. Even the age of sixty was an honorable age, but if a person reached the age of seventy he or she was considered to have fulfilled the whole life cycle of a human being.[4]

In the world of antiquity different ages were considered to be under the protection of different divine powers and especially under the influence of planets that, according to astrological wisdom, guided the life of a human being. The moon was the main guide during the first four years. Then, Mercury took over the guardianship of the life of the young person. From the age of fourteen to twenty-one, Venus was the main guardian. The adult person was under the protection of the sun until about the age of forty-five, then Mars, Jupiter, and finally Saturn took care of him or her. There were, of course, even more sophisticated assumptions concerning the influence of different planets on the life cycle and the fate of the human being. The natal constellation of the planets, according to common belief, influenced the personality or temperament, as well as one's fortune in life.[5]

Most of the life stages known to us from ancient texts tend to focus on the male life course. In this chapter the female life course will be reconstructed from fragmentary, mainly literary sources. In so doing, we begin with the section, "From the Womb to the Female Adolescent," which examines the period from the social birth to the age before marriage, and then move on to a discussion of betrothal and marriage in "Transition to Adulthood." The life of the mature women until old age is the focus of "Matronal Life."

FROM THE WOMB TO THE FEMALE ADOLESCENT: A GIRL IS BORN!

There are not many sources from antiquity concerning female childhood or childhood in general. As was the case with other subordinated groups in antiquity, children were usually defined as being unlike adults, particularly adult males. Behavioral differences between girls and boys received relatively little attention in literary sources.[6]

FIGURE 1.1: Scribonia Attica's tombstone. A representation of childbirth information. Terra-cotta bas-relief (28 by 41.5 centimeters), Necropolis of Isola Sacra, Ostia, first to second century C.E. (Photo credit: Museum of Ostia, Italy.)

The birth of a child did not automatically make it a member of the family. The acceptance of the father of the family, the *kyrios* in Athens and *paterfamilias* in Rome, was needed for a child to become socially born and to start its life course as a member of the family. The father of the family decided whether to keep the child or to abandon it. The decision depended on factors such as the size of the family and the economic situation. Poor families had to choose which children they could afford to keep, and wealthier parents had to think about their property and its division between their heirs after their death. If there were too many children, even in wealthier families, the expectation of a decent quality of life might not be fulfilled. There were, of course, other causes for the exposure of a baby, such as its poor physical condition or possible visible defects. Children, and especially female offspring, were abandoned for different reasons, even if the practice of exposure was less frequent than originally thought—as has been the subject of recent discussion.[7]

In most cases, the birth of a child was a happy and desired event. The role of a girl in the family depended, of course, on the question of whether she was the firstborn, the last born, or in between. The firstborn child created the next generation, and typically this birth delineated the stages of the life cycle not only for her but also for her parents and grandparents, if living. The birth itself was a dangerous process and required the help of midwives and the protection of divine forces. Artemis and Diana were the goddesses who helped in childbirth; Juno Lucina gave light to the eyes of the newborn; and Egeria and Carmenta, prophetic nymphs and givers of life, protected the child.[8]

In Athens, when a girl was born, tufts of wool were hung outside the door of her home. Five days later, the nurse took the baby and carried her around the family hearth followed by a cheerful procession of the family members (*amphidromia*). In Rome the front door was decorated with flowers after the birth of a child. There might have been a special ceremony in which the father raised the child ritually in his arms and in this way acknowledged it as his legitimate child.[9] After that, the child was accepted into the household and thought to be under the care of the family gods as well as those already mentioned. The family then arranged a feast for her; after that, exposure was no longer possible.[10]

In antiquity the average life expectancy was relatively low. According to many researchers the death rate for children between zero and five years of age was roughly one-third to one-half of all births.[11] As little children were considered very vulnerable, they were protected in many ways. In Rome, when a child was born, three men from the family were selected to perform certain rites. They were called after the three divine forces: Intercidona (symbolized by an axe, which protected the women giving birth), Pilumnus or Picumnus (who protected children with his pestle), and Deverra (she who sweeps the evil out). These three men performed sacred rituals to protect the newborn from evil powers and especially from the bad influence of the wild deity called Silvanus. The ritual activities took place during the night when the men walked around the house representing these deities. First they struck the threshold with an axe, after that with a pestle, and finally they swept it with a broom. These ritualistic actions were believed to prevent Silvanus, a terrifying god of the wild nature, from entering the house of the newborn. After the first days, special deities took care of every stage of a child's development, from its first steps to its first words.[12]

In antiquity parents gave children different kinds of amulets to protect the children from the evil eye and demons, as well as diseases and bad luck. A traditional amulet for little children was the *fascinum*, a pendant in the shape of a phallus. Young freeborn boys wore a *bulla* in Rome, but we know that in areas near Rome, in Lavinium, and in Etruscan cities, both girls and boys used amulets as a symbol of their status as freeborn children.[13] In early Christian families children were supposed to be under the special protection of the saints. According to Jewish and Christian traditions children were protected with Hebrew verses from the Torah or miniature Gospels, which were carried by children in small boxes.[14]

When a baby girl was accepted as a member of the family, the next step was to give her a name. In Greece the tenth day after the birth was dedicated to this special celebration and feast.[15] In Rome, according to Plutarch, the girls were named when they were eight days old and boys when they were nine days old; the day was called *dies lustricus*, purification day. Giving a name to a child emphasized the beginning of the development of a personal identity. Girls in Greece were usually given the feminine forms of the names given to the boys. Sometimes they were given names according to certain ideals, like Euphrosyne (happiness) or Eirene (peace).[16] Girls in Rome received their names according to their family names and the order of their birth, such as Claudia Tertia or Agrippina Minor. Individual names for daughters became common during the early imperial period.[17] After the naming of a child the process of socialization started immediately, as did growing up as a gendered human being.[18]

When the mother was not available, a wet nurse took care of the child by breast-feeding and caring for it.[19] A child then spent most of its time with the nurse. This practice was quite widespread in Greek and Roman antiquity, and not only in upper-class families.[20] Until the age of six or seven, for both girls and boys, socialization took place mostly within the household. According to the traditional view among scholars, unmarried girls lived with their little brothers and mothers in the women's quarters of their houses. In Athens, boys left their younger siblings when they were about seven years old to go to school. Their sisters stayed at home until marriage. Siblings were of central importance in the socialization process of children, and elder sisters and brothers were often important role models for their younger siblings.[21] Nevertheless, children in the home and its close vicinity were in contact with a large number of adults—family members and servants—who were influential in their upbringing.

Children's Activities

The construction of gender was reinforced by children's play and their toys. Different types of play were considered appropriate for girls and boys. As freeborn boys' games prepared them for public life in the community, freeborn girls were encouraged to play games related to their future roles as wives and mothers. According to the classical tradition, the girls of Sparta enjoyed the greatest freedom: they took part in sports and performed many roles publicly. It seems that some Etruscan girls had similar freedoms: in recent excavations, some types of sports equipment, such as *strigils* (a metal tool for scraping off sweat and dirt), have been found in the graves of Etruscan women.[22]

There is much and varied visual evidence from antiquity picturing children at play. Both girls and boys played with dolls, cymbals, rattles, tops, balls, clay animals, and the ubiquitous knucklebones (*astragoloi*). These toys were later dedicated to protective divinities. Games typically engaged in by boys were contests of strength and blood sports: cockfighting was very popular. In reliefs on tombs and sarcophagi, girls are often represented with birds or other pets. Frequently, these reliefs had religious connotations as well.[23]

Participating in the Community

Children participated quite actively in private and public religious life. In domestic cults, children—both girls and boys—were always needed. They assisted in sacrifices, carrying sacrificial tools, singing, and praying. In many rituals there were special qualities required from the young participants. In Athens, a child with both parents living (*paideis amphitaleis*) distributed bread to the guests in marriage rituals. In Rome, we find the same kind of requirements for children participating in rituals; they were supposed to be *patrimi matrimi* (with both parents alive).[24] Children were actors in several religious festivals, for they were thought to bring good luck. Girls were active especially in rituals that prepared them for their future roles in the family.[25]

The importance of religious rituals in the socialization of youngsters is evident in the classical world. In particular, noble girls and boys participated in public life by engaging in religious rituals and choruses, which were highly popular in Greece and Rome. Through these rituals and ceremonies, children were recognized and appreciated by wider circles than their family and neighbors. Young females defined as virgins performed their rites in their own groups—and at religious festivals they seem to have been differentiated from adult women and younger children as well—corresponding to the ritual grouping of young males. The visibility of young females might have been related to the status of their parents. Consequently, their prominence in rituals was a means for families to maintain their status from one generation to the next.[26]

The most revealing example of age-related service in ritual is from the Athenian sanctuary of the goddess Artemis in Brauron. Athenian girls between the ages of five and ten served as "bears" at the sanctuary during the festival held every five years.[27] For Athenian girls the age of ten marked a transitional point from childhood to a potentially marriageable age. The age of ten coincided with Roman preferences for the age of betrothal for girls, too. Service as a "bear" can be seen as a pre-menarche rite of passage for these girls who were entering the phase of puberty in their biological development. The ritual service to Artemis was a public action in the community that sought to control the transition from a girl to a pubescent or marriageable maiden by the public performance of service to Artemis.[28]

In Rome the maturation rites of boys were important milestones in the life of the community. Boys of fourteen to sixteen years consecrated their amulets, *bullae*, to the Lares (protectors of the family) during the Liberalia festival, the celebration of the maturation of teenage boys in Rome. One of the few instances where we find any information about the puberty rites of the Roman girls is in Arnobius's book *Adversus Gentes*, written in the fourth century C.E. In this text, Arnobius listed the old Roman customs. One of these consisted of presenting a maiden's garment, that is, a toga, to the temple of Fortuna Virginalis. According to Roman tradition Fortuna Virgo or Virginalis took care of new brides and brought them luck.[29]

Training for the Future

We have much more evidence about boys' education than girls' in both Greek and Roman society. According to the literary tradition, Sparta was perhaps the only ancient city that prescribed a general education for girls. Accordingly, it has been questioned whether Greek or Roman girls and women in general could read and write.[30]

In general, girls probably received training from older females, either family members or slaves. The part considered most essential in a girl's training for life, as a wife and mother capable of running a household, took place in her own home. In Rome, in wealthy families, both sons and daughters were often taught by a learned slave. A daughter in a wealthy Roman family did receive some years of education, making her a literate and educated person, a factor in the creation of her high status in adulthood.[31]

The *oikos* or *domus*, the home of wealthier citizens in Greece and Rome, was the central place for women, children, and slaves. Men spent time outside of the home in baths and outdoor activities in the agora or the forum, or taking care of family business with clients and freed slaves. Athenian girls and women, especially those of noble origin, were kept more strictly inside their homes than Greek men. During the Hellenistic period the rigid discipline of the Greek *oikoi* relaxed, and even high-born ladies could walk outdoors, but not without an escort. In Rome, the home was a meeting place for a *patronus* (the patron of the house) and his clients as Roman men kept an office (*tablinum*) inside their homes. We have also some information, mostly from Latin inscriptions, naming a wife of an important *patronus* as *patrona*, and consequently very probably receiving her clients at home as well. Even if women in Rome were in general more visible than in Greece, noblewomen lived much of their lives inside their houses, exceptions being celebrations of major religious or political festivals.[32]

Middle-class women, of course, took care of family business and could walk more freely on the streets and squares. In the countryside, lower-status women worked with their husbands and children outside in the fields, and in towns they worked at home and in workshops—as they had done for centuries. Textile workshops in particular were populated by female workers.[33]

FIGURE 1.2: Workshop sign, Pompeii. Location: Mostra Augustea, Rome, Italy. (Photo credit: Alinari/Art Resource, NY [ART39105].)

The socialization of girls took place at home, where they were expected to learn spinning, weaving, and sewing. Nevertheless, their mothers invited family friends and neighbors to the home. The patron of the house could, of course, invite his clients and friends home as well, and, especially in Roman families, it was customary to invite guests and organize dinner parties in which the female members of the family could participate.[34] In Rome, communal meals within the family were a popular custom. Especially in imperial families, children were expected to be present during mealtimes. The age at which children began to recline while eating is not entirely clear, but typically the turning point was marriage for girls and the assumption of the *toga virilis* for boys.[35]

From Slave Girls to Freed Women

In recent decades several studies have explored the impact of status on children: legitimate or illegitimate, freeborn or slaves, biological or adopted.[36] Slave girls started work at a very early age, around five. Normally children worked with their parents, girls helping with spinning wool, weaving, cleaning the house, and so forth. Sometimes even freeborn parents had to hire out their children to pay their debts.[37] Slave girls and boys in the domestic sphere could even study with freeborn children—especially in Rome—and they could form close emotional ties with the family, especially if a slave child was *collacteus* or *collactaneus*, breast-fed by the same nurse as the children of their master. Nevertheless, their whole life was dependent on their master or mistress. The childhood of a slave was not protected in any way. The owner was free to use slaves in whatever way he or she decided. Public opinion could influence the owner's acts, but sexual abuse or beatings of slave girls and young women were considered a private matter. A slave girl did not own her body, nor did an adult slave woman. It was not unusual for the owner to have sexual relationships and father children with his slaves.[38]

When a slave woman was freed in Rome, she finally won the right—in principle—to decide the use of her own body. The artistic expressions of this new social status are evident in thousands of epitaphs, statues, and decorations on the tombs of freed people in Rome. On these tomb *stelae*, freedwomen were represented with all the epithets of a traditional Roman matron in her highly respected *pudicitia* form. The Roman matron was technically untouchable. According to Roman law, adultery with a married woman of citizen status could bring harsh penalties. The family of *Liberti* appreciated their new status as freed citizens by erecting monuments, even in honor of their sons and daughters who had died prematurely.[39]

TRANSITION TO ADULTHOOD: THE BEST
DAY OF YOUR LIFE?

"I offer thee to wife, to get thee lawful children."[40]

In patriarchal societies like Athens and Rome, marriages were strongly patrilineal: a girl moved from her father's home into the home of her husband's family. Girls and women lived under their families' male guardianship all of their lives, first that of their fathers, then their husbands or guardians, and finally their sons when they came of age. A father gave his daughter, usually a young girl twelve to sixteen years old, away to a husband who was usually much older. An age gap of about eight to ten years or more was common in Greco-Roman society, although in Sparta the age difference between husbands and wives was less.[41]

The preparations for the girl's marriage might have begun several years before the actual wedding took place, through the parental search for an appropriate husband—preferably one of equal or higher social and economic status compared to the family of the bride. In both Greece and Rome girls were betrothed early—in Rome perhaps even a little earlier than in Greece, at the age of seven to ten. The girl's life in general was focused on a future of marriage and family life. Upper-class girls were usually betrothed earlier than those of the lower classes. Until the time of her first marriage, the girl usually remained in the house where she had grown up. Once the day of the wedding was set, preparations for the ceremony, her bridal outfit, and the dowry were begun.[42]

In classical Greece the legal system and dowry practices varied from polis to polis. If a father could not provide a dowry for his daughter, it would have to be produced by relatives or even by the city itself. The size of an Athenian dowry was, of course, dependent on the prosperity of the girl's father. When the marriage was to take place, the girl consecrated her toys to the temple of Artemis. Her hair was cut, and her girdle was offered to Athena Apatouria.[43] Then the bride took a ritual bath in water drawn from a sacred spring. These practices symbolized a transfer from childhood to adulthood and changed the status and identity of a celibate girl into a wife through the union of marriage. At the same time the bride underwent many significant transformations. The jewelry a bride wore at her wedding represented part of the wealth of the household, but by far the largest expense for her parents was her dowry. The bride and the groom prepared for the wedding by means of offerings, dedications, and sacrifices. These prematrimonial practices were seen as purifying and propitiatory rites.[44]

There were few alternatives to marriage in the classical world. In Athens, girls were usually married between the ages of fourteen and eighteen; in Rome girls could be legally married at the age of twelve, and boys at fourteen, but the norm was rather different. Girls were generally married in their late teens to young men in their late twenties. First marriages were usually arranged by parents or guardians, and personal emotions or feelings played little or no part in the process.[45]

In Greece the marriage was constituted by the acts of *engue* (pledge), *ekdosis*, and *gamos* (wedding feast). In Athens the bride was not considered a legal agent, and her presence was not necessary at the *engue*, where the arrangement of the dowry was settled. The wedding was designated by the terms *ekdosis* and *gamos*. *Ekdosis* means the giving away of the bride from father to husband in order to create an *oikos*.[46]

There were, of course, differences between the Greek and Roman gender and family systems. In Rome there were no legal obligations for a dowry to give validity to a marriage, even if it was a widespread custom. The dowry became the full legal property of the husband, or his *paterfamilias*, once it was handed over to him.[47] The verbal consent between the bride and groom fulfilled the *matrimonium*. In Roman marriage ceremonies, the gender order, and especially the roles of wife and husband, was established by the rituals. The formula pronounced by a bride, *ubi tu Gaius ibi ego Gaia*, "Where you are Gaius, I am Gaia," has been connected to these practices. The actual consummation of the marriage took place in the bedroom after the ceremonies. The day after the wedding, the groom would hold a dinner party at his house, and at this time the bride made an offering to the gods of her new home.[48]

One special distinction that differentiated Athenian or Roman female citizens from other women in antiquity was that only matrons could produce legitimate children who had full citizenship rights. Even if this seems self-evident, it meant that the status of Athenian "female citizens," especially after Pericles' Citizenship Law, and that of the Roman matrons from the Republican age on, was quite unique. To produce legitimate children was one of the most important duties of all citizens. Living in a legitimate marriage was a precondition for successful participation in the public life of the city. In this sense, the private sphere encroached on the political sphere. We should not underestimate the importance of this precondition in the differentiation of the lives of women in antiquity.

Furthermore, a citizen without offspring suffered from shame. A girl who was married and did not become pregnant in due time was defined as sterile and deserted. If she did not have any property of her own, her status was miserable. On divorce she would be returned to the house of her father or guardian, and it was unlikely that she would be sought for a second marriage.[49]

Peculiarities in the Roman Marriage System

As in Greek as well as Roman marriage, the focal question concerned the distribution of property: How much should the daughter take to another family by dowry or by inheritance? The particularities of the lives of women rested on this fundamental question.

Traditional marriage in Rome was called *matrimonium cum manu. Manus,* which literally means "hand," was a relationship in which the wife (and all her property) was under the jurisdiction of the husband or, if the husband was not juridically independent (*sui iuris*), even that of his father. She was regarded as being *filiae loco*, in the position of a daughter, in relation to her husband. Thus, the wife in *manus* marriage could possess no property of her own, and everything was under the control of her husband.[50]

The first and most traditional type of *manus* marriage was called *confarreatio*.[51] The ritual of *confarreatio* took its name from the use of cake made of spelt (*far*) in a sacrifice made to Jupiter. The *confarreatio* marriage survived into the empire because it was essential to the maintenance of state religion. The principal *flamines*, priests of Jupiter, Mars, and Quirinus, and the *rex sacrorum*, the priest named sacred king, as well as their wives, had to be born of parents married in *confarreatio*, and the priests themselves had to marry in this way. It was originally a marriage confined to the old families of pure patrician origin. The *confarreatio* marriage of the Flamen and Flaminica Dialis was virtually indissoluble.[52]

The second and more common type of *manus* marriage was called *coemptio*. It represented a "bride purchase," as the groom paid *nummus usus*, a penny, and received the bride in exchange. While this purchase was not a real sale, it symbolized the traditional bride purchases of earlier societies. Only five witnesses were required, and the wedding ceremony was much less formal than a *confarreatio*, but the bride still passed to her husband's *manus*.[53]

The third type of marriage is somewhat more unusual and was obsolete by the end of the republic. *Usus* was a practical marriage that did not require an actual wedding ceremony; it was a transfer to the *manus* of the husband by default after cohabitation. The only requirement for an *usus* marriage was that the man and woman cohabitate for one full year. The woman would then pass into her husband's *manus*. There was one loophole, however: she would not do so if, within that year, the woman stayed away for three consecutive nights (*trinoctium usurpation*).[54] From the second century B.C.E., *manus* marriages became rarer. The new form, called *sine manu*—already known in the Laws of the XII tables (450 B.C.E.)—by which the wife remained under her own father's control, became more popular.[55]

Sine manu marriages solved one of the main problems of marriages of daughters: When the female stayed under her father's control, the property she inherited did not merge with the property of her husband's family. If the daughter died without children, her property reverted to her original family. Of course, later on, women made testaments for the benefit of their children, but even these typically required the approval of the woman's original guardians if they were still alive.[56]

MATRONAL LIFE

Living with a Husband in Rome

At the end of the Republican and the beginning of the imperial era, in Roman families a close relationship between husband and wife was highly honored. One of the requirements for a valid marriage was the consent of both parties. The warm relationship between husband and wife was an ideal often venerated in private statues and reliefs as well as in inscriptions on tombs.[57] Whether these inscriptions represent genuine affection or simply public piety between the spouses is unknown. Perhaps some hint regarding the question of affection between spouses is given by the rise in divorces during the Hellenistic period in Greece and the late Republican period in Rome.

During the Augustan period, the new legislation made by this emperor highlighted the importance of marriage and the relationship between husband and wife in a manner that was unprecedented in the ancient world. Augustus made every effort to increase the number of citizens through a new family policy emphasizing family and marriage. Therefore, it is not surprising that the writers of the first century also emphasized the importance of marriage as a basis of the integrity and national identity of the Roman people.[58] The first marriage of a girl—as well as a young man—was normally decided by the parents, but when divorce became more frequent, women could influence the second choice and be more active in searching for a suitable candidate for her next marriage. Divorce in ancient Rome was usually a private affair, and only the parties involved were notified.

The custody of children was usually entrusted to the father and his family. There were, nevertheless, other solutions. According to the *Codex Justinianus*, the emperor Diocletian (reigned 284–305 C.E.) gave this answer to a woman named Caelestina who had petitioned him about her children after the divorce: "However, the appropriate judge will decide whether the children ought to stay and be cared for at the father's home or at the mother's after a marriage has been broken up."[59] Therefore, it was possible for a judge to rule in the mother's favor on such occasions.

Sexual Life Cycle

It has often been said that sexuality in antiquity lacked the modern categories of heterosexual and homosexual.[60] The differentiating characteristic in this cultural binary system was activity versus passivity, or penetrating versus being penetrated. Notions of Greco-Roman masculinity were based on being the active partner in sexual activity with a female or male. Active women, on the other hand, were not considered honorable but were perceived within the culture as *hetaerae* or prostitutes.[61] (More will be said on this topic in chapter 2.) Nevertheless, in classical Greece and Rome, sexuality was considered a part of ordinary life, and not sinful as such. Still, the chastity of women was one of the basic values held in antiquity. Girls started their active sexual life quite early. It was assumed that girls developed a desire for sexual relations with the onset of puberty. For freeborn girls, marriage was the only suitable arena for sexual relations, and they were expected to be virgins when entering married life. Why was virginity so highly esteemed and important?

For reasons that are explained in chapter 2, it was a common idea in antiquity that women were not capable of controlling their sexuality. From their teens on, girls were looked on as sexual objects. Epictetus mentions that "women from fourteen years old are flattered with the title of 'mistresses' by the men. Therefore, perceiving that they are regarded only as qualified to give the men pleasure, they begin to adorn themselves, and in that to place all their hopes."[62] According to this source, it was male attention that persuaded young women to become more interested in "pleasing men." Women had to be controlled and kept away from male non-kin.

We may assume that in patriarchal societies the sexual freedom of women has always been seen as a threat to the social and economic order. With regard to male concern over offspring and inheritance, it was central to this order that men controlled the reproduction of their women. In the background to this issue there were, as well, certain irrational assumptions on the preconditions of fertility: Only a purified land could produce good fruit. A woman whose reputation and origin was uncertain could carry polluted blood that would produce only prodigal offspring. This becomes evident when we look more carefully at the story concerning the Intermarriage Law (*Lex Canuleia*) in Rome during the early republic. According to Livy the high-born patricians were against the *Lex Canuleia* because they were afraid of contamination. Intermarriage between patricians and plebeians would bring them to the situation "that nothing might be pure, nothing unpolluted": "The son of such a marriage would be ignorant to what blood and to what worship he would belong." The threat of the mixture of pure and impure was one of the *longue durée* fears of the Romans.[63]

Furthermore, there were differences in sexual attitudes toward women according to the cultural background and age of a woman. Sexual life was considered a natural part of human life. Aemilia Pudentilla, a rich and noble lady from Oea, Roman North Africa, decided to marry Apuleius, a young and famous orator, in the middle of the second century C.E. This marriage became scandalous, and finally the local prosecutor challenged Apuleius to explain why Pudentilla married him after fourteen years of widowhood and why, being a much older woman, she accepted a young man. Fortunately, the answer of Apuleius—his *Apologia*—still exists. Apuleius points out that the physical illness induced by sexual abstinence drove Pudentilla to announce her intention of remarriage. Pudentilla's case reveals the standard negative arguments against older women, but at the same time it shows the attitude that an active sexual life was considered to be healthy even for older women.[64]

Pregnancies and Miscarriages

The life cycle of a woman could include marriages and miscarriages. In Rome, divorce, particularly in noble families, was frequent. Married life, as discussed earlier, usually started quite early. Fertility was low for young women, and children did not usually come until the late teens and beyond. Rates of miscarriages and infant mortality were high. Tullia, Cicero's daughter, who married very young, was on her third marriage when she finally became pregnant and produced her first child—which did not survive. Quintilian's wife had borne two sons before she died at the age of eighteen, but neither of the children survived after the age of five. Even for mature women, childbirth was a dangerous business. For example, Pliny the Younger states that both daughters of his friend Helvidius died during childbirth.[65] Soranus, the second-century Greek physician practicing in Rome, argued against very early intercourse on the basis that young bodies were not yet ready to produce children. Another threat for women was the use of unsafe methods of birth control and contraception methods that were very risky for women's health.[66]

One of the peculiarities of the Roman reproductive system was the passing around of fertile women from one husband and family to another. There are two well-known examples: Martia, first the wife of Cato and later of Hortensius, and Livia, first the wife of Tiberius Claudius and later of Augustus. Both were passed to another man even though they were pregnant by the first husband. It is not known how common this habit was in the circles of noble families. Nevertheless, according to Plutarch, "when a Roman man had a sufficient number of children to rear, another, who lacked children, could persuade him to the step, relinquished his wife to him, having the power of surrendering her entirely or only for a season."[67]

FEMALE EXPERIENCE AND SOCIAL EXPECTATIONS OF OLDER WOMEN

A woman who travels outside the house must be
of such an age that onlookers might ask, not
whose wife she is, but whose mother.[68]

In antiquity the attitude toward one's golden years was ambivalent. In classical literature from Hesiod to Virgil older people were often seen as a burden for the younger generations and old age in general as incorporating all the malevolent features of life. Furthermore, older women from a low stratum of society were often abused and usually ridiculed in classical literature. An old drunken courtesan attempting to cover her aging in order to remain younger looking is a common stereotype in the visual arts and satirical literature like the *Satires* of Horace.[69]

At the same time, the attitude toward old people was often respectful, as they still had power and wealth. As widows in particular, women in old age might, in practice, have enjoyed considerable authority because they controlled the family wealth to some extent.[70] This respectful attitude is evident in several realistic statues of older women that show the signs of aging without any hesitation. For those women—or for their families—the signs of aging were not a problem but a source of high status.[71]

According to Hesiod there was an old proverb: "Deeds belong to young people, council to those of middle years and prayers to old people." In the religious sphere the highly honored status and important position of older priestesses kept in mind the value of experience and age. In Roman hierarchical society, the high regard for age was a basis for venerating elderly upper-class women.[72] In the religious practices of the female cultic spheres like the Apollonian Sibyls and the Vestal Virgins, this attitude always played a central role. Even after death, these women were still honored in several ways. In Rome public funerals were organized to honor the memory of Roman matrons, especially those of families of consequence. This shows the central importance of the communal memory of the female members of the nobility.[73]

CONCLUSION: THE FEMALE LIFE CYCLE—WHAT A JOURNEY!

The premodern world has traditionally been seen as hostile toward women and children in general: emotional and physical violence and negligence in caregiving traditionally characterize the picture of the period. Undeniably, premodern societies were violent, and childhood in many respects was full of hazards even for the offspring of wealthy families. As we have seen, in antiquity, the average life expectancy was relatively low. However, this observation can be misleading when we study everyday life in local communities. The average life spans for ancient women and men are skewed by the high infant mortality rates at childbirth and in the early years of life. Nevertheless, there were differences in the life cycle between genders. The fact that the sexual life for girls could begin from the age of twelve certainly increased the number of deaths caused by childbirth and childbed fever. The deaths of small children and their mothers were an integral part of Greek and Roman life. Having passed the critical years of childhood, youth, and childbearing, women could expect to live a reasonably long time.

CHAPTER TWO

Bodies and Sexuality

ALLISON GLAZEBROOK AND NICOLA MELLOR

The body and sexuality have become important topics for feminist historians and gender studies in the past twenty-five years, generating a large corpus of scholarship. Much of this work reacts to Michel Foucault's seminal work, *History of Sexuality*, in particular, volume 2: *The Use of Pleasure*, and volume 3: *The Care of the Self*,[1] which identified gender as a social construction and sexuality as a social practice but ignored women and female desire. The body is an important locus for producing and displaying gender identity and difference, and it links gender to other identities, such as social and economic status and ethnicity. Most scholars today recognize that ancient discussions of the female body and sexuality highlight the secondary status of women in ancient cultures and women as objects of exchange and dispute between men. Despite the many restrictions imposed on women and their varied bodies by cultures more broadly, the ways in which their bodies were marked, represented, conceptualized, and regulated also reveal something of female autonomy and agency in ancient cultures through consideration of women's self-presentation and "transgressive" desires. While there is much diversity between and within the Greek, Roman, and Christian worlds, there are also important similarities in practices and attitudes. This chapter outlines the most significant similarities and differences in these areas and of necessity, given the nature of the evidence, focuses on Athens, Rome, and the early Christian world.

THE FEMALE BODY IN THE GRECO-ROMAN TRADITION

In ancient Greece and Rome, the female body and sexuality were directly connected to the concepts of *sôphrosunê* and *pudicitia*. Neither concept is easily translated into English. While these concepts apply equally to free men and women, gender affects the definition of each term.[2] Classical Athenian society expected female kin and particularly the married woman to manifest *sôphrosunê*. The primary characteristics of female *sôphrosunê* were a woman's sexual virtue and obedience to her father and husband.[3] In ancient Rome, *pudicitia* referred to the sexual virtue of the Roman *matrona*.[4] In both cultures, such virtue was suggested through behavior and dress and distinguished wives and daughters from slaves and prostitutes. Whereas the Roman woman could possess *pudicitia* as a quality, the Athenian woman attained *sôphrosunê* only through her containment in marriage and the wearing of the veil. Sexual impropriety, even if only implied, damaged the reputation of both Greek and Roman women, as well as the honor of her father and husband and any children. The connection between female sexual virtue and male honor led to restrictions on female behavior and dress, strict penalties for adultery, and strong differentiation (at least conceptually) between wives and prostitutes. At the same time, dress and adornment became a way for women to exert control over their bodies by enhancing their appearance and asserting their sexual virtue and social status.

Imagining the Female Body

In both Greek and Roman culture, conceptions of the female body paralleled images associated with the earth and fertility. In Greek and Roman mythology, earth was represented as a female goddess. The Greeks called her Gaia. According to Hesiod, she was a primordial goddess from whom the other gods were born. She was a mother and nurse to all living creatures on earth.[5] The Romans referred to her as Tellus and associated her with fertility, prosperity, and abundance. The emperor Augustus used her persona and associated traits to represent his new Rome: the *Ara Pacis* of 13–9 B.C.E. depicts Tellus surrounded by stalks of grain and livestock cradling two babes on her knee.[6] Imagery surrounding intercourse and procreation conflates human reproduction with the cultivation of the earth. The new bride is a field to be plowed: according to Menander, the father handed over the bride at the Greek wedding ceremony with the words, "I give my daughter to you for the plowing of legitimate children."[7] Plutarch refers to the production of children in marriage as the most sacred kind of sowing and plowing and to offspring as the crop and fruit of intercourse.[8] In Latin examples, Plautus and Lucilius use *arare* (to plow) and *molere* (to grind) as euphemisms for intercourse.[9] The unmarried girl was frequently described as a ripe fruit or flower about to be plucked. Sappho refers to a maiden as the ripe apple on the tree waiting to be picked. Persephone is picking flowers in a field at the very moment Hades springs forth from the earth and plucks her to be his bride. In his marriage hymns, Catullus refers to the bride in the bridal bed as having a face like a flower and to the untouched maiden as a flower in a fenced garden.[10] Greek and Latin agricultural terminology, such as *sulcus* (furrow), *ager* (field), *guai* (fields), and *kêpos* (garden), can refer specifically to female genitalia.[11]

Greco-Roman literature also associates the female body with excessive appetites. The archaic poet Semonides in his poem on women equates women with various animals: the sow woman, donkey woman, and weasel woman. In these examples, women are more bestial than human, with excessive appetites for food and sex. In the work of Hesiod, Hermes gives the first woman a doglike mind. She is also greedy, lazy, and sexually insatiable.[12] The excessive nature of female desire is a common stereotype of comedy. Aristophanes represents the wives of Athenians as overly lustful and always interested in sex in his women plays: *Lysistrata*, *Thesmophoriazusae*, and *Ecclesiazusae*. In his play *Lysistrata*, for example, the title character gathers the wives of Athens together in a summit to consider how to end the Peloponnesian war.[13] She suggests a "sex strike," and initially not a single woman is willing to agree, with one exclaiming, "But, whatever else you want. If I must, I am willing to walk through fire—rather this than give up sex." Euripides's *Hippolytus* reveals the lack of control women have over their desire. Phaedra is overcome with lust for her stepson, becoming ill and distraught. Euripides's *Medea* highlights *erôs*, physical lust, as a driving force behind Medea's destructive behavior. Depictions of female sexuality in Roman literature frequently emphasize the insatiability of a desiring woman. The orator Cicero accuses the matron Clodia of preying on young men to satisfy her passion. In Juvenal's sixth satire, another matron runs off with a gladiator, her social inferior, and the wife of the emperor Claudius becomes a willing brothel worker but, despite a night full of sex, remains sexually unsatisfied. Seneca accuses Augustus's daughter Julia of prostituting herself because of her lustful disposition.[14]

While Athenian wives and prostitutes could be distinguished through relative *sôphrosunê*, they shared a body that was by nature excessive and uncontrollable. It was only through marriage, male guardianship, and the veil that the excessive nature of the female body could be controlled.[15] The prostitute body, lacking a male guardian, represented the uncontrolled nature of the female body. In his speech against the prostitute Neaera, Apollodorus tells his audience that she began working with her body at a very young age and that once at a victory celebration she even had intercourse with slaves.[16] Both observations are intended to demonstrate her excessive appetite for sex. Similarly, Firmicus (fourth century C.E.) comments that a *meretrix* is a woman who understands the economic potential of her internal desires.[17] Roman literary texts suggest that the female adulterer had to be *togate*, wearing the toga, the dress of the female prostitute. The wearing of the toga demonstrated the female adulterer's affinity with the lustful nature of prostitutes and was thus symbolic of her rejection of the sexual virtue normally associated with married women.[18] Only social practice separates the "respectable" woman from the whore.

Whereas the body of the free male is an active body that penetrates, the female body is passive and hence a penetrated body. Sexual terminology in Greek and Latin highlights this difference between the genders. In ancient Greek references to marriage, it is the man who marries by taking (*lambanein*) a wife and bringing (*agesthai*) her into his home. The brother or father or grandfather of a bride pledges (*enguan*) her and hands her over (*didonai*) to her new husband.[19] Marriage is a transaction between two families, and the bride herself is not an active participant in the exchange. In Figure 2.1, in the depiction of a bride on a *pyxis*, a vessel for women's cosmetics or items of adornment, she stands with her feet together, not taking any steps, while a woman nudges her from behind and a man grasps her arm to lead her away. In sexual crimes against a male citizen's female kin, the offender is the *moichos*, and *moicheuein* refers to his activity, whereas the female partner is the passive object of the action (*moicheumenê*) or the one with whom he committed his crime.[20] Roman marriage also makes the bride an object of exchange between two families. Similar to in Greek, "to lead a wife" (*ducere uxorem*) refers to the husband at the time of his marriage. Latin verbs referring to sexual activity, whether involving the vagina (*futuere*), anus (*pedicare*), or mouth (*irrumare*), rarely employ females as subjects, but they are commonly the objects of these verbs.[21] Because of her passivity, the free female body is closer to the slave body than the free male body.

The Greeks also considered the female body to be a polluted body. Unlike her male peers, she lacked a fixed position in the ancient city: a girl leaves her father's household and joins the household of her husband at marriage. She experiences the birth of a child, bringing forth new life by violating the boundary of her own body. Her association with transitions and her lack of control over even the boundaries of her own body made her a polluted body.[22] Hesiod comments that a man should not wash himself with a woman's bath water.[23]

FIGURE 2.1: Wedding painter (fifth century B.C.E.). Wedding scene—perhaps the wedding of Peleus and Thetis. Red-figure *pyxis*. Inv. N 3.348. Louvre, Paris, France. (Photo credit: Erich Lessing/Art Resource, NY [ART30786].)

A fourth-century B.C.E. law code from Cyrene outlines the pollution and ritual cleansing for anyone coming into contact with a woman who has just given birth or miscarried and for a man coming from intercourse with a woman. Since woman was by nature already a polluted body, she was the one who washed and prepared the dead corpse (which was seen as polluting) for its funeral. The Roman attitude toward the female physical body was more ambivalent. A menstruating woman and menstrual fluid had a harmful effect on anyone or anything coming into contact with her or her fluid. Pliny comments that menstrual fluid can harm crops, dull knives, dim mirrors, and kill beehives. At the same time, it can cure certain diseases, and a menstruating woman can purge a garden of harmful insects.[24] Breast milk, however, always has an advantageous affect: it can cure disease and be a remedy against poison.[25] The Romans thus saw the female body and its processes as both dangerous and beneficial.

Performing the Female Body

While in the case of a free Greek man to be *sôphrôn* meant to possess self-control, a free woman was only *sôphrôn* when subject to the external control of a male guardian and when kept separate from non-kin males. Fathers, husbands, and adult sons were the *kurioi* (guardians) of an Athenian woman. Fathers had guardianship of daughters, husbands of their wives, and sons of their widowed mothers. The design of the courtyard house, with its high windows and internal courtyard, helped keep women from the gaze of men and safe from contact with male outsiders.[26] Although there is no evidence attesting to a *gynaikonitis* (women's quarters) as a specific part of the Greek house, male visitors were confined to the *andrôn*, a communal dining room. Such rooms did not normally have a direct view of the courtyard, and so women might be able to circulate freely through the house even when male visitors were present. Nevertheless, women did venture outside the house, either to fetch water or attend a festival or funeral. From Homer to Hellenistic sources, women donned the veil for such excursions. Three Greek words possibly refer to the veil: *krêdemnon*, *kaluptê*, and *kalumma*; however, it is not known if the terms refer to different types of veils or veiling.[27] Visual evidence attests to short shoulder-length veils, longer veils that cover the head and shoulders, and veils that are draped over the lower body and shoulders and easily lifted over the head as necessary.[28] Some women may even have had veils to cover their faces. They became an important element of attire when girls reached menarche and were a requirement of their dress as adults. Such garments protected the woman from contact with non-kin males, kept her body free from the male gaze, and through their encasement signified her *sôphrosunê*. Phaedra, in Euripides's *Hippolytus*, uncovers her head once she leaves her house and enters on stage.[29] This act unleashes her emotions and allows her to rave and hint at her shameful desire for Hippolytus. Without the veil, a woman was no longer contained and thus not *sôphrôn*. Even with the veil, the free woman had to exhibit appropriate emotional and behavioral responses in a particular situation. In encounters with men, she had to determine the appropriate use of her veil, whether or not it could hang freely or needed to be wrapped tightly around her body and face. When addressed or seen by a man, she must blush and lower her gaze. All of these habits identified her as *sôphrôn*. Spartan women, in contrast, appear to have exercised naked, like men, and even bore legitimate children with men other than their husbands.[30]

In ancient Rome, Roman matrons were expected to be *pudor*. Whereas Greek women required veils and male guardians to ensure their virtue, Roman *matronae* appear to have possessed such virtue without the need for external constraints. In the accounts of the rape of Lucretia in Livy and Valerius Maximus, the focus is on Lucretia as a moral subject.[31] The more extensive account is Livy's: Lucretia is raped by Sextus Tarquinius, the son of the Etruscan king. After the assault, she calls together her husband and father and narrates the events of the night. She ends by asking them to take revenge. Despite protests from her husband and father and their friends, she kills herself with a dagger to demonstrate her refusal to have intercourse with Tarquinius and affirm her *pudicitia*. Her aim is to prevent women from using her as an example to excuse any future lack of virtue. While the passage makes clear that the honor of male kin is closely connected to a woman's virtue, as in Greece, Lucretia's actions suggest further that *matronae* were ethical subjects who had control over their own sexual virtue.[32] Lucretia decides what action to take and makes her own judgment about her virtue, while ensuring that her act of *pudicitia* becomes known to the community at large.

Such a public display of *pudicitia* further separated Roman women's virtue from the virtue of Greek women. Unlike Athenian women, who normally avoided non-kin males and remained socially invisible until their names were inscribed on tombstones after their death, Roman wives needed to display their sexual virtue to the community. They had a public persona, receiving clients on behalf of their husbands and accompanying their husbands to social events, like dinner parties. Through ritual practice, behavior, and public honors, the Roman *matrona* demonstrated and proclaimed her sexual virtue publicly, enhancing her status and the honor of her husband.[33] Such display included the wearing of the *stola*, *vittae*, and the *palla*. The *stola* was a garment worn over the tunic. It reached to the wearer's ankles and was belted just beneath the breasts. Its characteristic V-neck and thick shoulder straps made it immediately recognizable. As an overgarment, it was superfluous to a woman's dress and likely uncomfortable on hot days and if engaging in any sort of physical activity. Literary sources associate the *stola* and *vittae*, woolen fillets used to bind a woman's hair, with the virtuous matron.[34] While not necessarily worn on a daily basis, these articles were likely important elements of dress for attending public ceremonies and performing rituals, when it was important for a woman to indicate her social status and virtue. Likewise, ancient writers equate the *palla*, a large rectangular piece of cloth draped around the body, with the ideal Roman matron and use it to signify a woman's virtue and social status.[35] The garment was worn over the left shoulder and either over or under the right arm. Its usual length was to the knees, and it could be drawn over the head to function like a veil. A woman might even use it to cover her face. Seneca advises women to cover their heads in this way to prevent the approach of men when in public. Although Gaius Sulpicius Gallus allegedly divorced his wife because she went outdoors with her head uncovered, veiling the head out of doors was at the personal discretion of a woman herself or a requirement of her family.[36] On the *Ara Pacis*, for example, while all the imperial women wear the *palla*, only some use it to cover their heads. It is unlikely that lower-class women wore the *palla*, since it would impede women when working, making it more important as a marker of social status than the *stola* because it indicated a woman who did not do manual labor.[37] Roman women also used jewelry, cosmetics, and elaborate hairstyles to indicate their status and distinguish themselves from other classes of women.[38] Female dress and adornment were equivalent to male status symbols, such as the *toga praetexta*.[39] The female body was thus a vehicle for the display of the status and wealth of a household.

FIGURE 2.2: *Ara Pacis*—detail. Detail of procession of Augustus's family. Museum of the Ara Pacis, Rome, Italy. (Photo credit: Janet H. Tulloch.)

Too much concern with beauty and adornment, however, was seen as a negative trait associated with laziness, luxury, duplicity, and a lack of virtue in both Greece and Rome.[40] In Greek sources, Semonides's mare woman is so concerned with her appearance that she neglects all housework. Hesiod's adorned first woman is not an active helpmate. Hesiod argues further that the adornment of women hides an evil disposition. In Xenophon's *Oeconomicus*, Ischomachus disapproves in particular of his wife's use of white powder, rouge, and platform shoes and claims such behavior is trickery and purposefully deceptive.[41] Too much concern for elaborate adornment aroused suspicion and indicated sexual impropriety or status as a prostitute.[42] Ischomachus reminds his wife that "wives who regularly sit around in grand style risk comparison with dolled-up, beguiling women."[43] At Rome, women adorned with cosmetics were thought to be hiding faults and hence duplicitous.[44] Lucilius suggests that an unfaithful woman adorns herself more elaborately when seeking lovers.[45] Juvenal accuses women of relinquishing their virtue in exchange for expensive jewels and other items of adornment.[46] Overadornment was perceived as a waste of time and money and was thought to be anti-Roman.[47]

Despite such anxiety, women appear to have enjoyed adornment as a way to exert control over their own bodies by enhancing their appearance and creating a social identity for themselves.[48] Among Greeks and Romans, emphasis is on a woman's red-and-white complexion as a marker of physical beauty. Skin free of blemishes was also an ideal. *Psimuthion* (or *cerussa* in Latin), a lead carbonate, was used for the face but could also be applied to the neck and arms to give women a paler complexion and cover any spots or wrinkles. Such pale complexions were an ideal of beauty going back to Homeric times.[49] Goddesses and mortal women are described as *leukôlenos* (white-armed) in the *Iliad* and *Odyssey*. Characters in Greek tragedy also use *leukos* (white, fair) to describe the neck, throat, cheeks, and hands of women such as Alcestis, the daughter of Creon, Antigone, and Iphigenia.[50] To add color to their faces, women used various substances as rouge for their cheeks. Greek sources mention *anchousa*, made from alkanet root. Roman sources also mention alkanet as well as *rubrica* (red ochre), *fucus* (a red dye from orchella weed), red chalk, and the lees of wine.[51] Roman women appear to have highlighted their eyes with soot, lampblack, or antimony, but eyes were not the main focus of their toilette, and if they wore too much, they might be considered coquettish or even be mistaken for a prostitute.[52] Greek wives do not appear to have used eye makeup. Substances for the lips are rarely mentioned in either tradition and thus appear uncommon.

In descriptions of prostitutes, it is their open display and purposeful manipulation of their bodies that the sources emphasize. Unlike female kin, who were visible only to certain men, the prostitute body was on display for all to see.[53] Greek comic poets speak of prostitutes lined up either naked or in diaphanous garments, and Attic vases show naked prostitutes with outstretched limbs revealing their full torsos.[54] Seneca's declaimers argue that the prostitute uses all kinds of bodily movements to attract men. He, along with other writers, describes her as *blanda*, alluring.[55] Prostitutes' public display in both Greece and Rome also included elaborate garments made from expensive fabrics. In contrast to married and marriageable women, Greek prostitutes drew attention to their eyes using *asbolos*, lampblack. They painted it on their eyebrows and around their eyes.[56] The statesman Alcibiades envisions himself wearing the dress of his courtesan in a dream. He also paints his face and outlines his eyes.[57] These examples suggest that eye makeup was a common element in the adornment of Greek prostitute women only. Cosmetics around the eyes would easily draw attention to this part of the face and shatter the deportment of female modesty necessary for married and marriageable Athenian women. In the mythical account of Herakles at the crossroads in Xenophon's *Memorabilia*, a similar contrast appears: the woman representing virtue adorns her eyes with *aidōs*, while Vice, or Happiness as she prefers to call herself, keeps her eyes *anapeptamena* (open wide).[58] Although no actual eye makeup is mentioned in either case, it is clear that the effect cosmetics have on the eyes runs counter to traditional ideas about a woman's sexual virtue. In addition to eye makeup, prostitutes might augment their breast size with padding, their hip size with a bustle, and their height with platform shoes.[59] Other women might also employ such tricks, but in doing so they risked being associated with prostitutes, accused of duplicity, and suspected of a lack of virtue.

Transgressive Bodies

While the Greeks and Romans did not practice sexual abstinence or devote themselves to a life of chastity, believing intercourse to be a regular feature of bodily well-being and care of the self, they did place restrictions on sexual behavior. Such restrictions differed according to gender. For marriageable and married women, only intercourse with a husband was permitted.[60] Since the goal of marriage was procreation and the inheritance pattern for both Greece and Rome was normally patrilineal,[61] there was much anxiety about female sexual loyalty. In the opening book of Homer's *Odyssey*, Telemachus says in regard to Odysseus, "My mother indeed says I am his, but yet I at any rate do not know. For no one, by his own means, knows his father."[62] It was expected that fathers and husbands kept the sexuality of their female kin contained and under their control so that a stranger might not contaminate the familial bloodline. In ancient Athens, *moicheia*, commonly translated as "adultery," was a sexual crime against a wife but also included sexual crimes against a citizen's daughter or sister.[63] In such cases, the woman was considered corrupted by a male lover. Nevertheless, her husband still divorced her, sending her back to her kin without her dowry. She was further banned from womanly adornment and attendance at public festivals, the main social outlet and public role for Athenian women.[64] If she ignored such prohibitions, any man could strip and beat her as long as he did not kill or permanently maim her. It also became acceptable for male kin to prostitute such a woman.[65] In this sense, such a woman lost her right to male protection as well as the few rights and privileges she had as a woman in the city of Athens.

In ancient Rome, it was permissible for a father or husband to kill an adulteress and her lover with impunity.[66] In 18 B.C.E., the emperor Augustus instituted new laws, known as the *lex Julia de adulteriis*, under which adultery became a crime against the state. Adulterers and adulteresses were now tried in a court of law, making adultery a crime against the state and no longer purely a family issue. If convicted, the individuals were sent into exile, with their property confiscated by the emperor. The new law also limited the circumstances under which a husband or father could kill an adulterous daughter or wife and her lover. A husband could kill only the lover caught in the act in his own home, and only a lover who was *infames* (such as a pimp, actor, or criminal), of slave status, or a freedman of the household. A father could kill his daughter and her lover with impunity if they were caught in the act in his own house or her husband's home. The husband normally divorced his wife without delay. A husband who did not divorce a wife accused of adultery could be charged with pimping. In addition to divorce and the loss of a part of her dowry, the adulterous matron had to be *togate*, wearing the toga, the dress of a prostitute.[67]

Since transgressive sexual behavior associated a woman with prostitution, Athenians and Romans developed an opposition between the prostitute and marriageable women as a way to enforce particular behavior in women, particularly elite women.[68] Although differences between wives, sisters, daughters, and prostitutes may not always have been apparent in everyday life, especially in Athens, in certain contexts, such as the law courts, the differences were exploited.[69] Apollodorus's famous statement, "We have *hetairai* for pleasure and *pallakai* for the daily care of our bodies, but wives for producing legitimate offspring and as a trustworthy guardian of our household goods," divides women into those available for sexual enjoyment and those available for the production of offspring.[70] In the course of the rest of the speech, Apollodorus distinguishes between wives and daughters and the *sōphrōn* behavior required of these women (chastity, prudence, and moderation), and that behavior that marks a woman, such as Neaera, as a prostitute—sexually available to anyone for pay, extravagant in her tastes, excessive in her behavior, and even arrogant.[71] Constructing a prostitute's behavior as the exact opposite of the wife's, sister's, and daughter's is also a strategy in other law court speeches. The speaker of Isaeus 3, for example, claims that the sister of an Athenian was the *hetaira* of the deceased Pyrrhus. He claims she was sexually available to anyone for a fee, attendant at symposia, and excessive in her behavior, while her brother claims she was Pyrrhus's legitimate wife. In both examples, the speaker presents the woman as a *hetaira*, while the opponent, we are told, claims her as a wife. Such distinctions reveal a fine line between being labeled a bad woman versus a good woman. While speakers also use accusations of sexual promiscuity against men, the consistency with which it is lobbied against women reveals how the existence of prostitution and prostitutes could work as a form of social control on female sexual behavior more generally. A woman herself or the man in charge of her would pay close attention to her behavior so that she would not be associated with a prostitute.

The same is true for late Republican and imperial Rome, with the most famous example being the portrayal of Clodia in Cicero's *Pro Caelio*.[72] Here the family and status of the woman are distinguished,[73] but Cicero uses wit, innuendo, direct accusation, and terms such as *meretricius* (of a prostitute) and *amica omnium* (friend of all) to establish her identity as no better than a prostitute.[74] Cicero constructs a boundary between two types of women, the *matrona* and the *meretrix*, and places Clodia on the side of the whore. A similar strategy appears in Seneca's *Controversiae*, a collection of rhetorical exercises by famous declaimers modeled on legal disputes from the early imperial period. Although often fictional cases, these exercises reveal how easily a female crosses the boundary between sexual propriety and sexual impropriety and how speakers manipulate such behavior to suggest her identity as a prostitute or wife and thereby gain disdain or sympathy for a woman. In 2.4, for example, a father recognizes his dying son's child, born to him by a woman working as a prostitute. Declamations disputing the legitimacy of the grandson emphasize the notoriety and promiscuity of the woman by claiming that the father of her child is uncertain and she herself known only too well. Supporting arguments present the woman as a mourning wife tending to a dying husband and claim she does not have the character of a prostitute, only the label. In another example, 2.7, a husband is suspicious of a bequest left to his wife by a young man and accuses her of adultery. He comments that her dress, walk, conversation, and appearance are not that of a faithful wife and associates her with *lenocinium*, a prostitute's allurement. He claims that she negotiated, like the most shameful women do (suggestive of prostitutes), for a higher price by at first rejecting the young man. Opposing arguments are less detailed but claim the wife behaved appropriately, with *pudicitia*, and ignored the advances of the young man. These declaimers construct the prostitute and wife as opposites and use sexual behavior associated with the prostitute to defame any woman and act as a check on her behavior and sexuality more generally. Roman women had to be careful to follow particular codes of behavior in their interactions with men in order not to harm their reputation or the reputation of their families.

Desiring Bodies

The sources reveal very little about the female sexual experience. The poetry of the Greek poet Sappho (late seventh to early sixth century B.C.E.) and the Roman poet Sulpicia (first century C.E.) represent the fullest accounts of female desire from the female perspective. Both writers hint that women did not conceptualize the sexual relationship using the penetrator/penetrated model that assigns a dominant role to one of the lovers.[75] Male-authored sources that consider female sexuality represent women as excessive in their desire and the sexually active woman as transgressive.[76] The ancient Greeks believed further that women, unlike men, had no ability to control their sexual urges and thus that women were always ready for sex. According to the Hippocratics and Plato, a woman's womb, not her conscious state, drove her sexual appetite.[77] The female body was also thought to expend a man's vital fluid and unman him. For these reasons, female desire was dangerous and destructive to men.[78] Hermes gives Odysseus strict instructions to follow before he has intercourse with Circe so that he is not incapacitated. Even then, Odysseus remains with Circe for a year until his men remind him about the need to return home. Hesiod warns against having sex with women in summer, when men are at their weakest. Medea's desire brings about the downfall of her brothers, her husband Jason, and the house of Creon.[79] For the Romans, female desire also emasculates men and causes them to neglect their duty. Dido's desire keeps Aeneas from founding Rome.[80] The elegiac poets become like slaves to their mistresses' desire.[81]

While there were many sexual opportunities for men, such as prostitutes, slaves, and boys, physical intimacy between husbands and wives was not simply a matter of procreation. Late fifth-century Athenian vase paintings depict marital and domestic scenes with Eros, suggesting desire for a husband on the part of women and the bride as an ideal.[82] Ischomachus tells his wife that regular physical activity will improve her complexion and make her more sexually attractive to him than the household slaves. He further claims that the physical pleasure he experiences with his wife is greater than with slaves, since his wife has intercourse with him of her own free will, whereas slaves are compelled to submit to him.[83] The Hippocratics argued that regular sexual intercourse was a necessary prescription for good female health.[84] Roman sources speak about the pleasure of sex between a husband and wife. Catullus's marriage hymn, for example, refers to the bride as "filled with desire for her new spouse."[85] Pliny the Younger writes of his desire in a letter to his wife.[86] While Greek and Roman medical writers write about female orgasm, the sexual preoccupation with penetration and the aversion to cunnilingus in literary references suggest that female satisfaction was not the primary concern of sexual intercourse.

Classical Greek writers frequently mention same-sex relations between men but only rarely consider such relations between women. In Plato's *Symposium*, the playwright Aristophanes gives a speech on love that ends with a reference to sexual unions between men, between men and women, and between women.[87] Plato calls women who love women *hetairistriai*. His specific comment on them is neutral in tone, but the passage makes it clear that the most valued relationship is that between two males. Scholars interpret the dearth of references in Greek male-authored sources in two ways: either such relations between women were not common, or men had no concern whether or not women had intimate relations with each other.[88] A major source on relations between women is the archaic poet Sappho. She directed her poetry at women, focusing on her desire for other women. She implores Aphrodite to help her in winning the desire of a new love interest and speaks of the physical pleasure shared with her female lover.[89] It seems likely that such relationships reflected the model of relations between men in which an adult lover had a youth as a beloved. Sappho was likely the elder partner in relationship with a young girl prior to her marriage.[90] Her relationships with females differ from those between men in that the latter focus on the pleasure of the adult male, while Sappho sought a relationship in which pleasure was shared.[91] The male poet Alcman (late seventh century B.C.E.) makes reference to erotic feelings between young women at Sparta. His *Partheneia*, performed by female choruses, immortalize the beauty of Spartan women and eroticize the female performers both as objects and as agents.[92] In the first *Partheneion*, the chorus of girls draws attention to their own beauty and highlights, in particular, the beauty of their chorus leader, *Hagesichora*.[93] In this way, such choruses invited their audience, likely including young men,[94] to admire their physical beauty and sexualize them. They further comment, "Hagesichora exhausts me [with desire],"[95] bringing attention to themselves as desiring subjects. Claude Calame argues that the public display of such feelings suggests that female eroticism was perhaps encouraged as a way to prepare young girls for the sexual relationship of marriage. Other scholars point to the similar age of these partners to argue against any pedagogical function for same-sex relations between women and postulate a kind of lesbianism similar to the modern Western world.[96]

By the Hellenistic period, women who preferred women over men faced disapproval.[97] For the Romans, relations between women were seen as a perversion and considered threatening.[98] Ovid refers to such desire in his *Metamorphoses* as previously unknown and unnatural.[99] At the end of the account of Iphis and Ianthe, Iphis transforms into a male and can now marry and love Ianthe openly. Order is thus restored. Martial unleashes some of his harshest invective against this practice.[100] The Romans commonly called a woman who sought pleasure with other women a *tribas*, a Greek word derived from *tribein*, meaning "to rub." Unlike other words derived from *tribein*, like *flagritriba* (wearer out of whips), and imported into Latin, the ending is not Latinized. The retention of the Greek ending associates the practice with Greeks and highlights the Roman disbelief in such practices between Roman women.[101] Despite the origins of the term, the Romans appear not to have envisioned the physical act between two women as rubbing but as involving some kind of penetration.[102] In this way, Roman writers masculinize such women. In some cases such women also penetrate boys and even men, demonstrating the unnaturalness of the female penetrator. There are no Latin sources on love between women from a female perspective.

THE FEMALE BODY IN THE EARLY CHRISTIAN TRADITION

Concepts and values about bodies and sexuality were central to the vision of Christianity advanced in the texts of the first millennium of Christian worship and reveal the female body to have been a potent symbol, particularly through celibacy, renunciation of signs of worldly wealth, and even bodily suffering.[103] Asceticism (a regimen of self-restraint, most notably in sexuality, food, drink, clothing, and property) was a highly discussed element in Christian texts, particularly in the late fourth to fifth centuries, that left an enduring legacy in the monasticism of the medieval period onward. Nevertheless, as Christianity spread through the Roman Empire, many preexisting values remained. Much of Roman and early medieval society at large continued to uphold the practices of marriage and of conventional display through the adornment of the body.

Transitions

The continued care of the body and display of feminine beauty and worldly wealth can be seen in the archaeological evidence of jewelry, cosmetic implements, and textiles. A particularly lavish cosmetic chest from the late fourth century, shown in Figure 2.3, survives as part of the Esquiline Treasure. It bears an inscription dedicating it to a Christian married couple, Projecta and Secundus. Not only does the image on the lid of naked Erotes indicate the sexually oriented hopes for their marriage, but Projecta is dressed in bridal finery and adornments. It was also still expected that a woman of good character would display some modesty in her clothing and behavior. Christian writers often particularly emphasized or extended this, suggesting that women should dress in "mourning" and praising shapeless clothing.[104] Some women were praised for keeping their bodies concealed even from physicians at times of injury or illness. For example, Gregory of Nyssa recounts that his sister Macrina would not seek treatment for a breast tumor, because "she judged it worse than the pain, to uncover any part of the body to a stranger's eyes."[105] Sexual propriety also remained a key expectation for women. Chastity was emphasized, but the concept of marriage as a once-only lifetime bond increased in currency and also began to be extended in theory to men, with a growing belief that sexual intercourse should take place only within marriage.[106] It is, however, hard to discern the extent to which the double standard for men's and women's fidelity in marriage was seriously disturbed.[107] Classical ideas of sexual excess as a particularly feminine characteristic, and of women as an alluring but terrible "trap" for men, continued unabated, with Clement of Alexandria (second to third centuries), for instance, suggesting that women should keep themselves covered and avoid flirtatious looks and glances in order not to tempt men.[108] A woman could therefore be held responsible for not only her own sexual behavior but also that of men, if she was judged to be arousing male lust. For example, the fourth-century holy woman Alexandra is said to have enclosed herself in a tomb because "a man was distracted in mind because of me and, rather than scandalize a soul made in the image of God to stumble, I betook myself alive to a tomb, lest I seem to cause him suffering or reject him."[109] In contrast, some celibate women (known as *subintroductae*

FIGURE 2.3: The Projecta Casket, Roman, ca. 380. A view of the top of the lid showing busts of a richly attired woman and man appearing within a wreath held by naked Erotes. They are identified by an inscription in Latin around the rim of the lid: "Secundus and Projecta, may you live in Christ." British Museum, London, Great Britain. (Photo credit: © The Trustees of the British Museum/Art Resource, NY [ART300539].)

or *agapetae*) chose to live with an unrelated celibate man, demonstrating that at least some Christians did not think that proximity to a woman was always a severe danger. This practice drew harsh criticism from ascetic writers such as Jerome and John Chrysostom, who did not see how these men and women could avoid the actual sin of breaking their vow of celibacy or having sexual thoughts and thus being "guilty of ten thousand adulteries, daily beholding them with desire."[110]

Even though ascetic Christianity tended to see women as innately tempting and simultaneously encouraged communities of women to live together, female homosexual feelings or practices continued to receive relatively scant attention.[111] The only clear source on female homoerotic practices in the growing ascetic communities of the fourth and fifth centuries is found among Bishop Augustine of Hippo's advice on good order in such establishments:

The love which you bear to each other must be not carnal, but spiritual: for those things which are practiced by immodest women in shameful frolic and sporting with one another ought not even to be done by those of your sex who are married, or are intending to marry, and much more ought not to be done by widows or chaste virgins dedicated to be hand-maids of Christ by a holy vow.[112]

Beyond the Needs of the Body

Two areas where Christianity (or at least segments of Christianity) did diverge from the mainstream of Greco-Roman society were in depreciating the body and renouncing sexuality on the grounds that physical and sexual needs or appetites hampered or were less important than the rewards of the afterlife. This presented a potential disadvantage for women in that they continued to be seen as more sexual and more "bodily" (living "more in accordance with the promptings of the inferior flesh than by the superior reason," as Augustine of Hippo put it) and their bodies were viewed as more polluting through, for example, menstruation or childbirth.[113] At the same time, these harsh perspectives on women also presented a means of achieving more appreciation for their pious actions because, through bodily suffering or privation, women could be noted and praised for transcending not only human nature but also their feminine "body-centered" nature.[114]

Before Christianity was recognized as an acceptable religion in the early fourth century, it faced opposition and, at several points, outright persecution. A number of Christians refused to renounce their religion and sacrifice to the gods and died in public torture and executions. Through bearing the gradual and painful destruction of their bodies, female martyrs could earn the same heavenly rewards as men. Furthermore, in accounts of female martyrdoms the female body became the site of Christian messages about spiritual strength because, through bearing physical pain, they not only gained the same admiration as male martyrs but also showed strength and endurance far beyond the physical and moral weakness expected of women. For example, in the martyrdom of the slave girl Blandina, it was

> feared that on account of the weakness of her body, she would be unable to make bold confession, [but] Blandina was filled with such power as to be delivered and raised above those who were torturing her by turns from morning till evening in every manner, so that they acknowledged that they were conquered, and could do nothing more to her. And they were astonished at her endurance, as her entire body was mangled and broken.[115]

Accounts of female martyrs also often directed the audience's gaze up and down the female body. The third-century martyrs Perpetua and Felicitas were "stripped and clothed with nets, they were led forth. The populace shuddered as they saw one young woman of delicate frame, and another with breasts still dripping from her recent childbirth."[116] This exposure of the female body—that may have shocked, disgusted, or titillated—captured the audience's imagination through images of the female body in a way that set women's bodily endurance as an example for all.

Once Christianity was established as a recognized and imperially supported religion, persecution became rare (though it could occur during conflict between rival doctrines), but the growing ascetic movement advocated similar rewards through the deprivation of bodily needs and appetites. In its view, a lifestyle of fasting, celibacy, and poverty (albeit variably defined) demonstrated that Christ's call was stronger than worldly values and bodily needs. Some strands of Greek and Roman philosophy had advised austere lifestyles, and scripture had encouraged spiritual goals over material goods and needs, but the main trend toward Christian asceticism began in the desert with famous male pioneers such as St. Antony and St. Pachomius, in whose footsteps followed both solitary monks and those living in communities of various types. Some women, such as Amma Sarah, are also known to have chosen this mode of hard desert life, but the real popularity of asceticism among women arrived with the urban asceticism promoted from the late fourth century on by writers such as Jerome of Strido, Ambrose of Milan, Gregory of Nyssa, and Augustine of Hippo. The idea of closing oneself off from the dangers of worldly society while still living in the city took off with a significant focus on women and particularly on the lifestyle for virgins and widows. The ascetic lifestyle of Paula, a senatorial widow in whose circle the ascetic writer Jerome of Strido circulated in Rome in the late fourth century, is summarized by him as follows: "She mourned and fasted, she was squalid with dirt, her eyes were dim from weeping."[117]

Asceticism was also an area in which Christians might be decried as heretics—for depreciation of the body stood very close to a rejection of the body as evil, as espoused by groups such as the Manicheans. Asceticism, therefore, did face opposition, and ascetic women could face accusations of excess or inappropriateness. One aspect of some women's rejection of mainstream standards of feminine behavior that attracted disapproval was their wearing of masculine clothing. While the trope of women disguising themselves as eunuchs to enter monastic foundations is likely to have been more a product of narrative techniques, it does seem that some women did change their dress and hair to give themselves a more masculine appearance.[118] The virgin saint Thecla, a role model for many Christian women, adopted men's clothing and hairstyle to mark her baptism and devotion to the way of life inspired in her by the apostle Paul during his visit to her city.[119] Such practices continued into the fourth and fifth centuries in some communities, but our knowledge of these is limited to prohibitions by incensed clergy.[120] Ascetic writers whose works survive took a dim view of such "excess" that went beyond their own modifications of appropriate female behavior. Jerome of Strido criticized women who "change their garb and assume the mien of men, being ashamed of being what they were born to be—women. They cut off their hair and are not ashamed to look like eunuchs."[121] This claim to masculinity represented a challenge to mainstream society, which still decried women assuming male roles or appearing as men.

Renouncing Sexuality

The most striking aspect of Christianity's influence on the discourse of female sexuality was its focus on female celibacy, and particularly virginity. The Roman and post-Roman worlds continued to see women's sexuality as tied to marriage, but the rhetoric of the fourth and fifth centuries, while vocally challenged by advocates of marriage, emphasized virginity for women as the ideal.[122] Virginity had been prized before the fourth century, but it was at this point in early Christianity that it became such a major focus in writings. Despite the waxing and waning of the popularity of virginity in both rhetoric and actual practice during the rest of the early medieval period, it continued in the long term to be regarded as the apogee of feminine achievement.[123] Virginity was also becoming an increasingly important theological concept in the late fourth and early fifth centuries, with writers such as Ambrose pushing for recognition of the perpetual virginity of Mary, mother of Jesus.[124] Although this did not become official dogma until 533, it indicates the level of spiritual importance given to the physical state of virginity. Accounts of martyrdoms also took on such a focus: The martyr Perpetua was a wife and mother, but later saints' lives and martyr accounts tended to focus on the virginity of the female martyr. For example, in the late fourth or early fifth century, in a set of poems by Prudentius called the *Peristephanon*, Prudentius mentions that Eulalia, Agnes, and Encratis are virgins, but the male martyrs are not described in terms of their marital status or sexual experience—including St. Paul the apostle, who had promoted sexual abstinence in his first letter to the Christian community at Corinth.[125] Virginity was praised as a renunciation of the social obligation

to marry and reproduce but also as an avoidance of a physical act that was
starting to be deemed repugnant by some theologians. A widow who decided
to renounce remarriage in favor of devotion to God was praised highly, but
her state was presented as spiritually less than that of the virgin, and so it was
not just the renunciation of an "unnecessary" social role that was at the heart
of the ideal of virginity—the act of sexual intercourse was seen, as in prevailing Greco-Roman medical theories, as something that irreversibly changed the
female body.[126] Ascetic writers were clear that "true" virgins needed to be pure
in body and in mind (particularly as they could then strengthen their position
by condemning virgins from heretic groups as impure in mind), but the purity
of the virgin body was seen as the crucial element.[127] For Ambrose, the Virgin

FIGURE 2.4: Saint Agnes. Gilded glass paste set into plaster. Fourth century C.E. Catacomb
of Panfilo, Rome, Italy. (Photo credit: Scala/Art Resource, NY [ART54534].)

Mary was a closed "gate," and Christ was born "without opening the genital seal. The barrier of modesty remained intact and the seals of integrity were preserved."[128] Similar imagery was employed to describe Christian virgins, who were "girded" by virtues and "an enclosure of modesty" or represented by the Song of Songs' image of the "fountain sealed."[129]

It is striking that such close attention was paid by male writers to female virginity and that the language used to discuss it could be extraordinarily sexual. The bridal imagery of the biblical Song of Songs, such as the bridegroom taking the bride into his chambers, was used allegorically to represent the intense relationship between Christ and the Christian, but this was rather sexually evocative when discussing a young woman's renunciation of the usual sexual obligations.[130] In the poems by Prudentius called the *Peristephanon*, the virgin-martyr Agnes is described as saying to the prefect at her trial, "You may stain your sword with my blood if you will, but you will not pollute my body with lust."[131] Continuing the erotic connotations of the staining of the sword, several lines later Prudentius's Agnes tells the executioner, "This lover, this one at last, I confess it, pleases me. I shall meet his eager steps half-way and not put off his hot desires. I shall welcome the whole length of his blade into my bosom, drawing the sword-blow to the depths of my breast; and so as Christ's bride I shall o'erleap all the darkness of the sky."[132] It is a striking passage designed to emphasize that Agnes has renounced the social expectation that she will be deflowered by a husband in favor of the penetration of the sword and a spiritual ecstasy and heavenly reward. As well as showing the continued link between female sexuality and fertility (despite the renunciation of that fertility), the textual eroticism of these girls suggests that female bodies, even when virginal, were an important tool through which male writers and their audiences could think about their own desire and longing for spiritual intimacy and fulfillment.[133]

For the women mentioned in such texts, it could be argued that the ideal of virginity (or the lesser ideal of widowhood or celibacy within marriage) offered women a new choice of sexuality. By choosing a life of virginity or sustained widowhood, they could avoid sexual intercourse with a husband chosen by their family and the "millstone" of successive childbirths. The seeming freedom of virgins and widows to travel, dispose of their wealth as they saw fit, and reject marital suitors at face value suggests a widening of opportunities.[134] We must be careful, however, not to overplay the significance or extent of this "freedom" since few women truly possessed the luxury of choice in the disposal of their sexuality. Women were encouraged to choose virginity by some of the prominent voices in Christianity but nevertheless needed to persuade their families first.[135] Despite having a renowned ascetic for a grand-mother, Melania the Younger was compelled by her wealthy family to accept marriage, and she failed to persuade her husband Pinianus to take up a life of celibacy within marriage, although he conceded that they would do so once they had children.[136] Marriage remained the norm, and a woman could not, for instance, use her spiritual aspirations to justify her refusal to have sex with her husband.[137]

Since the majority of the Christian world continued to choose marriage and procreation, virginity offered the benefit of an extremely rare status for women who chose (or were given to) it. Virgins such as Eustochium or Ambrose's sister Marcellina were unusual and showed the moral character of their families as well as the family's financial and political stability in affording to forgo a marital alliance using their daughter.[138] As a result, some families chose a life of virginity for their daughters even in infanthood, so the matter of "choice" and sexuality was more complex than women's individual decisions to avoid compulsory heterosexuality.[139]

CONCLUSION

As explored at the start of this chapter, Greco-Roman societies tended to see dress and adornment as signifiers of sexual status and propriety and sought to impose codes of sexual behavior on women by designating "excessive" adornment, cosmetics, and visibility as the marks of a prostitute. A woman's degree of conformity to these codes and signifiers demonstrated her relative *sôphrosunê* or *pudicitia*. Women were classified sexually as passive and weak against bodily appetites, but their fertility was valued highly when restricted to the role of wife. Christianity, then, consolidated some values and introduced others in a way that transformed the Greek and Roman legacy to later society. The disintegration of the Roman Empire into Germanic kingdoms in the West and the Byzantine Empire in the East brought a greater degree of cultural variation, but these variations developed in negotiation with Greco-Roman and Christian concepts and inherited many of the views of women's bodies and sexuality outlined in this chapter.

CHAPTER THREE

Religion and Popular Beliefs: Ritual Practices and Female Practitioners

JANET H. TULLOCH

Our current knowledge of ritual activities performed by actual women in Western antiquity is like a new cloth made from the hems of old skirts—some strips are plain, some are embroidered, and others have precious beads and mirrors stitched into the fabric. Overall, tremendous diversity exists across the length of the bolt. Despite its beauty and resilience, all of the cloth's sections have imperfections; the bolt itself, a stitched construction of fragments. There are many reasons for the state of our fragmented knowledge of ancient women's ritual practices, most notably the almost complete lack of visual or textual remains created or authored by women, the patriarchal slant of the sources that have survived, and the interpretative challenges of the physical evidence itself, including issues of dating, translation, historical context, authorship, and provenance.

While we know that mostly elite women performed authoritative roles in Greek and Roman religions as priestesses and benefactors, held ordained offices in early Christianity, and were synagogue leaders in early Judaism, it is important to recognize that women's religious authority between the years 500 B.C.E. and 1000 C.E. occurred within the ideological framework of entrenched patriarchal societies where the degree and types of women's ritual performance were sanctioned by male religious and state authorities. Practices outside of these patriarchal sancta were deemed witchcraft or heresy.

The origin of male regulation of women's ritual practice might be explained, according to Deborah Lyons, by an ethnographic model found in many cultures whereby a story or series of narratives circulate that serve to justify the religious control of *real* women. Typically, these stories relate that females in the culture's mythical past were forced to yield their sacred power as a result of their misuse of it, an act often caused by a "fatal flaw"—such as curiosity. According to these narratives, women were unwilling to share their power with men. Transposed into ancient Western cultures, this model suggests that the stories about mythical females such as the "Amazons from the East," Eve, Pandora, Medea, and early Christian women prophets—that is, the so-called "bad girls" of Western sacred history (from a male point of view)—were retold and embellished over time, eventually conflating the characteristics of the women in the stories with the "nature" of real women in the society. As the centuries passed, the storytellers and the listeners, perhaps unwittingly, helped to establish gender-regulated boundaries toward the divine through the reverence paid toward stories from "mythical times."[1] Whatever the mythological origins for justifying the regulation of women's ritual practice, we know that by the classical period in Greece (ca. 479–323 B.C.E.), female ritual agents and the rites they practiced were sanctioned by male-directed poleis. Add to this state of affairs a circulating discourse about "dangerous" women who practiced subversive rituals using magical incantations, and the eventual result was the complete loss of all female publicly held religious authority by the sixth century C.E. To wit, though some authority continued for deaconesses in the Eastern church, the last Western orders of deaconesses and widows were eliminated from Christianity by the Council of Epaon in 517 C.E. (It was also about this time, in 529 C.E., that the emperor Justinian either closed or placed Plato's academy in Athens under state control, thereby ending the academic freedom of its philosophers.) That men also possessed negative qualities seems to have been offset by the cultural practices of hero and emperor worship and the publicly saturated representation of an übermasculine pantheon of gods in both Greece and Rome. Not surprisingly, when all gods and goddesses were legislatively reduced to a single deity with Emperor Theodosius's imposition of Christianity in 391 C.E. as the only legitimate religion in the empire, that one god was male. With the elimination of the feminine divine through imperial decree, only Mary, the Mother of God (*Theotokos*), remained as a heavenly female power available to women and men. Anyone caught worshipping Mary as a goddess, however, was quickly condemned as a heretic.[2]

Against the brand of "the infamous feminine," this chapter presents a chronological summary by theme of what scholars do know about the ritual practices of ancient women. These women unquestionably contributed to the cultural heritage of Western religious traditions considered here, that is, the Greek and Roman religions, early Judaism, and early Christianity. Due to the timeline and space limitations of this volume, this chapter is by necessity an overview. There are, however, specific topics that are shared among the diverse religions that relate to our chapter's subheading of ritual practices and female practitioners: sacred regulations and access to the sanctuary, women's and girls' religious festivals, popular beliefs and superstition, and, especially, female priesthood and religious authority. It is these topics that are addressed in this chapter. The reader can find further material on all these topics in the bibliography—especially in the excellent sourcebooks on women and ancient religions. In the following sections, it is recommended the reader keep in mind the diversity of women, represented by our metaphor of the bolt of cloth. It is especially important to remember that these fragments are the ones that have survived the ravages of time, while others have disappeared entirely.

SACRED REGULATIONS AND ACCESS TO THE SANCTUARY

Sacred sites have always imposed restrictions based on the perceived purity of the humans who approached their sanctuary. In the Western traditions, the female body was viewed as particularly vulnerable to ritual pollution. From the fourth century B.C.E. on, Greek sacred laws described childbirth, miscarriage, abortion, and menstruation as occasions of female pollution,[3] and seminal emissions as sources of male pollution. While sex was seen as a source of ritual pollution for both women and men, events related to other aspects of reproduction polluted only women. While the honoring of female or male sexuality in religious festivals such as the women's Thesmophoria or the all-male cult of Herakles remained a focal point of sacred rites in early Greek religious practices, Robert Parker suggests that ritual pollution was probably the reason for restricting the presence of the opposite sex at these rites. According to Parker, it was for a similar reason that women were sometimes excluded from the cults of Poseidon, Zeus, and Ares, "all emphatically masculine gods." The epithet "Herakles, Woman-Hater" from Phocis suggests, however, an overt male anxiety related to the mere existence of women that undergirded the celebration of some male-only rites.[4]

In spite of women's occasional impure state, the honoring of female genitalia through ritual, gave sexually experienced women (i.e., married women) direct access to the divine both as priestess and as worshipper in rites dedicated to goddesses such as Demeter and her daughter Persephone (Kore). Earthenware figurines, identified as "Baubo," found in the temple of Demeter[5] and Persephone (fourth century B.C.E., at Priene, in Ionia)[6] suggest that female sexuality as late as the classical period was seen by both women and men as sacred, a power that, with the blessing of the male polis, was squarely in the hands of women to manage and regulate on behalf of the city.

Despite, or, as some might argue, because of, women's power of regeneration, all women in Greece had to contend with the purity regulations of sacred temples. Although these differed from place to place, extant Greek sacred laws provide some clues as to the types of ritual pollution shared among poleis in the Hellenistic and Roman periods. Occasions of female pollution that required the longest periods of purification were childbirth, menstruation, and miscarriage, with the latter carrying the requirement of forty days of purification.[7] As Andreas Bendlin has stated, "the male regulators of cult practice

FIGURE 3.1: Votive objects. Forty-eight small objects (miniature vases, terra-cotta figures) from the sanctuary of Demeter and her daughter Persephone in Priene. Hellenistic. Inv. FV 990230. (Photo credit: Ingrid Geske [ART400696].)

regarded the female body as particularly susceptible to pollution and hence in need of ritual regulation."[8]

According to Bella Vivante, throughout the Greek and Roman periods, there was a gradual shift of focus in women's rituals from sexuality to motherhood:

> By the Roman period the ecstatic fertility rites for both male and female deities were considered contrary to Roman moral sexual standards and were declared illegal at various times. . . . Roman women expressed their concern with fertility far more through rituals that emphasized motherhood.[9]

One might speculate that such a shift would have privileged *matronaes'* access to the sanctuary. While we certainly find the segregation of women's rites within the Roman Republic, participation in these rites seems to have been based on social as well as marital status. For example, when *matronae* (married women; mothers of legitimate children) washed a statue of Venus Verticordia on April 1 to ensure sexual morality, on the same day, *non-matronae* such as prostitutes or plebeians went to the baths to worship Fortuna Virilis to enhance their attraction to men. While slaves were excluded from the June festival of the *Matralia*, in which freeborn Roman mothers petitioned the goddess for the safekeeping of their children, slaves were honored at the July rites of the Capratine Nones.[10] While the December ritual of the Bona Dea was restricted to *matronae*, prostitutes were active in the April celebration of the Floralia and worshipped Venus Erycina at her temple on the Vinalia.[11] While marital and social status contributed to the segregation of Roman women's rituals preventing some women from accessing expressions of the feminine divine, there is no question that ritual pollution played a role in limiting women's access to the sanctuary in Judaism during the Second Temple period up to the temple's destruction by the Romans in 70 C.E.

In Judaism, purity laws kept women outside the Jerusalem temple at all times during their menses. Once they were ritually purified, they could advance no further than the second court, known as the women's court (although men could worship there too). Ritually purified Jewish men could advance to the third court but no further. (Only male priests were allowed to advance to the court of the priests, the final court before the Holy of Holies.) Joan Branham makes an interesting argument that the reason for women's segregation in the temple was not due to misogynist tendencies but rather to a potential rivalry between the two life-giving forces and purifying agents—sacrificial blood and women's reproductive blood. The acceptance of menstruants in the earliest synagogues, where sacrifice never had taken place, or no longer took place, would suggest that the potential rivalry of sacred power based on blood was no longer operative.[12] The question remains, however, if women's reproductive blood was indeed considered to be so potent (possibly even more so than male blood, given that ancient Levitical purity laws demanded that women who gave birth to a female child undergo twice the purification time: eighty days, versus forty days for male babies), why was women's reproductive blood perceived negatively in relation to sacrificial blood? Branham states that for Jewish, Greek, and Roman temples, an "absolute antipathy between the two fluids may [have] arise[n] from their *kindred or similar powers* of purification, life, and rebirth."[13] The question of who had ultimate authority over life, death, and rebirth, or what Branham calls "a certain tension in dominionship"[14]—the (male) god(s) or reproductive-aged women—seems to be the essence of the tension. Indeed, Branham states that "women would have wielded an immense religious power [in antiquity] had they been able to spill the blood of animals in rituals of fertility, propitiation, and purification and to control the natural processes of procreation."[15] Even though sacrifice was no longer performed in the temple, by the sixth or seventh century C.E., when Jewish prayer space, as Shaye J. D. Cohen states, "was becoming a surrogate temple," with sacred space increasingly differentiated by chancel screens and arks, Jewish menstruants were "explicitly prohibited from entering a synagogue and touching holy books and implicitly prohibited from reciting benedictions and reciting the name of God."[16] If Branham is correct, we must conclude that it was fear of women's reproductive blood *as the stronger source of ritual power* that was at the heart of ancient patriarchal purity laws—both Jewish and Greek.

Despite Christianity's early days of female initiative and power, women's leadership roles likewise collapsed under the strain of patriarchal culture and sacred space. Women's access to "the sancta," identified as being baptized, partaking in the Eucharist, or entering the space where the *ecclesia* (church) met, was an open debate by the early third century. Early Christian fathers vacillated as to whether menstruants should be allowed to touch the Eucharist or even enter the building where the *ecclesia* gathered.[17] Both sides used the New Testament story of the woman with the issue of blood who is cured by touching Jesus's robe as evidence for their position.[18] A chapter on purity laws in the *Didascalia*, a mid-third-century church document from Syria, may have been an attempt to set the record straight. The *Didascalia* maintained that for Christians, impurity was caused by sin, not uncontrollable states of nature.

Female and male Christians no longer needed to follow purity laws because
these laws were Jewish (or, worse, pagan), not Christian practices; therefore,
menstruants were allowed to touch the Eucharist and enter a church building.
States of ritual purity, the authors of the *Didascalia* argued, were no longer an
issue for Christians.

At around the same time, regulations or formal church orders limiting wom-
en's liturgical roles appeared with the circulation of the *Apostolic Tradition
of Hippolytus*. Up until the end of the second century, proscriptions against
women performing certain roles in the Church, such as teaching or baptizing,
were practiced in some—though not all—early Christian communities. These
proscriptions were justified by references to church "custom" or "tradition."[19]
Justification was based also on the second-century Christian interpretation of
Genesis, the first book of the Hebrew scriptures. According to this view, the
formation of Eve, the first woman in the Semitic story of human origins, came
after the formation of Adam, the first man. Therefore, women could not have
authority over men in matters such as teaching about the sacred since women
came second in the order of human creation. Early Christian exegetes largely
did not recognize that there are two human-origin stories in the book of Genesis, or at least two parts to the same story: Genesis 1:27 and Genesis 2:7–23.
The first part narrates the story of the Israelite god creating male and female at
the same time in "his" image.[20] It is the second story of how the Israelite god
created woman from Adam's rib that early Christian writers emphasized when
developing their theology of humankind.

A second passage from Genesis used to deny women ecclesiastical authority in the early Church concerns the story of Eve's deception by the serpent
(Satan) in the Garden of Eden (3:1–5). Although this deception brought the
knowledge of good and evil to the primordial couple, it also brought their
permanent exile from Eden. Eve, and through her all women, were blamed by
early Christian exegetes (and others who would follow this lead down through
the ages) for "losing paradise" for humankind. In his address to a female audience on the dress of women, Tertullian, a third-century North African church
father, stated, "and you know not that you also are an Eve? God's judgment
on [Eve's] sex lives on in our age; the guilt necessarily lives on as well. *You* are
the Devil's gateway."[21] Such a sex, according to this view, could never have
authority over men as teachers of doctrine or as priests. How early Christian
women responded to these proscriptions is discussed in the following sections,
"Women's and Girls' Religious Festivals" and "Female Priesthood and Religious Authority."

WOMEN'S AND GIRLS' RELIGIOUS FESTIVALS

In all ancient religions, cosmic order was regulated through a series of sacred holidays or festivals that made up the calendar year. Until Julius Caesar's recommendation to adopt the Egyptian solar calendar in the middle of the first century B.C.E., each city or territory in antiquity functioned according to its own ritual calendar. For ancient Greeks, time was based on a lunar month with each cycle named after a god, goddess, or monarch. As Janett Morgan has argued, women's religious festivals were a time of female movement in the ancient world, bringing women into the city streets and rendering them visible.[22] Set outside ordinary time, sacred holidays meant women could reconnect with old friends and meet new ones. Rituals could include fasting, sacrifice, mourning, feasting, athletic competitions, singing, dancing, processions, and play as part of the festival. In this section we present some of the more important women's and girls' festivals from antiquity, beginning with the Greeks and ending with a festival to honor the Virgin Mary.

Greek Festivals

Brauronia (Artemis)

The Greek goddess Artemis presided over transitions, especially the hazardous and morally ambiguous transition of girls from a *parthenos* (virgin) to a reproductive *gyne* (woman, wife). The goddess's protectors enforced strict rules of access to her illustrious temple in Ephesus, if an excerpt from Achilles Tatius's novel *Leucippe and Clitophon* is to be trusted: "Only men and [female] virgins were permitted here. If a non-virgin woman passed inside, the penalty was death, unless she was a slave accusing her master, in which case she was allowed to beseech the goddess."[23] Archaeological evidence for this festival includes *krateriskoi* (small two-handed cups) found at various Artemis shrines in Greece that date to the sixth and fifth centuries B.C.E. Images on the cups that show girls in tunics or nude, running and carrying crowns, branches, or torches, were once thought by scholars to depict actual rites of the Brauronia. More recent interpretations suggest the imagery depicts a mythical *arkteia* (ritual of prepubescent girls imitating she-bears).[24]

The Thesmophoria

Unlike the Eleusinian mysteries, which took place annually in September at Eleusis, the Thesmophoria, the all-female festival that was part of the cult of Demeter and Persephone, excluded children and virgins. In most Greek cities, the three-day festival took place during the month of Pyanopsion (September/

October). As already mentioned, the discovery of Baubo earthenware figurines in the temple of Demeter and Persephone at Priene suggests that the
role of female sexuality in the cosmological order was central to this festival.
In other words, fertility and agriculture were not the only subjects of the secret
rites. As Burkert states, "what is laid down may be called *thesmos* in [ancient]
Greek."[25] It is possible that Demeter's epithet as *thesmophorus*, or "law giving," meant that more than decayed animal remains from pits were laid down
at the goddesses' altar. As Morgan suggests, "Demeter is concerned with the
structure of communities and the maintenance of order within them."[26] Civi-
lized communities could not be sustained by the abduction and rape of young
girls (the fate of Demeter's daughter, Persephone). Rather, communities were
sustained by institutions and laws like marriage that were laid down to protect
female sexuality (Demeter's domain). As Morgan states of this festival, "the
drama of [the women's] abandonment of home, their movement out of the
house and into the political space of the city, reminds the male city of their
importance. Without wives, there is no city and no structure or order in the
community."[27]

The Adonis Cult

One festival open to all women that brought them into the open air but not
the city streets was the rites for the male nature god, Adonis. This festival was
celebrated on the rooftops of their homes, where women grew fast-growing
plants in rooftop gardens in honor of the youth, a favorite of Aphrodite. The
rooftop cries and loud lamentations of the women, possessed by grief for the
dead god, symbolized by the plants withered from the heat, could be heard
across the city.[28]

The Dionysia

According to the ancient Athenian festival calendar, there were both rural
and city Dionysia that took place in different months of the year (Posei-
deon and Elaphebolion, respectively) as well as the Lenaia, which occurred
during Gamelion (the month of marriage). The city festival was probably biennial by the third century B.C.E. while the rural festival took place
at least once a year. The role of women as civilizers, and symbols of the
household and order, is temporarily inverted in the Dionysia, as seen in the
mythical-ritual schema of Euripides's *Bacchae*, in which all the women of
Thebes are driven out of their homes to the mountains, "crazed of mind"
by the god of wine, wilderness, and vegetation. How much the description
of the rites from literary sources is fact and how much is fiction is unknown.
However, there exists an early third-century B.C.E. inscription from Miletus in

Western Turkey that attests to the regulation of the practices of priestesses and female worshippers of Dionysos:

> Whenever the priestess performs the holy rites on behalf of the city . . . , it is not permitted for anyone to throw pieces of raw meat [anywhere], before the priestess has thrown them on behalf of the city, nor is it permitted for anyone to assemble a band of maenads [*thiasos*] before the public *thiasos* [has been assembled] . . .
>
> . . . to provide [for the women] the implements for initiation in all the orgies. . . .
>
> And whenever a woman wishes to perform an initiation for Dionysos Bacchius in the city, in the countryside or on the islands, she must pay a piece of gold to the priestess at each biennial celebration.[29]

Another inscription from Miletus, in about the third or second century B.C.E., attests to the acts of Alcmeonis, a priestess of Dionysos who led the Bacchae (the followers of Dionysos) from the city: "to the mountain and carried all the sacred objects and implements, marching in procession before the whole city. Should some stranger ask for her name: Alcmeonis, daughter of Rhodius, who knew her share of the blessings."[30]

Roman Festivals

Ceres

The festival of Ceres in Rome culminated on April 19 after a week of games celebrating Ceres's role as the goddess who provided corn to Rome's plebian community. According to Ovid, worshippers of Ceres gave up sex for a period of nine nights at the time of the goddess's festival.[31] During her games, a torch was given out to all participants in imitation of Ceres, who searched for her daughter during the earth's darkness.[32] While relationships with fathers and daughters were not mentioned during the festival, due to the goddess's hostility toward marriage,[33] it seems that the rites were conducted in the open with none of the secrecy of the Thesmophoria.

The Matralia, festival of Mater Matuta (June 11)

This annual festival involved the offering of hot cakes to a goddess of uncertain origin (Greek? Italic?) with a temple in the Boarium Forum near the banks of the Tiber in Rome. It was celebrated by freeborn Roman mothers, who petitioned the goddess for protection of their children from harm. Slave girls, as Ovid tells us, were barred from the ceremonies because the goddess did not trust the service of female slaves, who gave away the secrets of their mistresses and fornicated with their husbands.[34]

The Vestalia

The Vestalia, by all accounts, was an ancient Roman festival that took place in June to honor the sacred fire beneath the earth and, by association, the fire that burns in all hearths and fosters all things.[35] In the Republic and the first few centuries of the empire, the home for this cult was in the Roman forum, although "satellite cults" may have existed in other parts of the empire.[36] Unlike

FIGURE 3.2: Statue of a Vestal Virgin. Location: The Garden of the Vestal Virgins, Roman forum. (Photo credit: Janet H. Tulloch.)

other gods and goddesses in Roman religion, the virgin goddess Vesta had no cult image, but her flame was housed in a round temple to mimic the shape of the earth. During the festival, the temple of Vesta was open for seven days.

Matronae were allowed to approach barefoot and make a food offering, perhaps in gratitude for the fire in their own hearth, which helped foster life in their household. The Vestals, the virgin priestesses of the goddess, offered cakes made of corn. During this festival all official business was brought to a standstill, and donkeys, which usually worked in mills to grind the grain, were given a special day of rest.

The Cult of Diana (August 13)

C.M.C. Green has suggested that as well as being the guardian of women in childbirth, "Diana was the *tutela* of the young."[37] In Rome her rites were celebrated at her temple on the Aventine Hill.[38] Both Horace and Catullus wrote verses to be sung together by young girls and "chaste" boys for the goddess.[39] Statius tells us that in Aricia, the most famous cult site for Diana in Latium, Diana's rites were performed at night by women carrying torches, who, after the rites, returned to Rome in a torchlight procession.[40] A fresco from the port of Ostia (near Rome) painted sometime during the third century of the empire shows girls and boys dressed as adult women and men in the act of staging such a torchlight procession. As part of this little procession, the girls and boys no doubt chanted the verses of Horace and Catullus in a local ritual drama performed for the goddess on her festival day.

Bona Dea

Although the goddess's festival day was May 1, a night sacrifice to the Bona Dea was performed by women in early December. This rite is interesting for two reasons. First, it did not appear in the formal festival calendar, which meant it was not under the authority of the all-male pontifical college. Second, it did not take place at a temple but in the home of a high-ranking Roman official. The goddess, Bona Dea, it seemed, "abhor[red] the eyes of males."[41] Vestals were known to have attended and may have assisted in the sacrifice of a pig. Men were most definitely not welcome, though it did not stop some from trying.[42]

Early Jewish Women and Festivals

Although Rosh Chodesh, or the appearance of the new moon, was traditionally a day of rest for Jewish women in antiquity when they did not have to spin, weave, or sew, because of their past righteousness, we have no evidence of how women might have celebrated this day. That it had some association with the on-coming of menses seems logical given the holiday's connection to the new moon. Unfortunately, we have no archaeological or epigraphic evidence that has come to light to support this conjecture—only the sparse literary evidence of the Talmud[43] and its commentary by Rashi (1040–1105 C.E.), a medieval French rabbi. There is no doubt, however, that some Jewish festivals held more appeal for women, including "Judaizing Christian" women, than others. Evidence for this latter practice comes from a letter written by John Chrysostom in the late fourth century. In this letter he chastises the men of his congregation for allowing their Christian wives to go to the Jewish "Feast of Trumpets," which clearly held an attraction for Jewish and Christian women.[44] Other than danc-ing barefoot in the marketplace, however, we have no records of what women and men did during these religious festivals.[45]

Early Christian Women and Festivals

The earliest extant list of Christian festivals was created by Furius Dionysius Filocalus, an artist employed by Pope Damasus in the last half of the fourth cen-tury to create the inscriptions for martyrs' shrines in the Roman catacombs. Not only did women participate in the feast days of these martyrs, but the richer ones among their numbers also contributed their private wealth to enlarging shrine sites to accommodate the increased flow of pilgrims.[46] Filocalus's list of the festivals held in the year 354 C.E. began with the birth of Jesus on December 25 and included Roman celebrations for individuals martyred in the third century, including North Africans, Cyprian, Perpetua, and Felicitas.[47] In Western Asia, women in Arabia who came from Thrace celebrated what might have been a women-only festival to the Virgin Mary by baking cakes and assembling to-gether. While the evidence for this practice dates to the fourth century, it is quite possible that the practice had been ongoing for some time, a possible survival from women's participation in Greek goddess festivals (see earlier discussion) or ancient celebrations of the Queen of Heaven: "For some women prepare a certain kind of little cake with four indentations, cover it with a fine linen veil on a solemn day of the year, and on certain days they set forth bread and offer it in the name of Mary. They all partake of the bread."[48] Such practices by the fourth century were considered by the mainstream Church as not only "silly" or a "ridiculous joke" but, more dangerously, heretical. From the point of view of the bishop who wrote the preceding words, "it is . . . through women the devil has vomited this [practice] forth." However, there is evidence of homilies (acephalous, anonymous, or attributed to John Chrysostom [349–407 C.E.]) for festivals of the Virgin Mary in the Greek church in the last half of the fourth century, celebrating both the Feast of the Assumption (August 15) and the Feast of the Annunciation (March 25).[49] These festivals were sanctioned by the Church and were certainly not female-only celebrations.

FEMALE PRIESTHOOD AND RELIGIOUS AUTHORITY

Within Greek religions, the *Pythia*, or Oracle at Delphi, is the earliest known position in which a woman served the divine in a cultic role. This role required that specific criteria be met by the woman who filled the position: "The *Pythia* was over the age of 50 when she was appointed, and thereafter lived a secluded, chaste and dedicated life; how she was selected is never explained, but the Delphian authorities may have chosen her from among a band of holy women whose task it was to tend the hearth in the temple."[50] The sacred office of *Pythia*, which continued until 391 C.E., was held until death. In her role as *Pythia*, the occupant took great care to purify herself before engaging in divination to seek the god Apollo's will on behalf of a devotee. Whether the *Pythia* functioned as a *mantis* (a seer), a *prophetis* (a speaker), a *promantis* (a foreseer) or aspects of all three types, her own agency within the ritual has long been debated by scholars.[51]

Although Greek literature has suggested the names of some *Pythia* at Delphi, of the 153 historical women listed as priestesses in Joan Connelly's "Index of Priestesses," only one name for this office has come down to us through historical sources, that of Theoneike, found in a third-century C.E. epigraph inscribed into a stone that is part of a Byzantine church.[52] Other sacred women from Greek religions are attested by literary, epigraphic, and archaeological evidence. In this section we turn our attention to this evidence for female priesthood and the religious authority of women down to late antiquity. As Connelly states, "It is the powerful analogy between house and temple that provides a critical foundation for female agency in Greek religion."[53] It can be said that this analogy holds true for most women holding religious office in antiquity.

It has been argued that in Greek and Roman antiquity male priests generally served male gods and female priests, female gods. While this statement has some merit, we cannot accept it as a truism. Women such as the *Pythia* at Delphi often served male gods in a cult capacity. Gods served by female priestesses included Dionysos/Bacchus, Zeus, Asklepios, Sabazios, and Hierokles. Male emperors were also served by priestesses as well as priests as

part of emperor worship in imperial cults during the Roman Empire.[54] Some
women during the Greek and Roman periods even held cultic roles in more
than one religion. We know from an inscription in Rome written in both
Latin and Greek that a certain Alexandria during her short life served both
Bacchus (Dionysos) as priestess and the goddess Isis as *pastophorus* (an aco-
lyte who carried the cult statue in processions).[55] We know of another woman
from the second century C.E., Tata of Aphrodisias, who was priestess of Hera
for life but who also served as a priestess to the imperial cult in the city of
Aphrodisias.[56]

In the Roman Republic, the religious offices to which women could be appointed included the priesthood of Ceres, Venus, Vesta, the Flaminica Dialis,
and the *regina sacrorum*. The women who occupied the latter two offices were
married to their husband-priests and participated in a joint priesthood. Divorce was not an option. While the evidence is mixed, priestesses of Ceres may
have been celibate during their occupation of this office.[57] The priestesses of
Vesta, or the Vestal Virgins, were selected between the ages of six and ten to
guarantee virginity. Continued chastity while in office was mandatory, upon
pain of death if the vow was broken. Like ancient Greece, the requirements for
women to be appointed to a Roman public religious office depended on elite
familial lineage, age, personal reputation, and marital status. Generally, candi-
dates for office were chosen by the *pontifex maximus* or his delegates. Women
receiving religious honors such as the dedication of a goddess's statue were
chosen by their female peers, although the initial group of women appears to
have been chosen by the all-male Roman senate.[58]

During the imperial period, new studies on gendered participation in public
life have allowed us to move forward from the traditional viewpoint that the
order of the Vestal Virgins in Rome was the only sacred public office open to
women and their younger female acolytes. Research based on several hundred
coins and inscriptions from Ephesus and the eastern Roman Empire shows
that women in the province of Asia began to serve in the high priesthoods of
the provincial imperial cults (i.e., worship of the emperor)—offices that were
previously restricted to men—by the first half of the first century C.E.[59] This
participation reached a record high during the years 201–50 C.E. in the Roman
province of Asia, when almost 40 percent of all high priesthoods in the provincial imperial cult were held by women.[60] After this time, women's participation
in the imperial cult dropped off due to internal crises in the empire and the
unstable mechanisms for emperor succession.[61]

Women were also active as ritual practitioners in oriental cults, especially the
popular cult of Isis that was transplanted across the empire from Egyptian soil.

FIGURE 3.3: Isis ritual at Pompeii or Herculaneum. With female, male, and child practitioners. Fresco. First century C.E. [ART62958].

Based on first-century frescoes showing cult activities found in Herculaneum and Pompeii, it is clear that female ritualists participated along with males in performing the rites of the goddess.

Women in Early Judaism

Greek inscriptions for Jewish women's leadership provide intriguing evidence for women as the head or ruler (*archisynagogos*) of the synagogue and/or Jewish community in the eastern part of the Roman Empire from the second to the fifth centuries C.E. Of the three published inscriptions found in Ross Shepard Kraemer's sourcebook of women's religions in the Greco-Roman world, two are funerary, and one is an inscription found on a fourth- or fifth-century chancel-screen post that was originally part of a synagogue. While these inscriptions do not explain the role attributed to these women, it is clear in the case of at least one woman, Rufina of Smyrna, that she was a very wealthy woman capable of building a household tomb that was not only large enough for the slaves raised in her household but also for her freed slaves.[62] Jack Lightstone has argued convincingly that based on similar inscriptional evidence the role of *archisynagogos* refers to the governance and administration of the Jewish community and synagogue in the diaspora, a privileged role that seems to have been held by transgenerational elite Jewish families. Evidence that the office of *archisynagogos* could be inherited is attested by a tomb inscription naming a small child as the occupant of this office.[63] In status and responsibility this role was similar to the Roman office of *decurion* (a municipal official) as fourth-century Roman legal texts suggest.[64] We also know of women who acted as an elder (*presbytera*) in their communities, which in some cases included authority as a member of the synagogue council.[65] Although scholars disagree as to the type of authority associated with these titles, Lightstone argues that inscriptional evidence for titles such as "father" or "mother" of the synagogue "seem to be honorifics bestowed on individuals in recognition of persistent or major benefaction, or in recognition of long service."[66] In other words, there seems to be a separate category for those individuals who gave for the upkeep of the synagogue but did not participate in its governance. Further evidence suggesting a distinction between "benefactor" and *archisynagogos* includes some late fourth-century inscriptions attesting to ten women who contributed some of their wealth to the completion of a mosaic floor in a Syrian synagogue. In these examples, the women's beneficence was part of a religious offering carried out as the "fulfillment of a vow."[67] Lee Levine cautions that the larger number of women named as a benefactor or *archisynagogos* in western Asia was not typical of Jewish practice in Rome or Palestine.[68] Therefore, their role as leader of the synagogue might have been due to the effect of a broader cultural acceptance of women's religious authority in that geographic area.

Women in the New Testament

Our knowledge of women's activities in the earliest Jesus communities is drawn primarily from the four Gospels in the New Testament. Although these gospels were assigned "authors" by later church tradition, none is an eyewitness account of the ministry of Jesus of Nazareth. The newest Gospel, John, with its stories of clever, independent women, is dated by most scholars to the last decade of the first century, approximately sixty years after the death of Jesus. Even the Gospel that most scholars consider to be the earliest, Mark, is dated between 40 and 73 c.e. While scholars generally agree that the Gospels include historical materials, the degree and identification of embedded materials (e.g., sayings that go back to Jesus himself, lines that are products of early church redactors) are highly contested.

In the Gospel narratives, women are frequently placed at key moments in the transmission of important announcements. We are told that Mary Magdalene, Jesus's mother Mary, Mary the mother of James and Joses, Salome, and others all accompanied Jesus to Jerusalem from the Galilee. Certainly, based on the social context of the Greco-Roman world, some of the women in Jesus's female circle would have been well-to-do women, "who provided for him out of their resources"[69] (i.e., they were patrons, while others were disciples who probably assisted Jesus in his ministry). Women in New Testament stories do not follow Jesus blindly but rather challenge him (Martha of Bethany), poke fun at him (the Samaritan woman), and intellectually challenge him (the Syrophoenician woman). In all four Gospels, women witness Jesus's death and are the first witnesses of his empty tomb. In Mark, Matthew, and John, Mary of Magdala is the first person to have a resurrection vision of Jesus. He speaks with and commissions her to spread the news, causing early church fathers to dub her "the apostle to the apostles."[70]

After the death of Jesus, women often acted as leaders in house churches where members of the movement met for worship, hospitality, and mission. Women who were active workers in the first century were itinerant missionaries who sometimes proselytized alongside a male spouse/partner (e.g., Prisca and Aquila; Adronicus and Junia); or who were coworkers with Paul, the apostle to the gentiles, in the movement to win converts (e.g., Prisca and her spouse Aquila; Tryphaena and Tryphosa; Euodia and Syntyche; and a woman called Mary); or who were wealthy benefactors offering hospitality (e.g., Lydia, the purple dye merchant of Philippi; Phoebe of Cenchreae) or were leaders of house churches (e.g., Nympha in Collossae; Prisca and Aquila in Rome, Ephesus, and possibly Corinth).[71] The label of deacon of the church at Cenchreae was given to Phoebe, Paul's benefactor, mentioned in Romans 16:1–2. At this point, before the death of Paul, about 62–65 c.e., early Christian communities were not yet organized under a single patriarchal and authoritative church. Leadership was based on how well a woman or a man was able to use his or her gifts, and how willingly, to serve the assembly of believers or provide resources, including financial ones, for the community to survive. As is clear from the names already listed, some of the same early leaders performed a number of these different roles.

Women in Early and Late Antique Christianity

As the early communities began to develop into a distinct religion, men and women took on various functions in their churches. Widows, the role of prophet, and the order of virgins, which either included or was exclusive to women, were not ordained offices,[72] though women who carried out these roles were expected to serve in specific ways. Ordained offices for women included deacons and deaconesses, widows in some instances, and presbyters (defined as elders or priests in early Christianity). The idea of women holding the office of presbyter is repeatedly condemned by fourth-century bishops when the early church, under Emperor Constantine and his heirs, began to hold its first synods and councils with a Roman emperor present. Nonetheless, epigraphic and literary evidence suggests women's continued existence in this role at least until the sixth century. Kevin Madigan and Carolyn Osiek's carefully documented study on ordained women in the early church shows that among the surviving evidence, at least ten women held the office of deaconess, presbyter, or *episcopa* (bishop).[73] It is almost certain that there were more than these ten who served in these offices, but further evidence eludes us. Despite the various church orders that outlined gender-specific roles for men and women in the early church, women continued to fill sacramental roles as needed whether it was against orthodox church practice or not. As Madigan and Osiek state, "What can be said with certainty is that the claim that women have never functioned as presbyters in the 'orthodox' church is simply untrue."[74]

By the same imperial decree of 391 c.e. that put an end to the funding of the Roman emperor cults, the fire at the Temple of Vesta in Rome was extinguished, and the order of Vestals was abolished. Even the ancient sanctuary of Apollo at Delphi was closed. A Christian emperor now sat on the throne of Rome. Theodosius's decrees, preventing public pagan practice by enforcing the closure of Roman temples, combined with the entrenched patriarchy of the Christian bishops meant that sacramental public roles for women in the empire were drying up. As positions with ritual authority began to evaporate, women found new ways to exercise religious influence through the development of leadership roles in urban monasteries in Rome (e.g., Marcella, 325–410 c.e.) and Roman Palestine (e.g., Paula and Eustochium, late fourth and early fifth centuries), eventually managing monasteries as abbesses across the hinterlands of a declining empire. Like priestesses, abbesses typically came from wealthy aristocratic families, using their wealth to either found a monastery or provide for its ongoing maintenance. Such institutions provided not only for those women with the luxury to choose a life of virgin celibacy but also for homeless, poor, ill, and physically disabled women. One of the most famous abbesses of Celtic Christianity is Hilda of Whitby (ca. 614–80 C.E.), founder of the double monastery at Whitby in Northumbria, England. Under Hilda's leadership, Whitby monastery became a major center for scholarship and education.[75] Christian women continued in these roles well into the Middle Ages but with reduced independence and power from their bishop overseers.

POPULAR BELIEFS AND SUPERSTITION

As in many parts of the world today, ancient people held beliefs and practiced rituals that were not always acceptable to the religious authorities. Kim Stratton has argued convincingly that behavior (positive or negative) perceived as "magic" in the ancient world was part of an active polemical discourse among elite groups vying for worldly and/or cosmic authority.[76] In other words, the label of sorcerer cannot always be taken at face value. For example, early Christians called the Roman gods "demons," while members of Roman cults accused early Christians of being secretive and practicing a *superstitio*.[77] Both accusers used labels associated with the dark arts to denigrate the legitimate religious practices of the other. With that caveat in mind, in this final section we briefly examine different types of evidence for a popular discourse that frequently targeted (but was not exclusive to) women as sorceresses and instruments of the evil eye.

According to Stratton, the concept of magic in recent Western culture dates back to elite Greek writers in the fifth and fourth centuries B.C.E. who associated magic with "barbarous activities, foreign rituals and dangerous women."[78] Love potions, curses against one's enemy, and remedies for an ailing body could all fall under the rubric of "witchcraft" depending on who was doing the labeling. One famous literary tale typical of the time relates the story of a young protagonist, Lucius, who after hearing numerous stories about the antics of female witches travels to the town of Hypata in Thessaly to learn the ways of the dark arts. The hero is accidentally transformed into a jackass by his lover, a female slave and assistant to the old witch in whose home he is a guest. In this cautionary tale of the dark arts known as *Metamorphoses* or *The Golden Ass*, by the Latin writer Apuleius (fl. 155 C.E.), Lucius must undergo numerous humiliations and beatings as an ass until he is eventually saved by the great goddess Isis. Although Roman stories like this one embeds "wizened old hags" as a stereotype, Stratton points out that the Greek female stereotype for a sorceress was generally a jilted wife.[79]

In real life, curses or spells were frequently inscribed on lead tablets (*defixiones*) and then placed in the ground, to be activated by the chthonic deities; others were buried near the graves of young children.[80] Those who had died prematurely were thought to hold a certain magical efficacy that would strengthen a curse. In late antiquity, even the icons of martyred saints were used to hide curses in the belief that the saint's spirit would activate the curse.[81] Pottery incantation bowls from the seventh or eighth century C.E. with Aramaic, Syriac, and Mandaic inscriptions written in ink show that ordinary domestic ware was used as a surface for magical incantations. About 150 of these bowls have been found in the area of Iraq, northeastern Syria, and southeastern Turkey. These bowls were found in homes under door thresholds or under the floor in room corners.[82] Depending on the incantation, the bowls' function was to repel and protect oneself and one's family from harm. Some incantations, like the one on the bowl pictured in Figure 3.4, effected a countercurse

FIGURE 3.4: Incantation bowl. With Aramaic writing from Iraq, eighth century C.E. © The Trustees of the British Museum [Registration number: 1980,0415.1].

against "women who curse." Other incantation bowls actually named names, both that of the suspected sorceress and the name of the client who commissioned the incantation bowl against individual "x" and his or her family. A shared use of inscribed polytheistic and Jewish symbols across religious and cultural boundaries makes identification of these artifacts with one particular religious group problematic.[83] In the example here, the incantation calls for an overturning of the woman who curses standing in public spaces, that is, fields and marketplaces, as well as sacred space, that is, a mountain, a temple, or a synagogue,[84] suggesting that the unnamed client (in this instance) was a Christian or a Muslim.

Finally, in the ancient world, fear of the "evil eye" was widespread, and spells were often cast to protect individuals against its potential harm. Like today in many parts of the world, protective amulets or signs were used on the body, in the home, and on the prows of ships to avert a harmful gaze. In some ways, the evil eye was the inverse of a "sacred gaze," a form of ritual seeing that involves an ocular exchange between a devotee and his or her god. Both forms of the gaze were a type of visual practice in the ancient world based on the belief that anyone could be affected by a negative or positive look, whether the source of that gaze was a cult image, an icon, a god, or a human being. During the time period covered by this volume, most people believed that the eye and soul were connected and thus that both could suffer or benefit from a particular gaze. The evil eye was a particularly powerful form of the gaze that was thought to enter the body of a victim through the pores of the skin as well as through the eyes.[85] However, direct contact with a human (or supernatural) agent was not necessarily required to effect harm on a human being. For example, simply viewing events at Roman festivals or burial ceremonies was considered to be harmful to Christian eyes. Elizabeth Castelli writes that for the early church fathers, "The [pagan] spectacles were the quintessential threat to Christian well-being because, through the power of the gaze, they incited feelings of desire and bloodlust. Because of the power of images that one encountered in the arena or at other spectacles, the soul became brutalized, coarsened, and assimilated to the violence and duplicity of the performances."[86] Death pollution through visual apprehension of dead bodies was another source of harm for both women and men according to both pagan and Jewish practices.[87] Perhaps this is why in Greek, Roman, Jewish, and early Christian burial practices, women, a group already identified with multiple occasions for ritual pollution, took on the responsibility of preparing the corpse for incineration/inhumation. While attitudes toward the dead changed throughout antiquity, most believers, whether pagan, Jew, or Christian, female or male, never lost their fear of the evil eye.

CONCLUSION

As we have seen, our stitched construction of fragments has in the end rendered some patterns of women's religious involvement in antiquity. Despite the increased restrictions on their ritual practice across different religions and the time period covered in this chapter, some women, especially those from noble families, those with substantial resources of wealth, or those who were born or married into religious families, were able to secure religious authority or a sanctioned ritual practice for themselves. Through their management skills, religious practices and leadership, as well as with their financial resources, women contributed to the development and cultural stabilization of the religions they practiced. In many ways these women continued to be the lifeblood of successive and competing religious regimes in Western antiquity, offering their life's energy and sometimes their lives in return for their "share of the blessings."

CHAPTER FOUR

Medicine and Disease

STEVEN MUIR AND LAURENCE TOTELIN

Between the civic doctor and self-help came a great variety of healers—circuit doctors going round the countryside from a home base in
a market town, wise women, magicians, druggists, faith healers and
quacks. . . . Our literary texts play down magical and folk healing: the
papyri and the long survival of such remedies reveal that for many people
such treatments had some value and, possibly, were all that was accessible.[1]

In this chapter, the discussion covers the various roles played by women in
the process of health care in the ancient Western world. Primary texts include
those in the Hippocratic and Galenic traditions, the influential gynecological
text of Soranus, Greek and Roman religious texts, magic papyri, and texts
from the New Testament, late antique, and early medieval Christian periods.
A number of issues need to be stated at the outset.

The preceding quote by Vivian Nutton suggests that there were options
involved in health care decisions.[2] In the ancient world, women were under the
authority of men who made decisions that affected their lives, including health
matters. In many cases, fathers or husbands authorized a line of treatment or
selected a healer. However, women probably had some role in the diagnosis of
their own health states and those of their family and friends. There is analysis
and choice involved every time someone categorizes a physical condition as
an "illness" and adopts strategies to deal with this condition.[3] In a pluralistic

health care system, like that which existed in antiquity, people selected from a number of healing modes (secular, religious, magical), consulted a particular healer, or chose to combine various modes and advice. In antiquity, a woman also faced daily choices as she administered a regimen for herself or for others.

The usual issue of androcentric and intermittent primary evidence is particularly acute in the case of women's health. In most societies, women are significant caregivers in the domestic arena (a largely private space), in terms of both remedies and palliative care.[4] The urgencies of illness and its economic impact on people living in poverty or at subsistence levels likely led women to seek inexpensive treatment, even improvise therapeutic methods. However, most ancient literary sources give detailed evidence only for the practices and concepts of "elite" medicine—the often expensive activities endorsed and undertaken by men trained in the art of medicine and practiced in the public arena. The roles of herbalists, midwives, wise women, wives, and mothers are less well attested or are unclear in our sources. The reader may regard the image on the Greek vase shown in Figure 4.1 and wonder as to its meaning. A woman is reading from a scroll, and a second woman is holding a small jar. Is this a woman reading a recipe for a healing draught and her assistant holding a batch of the preparation?[5]

FIGURE 4.1: Greek vase—detail. A seated woman reads from a scroll, and a standing woman holds a small jar. Red-figure vase, fourth century B.C.E., Athens. © The Trustees of the British Museum [Registration number: 1836,0224.27].

Various modes of therapy are at work in the time period covered in this volume: secular, religious, and magical. There is overlap between these fields, as scholars have noted.[6] Medical activity in the ancient world (both official and popular) was inclusive rather than exclusive—it combined many tactics and worldviews. Figure 4.2 illustrates a dual perspective: a physician conducts a medical examination under the supervision of the Greek healing god Asclepius.

An issue for the reader to keep in mind is the social dimension of life. In the ancient world, a person's social network (family, association, and town) was the starting point of that person's identity.[7] One person's actions had tremendous impact on others: for example, the prayers and sacrifices done by one person could be beneficial for many. Similarly, the authority and character of the healer was part of the therapy process. It is no coincidence that votive plaques at healing shrines show a human family approaching the divine family of Asclepius and his daughters (see later on)—both human and divine groups are involved in the healing process.

Here, discussion of women's healing is based on a model of three roles. The first is that of patient, where the woman is involved in a process of seeking

FIGURE 4.2: Roman seal sardstone. A physician examines a patient while Asclepius supervises. Sard, Roman, first to second century C.E. © The Trustees of the British Museum [Registration number: 1836,0224.27] 1912,0311.1.

personal healing. As already noted, a woman makes some choices relating to self-diagnosis and also the administration of treatment (whether that involves purchasing and taking a prescription, following a dietary or exercise regimen, reciting a spell, or going to a temple). The second role is that of medical practitioner. The woman is involved in the healing of another person. As a member of the patient's social network, the practitioner may act as the primary healer (as a midwife, for instance), or she may participate in the healing process in a variety of ways, such as assistant or facilitator. The third role is a medical authority. This woman's impact extends beyond the immediate treatment of a patient. Her recipes and advice are considered so valuable by a community that she affects many people beyond her own lifetime. An authority may be a model or example whose legendary reputation lives on in the stories and practices of later generations.[8] The reader will find intriguing evidence for each of these roles.

WOMEN AS PATIENTS

The compilers of the Hippocratic gynecological treatises, a series of medical texts composed in the fifth and fourth centuries B.C.E., divide their female patients into two categories: women of experience and women who lack it.[9] As a result of their inexperience, women in the latter category feel shame when suffering gynecological ailments and do not seek the help of physicians until it is too late. Women of experience, on the other hand, know their own body, can tell when they have conceived, can perform internal examinations on themselves, and actively participate in their treatment. The compiler of Diseases of Women, the longest Hippocratic gynecological treatise, recounts the story of a patient named Phrontis, whose knowledge and experience the physician can rely on:

> Phrontis suffered what women who are not purged from the lochia suffer and, in addition, she felt pain in the genitals; and touching she knew that there was obstruction; she said so and, after treatment, she was purged and she became healthy and fertile.[10]

This story calls for two comments. First, Phrontis is the only named patient in the Hippocratic gynecological treatises, which center their narratives on descriptions of diseases rather than on patient histories. This absence of named female patients, however, is a general characteristic of ancient medical literature. For instance, in the *Epidemics*, a series of Hippocratic medical texts that present themselves as collections of case histories, women are rarely referred to by their first names (see the example later on). Instead, a woman is named after her legal guardian (*kyrios*, "lord"): her father (e.g., Telebolus's daughter), her husband (e.g., Epicrates's wife), her brother (e.g., Harpalides's sister), or her master (e.g., the woman of Pantemides's house).[11] To name women after their legal guardians was traditional in antiquity, and this practice is especially understandable in a medical context. Indeed, it was the *kyrios* who sought and paid for medical help for the female members of his household. In the *Epidemics*, women whose legal guardians were not known were left entirely anonymous, as in the case of a woman "lying sick by the shore" three months into her pregnancy who suffered a fever with pains in the loins.[12]

Second, the outcome of Phrontis's story is worth noting. Thanks to her cooperation with the physician, she remained fertile. Thus, she was able to fulfill one of the most important roles of a Greek woman and one of the main concerns of the Hippocratic gynecological writers: the conception of children. For these writers, women's health was dependent on the good functioning of their reproductive systems. The writers considered women to be fundamentally different from men; in particular, women were characterized by their spongy and wet flesh that retained fluid in the form of blood.[13] Hippocratic women needed to rid themselves of this extra fluid through menstruation, pregnancy (when blood served as nourishment for the fetus), lochial flow (purgation after birth), or lactation (when blood was transformed into milk). In the absence of such purgation, disease was thought to ensue.[14]

The organ at the center of the Hippocratic woman's reproductive system was the womb. According to the Hippocratic compilers, the womb, when too dry, could move in the body in search of moisture. This organ traveled along a tube (*hodos*), never explicitly described but implied in a variety of ways, stretching from the mouth (*stoma*) of the womb (i.e., the vagina) to the mouth of the head.[15] The Hippocratics described these movements in a purely mechanical way (the attraction of dry by wet) and never compared the womb to a wandering animal as did the Pythagorean philosopher Timaeus, the central character of Plato's eponymous dialogue.[16]

Since 1980 there has been extensive debate as to whether the knowledge of the female body transmitted in the Hippocratic gynecological treatises was contributed by women or invented by male writers. The current consensus is that a polarization into male and female knowledge is not helpful in understanding these texts. Both men and women may have contributed knowledge; women may have contributed knowledge that was then expressed "through a male lens"; male writers may have invented some pieces of knowledge—all these scenarios are possible and not mutually exclusive.[17]

A similar conclusion has been reached concerning the numerous therapies and recipes listed in the Hippocratic gynecological treatises. Some recipes may have been contributed by women, but it is likely that pharmacological knowledge relating to female ailments was shared by men and women in antiquity, since female ailments often had far-reaching implications for the entire household, such as infertility.[18]

The treatments prescribed in the Hippocratic gynecological treatises consist in pharmacological remedies administered either externally (ointments, cataplasms), internally (drinks, electuaries), or vaginally (pessaries, fumigations); regimens and diets; manipulations of the womb; and sexual intercourse. In the administration of these various therapies, cooperation between the female patient and male physician was paramount, as was a significant degree of acceptance on the part of the patient. Many treatments were painful and/or long lasting, as in the case of a fumigation that had to be administered until the patient declared "that her sight [had] become dim and that she [was] about to faint."[19]

Not only did the Hippocratic gynecological writers conceive of women as being fundamentally different from men, they also criticized those physicians who treated women's ailments as if they were men's diseases.[20] In other words, these compilers argued for the existence of gynecology as an independent medical specialty. The independence of gynecology was not always recognized in antiquity; instead, the questions whether women had diseases of their own and were different from men was much debated.[21]

Writing slightly later than the Hippocratic gynecological compilers, the philosopher Aristotle argued that the male body was the norm from which the female body deviated. Aristotle's woman was a "deformed man" whose body was colder than that of a man. This coldness prevented women from heating up blood into seed and therefore from playing an active part in reproduction.[22] Aristotle's knowledge of the female body was, like that of the Hippocratic physicians, mainly derived from external observations. However, Aristotle also practiced some dissection on animals, thus paving the way for the major advances in anatomical knowledge, based on human dissections, of the Hellenistic period.

Interestingly, anatomical discoveries pertaining to the female body reinforced—not weakened—the Aristotelian conception of women as deformed men. The famous Hellenistic physician Herophilus described parts of the female body he had discovered through human dissection, two of which he named by analogy with the male system: the female "testicles" (i.e., ovaries) and spermatic ducts (i.e., Fallopian tubes). For Herophilus, women had the same sexual organs as men and suffered the same afflictions as men; however, he recognized that menstruation, childbirth, and lactation affected women only.[23]

Herophilus also observed the uterine ligaments that anchored the womb, thus making it impossible for this organ to move extensively.[24] Despite this anatomical observation, some later medical authors described the uterus as a wandering animal. Treatments (e.g., scent therapy) prescribed primarily against womb movements by Hippocratic authors remained popular, even with authors who rejected the notion of a moving womb; and Greek amulets against the ascent of the womb dating to the sixth or seventh century C.E. have been found.[25]

Soranus, a physician of the Methodist school active at the turn of the first and second century C.E., held similar views to those of Herophilus: women were affected by the same diseases as men but were alone in suffering the ailments related to bearing and feeding children. To the modern reader, Soranus's treatment of female patients in his *Gynecology* appears much more humane than that of the Hippocratic physicians. Soranus favored mild remedies such as bathing and massage and rejected harsh treatments such as emmenagogues, or a "ladder treatment" that required women to be hanged by their feet.[26] The Methodist physician considered menstruation to be an uncomfortable experience for women, saw intercourse as harmful, described the various ailments suffered by women during pregnancy, and recognized how traumatic childbirth and gynecological diseases could be for women.[27]

Soranus's *Gynecology* exerted a long-lasting influence on medical literature. It was excerpted by the Greek-speaking encyclopedists Oribasius (fourth century C.E.), Aetius (sixth century C.E.), and Paul of Aegina (seventh century C.E.). In the Latin-speaking world, the *Gynecology* was made available through translations, such as that of Caelius Aurelianus (fifth century C.E.), and adaptations, such as Muscio's *Genecia*, a question-and-answer text popular until the end of the twelfth century.[28] Whether Soranus also exerted an influence on the lives of individual women by putting his principles into practice is unclear, as he does not name a single female patient in his *Gynecology*.

Galen, the most famous physician of antiquity, on the other hand, records some of the relations he had with female patients (about twenty-five of Galen's stories are about female patients). Some of these women were illustrious enough to be called by their first names, such as Arria (who suffered from a weak stomach); others Galen named after their legal guardians, as in the case of the wife of Boethus who suffered from a "female flux"; others he referred to merely by their age and symptoms. With some notorious exceptions, Galen seems to have had little regard for women, whom he criticized for their lack of calm and their vanity and coquetry.[29]

From an anatomical point of view, Galen considered women to be inverted men, with the same genitalia as men but located inside the body rather than outside. Galen devoted a treatise to the anatomy of the uterus but was not particularly interested in female ailments, which he believed to be caused by "female semen."[30]

Physicians such as Soranus or Galen would have been an expensive choice for a sick woman and her family; often religious and magical healing were more accessible and less expensive alternatives. Regarding religion in general, and religious healing in particular, in the ancient world we must recognize the importance of ritual action and the role of a person's social network.[31] From the evidence of offerings, prayers, and other ritual actions, it is evident people considered actions to have expressed their piety effectively, and they expected some kind of practical (this-world) benefit such as healing as a reward or consequence. We note the group or social dimension of ancient religion—it seldom (if ever) was simply an individual matter. Thus, the religious actions of one person could well have been thought to facilitate the healing of another.

One type of ritual action was incubation at healing sites. Incubation was part of a pilgrimage process. People would travel to a sacred site, purify themselves, offer sacrifices and prayers, and then sleep there. They hoped to have a dream or vision, in which the healing god would appear and give advice or perform a miracle. Often the dream advice was a complicated or unusual set of actions to be performed, or a prescription to be taken. People often incubated for their own healing, and there is epigraphic evidence of women incubating at temples and being cured. Inscriptions at the Asclepius shrine at Epidaurus record several instances: there are cures of problematically extended periods of pregnancy, infertility, blindness, and tapeworm.[32]

Another type of ritual action related to Greco-Roman religious healing is ex-voto offerings. These objects were deposited at temples and shrines. They served as a potent promissory note[33] (a working spiritual gift in hope of a future benefit) or a thank offering (given in gratitude for a received benefit).[34] A variety of things might serve this function. Many of these objects are realistic renditions of body parts. Some apply to either gender (stylized renditions of ears or eyes), and in these cases it is impossible to determine whether a man or woman gave these objects. Other objects are gender-specific: small representations of a uterus or rounded breast give evidence of women's needs and involvement in ex-votos. Still other ex-votos are plaques with inscriptions or illustrations of scenes of offerings, dreams, or miraculous healings. At times, these objects appear to be stock and mass-produced, while others clearly were commissioned specifically by the donor. The image of the leg shown in Figure 4.4 bears a dedication thanking Asclepius and Hygieia.

FIGURE 4.3: Ex-voto offerings. Terra-cotta models of breast, eye, ear, womb, third to first century B.C.E. © The Trustees of the British Museum [Registration number: 1865,1118.119].

A third sort of religious action was an appeal to a holy man for a cure. A few examples from the accounts of Jesus's healing ministry provide data on the issue of women's health. The episode of the woman with the flow of blood illustrates the active role of a patient seeking healing.[35] In Mark's Gospel, we hear of a woman who had heard of Jesus and then deliberately sought him out, confident he would heal her. She reached out and touched Jesus's robe and was healed. Jesus commended her initiative, saying, "Your faith has saved you." The account stresses the active role she has played in her healing.[36] Caesarius of Arles (sixth century) provides evidence of the power of the holy man within a Christian community in southern France.[37] The biography of Caesarius shows that many people came to him for healing, including women.[38] St. Martin of Gaul (sixth century) was another Christian holy man with legendary healing powers.[39] His shrine became a pilgrimage site, and sick people visited it in a way similar to the Asclepius shrines in the Greco-Roman period. Many of the texts relate to the healing of women.[40] A funeral eulogy by the fourth-century church father Gregory of Nazianzus provides evidence of a woman's creative initiative in her own healing.[41] In this sermon, Gregory praises his sister Gorgonia. She had endured a horrific accident and was at the point of death. She managed to make her way to a private chapel late at night. She prayed fervently at the altar, touching it as the woman with the flow of blood had touched Jesus's cloak. Then, says Gregory, "she anointed her whole

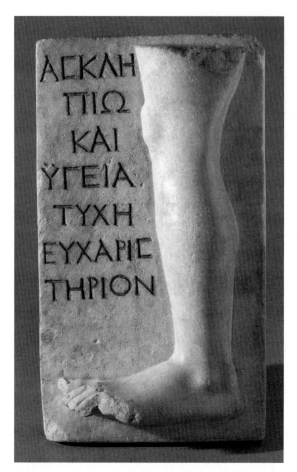

FIGURE 4.4: Ex-voto relief in the shape of a leg, dedi-
cated to Asclepius and Hygieia. First to second century
C.E., excavated from the shrine of Asclepius. © The
Trustees of the British Museum 1867.0508.117. The
Greek inscription reads, "[To] Asclepius and Hygieia
[from] Tyche, [as a] thank offering."

body with a medicine she had devised herself: having privately stored away some
of the sacraments . . . she now mingled them with her tears."[42] Out of this most
unusual self-administered ritual came Gorgonia's healing.

Like religion, magic involves accessing the supernatural world for benefit.
Using magic is an active process, whether one consults a magician, buys a
charm and then chants it regularly, or drinks a magic potion. The element of
choice and commitment is as great as when a woman self-administers a secular prescription. The Greek magic papyri collection has many texts of charms

for relief from illness or affliction. Like the ex-votos discussed earlier, at times these charms are gender-neutral (relating to fever, headache, or eye and ear problems) and could have been used by men or women. A few clearly deal with women's issues (hardening of the breasts, pregnancy and birth, or problematic menstrual flow).[43] Amulets were also used in gynecological contexts, as already mentioned. Amulets with birth scenes, to be used during labor, have been preserved. For instance, an amulet of the British Museum, shown in Figure 4.5, represents a woman giving birth on a seat, gripping handles, with legs apart, feet resting on a stool.[44]

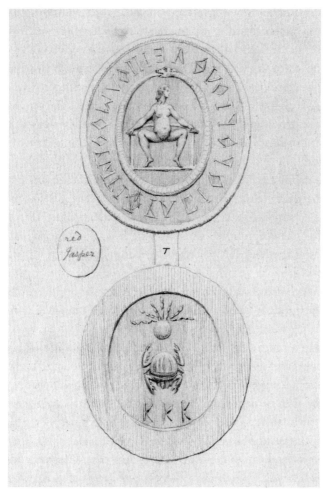

FIGURE 4.5: Drawing of childbirth on an amulet. Red-jasper amulet. Woman on a birth-stool. © The Trustees of the British Museum [Registration number: 2010,5006.585].

Objects associated with holy men in a Christian context function in a similar way to amulets in a pagan context. In the early medieval period, people would use relics to self-administer healing power for themselves or to help those in their family. Sometimes the people of the parish would use these objects in unconventional manners, and it was difficult for the church to control these practices.[45] Oil that the sixth-century Saint Caesarius had consecrated was kept in homes, and was used (on the initiative of household members) to effect self-cures or a cure for others. The case of a woman named Agretia is dramatic. She had an ailment like the woman with the issue of blood.[46] She demands to have a piece of the bishop's clothing that he had recently worn, and eventually a church officer obtains this item for her. She places the object on her body and is healed.[47]

We also have records of sermons that Caesarius preached.[48] Evidently in his area there was a lively belief and practice relating to the sacred or magical power of objects. It is likely that these beliefs reflect both pre-Christian and Christian views, and the two systems were in competition.[49] In one sermon, Caesarius urges people to receive sacraments and prayers in church for healing rather than resort to magic.[50] Another sermon provides significant evidence about the actions of some women:

> Those to whom God is unwilling to give children should not try to have them by means of herbs or magic signs or evil charms. . . . Just as women whom God wants to bear more children should not take medicines to prevent their conception, so those whom God wishes to remain sterile should desire and seek this gift from God alone.[51]

Sermon 52.5–6 criticizes women who seek the healing of their sons by means of magic (consulting a soothsayer, oracle, witch, or "nurse") rather than resorting to the church.[52]

The reader will see that although secular, religious, and magical medicine have been presented as separate entities, the overlap between the three forms of healing was at times significant. For example, although Soranus considered magical amulets to be ineffective, he did not begrudge women the right to use them when they suffered uterine hemorrhage, in order to keep them "more cheerful," anticipating the placebo effect.[53] It is also apparent that although women patients were under the control of men, they sometimes had choices regarding their healing. Women were also expected to take an active part in their cures by complying with time-consuming regimens or traveling to a healing temple or shrine. At times that active role was so pronounced that the boundary between the patient and the healer became blurred.

WOMEN AS HEALING PRACTITIONERS

A grave monument dating to the mid-fourth century B.C.E., shown in Figure 4.6, celebrates the life of a woman named Phanostrate, described as a doctor (*iatros*) and midwife (*maia*).[54] The word *maia* could be an informal title given to any experienced woman who had assisted neighbors and family members in childbirth, but the word *iatros* hints at a more formal medical occupation. Phanostrate's stele is the earliest such preserved monument commemorating a woman skilled in the healing arts.[55] The majority of these monuments focus on the family relationships and virtues of the deceased rather than on her professional occupation, but some are nevertheless useful in gaining an understanding of the role of women in healing.[56] For instance, in Figure 1.1, the bas-relief on the tomb of Scribonia Attica (mid-second century C.E.), a midwife buried with the physician M. Ulpius Amerimnus, represents a scene of childbirth that is very similar to the written description found in Soranus's *Gynecology*: the parturient is seated and supported by another woman, while the midwife examines the advancement of labor with her hand, turning her head away to preserve the patient's modesty.[57] An interesting inscription can be found at the base of a statue offered by Antiochis of Tlos in the late first century B.C.E. or early first century C.E.: "Antiochis, daughter of Diadotos, of Tlos, marked by the council and people of Tlos for her experience in the medical art, erected this statue of herself."[58] Interestingly, Galen also knew one or two women named Antiochis: he quotes two remedies "of Antiochis" (an emollient and a remedy for the spleen) and mentions an Antiochis as the dedicatee of a pharmacological treatise by Heraclides of Tarentum, the famous empiric physician (first century B.C.E.).[59] It is possible, although impossible to prove, that the Antiochis(es) of the literary tradition and that of the epigraphic tradition are one and the same person, a female healer highly regarded by her male colleagues and by her patients.[60] In any case, this example illustrates the difficulties encountered in bringing together the epigraphic (or papyrological) traditions and the literary tradition (medical or otherwise)—a literary tradition in which women healers are often regarded with suspicion or passed over in silence.

The Hippocratic corpus contains very little information on women's roles in healing. There are only three explicit mentions of female healers in the Hippocratic texts, all in relation to childbirth.[61] The Hippocratic corpus also refers to "other women" who helped women in labor.[62] Whether these shadowy women practiced midwifery for a living or were simply knowledgeable female relatives is unclear; the Hippocratics might have intended this ambiguity in order to account for a variety of circumstances.[63]

FIGURE 4.6: Stele of Phanostrate. Midwife *(maia)* and physician *(iatros)*, fourth century B.C.E. Attic stele; Athens, National Archaeological Museum, NM 993. Photo credit: National Archaeological Museum, Athens. © Hellenic Ministry of Culture and Tourism/ Archaeological Receipts Fund.

Some scholars have suggested that female healers do not appear in the Hippocratic corpus because its compilers were interested only in cases of difficult births, whereas midwives—or simply experienced women—attended uncomplicated births.[64] However, it may also be the case that the Hippocratics deliberately erased women healers from their narratives in a bid to appropriate for themselves an area of healing that was usually seen as woman's business, in a bid to control female reproductivity.[65] It is certainly not the case that women specializing in midwifery did not practice at the time of composition of the Hippocratic gynecological texts, even though a late text claims that the first midwife, Agnodice, was trained by Herophilus.[66] We have already encountered

the fourth-century Phanostrate, and one can also mention the Platonic dialogue in which Socrates claims to be the son of a midwife and to be a midwife
to men's ideas.[67] Socrates' midwife is an old woman who induces labor through
a creative combination of chants, charms, and drugs.

It is impossible to determine whether the Hippocratic gynecological writers intended their works to be read by some midwives.[68] Neither can we as-
certain whether Herophilus had an audience of midwives in mind when he
wrote a treatise entitled *Midwifery*, which is unfortunately lost to us.[69] On the
other hand, Soranus makes it clear that midwives should read—or have read to
them—his *Gynecology*. The beginning of this text contains a description of the
perfect midwife, who in addition to being literate should love her work, have
her wits about her, and be clean and robust.[70] Also writing with an audience of
women in mind was Muscio, who in his adaptation of Soranus's *Gynecology*
insisted that he wanted his work to be straightforward enough to be understood by midwives.[71]

Soranus's portrait of a midwife was one of an ideal female healer.[72] Not all
midwives kept their calm in difficult situations, if we may believe Galen's story
of how he healed Boethus's wife from a female flux.[73] As to the requirement
of devotion to one's job, one might consider a fifth-century text that describes
how a woman working in a wine shop was called to assist a woman in difficult
childbirth while serving a client.[74]

So far, the discussion has centered on cases where women performed
straightforward healing roles. Our discussion now turns to more complicated cases of what might be called "vicarious healing." In cases of incubation at sacred healing sites (sleeping in the temple precincts in hope of
a dream-vision), we have evidence of at least a few examples of vicarious
incubation. Specifically, a person would travel to a site, perform rituals of
purification and sacrifice, sleep overnight, and obtain a benefit for someone
else.[75] The following ancient source gives a rare personal account of religious
healing. Briefly, a son has traveled to the shrine of the healing god Asclepius
with his sick mother. They pray together, she is cured, and they thank the
god through sacrifices. Then the son becomes stricken with illness. The
son and mother again sleep in the temple precincts in the hope of a dream-
vision. This portion of the account describes the mother's role from the son's
perspective:

Heavy in the head with my troubles I was lapsing half-conscious into
sleep, and my mother, as a mother would for her child (and she is by
nature affectionate), being extremely grieved at my agonies was sitting
without enjoying even a short period of slumber, when suddenly she

perceived—it was no dream or sleep, for her eyes were open immovably, though not seeing clearly, for a divine and terrifying vision came to her. . . . When she had recovered herself, she tried, still trembling, to wake me, and finding that the fever had left me and that much sweat was pouring off me, did reverence to the manifestation of the god, and then wiped me and made me more collected.[76]

The mother and son compare notes and find that they each had a vision of the god, and at that moment the illness stopped. This account shows the group aspect of healing, as the mother and son facilitate each other's cure.

The most basic form of religious action in the Greco-Roman world was sacrifice. Gifts to the gods were thought to be pleasing and to result in rewards not only to the donor but also to the group associated with the donor (family, association, or town). In *The Women Sacrificing to Asclepius*, a third-century B.C.E. mime by Herondas, the temple warden says, "Your sacrifice, woman, has been well accomplished and with favorable presages. No one has evoked Paion more efficaciously than you have. Hail, Paion! Be favorable to these women for their good offerings, and if they have husbands, to them also and to their near kindred."[77] These women achieved the promise of good health for their families through their sacrifice.

Prayers could be given to the gods, and petitions to holy men. In accounts of the philosopher and wonder-worker Apollonius of Tyana (late first century C.E.), we hear of a woman seeking exorcism on behalf of her sixteen-year-old son who is possessed by a devil. Her action facilitates his cure.[78] In the New Testament, we find the story of a Syrophoenician woman who wants healing for her daughter; her initiative is remarkable. Despite an initial rebuff from Jesus, the woman persists and gives a clever rejoinder to Jesus's statement. Jesus commends this woman's initiative, and her daughter is healed.[79] In John 11:1–44 the sisters of Lazarus persistently ask Jesus to help their dying brother. Lazarus is brought back to life through the prayer of Jesus. In each of these accounts, the strong initiative and faith of the women is rewarded by the healing of a relative. Accounts of the lives of Christian saints such as Caesarius of Arles[80] and Martin of Gaul[81] continue the theme of women seeking healing on behalf of others.

The account of the women who accompany Jesus in Luke 8:1–3 is brief, but it offers interesting evidence of another type of role for females in the healing process. In the story, these women have been healed or exorcised by Jesus. The fact that some of the women are named indicates their importance in the later collective memory of Luke's community (perhaps as role models or authorities;

see the next section). The women are described in Luke 8:3 as traveling with Jesus (perhaps as disciples) and "providing for him out of their resources." It is likely that what we see here is a system of reciprocal patronage or an exchange of benefits. Jesus has given the women a valuable gift—divine healing. The women respond by being sponsors of Jesus's ministry, including healing.[82]

It is useful to read the preceding New Testament text in conjunction with the description of Jesus sending out seventy of his followers in Luke 10:1–12, 17–20.[83] The unnamed group of seventy in Luke are sent out "two by two" (10:1) in an itinerant ministry similar to that of Jesus: they travel to Galilean villages, share a meal with the locals, heal the sick, and proclaim that the Kingdom of God has drawn near at that place. The historical Jesus scholar, John Dominic Crossan, offers a credible hypothesis concerning these two texts: "I wonder . . . if what we are initially or primarily dealing with is healed healers? Is this what Jesus did with those whom he himself healed and who wanted to join his movement? He sent them out to do likewise?"[84] The reader may find here evidence of male-female team ministry in early Christianity. In ancient Mediterranean society, a respectable woman could not travel by herself—she needed to have a male escort. It usually was not socially acceptable for a man to visit the home of a single woman. The seventy who were sent out "two by two" in some cases could have been women paired with men, and these female disciples could then visit the women of a village. The apostle Paul speaks of women engaging in ministry with men, when he mentions the "sister-wife" (*adelphēn gynaika*) who accompanies a male apostle-missionary.[85] In Paul's letter to the group at Corinth, he describes the gifts of the Spirit as including healing or cures (*charismata iamatōn*) and those who served the group as having such gifts of healing.[86] Nothing Paul says suggests that it is only men who are granted spiritual gifts. Paul's famous statement in Galatians 3:26–28, concerning a new identity through Christ ("neither male nor female"), suggests that in the early Pauline communities, the conventional social and gender distinctions were viewed as secondary. The reader may well suppose that at times early Christian women did act as healers.

The family connection in healing is also important. Isis, a mother goddess in Hellenistic Egyptian religion, and Hygieia, the daughter-assistant of the Greco-Roman healing god Asclepius, show societal recognition of the role of women in health issues, recast as religious discourse and healing action. Many votive plaques show a family approaching the family of Asclepius. There is mirroring of human and divine families in these scenes: the two groups cooperate in the process of achieving healing.[87] Many shrines to Asclepius had statues of both the male god and his daughter Hygieia.[88]

As already noted, mothers and wives usually are significant caregivers in the home. With that in mind, household objects and women's jewelry offer intriguing evidence of women's involvement in Greco-Roman religion, and clues to women's roles in healing. Roman homes had a small shrine (a *lararium*), and often these worship spaces had a variety of little statues of gods and spirits. The members of the household chose the figures, arranged the space, and made small offerings on a regular basis. We have evidence of Isis and Hygieia/Salus statues in some of these domestic shrines. Isis and Hygieia were also popular figures on signet rings. It is likely that these rings had an apotropaic function (guarding against problems), but perhaps they also served an empowering function. It is reasonable to assume that a woman wearing a ring with a healing god or deity associated with health would consider that she was connected to the deity and receiving power to assist her in her daily tasks.[89]

Interestingly, early Christianity helped to develop the concept of a community health care system. Within the Greco-Roman world, the prevailing practice was that people only looked after their ill family members. The idea that the community had any responsibility for ill people was largely unknown. One thesis in Rodney Stark's *The Rise of Christianity* (1996) is that the charitable care provided by early Christians was an innovative market advantage that prompted outsiders to join the group and contributed to the eventual success of the Christian religion.[90]

In the office of a Christian bishop (*episkopos*), the reader will find evidence of still another type of female role in healing. A man known as a "server" (*diakonos*) assisted the bishop. In some cases, we see reference to a "female server" (*diakonē*).[91] Relevant for this chapter are the roles these women played in women's health care.

Church manuals of the second through fourth centuries show that female deacons did several things related to women's health. First, both male and female servers acted on behalf of the bishop and visited the sick and poor members of the congregation, with deacons visiting men and deaconesses visiting women. They would pray, share a communion meal, and at times anoint a person with consecrated oil. These religious activities were thought to convey not only spiritual but also physical benefits. Second, deaconesses did charity work and palliative care. They sat up with sick women during the night, changed dressings, perhaps brought food, and in general were a great comfort. One church text says the following: "A deaconess is required to go to houses of the heathen where there are believing women, and to visit those who are sick, and to minister to them in that of which they have need, and to bathe those who have begun to recover from sickness."[92] Third, there are a few references to the "laying on of hands" by widows (celibate mature women), a practice that may refer to charismatic healing,[93] a liturgical blessing, or some combination of the two acts.[94]

Thus, we recognize the important role of women in the team health ministry of early Christianity—and we may speculate that at times these women took initiatives apart from what the bishop had ordered, even to act directly as healers. Tertullian suggests that some women acted on their own authority (at least within so-called heretical or unorthodox Christian groups): "These heretical women, how bold they are! They dare to teach [men], argue [against men], enact exorcisms, promise cures, even baptize."[95] The fourth-century church writer Gregory of Nazianus (mentioned earlier) gave a eulogy to his mother, Nonna, which provides evidence of a woman's actions healing another. Gregory praises Nonna's effective prayers on behalf of her seriously ill husband (Gregory's father). As described by Gregory, his mother dramatically prays during a public Easter vigil, calling out for (in effect, demanding from God) her husband's healing. The old man recovered.[96]

We have one source relating to a sixth-century Christian holy woman, Saint Monegunde of France.[97] Like her male counterparts, she was thought to have healing powers during her lifetime, and after her death through her relics. Her brief biography contains accounts of her prayers healing many people, both men and women. One account relates a dramatic episode of this Christian healer imitating the actions of Christ:

> A certain woman brought to her [Monegunde] her daughter who was full of ulcers. . . . The Saint prayed, took saliva from her mouth, anointed her running sores with it, and made this young girl well by the help of the same virtue used by Him [Christ] Who, with some dust and spittle, formed the eyes of one born blind.[98]

The issue of witches and female magicians in Greek and Roman society is another area where the reader may suppose the involvement of women as practitioners: those who claimed magical powers could heal as well as harm.[99] Healing is a complex act, and the simple division of roles into healer and healed does not convey the subtleties of human action, as is evident in the cases of vicarious healing. Further, some male sources might have tried to play down the role of female healers, and the reader may suspect an element of competition in the medical marketplace. The area in which women were most active was gynecology/obstetrics, but their expertise could extend to other areas. As the next section shows, women could achieve high status through their healing role and take on the role of an authority.

WOMEN AS MEDICAL AUTHORITIES

From the beginnings of Greek literature, women are frequently presented as possessing pharmacological knowledge. In book 4 of the *Odyssey*, Helen learns the art of drugs from the Egyptian Polydamna, and in book 10, Circe transforms Odysseus and his men into pigs by means of a drug. The fragmentary tragedy of Sophocles entitled the *Rhizotomoi* (the root cutters) portrays Medea gathering pharmacological herbs.[100] Finally, in comedies, ordinary women were sometimes represented concocting love philters and poisons.[101] Women in Greek literature, it seems, most often used their pharmacological knowledge to negative ends.

As already noted, it is impossible to determine whether any of the pharmacological recipes preserved in the Hippocratic corpus were contributed by women. On the other hand, many recipes preserved in the writings of (male) medical authors active in the first centuries of our era are attributed to women. It is better to refer to these women as "authorities" rather than "authors" of these recipes, as many may never have written anything—they simply lent their names to the remedies.[102]

Some of these female contributors are presented as semi-anonymous: they are identified by their place of origin, their profession, or their marital status, but they are not named. For instance, in his *Composite Remedies*, the pharmacologist Scribonius Largus (first century C.E.) tells us how he went to great lengths and expense to obtain a remedy for pains in the colon from a woman whom he identifies by her geographic origin (Africa), her place of residence (Rome), and her social status—she was a *muliercula*, a dismissive term often used for a woman of low status. However, Scribonius does not indicate where the African lady obtained her expertise in curing diseases of the colon; we do not know whether she was a professional healer or not.[103]

Scribonius also lists a remedy against epilepsy he obtained from a woman he identifies by her place of residence (Rome), her marital status (*matrona*), and her virtue (*honesta*). The expression *matrona honesta* seems to indicate she held a higher social status than the *muliercula* of the previous story. Again Scribonius does not tell us where this matron obtained her medical expertise.[104] The same author relates another account of a semi-anonymous female authority, "the Syrian woman of Gadara," to whom a magic charm is attributed.

Evidently an authoritative female magician, her remedy was recommended to be used for an inflammation.[105]

It is important to note that the use of semi-anonymity in ancient pharmacological texts is documented in cases of men's remedies as well.[106] However, in the case of male informants, semi-anonymity is restricted to people from the lowest strata of society (peasants or country doctors); "honorable" male informants (that is, educated city physicians) are usually named. In contrast, women are often presented as semi-anonymous whatever their social status. Semi-anonymity allowed medical writers to establish a distance between themselves and sources they judged to be inferior, whether due to low social status or gender.

Not all women contributors to the fields of medicine and pharmacology were left unnamed, however. The women named by ancient medical writers include the aforementioned Antiochis, Aquilia Secunda, Aspasia, Cleopatra, Elephantis, Eugerasia, Lais, the Lybian Fabilla, Metrodora, Olympias of Thebes, Origeneia, Romula, Salpe, Samithra, Sotira, Spendusa, Thais, and Xanita.[107] With the exception of Aquilia, Fabilla, and Romula, all women listed have Greek names. The same phenomenon is observable in the case of named male authorities. Medicine was very much a Greek art, in the hands of Greek practitioners, even in the early Roman Empire.

Modern scholars sometimes assume that these female authorities were real women practitioners in the medical arts.[108] In some cases, such as Antiochis, this may well be true; however, some names of female medical authorities appear to be pseudonyms. As pointed out by Rebecca Flemming, in the first centuries of the Common Era, "pseudonymity was rife, if not *de rigueur*," and "the creation of a fictional female voice had a particular allure"—one can also add that it lent a vicarious authority to the author.[109] Let us now turn our attention to some of these female authorities whose names we should approach with caution.

Pliny the Elder names a certain Lais in relation to abortives and a remedy against the bite of rabid dogs.[110] Lais was the name of one of the most famous courtesans of antiquity: Lais of Corinth (fifth century B.C.E.). The name Lais was probably used as a pseudonym by generations of women who wanted to share the success of the beautiful Corinthian. That abortive recipes were circulated under that name does not come as a surprise.

Pliny also gives us six remedies by Salpe, the *obstetrix*. Among these remedies one can find one cosmetic recipe (a depilatory) and a recipe for an aphrodisiac, involving an ass's penis.[111] Athenaeus, on the other hand, mentions a Salpe from Lesbos, author of frivolous works (*paignia*).[112] Scholars have debated whether these two Salpes were the same person, but this seems to miss the point: "Salpe" was most probably a pseudonym—a mask—used to confer authority onto a certain type of literature characterized by its sexual content.[113] That "salpe" was also the name of a fish only adds to the suspicion, as fish and courtesans were often associated in ancient literature.[114]

"Salpe" contributed to the closely related fields of eroticism, cosmetics, and advice on female reproduction. The same nexus is observable with "Elephantis": Pliny mentions her as an authority on abortives; Galen cites one of her cosmetic remedies (a remedy against alopecia); and Martial and Suetonius knew her as an author of erotic manuals particularly appreciated by the emperor Tiberius.[115]

"Cleopatra" is yet another authoritative name in these three fields: Several cosmetic recipes bearing her name are preserved in Greek medical writings; they were extracted from a recipe book entitled *Cosmetics*. In the Latin medieval tradition, she is known as an authority on gynecology, and there are indications that she is remembered in the Arabic tradition as a writer on *aphrodisiaca*.[116] Cleopatra's *Cosmetics*, of which the writings of Galen and Paul of Aegina (seventh century C.E.) preserve extracts, was certainly not composed by the famous queen of Egypt: none of her early biographers specify that she wrote on medical topics.[117] Moreover, the work is not mentioned by any of the major medical writers active in the first century C.E. Although it is possible that a real woman named Cleopatra composed the *Cosmetics* at the end of the first or beginning of the second century, it is more plausible that the name Cleopatra was intentionally chosen as a pseudonym by the compiler of the text. As a pseudonym, this name was a particularly good choice: the queen of Egypt was famous for her beauty and her taste for luxury. Moreover, the connection with Egypt must have given a particular cachet to the treatise since the country was famous for its production of scented oils and ointments.

This choice of pseudonym was so good that later medical compilers were convinced that Queen Cleopatra had been active in the field of cosmetology. Thus, Aetius, writing in the sixth century C.E., included a recipe in the eighth book of his *Medical Collection* for an unguent of Queen Cleopatra, costly and pleasant.[118] Another recipe to make the face bright, attributed to a queen named Cleopatra—this time Cleopatra Berenice—appears in Metrodora's collection of recipes.[119]

The Greek tradition has preserved only the cosmetic recipes of Cleopatra, but in the late antique Latin tradition, her name is attached to two gynecological writings: the *Gynaecia* and the *Pessaria*. The *Gynaecia* exists in two versions (long and short) and covers a variety of gynecological issues and treatments; the *Pessaria* is a collection of twenty recipes for pessaries (i.e., vagi-nal suppositories).[120] We do not know whether the *Gynaecia* was originally composed in Greek and then translated into Latin or composed directly in Latin. In favor of the Greek origin of the Cleopatra gynecological tradition, we cite a manuscript of Soranus in which Cleopatra is said to have received gyne-cological illustrations from a certain Olympias of Heracleia.[121] That Olympias bore the same name as an authority in women's matters known to Pliny and as the famous mother of Alexander the Great could be merely a coincidence. It is impossible to prove her identity.[122]

Finally, in the Arabic tradition, the author Qustā ibn Lūqā (820–912 C.E.) mentions a book on aphrodisiacs by Cleopatra.[123] Thus, "Cleopatra," the name of a queen famous in antiquity for her love affairs and skills in the art of seduc-tion, conferred authority on all matters of knowledge pertaining to women's health and reproduction in later centuries.

The royal status of Cleopatra certainly added potency to the medical mate-rial transmitted under her name. Similarly, the name Aspasia, that of a medical authority quoted on numerous occasions by Aetius in his book on gynecologi-cal matters (book 16), may have lent both sexual and political power to her medical advice. Indeed, Aspasia was the name of Pericles's (ca. 495–429 B.C.E.) highly educated mistress.

The final female authority we would like to consider is Metrodora, whose name is attached to the treatise *From the Writings of Metrodora, Concerning Women's Afflictions of the Womb*, preserved in a single Greek manuscript.[124] This treatise, whose date is uncertain, includes a long section on gynecology, as well as recipes for aphrodisiacs and beautifying products. In the absence of in-depth scholarly work on this text, it is impossible to determine when this text was compiled, and whether it was authored by a woman or not.[125]

In the medical tradition, female names were used to confer authority not only on material that we would consider to be gynecological in nature but also on cosmetic and erotic material. Cosmetic recipes purported to enhance wom-en's beauty, and hence their sexual power; gynecological treatments enabled women to enhance or check fertility; and erotic advice helped them to become better lovers. Whether the authors were actually men seems irrelevant. Female pseudonyms were considered fit for these works because it was assumed that nobody would have known more about female sexuality, ways to cure sexual diseases, or ways to enhance beauty than a woman. In the words of Flemming, in medical writings, women were made to perform a "heavily gendered func-tion."[126] However, remedies ascribed to semi-anonymous women, such as the remedy against epilepsy by the honest Roman matron, hint at what might have been closer to the reality, that is, women's activity in all areas of medical practice.

The preaching and publication of Christian textual material is another area where men played a dominant role, yet here too we see female figures cited from time to time. Here, women are referred to not as medical authorities but as role models of faith and piety. The episodes of the sister and mother of Gregory of Nazianzus[127] were preached in church eulogies and later published. These texts gave those women the role of exemplars in later time periods. Some biblical women also fit this category. The account of the woman with the hemorrhage in Mark 5 was preached in many sermons during the patristic and medieval periods. Church histories also state that a statue of this woman was credited with miraculous healing powers well into the sixth century.[128] It is likely that these women caught the imagination of women, who looked to them as they themselves sought healing or did healing for others.

CONCLUSION

As we have discussed, there was significant overlap among "secular," "religious," and "magical" modes of healing. Female medical authorities may have written on gynecology, cosmetics, and other areas pertaining to woman's lives. More significantly, however, a simple contrast between male healers and female patients does not do justice to the subtle social dynamics of the ancient Western world between the fifth century B.C.E. and the seventh century C.E. and beyond. In this time period, and particularly in the channels of elite medicine, it is evident that men's authority was significant and at times determinative in assessing women's health states and prescribing modes of treatment. However, even within the confines of a patriarchal system, women likely made significant contributions in assessing their health states and facilitating their healing or that of others. In the areas of home remedies and religious healing, it may be the case that women had more scope for improvisation and initiative. In short, whether ancient women were patients, medical practitioners, or authorities, they all played important roles in the healing process and may justly be called "healers."

CHAPTER FIVE

Public and Private

KRISTINA MILNOR

Like the inhabitants of many premodern societies, ancient Greeks and Romans saw the world as divided into two spheres: the public realm of men, which encompassed the arena of civic interactions, especially economic exchange, politics, and the military; and the private realm of women, centered on the household, family, and domestic tasks of daily life. As early as Homer's *Iliad* (eighth century B.C.E.), the poet divides the landscape into two distinct worlds, that of the battlefield, where men meet and fight, and that of the city, the Trojans' home, which is represented as primarily inhabited by women.[1] Most of Homer's text takes place, of course, on the battlefield, while the interior of the city generally finds a place in the narrative only when one of the male heroes enters it. This reflects the traditional sense among the ancients, especially the classical Greeks, that the "privacy" of women's domestic world meant that it had no place in "public" speech: as Pericles famously put it in his funeral oration (430 B.C.E.), the greatest glory of a woman is not to be spoken of, for either praise or blame.[2] When women *were* praised in the ancient world, it was generally for their adherence to and performance of traditional domestic virtues such as childrearing and wool working. Numerous funerary epitaphs can be cited, including that of Claudia (Rome, second century B.C.E.), which expresses admiration for the dead woman's affection for her husband and nurturance of her two sons and concludes simply, "She kept her house, she worked with wool." The underlying assumption in such praise was, however, that the domestic sphere was women's right and natural home, so that, for instance,

Cicero sharply criticized the philosopher Plato for suggesting that the ideal state would provide equal opportunities for male and female participation in governance: "How great will be the misfortune of that city in which women assume the offices of men!"[3]

At the same time, however, there is also evidence that the prevailing ideology of separate gendered spheres was challenged in both representation and practice. Again, as early as Homer's *Iliad*, we find the hero Hector returning to his house in the city to find that his wife Andromache is not at home; instead, he finds her on the wall of the city, looking out over the fighting troops, where she laments her disempowered role as a woman and makes some suggestions about how her husband should conduct the day's battle. Aristophanes's comedy *Lysistrata* (411 B.C.E.) depicts a revolution by Athenian women who, unhappy with the lack of progress being made in the war between Athens and Sparta, stage a strike and force their male relatives to negotiate a peace treaty. Women-only religious festivals in Athens such as the Thesmophoria allowed women to take over public space, at least temporarily. Within Roman culture, women's restriction to the domestic sphere, away from public life, seems often to have been the site of contradictions and contestation. Thus, for instance, the historian Livy recounts the story of Lucretia, who goes down in Roman history as a preeminent example of domestic virtue: her husband proposes a contest to his friends over which of their wives would be found to be attentive to the home while their husbands were away at war; while the others' wives are discovered out at dinner parties, Lucretia is found in the center of her house, weaving with her handmaidens. When she is raped by a member of Rome's ruling family, she insists that she cannot live with the shame and commits suicide. This incident becomes the catalyst for the first great political revolution in Roman politics, as her male relatives rose up in anger against the prince who attacked her and overthrew the monarchy in favor of a republican government. Lucretia's performance of domesticity is thus the direct cause of her entry into the public history of the Roman state, which is then transformed because of her adherence to traditional feminine virtues.

In this essay, therefore, I discuss the ideals and ideologies that framed men and women's experience of the public/private dichotomy in ancient Greek and Roman culture. But I also focus on the ways in which those ideologies were resisted, at least in part because they already contained certain contradictions that were ripe for exploitation. For instance, although it is clear that the dominant norms of ancient cultures insisted that women should be as invisible as possible, confined to their homes and away from the public eye, nevertheless those same cultures spent a great deal of time discussing and describing that confinement, thus verbally violating the invisibility they sought to prescribe. Thus, in addition to the occasional act of genuine resistance performed by women and men who supported them, we find that the gendered division of the spheres—even and perhaps especially during times of heightened anxiety on the part of cultural conservatives—was always a site of a certain amount of ambiguity and contestation. Indeed, it is in many ways more productive to consider the separation of the sexes in ancient societies less as a fact of life than a problem to be negotiated, both in representation and reality.

CLASSICAL GREECE

I will begin chronologically, with classical Athens. Too little information survives from other city-states in the ancient Greek world to make very many pronouncements about the nature of female roles there, although tantalizing fragments can sometimes be found: Herodotus, for example, tells us that the Spartan queen Gorgo was responsible for deciphering a coded message sent to warn her state of the impending Persian invasion in 480 B.C.E.[4] Thus, not only does Gorgo seem to have been accorded access to the document in question, but she had the education and background to read it; moreover, Herodotus himself memorializes her entry into public affairs by recording her actions in his "public" history of the Persian wars. The fact of the matter, however, is that the vast majority of our textual evidence concerning women's lives in the classical period comes from the vibrant literary and cultural scene of Athens. In addition, the archaeology of household life has progressed greatly in recent years, which has provided a certain amount of further information about domestic patterns in communities like Delos and Olynthos.[5] Yet even in the cases where we have good, careful excavation records of individual dwellings and their material contents, "finding" women in the household—let alone identifying attitudes toward their roles there and in the public sphere—is difficult. There remains, therefore, a great deal to be done, and even the information we do have is open to different interpretations.

One example of this is a social and structural phenomenon known as the *gynaikonitis*, or "women's quarters," that part of the house to which women were supposedly secluded to keep them away from the eyes of men. There is a certain amount of textual evidence supporting the existence of *gynaikonites* in classical Athens. For instance, in his speech *On the Murder of Eratosthenes*, the orator Lysias has the speaker—the defendant—describe the layout of his house and how it was apportioned to the male and female inhabitants: "My little house is on two floors, with equal space upstairs and down for

the 'gunaikonitis' ['women's quarters'] and the 'andronitis' ['men's quarters'].
When our child was born its mother fed it; so that she should not endanger
herself going downstairs each time the baby had to be washed, I lived upstairs
and the women below."[6] In a similar vein, Xenophon's *Oeconomicus* also describes a household with a distinct *gynaikonitis* and *andronitis* (9.5), although
in that instance it is clear that the people so separated are slaves: the speaker
notes that there is a locked door between the two areas so that the inhabitants cannot reproduce without the master's permission. In Lysias's description,
however, it is clear that the mistress of the house used the *gynaikonitis* along
with the slave women, but the speaker also indicates later in the speech that
the couple regularly shared a bed in the *andronitis*, with the wife descending
to the women's quarters only when the baby needed care. Moreover, the point
of the house description in the speech is that the defendant wishes to explain
to the jury how his wife was able to conduct an adulterous affair without his
knowledge. The fact that the *gynaikonitis* is located on the ground floor en-
ables the adulterer to enter and leave in secret. Thus, on one level, the speaker
of Lysias 1 is certainly attempting to draw on the jury's understanding that
women who are not kept as far away from "outside" men as possible are in
danger of sexual transgression; on the other, his description of his household
arrangements shows that seclusion was not the only principle dictating the
placement of the women's quarters.

Indeed, scholars have put a certain amount of energy into identifying *gynaikonites* in the architectural plans of classical Greek houses but have met
with only limited success. In a well-known article from 1983, Susan Walker
claimed to have identified a *gynaikonitis* archaeologically,[7] but subsequent
scholars have been less convinced by her evidence and have argued that no
archaeological evidence of women's quarters can be found in Greek houses.[8]
Given these difficulties, it has been argued that we are dealing here with a difference between ideology and social practice, between what people write and
say about themselves and the way in which they actually live their lives.[9] Moreover, it has been pointed out that much of the textual evidence that indicates
a strict seclusion of Greek women comes from (later) Roman sources: thus,
the Roman architect Vitruvius describes Greek houses as having two distinct
courtyards, one larger and more open for the men and one smaller and more
private for the women, into which men are not allowed. Yet it is important to
remember that Vitruvius provides this description only as a way of contrasting
with the design of Roman houses, which do not distinguish space by gender.
The Roman biographer Cornelius Nepos is even more explicit in the preface to
his *de Excellentibus Ducibus Exterarum Gentium* (6–7):

For what Roman would be ashamed to invite his wife to a dinner party? And in what family does the mother of the household not occupy a central place in the home and move about through the crowd? But the situation is very different in Greece. For she is not invited to dinner, unless it is with close relatives, nor does she sit anywhere other than the innermost part of the house, which is called the *gynaikonitis*, into which no man goes except a near relation.

Again, like Vitruvius, Nepos adduces the idea of the *gynaikonitis* not as a neutral fact but as a means of measuring the cultural differences between Greeks and Romans. As I discuss later on, it is clear that the two societies had distinct understandings of the "correct" relationship between women and the public realm. Nevertheless, the Roman representations of Greek women's domestic seclusion do not express neat historical facts but rather the desire of the later culture to claim difference and a certain superiority over their Hellenic neighbors.

In an important study from 2003, Lloyd Llewellyn-Jones argues that the role of formal domestic seclusion in Athens, at least for the classical period, has been exaggerated. He goes on to note that "the *separation* of gendered spheres of activity does not suggest absolute subjection or seclusion for women and does not bar them from having social and public roles of their own—as long as they stay within the expected confines of correct female behaviour."[10] Part of maintaining those confines seems to have been the widespread practice of veiling in public, which became (Llewellyn-Jones contends) a means for "respectable" women to maintain their gendered privacy even while participating in activities outside their houses. He quotes a fragment from the sixth-century poet Theognis of Megara in which a woman remarks, "I despise the wicked man, and, veiling myself, I pass by, holding aloft a mind light like a little bird's."[11] Women were able to hide even in public space by carrying a kind of portable privacy along with them. Interestingly, Llewellyn-Jones also suggests that a kind of veil known as the *tegedion* (literally, "little roof"), which may have covered the full face rather than simply the head, came into increasing popularity in the Hellenistic period (late fourth to early third century B.C.E.).[12] This was precisely the time when certain women were becoming more and more publicly visible in the Greek world, in religious positions, in ceremonial civic offices, and as patrons of public works. This shift in women's roles in Greek city-states seems to have been caused by a number of different factors: the influence of Hellenistic ideals of politically powerful queenship, the shift in property-ownership practices and corresponding greater economic independence for women, and the importance of female representatives of elite families in the public sphere.[13] If, however, Llewellyn-Jones is correct that this rise in formal, public roles for women went hand-in-hand with a greater insistence on veiling, we may detect a certain paradox in the ideologies that lay behind the physical and visual seclusion of Greek women.

On the other hand, whatever the actual physical mechanisms that sought to confine ancient Greek women, it is clear that there were powerful cultural pressures on women to remain in their "proper" sphere of home and family. When Plato in the *Republic* argues that women could and should have almost as much power and prominence in the ideal state as men,[14] because they have similar natural capacities, he is clearly expressing a radical idea—one for which, as I already noted, he was sharply criticized by Cicero. Elsewhere in his writings Plato seems closer to a mainstream Greek view of women's nature, as, for instance, in the *Laws*, where he criticizes the practice of leaving women's activities ungoverned by legislation; as he notes, "for to fail to regulate women is not only, as you might think, something which affects half of the whole matter, but, as much as women are naturally inferior to men in regard to virtue, by so much it is more than twice as important [to regulate their behavior]."[15] He goes on to remark that women are more accustomed to secrecy and darkness and for that reason resist any attempts to expose their actions to the view of others. The philosopher thus represents women not just as belonging in the private sphere physically but discursively as well: he sees the very act of legislating about them as a popularly unacceptable attempt to bring them "into the light." In the *Laws*, Plato suggests that this general Greek attitude is logically objectionable—because of their greater weakness of character, women need to be more controlled by law, not less—but his words nonetheless reflect the same ideological bias that would keep women separate and confined to the domestic world.

A more standard classical Greek view is represented by Xenophon in his *Oeconomicus*. The text is a philosophical dialogue in which Socrates "learns" how to be a good householder, based on the example of a young man, Ischomachus, who explains how he taught his wife how and why to manage her domestic duties. As part of his lesson to her, Ischomachus describes the origins of the gendered public/private dichotomy: When the gods created the world, they saw that the labor of living needed to be divided into two halves, since it was necessary for someone to go out into the world to hunt and farm and someone else to stay at home to perform the household tasks. Accordingly, they divided human beings into two types, those who were brave and powerful and thus naturally ordained to take care of "outside" work—men—and those who were more fearful and emotional, which suited them to "inside" duties, namely women.[16] Xenophon's speaker actually takes some pains to make it clear that there is not hierarchy between the two halves of the social world and the corresponding genders that belong to them; he describes the pair as existing in a mutually beneficial partnership (7.18), in which, although women are weaker both physically and mentally, men and women have equal capacities for memory, attention, and self-control (7.27). Thus, the *Oeconomicus* sees the gendered public/private dichotomy as both the cause and the symptom of the different natures of men and women but—at least overtly—refuses to attribute greater value to the public work of men.

At the same time, however, the overarching idea behind this section of the *Oeconomicus* is that Ischomachus must educate his new wife about how to care for her household correctly. That is, the "natural" divide between the sexes and their spheres of expertise, so carefully explained in the earlier cosmology, is instantaneously deconstructed. Ischomachus, it turns out, is the source of knowledge about both the outside, public tasks of men and the inside, domestic ones of women. In fact, Ischomachus repeatedly employs metaphors from civic life in his advice about the wife's domestic duties, such as "Then I directed my wife to make regulations, and to supervise their enforcement within the household, and whenever she thought fit to demand an accounting of its inventory, in the way a captain of the watch might demand an accounting from his guards and inquire if everything is in good order, as the council investigates the cavalry."[17] Ischomachus's language, then, further deconstructs the expressed divide between the world of men and that of women by suggesting that the forms and models of the male world can be applied easily to the female one. On one level, Xenophon's point seems to be to create a philosophical continuity between orderliness in the home and in the polis—thus showing, as seems to be the goal of the dialogue, that in order to be a good citizen a man must also be a good householder. At the same time, however, the substitution of male civic knowledge for female domestic expertise in the episode between Ischomachus and his wife also implies—even though Xenophon overtly denies it—a hierarchy between the two.

These philosophical explorations and explanations of the gendered public/private dichotomy in classical Athens certainly suggest the existence of powerful ideologies and cultural practices that restricted women to the domestic sphere. Nevertheless, even within Plato's and Xenophon's writings, there is a resistant undertow—a kind of anxious discursive return to the question of why and how society functioned by attempting to render half of its freeborn population invisible. On a wider cultural level, this can also be seen in many of the tragic plays that were presented in Athens during the fifth century B.C.E. The onstage space of tragedy was generally constructed as an outside area in front of a house or palace, with a door allowing access to the "inside" of the dwelling. Thus, as Froma Zeitlin has noted, "the ordinary business of entrances and exits, of comings and goings through the door of the house, maintains a symbolic dialectic between public and private, seen and unseen, open and secret, even known and unknown."[18] This dialectic is grounded in the gendered divide between the feminine domestic interior—invisible to the audience—and the masculine public space of the forestage. Yet women often play important roles in tragic plays and, by extension, in that public space. Indeed, Zeitlin goes on to argue that much of classical tragedy is built around the conflict between the sexes over ownership and control of inside and outside: "But in the contest over rights to control domestic space that the stage conventions exploit, the woman and not the man, by reason of her close identification with the house as her intimate scene, consistently rules the relations between inside and outside and shows herself as standing on the threshold betwixt and between."[19]

This is not to say that tragedy unambiguously empowers women but rather to point out that the tragic plays represent a popular cultural form in which questions about the gendered public/private dichotomy could be and were negotiated. Thus, for instance, the first scene of Sophocles's *Antigone* is a conversation between the heroine and her sister that takes place on the forestage, identified as the space "beyond the gates of the courtyard."[20] As M. W. Blundell remarks, "There is an element of transgression and risk in the fact that two young unmarried girls are outside the palace gates, rather than inside in the space culturally defined as female."[21] Later on in the play, the conservative and repressive King Creon will attempt to suppress the sisters' rebellion by sending them into the palace so that they will not "wander about, unruly."[22] At the same time, the first scene depicts the conflict between Antigone, who insists on her responsibility to defy the public authority of the king, and her more cautious sister, who argues that women must remember their correct place in the hierarchy and obey the authority of men. The space before the palace, therefore, is an appropriate one for their interaction: it is public place but within sight of the domestic sphere of the palace/household, so that it represents a kind of liminal zone in which the two women can negotiate their opposing views of the correct female relationship with masculine civic authority. A similar spatial gesture can be seen in Euripides's *Medea*, where the heroine begins her first speech by announcing, "I have come out of the house," and goes on to lament the disempowerment that women suffer in their domestic relationships as daughters and wives. Of course, many of the things that Medea criticizes—the fact that women are forced to marry men not of their own choosing, that they are entirely subject to their husbands' whims after marriage—are not actually true of Medea herself. She is, as the play goes on to show, an anomalous example of femininity, caught between the demands of her sex and her adherence to a masculine heroic code.[23] Her unique position between male and female values is heralded by her delivery of the speech concerning the domestic lives of women in the public space of the forestage.

A more extended meditation on the process and politics of a woman's emergence into the public sphere can be found in Euripides's play *Phoenissae*. The play has a complicated structure, but one of its most important subplots concerns Antigone, earlier made famous in Sophocles's play by her staunch and "unwomanly" defiance of her uncle Creon's authority. Euripides's play recounts some of the same events as Sophocles's, particularly with regard to Antigone. She is the daughter of the doomed king Oedipus, whose cursed fate—he unwittingly killed his father and married his mother—carries on to his incestuously conceived children: his sons kill each other in a civil conflict over the city, and when his brother (and now king) Creon forbids the burial of one of them, Antigone takes it on herself to defy the order and give her brother the last rites. In Sophocles's play *Antigone*, the heroine opens the play already decided on the course of action she will take, determined to act against the public decree and thus insert herself into the world of politics. In Euripides's *Phoenissae*, on the other hand, Antigone begins as a traditional young woman, so modest that she must be persuaded by her tutor to stand with him on the roof of the palace and observe the battle below.[24] Later in the play, her mother, Jocasta, drags her out onto the battlefield in a doomed effort to prevent the conflict between her brothers; Antigone goes, but protesting, "I shrink from the crowd" (1276).[25] Finally, however, once she has observed the death of her brothers and heard Creon's decree against burial, she takes her place on the forestage, symbolically casting off her maidenly veil (1485–91) and singing a song of grief for the fate of her family. She goes on to refuse Creon's order that she return to her room in the palace to await marriage (1636–38) and to announce her intent to defy his edict forbidding burial of her brother (1657). She even takes up a sword on which to swear her commitment to this course of action (1677). She has been transformed from a traditionally modest, maidenly girl into a powerful political actor, a change that is symbolized by her movement from the interior of the house to the center of the stage.

One scholar has argued that Antigone's transformation in the *Phoenissae* is essentially a commentary on the exclusion of certain categories of persons from participation in Athenian democracy: following her brother Eteocles's speech at the center of the play, which refutes the idea of a natural or divinely sanctioned idea of "justice," Antigone shows the merits in "the rejection of prescribed categories and the affirmation of an individual, male or female, making choices, speaking freely without deference to authority or societal expectations."[26] Thus, in many ways, the *Phoenissae*—among other Greek tragedies—represents a remarkable artistic meditation on women's place in Athenian society. On the other hand, it is clear that as a young, unmarried woman, or *parthenos*, Antigone would have held a cultural position in the eyes of classical Athenians that may have partially legitimated her participation in public affairs. It has been pointed out that there were numerous public religious festivals in Athens that accorded important roles to *parthenoi*, in which the girls' virginity was put on display and used in the service of the gods and the state.[27] Certainly, there were other festivals—most notably the Thesmophoria—in which mature, married women were the most important participants: this was a secret, female-only fertility celebration dedicated to Demeter, goddess of the harvest, birth, and marriage. Importantly, however, the Thesmophoria was a "private" celebration, whose rites were so closely guarded from male scrutiny that we now know almost nothing about them.[28] Thus, while the proven fertility of mature women, and the presumed wisdom and experience of old ones, was ritually harnessed for the good of the city, this could be done only under circumstances that preserved the privacy of their position.[29] By contrast, *parthenoi*, in part because their virginity mirrored that of the city's patron goddess Athena, were able to appear and serve in public.

Another way in which Greek women achieved a certain presence in public affairs through religion was by means of holding priesthoods. These were generally in the service of female gods, although there were a few notable exceptions such as the priestess of Apollo at Delphi, one of the most important religious sites in the Greek world. Unlike the participants in festivals like the Thesmophoria, however, it is clear that most of these priestesses, especially those who served city-specific cults, were exclusively aristocratic women. This became increasingly true into the Hellenistic and Roman periods, when it is clear that euergetism—the act of privately funding public projects for the city— was an important aspect of both male and female priesthoods. This meant two things: first, that the women who held such priesthoods were those whose families had significant wealth, to which women had greater access under the inheritance laws and practices of the later periods, which were far more favorable to daughters, wives, sisters, and so on (see later on); and, second, that the women in such positions became increasingly prominent in civic venues, as the sponsors of monuments, building projects, and other public works.[30] We thus know a great deal more about the activities of aristocratic Greek women in the Hellenistic and Roman periods. It is important to note, though, that—as with much of antiquity—the lives of the women about whom we hear do not reflect those of all women. Considerably less is known about the circumstances of even the middle class, let alone the genuinely poor. We might hypothesize that those without servants to, for instance, fetch water from city wells or buy produce at the market had a greater informal presence in public space than their wealthier sisters. In contrast, and especially in the later periods, formal public positions and commemoration in public documents such as inscriptions were confined to the richest segment of female society.

REPUBLICAN AND IMPERIAL ROME

As I have already noted, Roman society had a quite different understanding of the "correct" relationship between women and the public/private dichotomy. I have already narrated the story of Lucretia, whose rape and consequent suicide were the motivating causes for the creation of the Roman Republic, but early Roman history contained many other, similar stories that seem to show the centrality of women and family life to Roman politics. Thus, for instance, another important story, recounted in detail in several different sources, is that of the Sabine women. During the time of Romulus, who, according to tradition, founded the city of Rome in 753 B.C.E. and served as its first king, there was a dearth of women in the new community's population, such that, according to one historian, it was feared that the city would not last beyond a single generation because no children would be born.[31] Romulus's solution to the problem was to invite the neighboring communities, including the Sabines, to a festival; once they were there with their families, the Romans attacked and kidnapped the eligible women, carrying them off to Rome to serve as wives and (future) mothers to the Roman population. Needless to say, the Sabines and other neighbors took this action to be amiss and declared war in an attempt to retrieve their female relatives, but the women themselves interceded on the battlefield, saying (according to the historian Livy), "We are the cause of this war, of the injury and slaughter of our husbands and fathers; better that we should die than that we should live without either of you, as widows or orphans."[32] Moved by this appeal, the two sides reconciled and agreed to live together as a single community.

What is particularly interesting about this story is the way in which it provides an etiology and rationalization for Roman imperial expansion by "domesticating" it: by seizing and marrying the Sabine women, the Romans

are able not only to ensure their city's continued survival into the next generation but also to incorporate the rest of their families into the Roman state. Like
the story of Lucretia, therefore, the story of the Sabine women suggests that, far
from being peripheral to Roman politics, women and family life were in some
instances central to it. Of course, it is also true that Roman historians sometimes use the presence of women in public affairs as a sign of degeneration and
the depravity of certain historical moments. One example of this is the portrait
of Sempronia that is included in Sallust's narrative of the conspiracy of Catiline
to overthrow the Roman state in 62 B.C.E. According to the historian, she was
one of a number of women with loose morals who participated in the plot; she
actively pursued men rather than allowing herself to be pursued, and she was
possessed of a number of noteworthy accomplishments and skills, including
a certain "manly daring" (*virilis audacia*) that distinguished her among the
conspirators.[33] Scholars have noted that, whatever the actual historical facts of
her life, the presence of Sempronia among Catiline's followers in Sallust's narrative is a way for the historian to show the monstrous qualities of those who
participated in the plot. Sempronia's lack of traditional feminine virtues, her
high level of education, and her refusal of womanly passivity all serve to characterize not only her but also the kind of men who would associate with her.
For Sallust, both the Catilinarian conspiracy itself and the participation of such
a woman in it show the corruption of traditional masculine public virtues.[34]

   The difference between the Sabine women and Sempronia is not, therefore,
their presence in public: both stories turn on the idea that women sometimes
can and do participate in the civic affairs of the Roman state. Critically, the
Sabine women do so while still maintaining their domestic identities, so that
when they intercede between the two armies, they do so as wives, daughters,
and (future) mothers. Sempronia, on the other hand, is a monstrously abnor-
mal exemplar of her sex, and her association with the conspiracy of Catiline
serves to prove simultaneously her degeneracy and that of the political movement of which she was a part. Whereas classical Greek myth, culture, and
history always viewed any presence of women in public with a certain suspicion and anxiety, the Romans differentiated between women who were able
to maintain their traditional domestic roles even in the midst of civic turmoil
and those who were not. Indeed, one of the lessons that can be drawn from
both the story of Lucretia and that of the Sabine women is that the traditional
feminine domestic virtues of the women in the story triumph over the bad
behavior of the men, bringing a much-needed sense of heroism and nobility to
a time of public strife. In this sense, these historical myths emphasize the idea
that women's participation in civic affairs could be not only acceptable but

necessary, as long as they were able to remain faithful to the private values that they were imagined to embody.

The stories of Lucretia and the Sabine women come from the period of "Roman historical myth"—the time before we, or Roman historians, had good sources on which to rely—and therefore they represent a kind of quasi-religious understanding of how and why Rome grew into a mighty empire from its humble beginnings. Yet even once we enter the period of the later republic, when we begin to have real historical records of women's activities, we continue to see expressions of the complex relationship within Roman society between women and public life. Thus, for instance, we have fragments of two letters by Cornelia, mother of the revolutionary Gracchi brothers, in which she castigates her son Gaius (154–121 B.C.E.) for stirring up political trouble after his brother's assassination: "You will say that it is a fine thing to take revenge on enemies. This seems like a great and lovely thing to no one more than me, but only if it is possible to accomplish it with the state unharmed."[35] These fragments are preserved by the historian and biographer Cornelius Nepos, writing almost a hundred years after the events described, and most scholars are dubious that the words are authentically by Cornelia; nevertheless, both Nepos and Cicero not only believe them to be real but see nothing strange or reprehensible in a mother giving advice to her son about his political actions.[36] Again, however, it is clearly in the context of such traditional female roles (mother, sister, wife) that such activities were rendered acceptable. This is underscored by another remarkable primary text, the so-called *Laudatio Turiae* ("Funeral oration in praise of Turia"), an inscription from the end of the first century B.C.E. that records the life of an unnamed women who lived through the civil wars that afflicted the Roman state during the middle of the last century B.C.E. Her husband, who delivered the speech before it was inscribed on her tomb, praises her for her *domestica bona* ("good domestic qualities")[37] but also for her intercession on his behalf with the triumvir Lepidus after the husband himself had been banished from Rome for political reasons. "Turia's" behavior as a good wife thus included, in her husband's mind, taking his part in public affairs when he was not able to do so.

Indeed, it would seem to be no accident that women tend to be prominent in the history of Roman politics during times of political strife. This is especially noticeable during the civil conflicts that brought down the Roman Republic and led to the establishment of the empire—essentially a hereditary monarchy—under the *princeps* Augustus in 27 B.C.E. During the years of civic turmoil that led up to this point, we find women often emerging into the public eye simply because their male relatives have been rendered indisposed (by injury, exile, or death) due to political vicissitudes. The great Republican matron Fulvia, who would later be married to Mark Antony, first emerged into the public consciousness after the death of her husband Clodius in 53 B.C.E.; in the role of "grieving widow," she whipped up the emotions of his supporters against his enemies by dramatically displaying his mutilated body in the atrium of her home.[38] Nine years later, she employed a different version of the same act, performed in a more public space: In 43 B.C.E., the Senate attempted to declare Antony an enemy of the state, but Fulvia gathered together her mother-in-law and her son and spent the whole night before the vote visiting the homes of prominent senators. The next day, they also showed up at the doors of the Senate house, dressed in mourning and wailing lamentations.[39] Servilia, mother of Brutus, the assassin of Julius Caesar, was also instrumental in handling her son's affairs in Rome after he was forced to flee from the capital city. Cicero reports a strategy meeting that he held with her in July of 43 B.C.E. to discuss whether Brutus should bring his army to Italy. Writing of the meeting to her son, the orator called her "a very wise and industrious woman, whose attention is always turned to you."[40] Another meeting was subsequently held in Antium, attended by Brutus and his fellow tyrannicide Cassius along with Servilia, Tertulla, and Porcia—the latter two being Brutus's half sister and second wife.[41] From Servilia's reported comments during the meeting, it is clear that the women were included because they had direct access to the political institutions (such as the Senate) in Rome, while their male relatives were isolated in the provinces.

In other words, during these times of civic upheaval, women were able to be active in public affairs precisely because their gender protected them from the consequences that their male relatives suffered for their political activities. At the same time, however, it is clear that the line between civic and domestic affairs was never drawn as brightly in Roman culture as it was in classical Greece. One illustration of this has been seen in the material remains of Roman houses, as they are preserved in the ruins of Pompeii and Herculaneum, two communities destroyed by the eruption of Mount Vesuvius in 79 C.E. This disaster was unfortunate for the inhabitants of the Bay of Naples but a boon for archaeologists, insofar as it provided us with a remarkable collection of Roman houses to study. Of course, the point may be made that the domestic spaces of Pompeii and Herculaneum only represent those of a fairly specific place and time, but nevertheless the evidence preserved there means that it is possible to say a great deal more about Roman domestic practices than Greek ones. In addition, Rome also left us the written work of the architect Vitruvius, whose technical handbook *de Architectura* includes an entire book on proper methods of designing and building a house. In an important study, the scholar Andrew Wallace-Hadrill used Vitruvius to "read" Pompeian house plans and argue that, where the modern world locates the boundary between public and private space at the front door of the house, the Romans understood parts of the domestic dwelling to be public space.[42] As Vitruvius says,

> When [the different rooms] have been laid out in relation to the quarters of the sky, then it must be considered by what rationale, in private houses, places reserved for the owners of the house and those commonly shared with outsiders should be built. For the "reserved" places are those into which not everyone can come without an invitation, such as bedrooms, dining rooms, baths and other places which have related functions. The "common" rooms, however, are those into which ordinary people can come by right, even if uninvited; these are the vestibule, the inner court-yard, the peristyle, and other places which are able to be devoted to the same kind of use.[43]

As I noted earlier, Vitruvius sees gender as the most important social distinction expressed in the design of the Greek house; in describing the Roman house, however, his focus is on status differences, between the "reserved" rooms and those open to "ordinary" people.

Unlike the ancient Greeks, therefore, who seem to have mapped the dichotomies public/private, civic/domestic, and male/female neatly onto one another, the Romans had a more complicated understanding, not just of the relationship between women and public affairs, but more generally of that between the domestic sphere and civic life. Marriages among the elite, for instance, which were traditionally left to women to arrange, were often used as an avenue of forming political alliances. Thus, when Pompey was trying to cement his relationship with Julius Caesar and Crassus in the first triumvirate (59 B.C.E.), he married Caesar's daughter Julia; similarly, Caesar had married his third wife, Calpurnia, the same year to ensure the support of L. Calpurnius Piso, who was consul in 58 B.C.E.[44] One noteworthy negative example is the marriage of Cicero's daughter Tullia to Publius Cornelius Dolabella, which was arranged by Cicero's wife, Terentia, while the orator was in exile and without his knowledge. Terentia seems to have been pursuing her own agenda, as Cicero and Dolabella were on opposite political sides and Cicero was put into an extremely awkward position with his allies by the match.[45] As I noted, the practice of creating and maintaining political alliances through marriage was a long-standing one, but it is also clear that it became increasingly important toward the end of the republic as power became concentrated in the hands of fewer and fewer families. The traditional "domestic" power of women to contract these alliances correspondingly grew in importance.

Another factor that had a significant influence on Roman women's roles and visibility in public affairs was their ability to own property and inherit family money under Roman law. While women in classical Athens could have no independent financial standing, Roman women enjoyed comparative economic self-sufficiency, especially toward the end of the republic and throughout the empire. Although most women were formally under the supervision of a male tutor or "guardian," our sources make it clear that women often took charge of their own affairs. Thus, Cicero speaks with admiration of Caecilia Metella, who assisted the poverty-stricken Sextus Roscius of Ameria with both her social contacts and money.[46] In 45 B.C.E. the orator himself borrowed money from a certain Caerellia, of whose lending practices his friend Atticus apparently did not approve.[47] One of the largest buildings in the forum of Pompeii was one given by a woman named Eumachia, whose name and position (*sacerdos publica*, or civic priestess) were prominently displayed on its facade.[48] Another, more temporary sign elsewhere in the city offers for rent part of a large property belonging to Julia Felix.[49] One of the most noted episodes of the second triumvirate occurred in 42 B.C.E. when the magistrates tried to impose a tax on 1,400 of Rome's wealthiest women, a move that was thwarted by a group led by Hortensia, who lived up to her family's reputation for eloquence by delivering a speech before the tribunal in the middle of the Roman forum. That speech was preserved, read, and praised by later generations.[50] Although its original text has not survived, the second-century historian Appian preserves a version in which Hortensia is made to argue that women's formal exclusion from public affairs should protect their property from public taxes, especially those that are to be used in the pursuit of civil conflict: as Appian has her say, "Why are we to share the punishments, we who did not take part in the crimes?"[51]

The women discussed in the previous paragraph were clearly those who had access to family money, but it is also worth noting that we hear of a significant number of Roman women who worked outside their homes. We have little evidence of women employed in the professions—the occasional appearance of women in the law courts, representing themselves or others, is clearly an anomaly and very much treated as an unnatural intrusion into the male sphere.[52] There are some references in ancient sources to women bankers, but this probably points more to their role as private or semiprivate moneylenders:[53] a certain Otacilia Laterensis appears in Valerius Maximus's *Memorable*

Words and Deeds attempting to claim back a fraudulent loan from a former lover;[54] there is also a case recorded in the *Digest of Roman Law* where a Manilius is trying to recover some money placed on deposit with an unnamed woman.[55] A woman named Faustilla seems to have worked as a pawnbroker in Pompeii and is reported to have lent money against some basic items of clothing.[56] Far more common, however, are women engaged in the medical profession. They are most frequently found specializing in the care of women, like the female medical personnel whom the second-century doctor Galen encounters when treating the wife of the former consul Flavius Boethus: the author describes himself as working alongside these midwives to cure the patient's "female flow" and praises one of them as "thoroughly knowledgeable about her business."[57] Occasionally we even find evidence that suggests there were female practitioners of general medicine, such as the aunt of the fourth-century C.E. poet Ausonius, Aemilia Hilaria, who was (according to her nephew) "expert with the medical arts in the manner of men."[58]

Yet as we move down the social scale to crafts and small mercantile businesses, especially those relating to food production, women grow increasingly common. Female proprietresses of, for instance, cookshops, taverns, and market stalls, are well represented in both the epigraphic and visual record. Women who worked in the notoriously dissolute *caupinae* or *tabernae*, however, were often seen as morally compromised, so that, for instance, they were considered under Roman law to have the same status as prostitutes.[59] The early third-century jurist Ulpian remarks in the *Digest of Roman Law*, "We would say that a woman openly practices prostitution not only when she sells herself in a brothel, but also when she flaunts herself (as is common) in a tavern or somewhere else."[60] He goes on to note that women sometimes secretly manage prostitutes by pretending they are servants in an inn.[61] An interesting legal distinction arises under the emperor Constantine between a woman who owned or managed a tavern, who was allowed the same status as a Roman *matrona*, and those who actually served the patrons and were therefore considered to live degraded lives.[62] This suggests that it was indeed the "public" nature of a working woman's role that made it problematic for Roman men, since the law implies that the owner of the tavern is less morally compromised because she does not expose herself to the (male) customers.

At the same time, however, Constantine's distinction also points to the ways in which moral standards were intertwined with class differences: the proprietress of the cookshop has a higher status because her greater wealth (as the owner of the business rather than one of its workers) allows her to maintain it. In fact, there is some evidence that, for such "middle-class" women, the display of domestic virtues was both evidence of and a contribution to maintaining a particular position in the social hierarchy. Natalie Kampen has analyzed a wide range of visual depictions of women engaged in mercantile activities and concludes that there is little difference between the iconographic tropes employed to show male and female small-scale vendors. Once we move into the world of the rich merchant or artisan, we find no images of businesswomen, even though we know from other sources that women did participate in business at this level. Women appear in these representations alongside their merchant husbands only engaged in domestic or private activities such as spinning or having their hair dressed.[63] Similarly, a certain large and elaborately carved funerary monument celebrates the wife of a wealthy butcher as "pure, chaste, ignorant of the crowd, and faithful to her husband." The tomb's announcement of domestic virtues, as well as its scale, claims a particular social status for the deceased and her (still living at the time of its production) husband.[64] The point is that it seems to be at this middle-class level of Roman society— below the aristocratic women who gave money for buildings and participated in politics, above the working women who engaged directly with the public— that the display of the domestic ideal and the "privacy" of female life had the most urgency.

Nevertheless, it is clear that all women in Roman society existed to a greater or lesser extent within the confines of a moral discourse that saw the performance of conventional "domestic" virtues as the highest measure of a woman's success and that correspondingly often associated public visibility with moral transgression.[65] On the other hand, one of the things that distinguishes Roman women's position from that of their classical Greek sisters is the way in which some were able to harness that moral discourse and use it to create positions of power for themselves. This can be seen in the history of the early Christian church, where, partly because most communities at the time were centered on assemblies located in houses, women had more access to leadership and authority, since the home was already their domain.[66] In a similar vein, but more abstractly, under the empire, the women of the imperial household became increasingly influential as the emperor and his family became the central political force in the Roman state. This process began with Livia, wife of the first emperor, Augustus, and mother to his successor, Tiberius, who is remembered as having had significant influence over both men; her husband apparently valued Livia's advice so highly that he communicated with her in writing and had copies of her letters placed in the official archives.[67] She and her sister-in-law Octavia also sponsored significant building projects in Rome, a time-honored way by which the Roman elite displayed their wealth and influence in public. At the same time, however, Livia's public acts were understood as arising out of her domestic roles: one of her major construction projects, the shrine that she built to Concordia, looks to the traditional "fellowship" between husband and wife; she is also portrayed in contemporary and later sources as exercising toward the Roman people the kind of benevolence that befits a nurturing mother.[68]

As the empire grew older and one dynasty gave way to another, imperial women's roles within the family remained both important and highly visible. One circumstance that assisted in this was the fact that the women of a dynasty could often outlive a generation or two of their male relatives, who might be killed in battle or through treachery.[69] This meant that they could serve as an important binding link between reigns: emperors such as Claudius, Hadrian, and Marcus Aurelius all cemented their own positions by marrying women more closely related to previous rulers than they were themselves. The Severan dynasty (193–235 C.E.) gave birth to a number of extremely influential women who followed in Livia's footsteps. They included Julia Domna, who was married to the emperor Septimius Severus and was mother to his successor, Caracalla. Subsequently, her older sister, Julia Maesa, is reputed to have used her money and influence to secure the succession of her grandson Elagabalus to the throne; when he proved unsatisfactory, she used her power to replace him with his cousin Alexander Severus.[70] In the third century, due to the instability of the empire and the passing of the throne by military coup rather than succession, women played a lesser role, but when the imperial "house" reasserted itself after the demise of the Tetrarchy, female members of the imperial family return to view and continued to play important roles in establishing and legitimizing the rule of aspirants to the throne. Women such as Helena Augusta, first wife of Constantius Chlorus and mother of Constantine I, not only are reported to have assisted their male relatives from behind the scenes but also seem to have taken on genuinely "public" roles: Eusebius reports that Helena made state visits, traveling across the eastern provinces, bestowing gifts on various communities, and encouraging the military.[71]

As the empire became Christianized, and the center of power moved to Byzantium in the east, imperial women continued to have significant influence, from Aelia Galla Placidia (392–450 C.E.), who was the daughter, granddaughter, and half sister of four different emperors, to Theodora, wife of Justinian I (500–48 C.E.), who seems to have managed the affairs of the imperial family with an iron hand and was the sponsor of numerous public buildings and works of art. The growth in importance of the Virgin Mary and her icons in the Byzantine church also gave women a way of claiming a certain kind of religious authority even in a world that continued to be dominated by men.[72] The fact that women maintained the right to inherit money meant that widows, especially, could wield influence through their control of family funds. Thus, while it is clear that women's lives were still framed by the idea that they most properly belonged to the private or domestic sphere, they nevertheless were able to continue to find ways to have a place in public matters—sometimes by subverting the domestic ideal, sometimes by using it. In this, they followed the lead of earlier women, both Greek and Roman, who had similarly found ways to make their presence felt in the areas of the social world traditionally controlled by men, despite the ideological and gendered divide between the public and private spheres.

CHAPTER SIX

Education and Work

MARCIA LINDGREN

We know very little about the vast majority of women in the ancient world who were working wives and mothers. We can glimpse only traces of their lives from inscriptions on tombstones and from letters that have survived in Egypt and Britain. The women who gaze out from mummy portraits seem almost alive, yet they cannot tell us about their daily lives, whether they were educated, or how they contributed to the economies of their households and communities.

Many factors make it difficult to get a clear picture of women's lives in the ancient world. First, we are dependent on the evidence that has survived. Some geographic areas and some time periods are underrepresented or not represented at all. Second, how are we to interpret what remains? Textual sources are problematic for many reasons. Nearly all of the texts that survive were written by elite males about their own concerns. Writings by women constitute only a small percentage. When male authors do write about women, they tend to be the mothers, wives, and daughters of important men, or they are outstanding in some other way, renowned for their virtue or vice. Our evidence, therefore, is skewed away from women and ordinary people, particularly those of the lower classes. Depictions of women in poetry and drama do not necessarily tell us about the lives of real women, and forensic speeches involving women distort reality for their own purposes. Inscriptions on women's gravestones tend to be conservative, even anachronistic. They are more likely to praise old-fashioned virtues and favor domestic skills over intellectual and other accomplishments. Legal texts can be equally problematic, for they may or may not reflect actual practice. In addition, Roman juristic texts are late compilations full of contradictions. Visual representations of women are even trickier than textual sources. Artistic and funerary depictions, for example, are often idealized, and just because a woman is depicted with a book-roll or a writing instrument does not necessarily mean that she could read or write. Finally, cultural differences between the ancient world and our own make it difficult to grasp the realities of life for women who lived two thousand years ago. One important difference is the rigid patriarchal social structure that favored men and subordinated women, but probably the most important cultural difference is the institution of slavery and its unquestioned acceptance in antiquity.

Aristotle's view that slaves were inferior human beings deserving of their low status was shared by most Greeks and Romans.[1] Not even Christianity had a mitigating effect on attitudes toward slavery.[2] In fact, the culture of slavery was so

FIGURE 6.1: *Literate(?) baker and his wife*. The baker Terentius Neo and his wife. Fresco. Pompeii, first century C.E. Museo Archeologico Nazionale, Naples, Italy. (Photo credit: Vanni/Art Resource, NY [ART382542].)

entrenched in the ancient world that slaves, upon being freed, purchased slaves. For the most part female slaves were spared dangerous jobs involving heavy physical labor, but many endured hazardous living conditions working as prostitutes.

Slaves were easily acquired through purchase, inheritance, or reproduction (an infant born to a slave woman was considered the property of her owner). Individuals became slaves through various means. Many were born into slavery. Others, both children and adults, were captives of war, kidnapped by bandits, or sold by family members who could not afford to keep them. Another source of slaves was the Greco-Roman practice of abandoning unwanted infants, usually females, and leaving them to die of exposure. Since exposed infants were presumed to be slaves, they could be taken in by anyone. There was no comparable tradition among the Egyptians or Jews, who apparently raised all of their children.

Slaves were considered property, similar to livestock,[3] and therefore lacked the rights and protections of free citizens. The most critical distinction was that slaves had no legal protection from physical assault. Some slaves were treated humanely by their owners, while others endured harsh, sometimes life-threatening punishments. Since slaves *were* property, they could not own property, except through the mechanism of the *peculium* (small savings, private property). Although legal marriages between slaves were not permitted, a marital arrangement (called *contuberium* by the Romans) was possible. A slave mother had no legal claim to her child, and as far as the law was concerned, the child had no father. Moreover, until the late empire, slave families could be separated arbitrarily by an owner. Unlike their Greek counterparts, Roman slaves had some hope of freedom. They could be manumitted by their owner, through their owner's will, or by purchasing their own freedom. Furthermore, they could eventually become citizens, and their sons would even be eligible to hold office. After manumission slaves retained certain obligations to their former masters, and many continued on as paid employees, particularly women with limited skills. These options created complex social networks and led to far greater social stratification among the Romans.

EDUCATION OF WOMEN

A man who teaches a woman letters should know that he is providing poison to an asp.

Menander (Athens, fourth century B.C.E.)[4]

In the modern world education implies literacy, but this was not necessarily the case in antiquity. When Greece was emerging from an oral culture during the archaic period, the ability to read and write was far from a necessity. The spoken word still carried greater power than the written word. Literature was and would continue to be primarily oral, and the inability to read and write did not handicap ordinary citizens or prevent them from participating fully in private or public life. In fact, the notion that every male citizen should know how to read and write did not appear until the classical period.[5]

Overall literacy rates cannot be determined with any precision, let alone for subgroups like women and slaves. Estimates have been made, nonetheless, with scholars reaching vastly different conclusions—often from the same evidence. Efforts have been complicated by several factors, apart from the absence of any quantitative data. First, any definition of literacy must address the question of levels. Susan Guettel Cole defines literacy simply as "knowledge of the alphabet and the ability to write one's own name and to read simple formulaic expressions," while William V. Harris differentiates among "semi-literacy," "scribal literacy," and "craftsman's literacy."[6] Another complicating factor is that reading and writing are separable skills with separate functions and separate evidence. One cannot assume that just because a woman could read she could also write, or vice versa. Furthermore, in many parts of the ancient world literacy involved more than a single language. Another factor has to do with the use of intermediaries in antiquity; a person, whether literate or not, could "write" by dictating to a scribe employed for the purpose or could "read" by listening to a reader. Finally, estimated literacy rates have been affected by the tendency to generalize favorably about female literacy from the evidence of a few exceptional women. In spite of these complicating factors, we can safely say that at all periods the majority of people, men and women, were illiterate and that fewer women were literate than men. In terms of overall literacy, Harris posits only 5 to 10 percent in Attica during the classical period, 20 to 30 percent in some Hellenistic cities, and less than 15 percent in Italy during the late republic and early empire.[7] It is also safe to say that during most periods literate education was confined to the social elite.

Although there were schools in Greece by the early fifth century B.C.E., there is little evidence for the education of girls before the Hellenistic period (see the following on the notable exception of Sparta). In some Hellenistic cities private benefactors played a crucial role in extending a basic education to all freeborn children, including girls.[8] Until the Romans mandated municipally supported schools throughout the empire in the second century C.E., educating children was for the most part left up to individual families, who could teach their children themselves or pay someone else to do it.[9]

Many factors influenced whether or not a child received an education. Cost was an important consideration, and not just the expense of schooling, but also the loss of a child's labor or earnings while in school. High socioeconomic status improved the chances of receiving an education, but education for girls was more dependent on social status than it was for boys.[10] Residing in a city increased access to schools, although boys were more likely to go to schools than girls.[11] Parental attitudes toward education were critical, since without parental support there could be no instruction. In many households mothers took an active role in educating their young sons and daughters. Fathers also were involved, either in teaching their children or in supervising their education. Ancient sources tend to attribute a daughter's intellectual success to her father, while young men seem to have been influenced by educated mothers. After marriage, a young woman's husband could be important in her ongoing education. In fact, male relatives seem to have been crucial in securing a young woman's access to higher education or specialized training. (See the case of Sulpicia, discussed later on.) Still, it is unlikely that all upper-class families educated their daughters or that many girls went beyond the primary level. Those who did must have had extraordinary motivation and support.

Subjects and Levels

The nature of education did not change much over a thousand-year period.[12] Ancient education was firmly grounded in literature, which was used to teach grammar as well as mythology, geography, and morals. Instruction involved listening and speaking, with a strong emphasis on recitation and memorization. Greek school exercises culled from the comedies of Menander could be openly misogynistic: "Do not trust a woman, even when she is dead" and "Through women, all evils happen" are typical examples.[13]

The Romans modeled their education on Hellenistic Greek practice but excluded physical education. Children typically began primary instruction at age seven and continued until age eleven or twelve. At this level they learned letters and numbers. The next stage was grammatical instruction, which lasted until about age fifteen. Students learned grammar, literature (almost exclusively poetry), and mythology. By the late republic, Greek was taught along with Latin in Roman schools, and this continued until the empire was divided into East and West in the late fifth century. For young men completion of grammar school coincided with assuming the toga worn by adult males. At this point a youth either began military service or went directly to rhetorical school, which focused on oratory as preparation for a career in law and politics. Elite Roman males frequently went abroad to complete this advanced education, which often included the study of philosophy in addition to rhetoric. For upper-class Roman girls, however, marriage typically cut short their education at age twelve to fifteen, before they had completed grammatical instruction.[14] Theoretically, a young woman's education could continue after marriage, but only with her husband's cooperation and only if pregnancies and household duties did not interfere. An older, educated husband could even take on the role of mentor to a young wife. Thus, even an elite woman's education consisted of only primary and some grammatical instruction and rarely included an advanced rhetorical or philosophical education.

Education and Spartan Women

Sparta was unique among the Greek poleis in that education for girls was mandated and subsidized by the state. Just because Spartan girls were educated, however, does not mean that they all could read and write. Harris says that literary education, especially writing, was not a high priority in Sparta and that "literacy is likely to have been restricted . . . to a small number of men and a still smaller number of women."[15] As in other parts of Greece, illiteracy did not put girls at a disadvantage or prevent them from participating in state-sponsored activities. The young women who danced in choral competitions need not have learned their songs from a written text. The most important subject for Spartan girls was physical education (gymnastics and sports), followed by *mousike* (playing musical instruments, dancing, and singing), and possibly some reading and writing. The Spartan emphasis on physical training goes back to the seventh century B.C.E. and the constitution traditionally ascribed to Lycurgus, a legendary Spartan lawgiver. It was believed that the primary responsibility of a freeborn woman was to produce children and that offspring were healthier if both parents were strong. In Sparta slaves performed domestic tasks, and so there was no need for freeborn girls to become skilled in these areas, with the exception of weaving for ritual purposes. Since education for males focused on physical and military training, leaving little time for other subjects, the cultural training of girls may have been superior to that of boys.[16] Ancient sources mention two female poets (although no works survive) and several female philosophers, while Spartan men had a reputation for being "uncultured."[17] The education of Spartan girls continued until they married at age eighteen to twenty, significantly later than other Greek women, who typically married at age fourteen.

Ancient Attitudes toward Educating Women

On a philosophical level, there were few objections to educating women. Plato made a strong case for educating women alongside men in all subject areas, including the arts, gymnastics, and military training.[18] Even Aristotle, who did not have an enlightened view of women in most matters, thought that children and women should receive an education because they were part of the greater world.[19] Aristotle's student Theophrastus, on the other hand, was in favor of educating women just enough to run a household, since any further education would make them lazy, talkative, and interfering.[20] Quintilian, a Roman teacher of rhetoric, believed that *both* parents should be educated for the good of the child.[21] By the end of the first century c.e. philosophers also supported education for women on moral grounds. Musonius Rufus, for example, believed that a philosophical education for women would help them attain moral excellence on a par with men.[22] All of this high-mindedness should not be mistaken for early feminism or support for women's equality, however. Plato, Aristotle, and even the authors of the Spartan constitution wanted what was best for the state, and Quintilian, what was best for the child. For them equal education for women was a by-product, not an intended consequence. Moreover, a philosophical education was intended not to prepare women for new roles but to make them more agreeable and effective in their traditional roles.

Benefits of an Education

Without subsidized education for all classes, there must be compelling incentives to educate children. Male citizens were educated so that they could participate in public life and assume roles of authority. Since women did not participate directly in civic life, the benefits of an education were not as clear. On a concrete level, training for a profession such as teaching or medicine enabled women of the lower classes, including freedwomen, to make a living. An educated housewife could assist in the education of her children, manage the household more effectively, and maintain or even improve her husband's social standing by reflecting well on him. On a deeper level, literacy and numeracy gave women an element of control over their lives—protection against deceit and greater knowledge in business matters.[23] In a paternalistic society where most women had the same legal standing as their children, and where wives were much younger than their husbands, marriage was, by definition, an unequal partnership. An education could put a woman on a more even footing with her husband, so that she could be an informed companion. Moreover, "literacy had a deeper function for women [than it did for men] and allowed them to be an integral part of a society that was fundamentally literate in the sense that many people were familiar with literate modes, if not themselves literate. . . . Archives containing letters of particularly distinguished women . . . show that education left permanent traces in them and to some degree shaped their thinking."[24]

WOMEN'S WRITING

Women used their literate educations to write letters, poetry, and scholarly works. Their writings can be classified as literary or documentary. In the literary category, poetry—especially lyric and elegiac verse—predominates, but an astonishing variety of other types is also represented. The term *documentary* applies to nonliterary writings such as letters and inscriptions. It is important to remember that these writings represent a small minority of women.

Documentary Writing

Documentary writing is a rich category that encompasses letters (private and business correspondence), legal documents (contracts), inscriptions (including handwritten dedications, curses, and inquiries to oracles, as well as formal inscriptions on stone paid for by women), and even graffiti. Although documentary writings are difficult to interpret, they offer a more direct conduit to the everyday concerns of real women. In this regard, private correspondence never intended to be shared with others is of special interest.[25] The following invitation to a birthday celebration provides a glimpse into two women's lives at a military outpost on the Roman frontier in about 100 C.E.:

> Claudia Severa to her [friend] Lepidina, greetings. On the third day before the Ides of September, sister, for the day of the celebration of my birthday, I give you a warm invitation to make sure that you come to us, to make the day more enjoyable for me by your arrival, if you are present. Give my greetings to your [husband] Cerialis. My [husband] Aelius and my little son send him their greetings. [Second hand] *I shall expect you, sister. Farewell, sister, my dearest soul, as I hope to prosper, and hail.* [Back to first hand] To Sulpicia Lepidina, [wife] of Cerialis, from Severa.[26]

Severa used a scribe (the first hand) but added her own closing (the second hand, in italics). Both women were officers' wives who had accompanied their husbands to Vindolanda in northern Britain. Severa, Lepidina, and their husbands were themselves from Batavia, a province that only recently had been granted Roman citizenship. Alan K. Bowman points to the surprising level of literacy in this remote community.[27] The documentary evidence from Vindolanda reminds us that the Roman military was an effective vehicle for education and acculturation in the provinces.

Literary Writing

The writing and preservation of literary texts by women was influenced by ancient concepts of public and private. In antiquity the "publication" of poetry involved public performance. Respectable women were considered part of the private world. Even if they did write, their work normally was not circulated outside the family and was not intended for publication. Compared to some 3,200 authors in the Greek canon alone, there are only about one hundred women who are known to have written in Greek and Latin from the seventh century B.C.E. to the fifth century C.E., and the works of only fifty-five of those women have survived.[28] Some of these are no more than scraps of text quoted in other authors or were found in Egypt on fragments of papyrus. It is important to note that men and women who wrote poetry and other types of literature were not paid for their work and did not receive compensation when their manuscripts were copied.

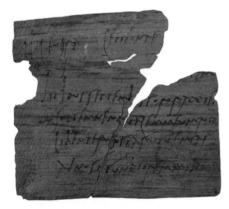 

FIGURE 6.2: Invitation to a birthday party. Roman writing tablet with a letter written in two different hands. It invites Sulpicia Lepidina, the commander's wife, to a birthday party. Roman Britain, ca. 100 C.E. From Vindolanda (modern-day Chesterholm, Northumberland, Britain). Inv. PY 1986,1001.64. British Museum, London, Great Britain. (Photo credit: © The Trustees of The British Museum/Art Resource, NY [ART351268].)

Some Greek women not only wrote poetry but also gained fame by doing so. In the *Palatine Anthology*, Antipater of Thessalonica praises "nine earthly muses," the most famous of whom was Sappho of Lesbos (early sixth century B.C.E.). Sappho's lyric poetry was highly regarded by men and women throughout antiquity and still commands a readership, although only fragments of her work remain. She profoundly influenced later poets such as Catullus, Horace, and Ovid. Representing the classical period are the poets Myrtis from Boeotia (no remains), Praxilla from Sikyon on the Corinthian Gulf, and Telesilla of Argos. The legendary Corinna from Boeotia, who belongs to either the fifth or the third century B.C.E., was said to have defeated Pindar five times. Finally, there are four Hellenistic poets whose works were preserved in the *Palatine Anthology*: Anyte from Arcadia ("the female Homer"), Nossis from Locri in Magna Graecia (known for epigrams), Moero (a writer of lyric, epigram, and epic), and Erinna from Teos or Rhodes (compared in antiquity to Sappho and Homer; author of "The Distaff").

The burgeoning of female poets during the Hellenistic age likely is related to improved educational opportunities for women. Plant credits the strong literary culture for the survival of their works: "This is in part due to the development of a new genre of poetry intended for written publication [epigram], the creation of anthologies and the collection of books. The establishment of the Library and Museum in Alexandria promoted literary and scholarly work, creating a strong literary culture and discerning readers for women's poetry, and a means by which that poetry might be preserved."[29] None of these poets lived in Alexandria; however, the city's positive cultural effects were felt throughout the Hellenistic world. Plant also sees proof of a wide readership in the fact that female poets were satirized in comedy and other literature.[30]

In contrast to the classical and Hellenistic ages in Greece, the Roman period produced few female writers. Only the poetry of Sulpicia survives from the so-called golden and silver ages of Roman literature, and we know of only a handful of other female writers.[31] Assuming that a woman did receive an education beyond the primary level, other factors conspired against her. The influence of ancient notions of public and private behavior for women has been noted already. Second, the literary process was a male enterprise, with talented male writers having access to literary patrons and their coteries. Third, the conditions for the proliferation of women's poetry during the Hellenistic period (mentioned earlier) were absent at this time. There were bookshops in Rome by the late republic (books were considered luxury goods) but no public libraries until 39 B.C.E., only private collections. There is no mention of women using the public libraries, and it has been suggested that perhaps they were excluded, if not by law, then by custom.[32] Assuming a woman gained access to and survived the literary process, her writing was still subject to the vagaries of textual transmission from antiquity to modern times.[33] It is easy enough to surmise why Sulpicia's elegies survived. We know that she was the niece and ward of Valerius Messalla Corvinus, an important literary patron, who must have given his niece an education as well as unparalleled access to his circle and the literary process. Thanks to this connection, her small collection of poetry became attached to the corpus of Tibullus and tagged along on his manuscripts through the ages. The case of Sulpicia demonstrates the importance of male relatives in securing access to education and the traditionally male pursuit of poetry writing.

Women also wrote in areas as diverse as history, philosophy, musical theory, grammar, literary criticism, astronomy, travel, medicine, sex, mathematics, drama, prophecy, alchemy, and theology.[34] Although even an overview of these writings is beyond the scope of this chapter, several names and categories are worth mentioning.

The rise of Christianity afforded women an opportunity that had not existed before. Instead of marriage, they could choose celibacy and a life of study and contemplation.[35] If a woman decided to write, she now found an audience beyond her family in the larger community of the church. By the late empire not all education was based on the literature of classical antiquity but also on scripture and the writings of the church fathers. The earliest surviving Christian literature by a woman is "The Martyrdom of Perpetua," a young mother's account of the events leading up to her death in 203 C.E. at Carthage.[36] A few select women continued to receive a classical education in addition to Christian instruction, and at least two women integrated this knowledge by writing centos. Taking its name from the Latin word for "patchwork," a cento is a poem created entirely from the lines of another poet. The cento co-opts whole lines or two half lines but rarely two consecutive lines from the source poem. In the fourth century, Proba, a Christian convert from a distinguished Roman family, wrote an influential Virgilian cento on the life of Jesus.[37] A century later the empress Eudocia composed a Christian cento in Greek based on the works of Homer.[38] One of the most well known women in antiquity was Hypatia, a Neoplatonic philosopher and the only non-Christian woman we know of who chose celibacy over marriage.[39] Hypatia was a distinguished mathematician, astronomer, and teacher of both pagans and Christians at Alexandria.[40] In 415 C.E. she was killed by a Christian faction who blamed her for a continuing dispute between the church and local officials. The genre of travel literature is represented by the wealthy, unmarried Egeria, perhaps an abbess, who traveled from her home in western Spain to the Holy Land in the early fifth century.[41] Egeria's *Itinerarium*, addressed to her "sisters," is an account of that pilgrimage. During the tenth century Hrotswitha, a canoness in Saxony, wrote plays, epics, poetry, and history on Christian themes from a feminine perspective. Her prolific writings in Latin reveal a close familiarity with classical literature.[42]

WOMEN'S WORK

Women's work is the loom, not assemblies.

Menander (Athens, fourth century B.C.E.)[43]

In antiquity individual households and communities depended on the labor of women and girls, who performed tasks that were surprisingly similar whether they were slaves, freed, or freeborn and whether the work was compensated or not. Most paid jobs for women evolved from such traditional unpaid domestic activities as child care, food preparation, and cloth production. Women worked at these jobs out of necessity, to provide for themselves and their families.

The configuration of property rights in the ancient world affected women's economic opportunities. Athenian women had limited property and inheritance rights and were prohibited from financial transactions over a certain amount. Because of these limitations, they did not engage in large-scale commerce or lend money.[44] Roman women, on the other hand, could own property (provided they were *sui juris*), inherit property, and make wills. Roman women, freed and freeborn, used their capital to make loans, invest in businesses, and even engage in large-scale commerce. Some wealthy women, such as Eumachia of Pompeii, also made noteworthy public benefactions and were patrons of men's trade guilds.

The family was the basic economic unit in antiquity, with both production and consumption centered on the household.[45] In his treatise on household management, Xenophon portrays a god-given division of labor in which women are naturally suited to care for what is inside the house (provided they are properly instructed by their husbands), while men are meant to take care of what is outside.[46] Xenophon's dichotomy not only accurately represents the types of jobs that men and women performed throughout antiquity but also symbolizes the exclusion of women from many civic functions. Perhaps its only shortcoming is that it fails to take into account the overlap between domestic and commercial activities in antiquity, for many commercial enterprises (such as cloth production) took place in the home.

Greek and Roman women provided skilled labor or worked in sales and services. Studies of Roman occupational inscriptions indicate that the range of women's jobs was much narrower than men's—about 35 for women compared to 225 for men in one study.[47] Women were employed in service (making and serving of food, prostitution), sales (foodstuffs), crafts (cloth production), luxury trades (perfume), and skilled jobs such as hairdressing and goldsmithing.[48] In these areas women were almost entirely excluded from supervisory or administrative positions, however.

Textile Production and Its Symbolic Value

Archaeological evidence links women with spinning and weaving as early as the Neolithic period, and evidence from Linear B tablets shows that women as well as men were involved in commercial textile manufacture during the Greek Bronze Age.[49] Women produced cloth for use in their own households and sold the surplus as one of the earliest commodities. Since spinning and weaving had been associated with women of all social strata from prehistoric times, they came to symbolize not just the feminine but also female virtue. In Homer's *Odyssey*, Penelope puts off the suitors by weaving a shroud for her father-in-law and in so doing symbolizes her ongoing fidelity to the absent Odysseus. In Roman legend, Lucretia proves herself to be the most virtuous wife when her husband and his companions surprise her late at night as she works at her loom. Even the sophisticated women of the imperial family were involved in domestic textile production.[50] On the other hand, spinning and weaving could carry an ominous subtext of entrapment or deceit. In the *Odyssey* both Calypso and Circe are working at their looms when they first appear. Odysseus is detained by these sexually demanding goddesses, who delay his homecoming.[51] Even the virtuous Penelope weaves a web of deceit—from the suitors' point of view—since at night she secretly unravels her work of the previous day. Thus, in literature even the most revered women's work could be connected with fear and suspicion.

Child Care

For those who could afford them, wet nurses and nannies were probably the most valued domestic workers in antiquity. The Greeks and Romans recognized that these women were mothers by proxy and could have an important influence on the development of the children they cared for. Thus, families sought nurses of good moral character who spoke excellent Greek or Latin.[52]

Children and their nurses developed close, emotional bonds that often lasted a lifetime. Faithful service was rewarded with manumission for slave nurses and with laudatory inscriptions on tombstones. Nurses also appear in epic and drama; Odysseus's old nurse, who recognizes him from the scar on his foot, comes to mind. Ancient male writers deplored the practice of hiring others to do what a mother should do herself and praised elite women who nursed their children themselves.

Agriculture and Food Production

The ancient economy was predominantly agricultural. Women were involved in all stages of food production and preparation: herding and caring for animals, grinding grain, baking bread, and making wine and beer. Women also sold what was not consumed within the household and were employed in commercial food production.[53] Female agricultural workers, including slaves, were involved in all aspects of farm labor, but their primary employment was domestic (cooking, cleaning, wool working), in contrast to the later American South, where slave women worked in the fields all day and did housework in their downtime.[54]

Household Slaves and Freedwomen

In the large urban households of Rome, slave women and freedwomen worked as clerks, secretaries, hairdressers, masseuses, spinners, weavers, clothes folders, midwives, wet nurses, and entertainers.[55] Male slaves performed some of these tasks as well, but they also worked outdoors in jobs done exclusively by men. A typical urban slave probably had more than one job. Specialization was possible only in larger households, where slaves sometimes were given training by their owners for specialized tasks. Some slave women did not have a particular job but seem to have been simply the companions of male slaves in the household. Treggiari estimates that over 45 percent of the female staff was married.[56]

Educated Professionals

Some women—slave, freed, and freeborn—trained and worked as physicians or midwives, while others were scribes, readers, or secretaries. Still others were schoolteachers, especially at the lower levels. Hermione, a woman who lived in Egypt in the first century c.e., may have been a teacher of Greek grammar.[57] In spite of the pastoral epistles' view that women should not teach the lessons of Jesus but rather be silent and deferential to men, early Christian women did become teachers and leaders of household churches. Proscriptions against

FIGURE 6.3: Mummy portrait of Hermione, *grammatikē* (grammar teacher, or simply educated woman). Egypt, first century C.E. © Girton College, Cambridge.

women teaching church doctrine were either modified or simply ignored by women teachers in early church assemblies.[58]

Performers

Jobs in entertainment were among the least respectable professions for both men and women in antiquity. Female musicians, singers, and dancers were employed for public and private functions; some elite Roman households even kept them on staff. Women also are known to have fought as gladiators, and although this probably was not common, it went on for several centuries.[59] In theatrical productions women's roles ordinarily were played by men, but women did act in the popular Roman mimes. Since these actresses performed bawdy skits (and even sex acts) onstage wearing little or no clothing, it is no wonder they were assumed to be prostitutes.

PROSTITUTION

A prostitute and a teacher of rhetoric have the same tears.

Menander (Athens, fourth century B.C.E.)[60]

Prostitution became institutionalized early on as a societal necessity. By the early sixth century B.C.E., prostitution was legal in Athens.[61] The origins of prostitution have been linked to so-called temple or sacred prostitution in Greece and the Near East. Sacred prostitution, however, is a modern label that has been applied to several ancient practices, including prostitution by temple personnel and prostitution with a portion of the proceeds dedicated to a god. Its existence has been disputed on the grounds that there is no direct, contemporary evidence to support the concept.[62] Rome probably had brothels and common prostitutes as early as the fourth century B.C.E. due to the Hellenizing influences of the Greek cities of southern Italy. After the defeat of Hannibal in 201 B.C.E., Roman expansion to the east accelerated the process.

Although prostitution is not an unfamiliar concept, formulating a definition can be problematic. In order to distinguish prostitution from other sexual arrangements, definitions often rely on three criteria: promiscuity, payment, and the emotional detachment of the participants.[63] This tripartite definition, however, excludes arrangements involving slaves who did not receive payment directly and who participated involuntarily. Madeleine Henry broadly defines the prostitution of women as "the exchange of a female's sexual service, with or without her consent, for some other resource."[64] This definition, while perhaps overly inclusive, is preferable because it encompasses the full range of circumstances, from the household slave or brothel worker to the sophisticated Athenian *hetaira* who accepted expensive gifts from her clients.[65]

In antiquity prostitutes were of all ethnicities. They were both male and female, but females far outnumbered males. Although many more worked in cities, prostitutes also worked in rural settings, essentially wherever there were clients. In terms of rank, prostitutes ranged from streetwalkers and brothel workers all the way to high-priced courtesans who lived independently and had exclusive relationships. Household slaves constituted an important category of unpaid sex workers, since owners had unrestricted access to their slaves. Evidence points to a high degree of permeability among female occupations in the service industries of food, sex, hospitality, and entertainment and to the often part-time and temporary nature of this employment.

In Athens, *pornai* ("paid women" or "whores"; singular *pornē*: the related verb means "to sell") had multiple short-term clients and generally served the lower classes. These women were slaves or free noncitizens who worked in the streets or in brothels and were paid by the sexual encounter. *Hetairai* ("female companions"; singular *hetaira*) were mostly free resident aliens who served the upper classes. They were paid by the evening or could have an exclusive, long-term arrangement with only one man. The term *pornē* was derogatory, while *hetaira* was euphemistic, although the terms are used interchangeably throughout Middle and New Comedy.[66] The *hetaira* accompanied a man to a symposium (drinking party from which respectable women were excluded) or was hired by the host as entertainment. As well as providing sexual services, these women took part in the drinking, gaming, and conversation. The top *hetairai* were educated and valued for their beauty and intelligence. The most well-known and influential Athenian *hetaira* was Aspasia, companion to the statesman Pericles. According to Plutarch, Aspasia not only trained young courtesans but also taught rhetoric and was so intelligent that Socrates brought his students to listen to her.[67]

The most common terms for Roman prostitutes were *scorta* ("skins" or "sluts"; singular *scortum*) and *meretrices* ("prostitutes"; singular *meretrix*: the related verb means "to earn"). Although most were slaves, some were freedwomen or even freeborn Romans. Those at the higher end of the scale were comparable to Athenian *hetairai*. At the lower end they worked in brothels, in one-room cells opening onto the street, at the baths, along streets and roadways, and among the tombs outside of towns. Women who served food and drink at inns, taverns, and lunch counters were assumed to be available for a price. Others followed the army or traveled to public festivals. Some female prostitutes wore the toga, the traditional garb of the Roman male citizen. The female version of the toga probably was colorful and lightweight and made it easy to distinguish prostitutes from respectable women, although the toga was only one of many choices of apparel for prostitutes.[68] Those at the bottom of the hierarchy wore very little or nothing at all.

In Greece brothels were either taxable private enterprises or state-run entities, while in Italy prostitution was an entirely private business that benefited the state through taxes. For the Romans prostitution was a business like any other, and the number and location of brothels appear to have been based solely on financial reasons, not the result of moral zoning.[69] The number of clients a prostitute served per day was inversely proportional to her fee.[70] Thomas McGinn estimates that prostitutes who charged two *asses* (small Roman coins) saw from fifteen to twenty clients per day, while those at the upper end charged eight to ten *asses* and served only about five clients. Since the price of a loaf of bread was two *asses*, an encounter was affordable for the average soldier, who had a daily discretionary income of about four *asses*.[71]

Social and Legal Aspects of Prostitution

The majority of Athenian prostitutes were slaves who worked in brothels under deplorable conditions. The situation was different for *hetairai*, who had more freedom and independence than respectable Athenian housewives. They could walk about freely in public and own and manage property without the supervision of a male guardian. Since a wife did not participate in her husband's social

FIGURE 6.4: Interior of Pompeiian brothel. First century C.E.
Photo: Fotografica Foglia. House of the Lupanare, Pompeii,
Italy. (Photo credit: Scala/Art Resource, NY [ART180959].)

or intellectual life, companions also filled that role. Because *hetairai* were educated and enjoyed many freedoms that are valued today, it may appear that
being a companion was preferable to being a wife. Although they were free, *hetairai* were noncitizens and therefore could not legally marry Athenian citizens.
Their children were considered illegitimate and could not inherit from citizen
fathers. Furthermore, Pomeroy reminds us, we know of prostitutes who tried
to pass as respectable wives, while we know of no citizen wives who wished to
be companions.[72]

Roman wives had much greater freedom than their Athenian counterparts. They entertained guests, accompanied their husbands to dinner parties,
and were free to converse with other men. When legislation made adultery a

criminal offense, Roman women registered as prostitutes so that they could not be prosecuted for adultery. The Senate closed this loophole by prohibiting women of the senatorial and equestrian orders from the profession.[73] Although prostitutes had to register with an official and pay a tax, there does not seem to have been much oversight beyond keeping public order.[74] Most free persons probably went into prostitution for financial reasons and because there were limited employment options for women. Some girls as young as nine years old were tricked into the profession by unscrupulous pimps who promised food and clothing.[75] The emperor Caligula reportedly coerced impoverished members of the elite to prostitute themselves in a palace brothel.[76] Still other upper-class Romans performed voluntarily as actors, gladiators, or prostitutes.[77]

Under Roman law men and women who followed certain "infamous" professions were prevented from fully exercising the rights of citizenship. These occupations included prostitute and pimp as well as actor and gladiator. On this basis male citizens were excluded from juries, magistracies, and the army. Moreover, juries were to disregard their testimony, and if convicted they could be punished more severely than others.[78] Female prostitutes were not permitted to marry freeborn Roman citizens, to participate in the same cults as respectable women, or to bring charges in court under any circumstances. Limits also were placed on their ability to inherit. Since sexual assault against a prostitute was not considered a crime, they had little personal protection.[79] Despite these legal disabilities and their marginal social status, some prostitutes, actors, and gladiators became celebrities and the paramours of influential men and women.

Ancient Attitudes toward Prostitution

The primary purpose of marriage in antiquity was to obtain legitimate children to inherit a family's wealth. Wives were necessary not only to produce these heirs but also to be guardians of the household's integrity, its wealth, and its cult. Men could have a range of sexual partners outside of marriage (mistresses, concubines, prostitutes, and slaves), although respectable women were off-limits. A woman, on the other hand, could have only one legitimate sexual partner, her husband; any other liaison was considered adultery. (For information on penalties for adultery, see chapter 2 in this volume.)

Since prostitution was legal, neither prostitutes nor their clients were committing a criminal offense. However, as we have seen, if they were not already slaves, prostitutes and procurers experienced a diminution of civic and personal rights, while their clients suffered little, if any, stigma. In other words, shame and dishonor attached to the prostitute and the pimp rather than to the institution or the customer. The Greeks and the Romans rationalized that prostitution was necessary to prevent men from committing adultery, thus protecting women and the family. Further, the availability of male prostitutes prevented young citizen men from being raped. These attitudes changed, however. Arguments appear in rhetorical exercises that not only do men who have prolonged affairs with courtesans waste their money and neglect their duties, but their frequent absences also force their wives to commit adultery.[80] The Greco-Roman notion that female sexuality needed to be controlled persisted through late antiquity. With Christianity came an emphasis on chastity, even celibacy, for men *and* women. The sexual double standard was no longer operational, at least in theory; now marital fidelity was expected of husbands as well as wives. Men, as the stronger sex, were warned not to yield to passion, except possibly with their wives for purposes of procreation.[81] There was no role for prostitution in Christian sexual practices.[82] Reality, of course, was another thing.

Augustine reluctantly acknowledged that prostitution was a necessary evil and supported segregating brothels rather than outlawing them.[83] The Christian emperor Leo I tried (unsuccessfully) to ban prostitution altogether.[84] Seventy-five years later the emperor Justinian, who wished to marry a former actress and prostitute, repealed laws that would have prevented him from marrying her legally. Since he was sympathetic to the plight of the prostitute, he also passed legislation preventing young women from being tricked or forced into prostitution[85] and converted a palace into a convent for former prostitutes.[86] In late antiquity, stories of the conversion and salvation of prostitutes became popular.[87] The story of Mary Magdalene, who according to a late sixth-century tradition, begun by Pope Gregory I, was saved from a life of prostitution by Christ, falls into this category. Until the twentieth century, when the Magdalene's identification as a prostitute was overturned by the Roman Catholic church, her story of repentance had much in common with that of Saint Pelagia, Antioch's foremost actress, dancer, and courtesan before she renounced her profession and converted to Christianity.[88]

EDUCATION, WORK, AND THE STEREOTYPING OF WOMEN

The ideal woman did not change much over time. She was a wife and mother, a household manager par excellence who exemplified the traditional virtues of chastity, industry, and obedience. She appeared in legend, or she was a real woman co-opted and mythologized as a model for other women. Women who defied this feminine ideal, whether in literature or in real life, served as powerful negative exempla. Ordinary women who broke stereotypes were criticized simply because they were educated or crossed the boundary between private and public life.

The phenomenon is unmistakable and pervasive. Male-authored texts associate educated, knowledgeable women with sexual promiscuity,[89] and writing openly on certain subjects earned poets like Sappho, Praxilla, and Nossis an unsavory reputation. The *puella docta* of the Roman elegists was portrayed as a Greek *hetaira*—intelligent, independent, and promiscuous—and her married counterpart, the *matrona docta*, was more accomplished than a respectable woman needed to be.[90] The only positive stereotype involving the educated woman was the Roman "ideal of educated motherhood," exemplified by Cornelia, mother of the Gracchi, who was praised because her erudition benefited her children.[91] Stereotypes by definition do not take into consideration the shadings of real life, and there probably were not clear distinctions between respectable and promiscuous women. We have seen that there was fluidity among occupations involving food, hospitality, and entertainment and that women working in these fields were assumed to be sexually available. Although commerce was disparaged by upper-class Romans, the notion of payment does not appear to be the objection to these working women. Rather, attitudes toward pleasure and public display seem to be significant.[92] Moreover, in the minds of the ancients there was an exceedingly fine line between promiscuity and prostitution. In Mesopotamian documents and the Hebrew Bible, female prostitutes are often indistinguishable from sexually available or promiscuous women.[93] The Greeks and the Romans made use of the same ambiguity in comedy, forensic oratory, and invective poetry. In short, the term *prostitute* or *whore* seems to have been applied broadly to *any* woman who transgressed social norms.

CHAPTER SEVEN

Power

LYNDA GARLAND

POWERFUL WOMEN IN CLASSICAL GREECE

The majority of the historical sources for classical Greece, the period from 478 to 323 B.C.E., were written by Athenians for a primarily Athenian audience, and each type of ancient evidence—historical sources, tragedy, comedy, lyric poetry, artistic and epigraphic sources—presents a different, and partial, view of the role and position of women. Almost all of it was, of course, written by men for a male audience who would have been shocked at the concept that women might have held positions of power. In Athens it was unusual for citizen women to be specifically named in the sources.[1] Athens, however, was not a typical Greek city, and women in Sparta and in other Doric cities such as Gortyn in Crete appear to have enjoyed considerably more status and latitude in behavior than women in Athens. Spartan queens in particular could play an important part in the governance of the state while their husbands were engaged in warfare.[2] One role in which women in Athens and elsewhere could enjoy prominent status was that of priestess; this role held great social importance, involving regular public duties, such as those of the priestesses of Athena Polias and Athena Nike in Athens. Myrrhine, priestess of Athena Nike, was chosen by lot from Athenian citizen women and served for life: inscriptions authorize her annual payment and perquisites (fifty drachmas and the legs and hides from public sacrifices) and a prominent seat in the theater of Dionysos. The priestess of Athena Polias was also arguably one of the most important women in the city. The position was always held by a member of the Eteoboutadai clan, thought to be descendants of the original kings of Athens. The position was held for life (one priestess, Lysimache, served for sixty-four years), and she officiated at the four-yearly festival, the Great Panathenaia.[3] The oracle of Apollo at Delphi, which was the most highly regarded in the Greek world, spoke through the *Pythia,* a woman priest responsible for delivering oracles to those who came to consult the god. Sitting on a tripod in the temple, she responded to questions on both personal and political matters, generally in prose, but occasionally in poetic hexameters. Three women from Delphi served in rotation, and the fact that at least one *Pythia* was dismissed after allegations of bribery suggests that these priestesses had full responsibility for their content and delivery of their responses.[4]

Women's lack of political power in classical Greece does not, however, imply that they were without authority in their own sphere, which in some cases may have covertly spilled over into the public domain. In accounting for all the evils of this world, Hesiod, writing in about 700 B.C.E., depicted the gods' creation of the first woman, Pandora (the all-endowed), as a punishment for Prometheus's having stolen fire from Mount Olympus and given it to mortals. Each of the gods gave Pandora a "gift" so that on their behalf she could wreak vengeance on men. Not only was Pandora made innately wily and deceitful, but out of curiosity she opened a jar and released all evils, such as toil, sickness, and disease: only hope remained inside the jar. This attempt to explain the existence of human misfortune and drudgery through the creation of this archetypal woman appears in both *Theogony* and *Works and Days*; Hesiod obviously thought the story said much about womankind. Woman is part goddess, part human, and part beast, and her arrival signifies the beginnings of all evils on the earth.[5]

A similar portrayal of women as formidable and unprincipled is seen in classical tragedy, and it is difficult to tell whether Athenian heroines like Sophocles' Antigone were intended to be, or would indeed have been seen as, representations of contemporary women. The plots of such tragedies, in which women are shown as powerful rulers in their own right, such as Clytemnestra, or obstinately opposed to male domination, like Antigone and Medea, were based on well-known mythological tales. As a result, the poet's point of attack has to be deduced from the choice of tale and the way in which the traditional plot has been adapted to reflect contemporary issues. Medea, for example, the witch and barbarian princess who helped Jason to escape from Colchis with the Golden Fleece, is presented by Euripides in 431 B.C.E. to highlight the problems faced by a wronged wife, who is simultaneously a foreigner in Athens with no family to defend her rights. Euripides appears to have been the first to present Medea as getting revenge on Jason, her children's father, by murdering her own children and by killing Jason's new bride and her father, the king of Corinth.[6] In Aeschylus's play *Agamemnon*, Clytemnestra, queen of Mycenae, infuriated by the sacrifice of her daughter Iphigeneia to gain favorable winds for the Greek fleet to sail to Troy (Clytemnestra had gone to Aulis believing that Iphigeneia had been summoned there to marry Achilles), had ruled during the ten years of Agamemnon's absence at Troy, taking his cousin Aegisthus as her lover. When Agamemnon returned home, she murdered him along with his concubine Cassandra.

While in many ways a Lady Macbeth figure, Clytemnestra believes she has good reason for her actions. Her speech to the chorus describes the exultation with which she committed the deed in language rich in the symbolism of fertility: his murder has given her new life, and her third and final stroke specifically is made to Zeus, "in thanks for prayers accomplished." As she says, "This man filled a mixing-bowl of evil curses, which he has returned and drained himself." He thoroughly deserved his fate. She speaks of him as a sacrifice to the gods, over which she could pour libation. That her husband, and her son Orestes, who is to kill her in a further act of revenge, think differently highlights the gendered viewpoint, which the Athenians may not have agreed with but which they could not help but respect.[7]

One of the earliest and greatest of Greek poets, Sappho of Lesbos, writing in the early sixth century B.C.E., was said by the Parian Marble to have spent some time in exile on Sicily, though her poems show little trace of interest in the turbulent politics of the island. In her work she gives a gendered view of power, and in a fragmentary poem that describes her daughter, Sappho rejects all the wealth and power of Lydia (home of the wealthy tyrant Gyges) and all masculine values in favor of her lovely daughter and the emotional bond among women. Elsewhere, she contrasts male desires (infantry, cavalry, and ships) with the more emotional ones of women, as reflected in Helen of Troy, "she that far surpassed mankind in beauty," who is shown as an autonomous agent in her decision to leave her husband, child, and parents for love. Helen in her beauty reminds Sappho of Anaktoria, "who is no longer near," and this brings the reader back to Sappho's own desires and the ways in which they are the antithesis of masculine aims and ambitions: "I would rather see her [Anaktoria's] lovely walk and the bright radiance of her face than the Lydians' chariots and fully-armed infantry."[8]

Greek historians present some vignettes of women capable of wielding power. While the Athenian historian Thucydides never mentions a woman by name, Herodotus in contrast takes a specific interest in commenting on non-conventional women. One of these is Artemisia, tyrant of Herodotus's own hometown, Halicarnassus on the southern coast of Asia Minor, close to the island of Rhodes. Interestingly, while sometimes considered a "barbarian," Artemisia was Greek, ruling the city even though she had a son of age to reign, having assumed power after the death of her husband. She commanded five triremes and was one of the many Greek contingents that supported the Persian king Xerxes's campaign against the Greek mainland in 480–479 B.C.E. Herodotus, who must have had detailed knowledge of the circumstances of her involvement in the war, makes clear that she joined the expedition not from compulsion but from "courage" and that she took a very active part in events, advising Xerxes not to fight at sea, advice that he appreciated even though he did not follow it. She was also clearly on board and in command of one of her own ships at the battle of Salamis. In order to escape the pursuit of an Athenian ship once the tide of battle was securely in the Athenians' favor, Artemisia deliberately rammed one of the ships on her own side—not a Persian ship, but a Greek ship from Calynda that was fighting for the Persians. The Athenian ship pursuing her lost interest, thinking that she was on the Greeks' side, while Xerxes, who was looking on and thought that she had sunk one of the enemy, commented, "My men have become women, my women men." Herodotus neither criticizes her involvement in battle nor her action at Salamis, merely stating that she was lucky that no one from the Calyndian ship survived. He also states more than once that of all Xerxes's advisers, Artemisia was the most dependable. On his retreat, Xerxes entrusted his illegitimate sons to Artemisia to transport them to Ephesus.[9]

As well as citizen women, Athens had educated noncitizen women among its residents, often foreign-born *hetairai* (companions). Certainly Aspasia of Miletus, Pericles's sexual partner, is described as educated and articulate; she is mentioned by Aristophanes, Plato, and Xenophon, while the philosophers Aeschines and Antisthenes each named a dialogue after her (both are now lost). There was a tradition that she wrote Pericles's speeches for him, including the important *Funeral Oration* for the dead in the first year of the Peloponnesian War (431 B.C.E.). Attacks on Aspasia by comic poets are rather aimed at Pericles; she is blamed for both the siege and defeat of Samos as an enemy of her home, Miletus, and for the outbreak of the Peloponnesian War. Clearly, dramatists overemphasized the influence that Aspasia had on Athenian politics, but it can be assumed that there was concern at an educated and articulate foreigner being Pericles's partner.[10] Athenian comic dramatists display women taking an interest in politics. Lysistrata, in the play of that name, unites the women of Greece into forcing their menfolk to make peace with Sparta by taking over the acropolis and treasury and by going on a sex strike until the men agree to stop the war. She describes her husband's reaction when she tries to talk to him about the war and decisions made in the assembly: "And he'd glare at me and say that, if I didn't weave my web, I'd really have a headache to complain about: 'For war should be men's concern!'" No doubt this was the conventional response when women attempted to take an interest in politics. Nevertheless, when Lysistrata speaks about the current state of affairs in Athens, she is meant to be taken seriously even though she is a woman, and she clearly articulates that war has an impact on women, whose sons die in battle.[11]

Women in classical Sparta enjoyed far more independence than women elsewhere in Greece due to the men's full-time participation in the army and life in barracks up until the age of thirty. Moreover, heiresses could inherit property in their own right rather than simply transmitting it to males of the family. By the fourth century B.C.E., women controlled considerable amounts of wealth. Aristotle calculates that in his own time (the late fourth century B.C.E.) women owned some two-fifths of Spartan land and discusses the lack of control exercised over Spartan women: Spartan men were "ruled by them." He points out the problems caused by the number of heiresses and the failure to limit the size of inheritances and dowries.[12] Spartan women had considerably more freedom than women elsewhere in Greece and could engage in activities unheard of elsewhere, not merely athletics and gymnastics, but ones that demanded control of property and were generally part of the sphere of men. Cyniska, daughter of King Archidamus II, won the chariot race at the Olympic festival in 396 and 392 B.C.E. As racing was an expensive hobby, Spartan women clearly controlled a large proportion of Sparta's wealth as early as 396 B.C.E. Cyniska was the first woman victor at these games; the occasion was celebrated by the erection of a hero shrine to her at Sparta and a statue of her by Paellas that was dedicated at Olympia. Another Spartan woman, Euryleonis, won the same event in 368 B.C.E. Certainly, by the third century, most of Sparta's wealth appears to have been controlled by women.[13]

One of the only Spartan queens whose actions and impact on Greek history are recorded is Gorgo, the daughter of Cleomenes I, wife of Leonidas and mother of Pleistarchus. Plutarch quotes her words as exemplifying Spartan austerity and dedication to the state, like those of other unnamed Spartan women who preferred to see their sons dead than dishonoring Sparta. When a foreign woman said to her, "You are the only women who can rule men," Gorgo was said to have replied, "That is because we are the only ones who

give birth to men." Gorgo when only eight or nine had warned her father
Cleomenes against being bribed by Aristagoras of Miletus, and as Leonidas's
wife, she had advised the Spartans on how to decipher a wax tablet from
Demaratus secretly warning the Spartans of the Persians' impending invasion.
In Plutarch's *Sayings of the Spartans*, Gorgo is said to have asked her husband,
Leonidas, when he left for Thermopylae, what instructions he had for her; his
reply was, "To marry good men and bear good children." As far as we know
she did not remarry. Gorgo herself would have been a considerable heiress as
Cleomenes's only child, and her marriage to her uncle Leonidas, her father's
half brother, would have kept the wealth firmly within the Agiad house, add-
ing to her position and influence within Sparta.[14] Spartan queens became even
more influential in the Hellenistic period. Archidamia, grandmother of King
Agis IV, not only aided her grandson in his reform of Spartan customs but
had earlier led female troops, fighting against Pyrrhus of Epirus when he attacked Sparta, and was murdered along with her daughter and grandson in
241 B.C.E.[15]

Greek women from the families of tyrants (tyranny was a form of nonin-
herited monarchy) are shown as proud of their family descent and status in
epitaphs that demonstrate that connection and wealth were extremely important to these women and those belonging to them: in the grave stele that speaks
to the passerby on her behalf, written by the poet Simonides, Xanthippe boasts
that she is not only the "glorious" wife of Archenautes but also the great-
great-granddaughter of Periander, tyrant of Corinth in the early sixth century
B.C.E. Four generations on, it is this relationship with Periander, "who once in
high-towered Corinth, where he was sovereign, commanded the people," that
still defines Xanthippe's perception of why she should not lie in death "unnamed."[16] A very similar epitaph, also by Simonides, praises Archedike, wife of
the tyrant Aiantides of Lampsacus, and daughter of Hippias, tyrant of Athens
(527–510 B.C.E.). Hippias had married his daughter to Aiantides shortly before
his expulsion from Athens because of Aiantides's connections with the Persian
king Darius, in case Hippias should have to flee to Darius's court at Susa.
Significant is the epitaph's total failure to mention Archedike's husband, Aiantides, an unthinkable act had he still been in power; the tyranny therefore must
have been overthrown before Archedike's death. Her distinction and rank in
this epitaph is based not on the importance of her husband but on her relationship to Hippias, "who was greatest in Greece of those of his time," linked to
the fact that she was daughter, wife, sister, and mother of tyrants. Nevertheless,
written in a city that had removed its tyrants, the epitaph is careful to mention that she was not given to "unseemly arrogance," implying the status and

power with which women like Archedike and Xanthippe were associated and
which they saw as their own.[17]

Women's political role intensified with the rise of Macedon in the fourth
century B.C.E. and in particular with the marriage of Olympias, daughter of
Neoptolemus I of Epirus, to Philip II of Macedon. Philip's fifth wife, and mother
of his heir, Alexander III (the Great), she brought him control of the kingdom
of the Molossians. Despite her status, Philip had other wives—foreign princesses like herself. His last marriage, in 336 B.C.E. to Cleopatra Eurydike, a
Macedonian and niece of the general Attalos, challenged Olympias's position
and the status of her son as Philip's heir, leading to a serious break in Philip's
relationship with both. When Philip was murdered by Pausanias, one of Philip's ex-lovers, suspicion was extended to Olympias, who later avenged herself
on her rival by murdering Philip's new wife Cleopatra and her baby daughter.
Now secure in power due to the position of her son Alexander, Olympias sent
numerous letters of advice to him while he was on campaign in Asia and clearly
kept him informed in his absence about the activities of Antipater, who was
regent in Macedon. She may also have played an important role in Alexander's
career through assuring him of his divinity as the son of Zeus, who was said
to have cohabited with her in the form of a giant snake prior to Alexander's
birth; that he was the son of Zeus was later confirmed by the oracle at Siwah
in Egypt. After Alexander's departure to Asia Minor, she played an important
part in politics and at one point returned to Epirus, which she ruled as regent
for her grandson Neoptolemus.

POWERFUL WOMEN IN THE HELLENISTIC PERIOD

After Alexander's death, Olympias remained in Epirus as an opponent of the
Macedonian regent, Antipater, until 317 B.C.E., when she sided with the regent Polyperchon against Cassander, Antipater's son, and Eurydike, wife of
the titular king Philip Arrhidaeus, Olympias's stepson. Motivated by the wish
to protect the Macedonian throne for her grandson in the face of Cassander's
aggression, she invaded Macedon with the help of Polyperchon. At this, Eurydike committed suicide, and Philip Arrhidaeus was murdered, with many of
Cassander's supporters massacred. Olympias in turn was to be defeated by
Cassander at Pydna in 316: her army deserted, and she was executed after being
condemned for her many executions. The Bactrian princess Roxane, mother of
Alexander's posthumous son, Alexander IV, was also captured by Cassander
at Pydna in 316 and later murdered with her child at Amphipolis, probably in
311. While both Olympias and Roxane had enjoyed extensive influence as the

mothers of royal sons, it is very clear that neither was capable of dealing with the armies wielded by Alexander's successors in their struggle for power.[18]

Olympias struggled, not unsuccessfully, for a role in Macedonian politics, though during her son's reign rather than that of her husband Philip; she was to be a role model for queens in the Hellenistic period that followed Alexander the Great's death. Other Macedonian women of note included Phila, daughter of Antipater and Cassander's sister, who became the wife first of Craterus and then of Demetrius Poliorcetes, and mother of Antigonus Gonatos. On the basis of Phila's position, Demetrius proclaimed himself king of Macedon in 294 B.C.E.[19] Another was Alexander's sister, Cleopatra, who married her uncle, Olympias's brother, Alexander king of the Molossians, in 336 B.C.E. and ruled for their son Neoptolemus while her husband was on campaign in Italy. After his death she ruled successfully as regent, receiving shipments of grain and acting as the religious head of state. Later, she lived at Pella with her children. To strengthen their position, she offered to marry Leonnatus, one of her brother's Companions, after his death in 323 B.C.E. When Leonnatus was killed at Lamia in 322, she went to Sardis in the hope of marrying Perdiccas, another of the Companions, where she was courted by a number of Alexander's successors until she was imprisoned by Antigonus the "One-Eyed." She then attempted to flee to Ptolemy in Egypt but was captured and returned to Sardis, where she was murdered, presumably at the instigation of Antigonus, but given a royal funeral, as befitted the sister of Alexander the Great.[20]

Artemisia II of Caria, on the coast of Asia Minor, is an unusual example in this period of a woman ruling in her own right after governing with her brother-husband Mausolus until his death in 353 B.C.E. Between 353 and 351 she skillfully maneuvered between the Greeks and the Persians, honoring her husband's memory by commissioning preeminent Greek writers to eulogize his memory. She also commissioned the construction of the 106-feet-high (49-meter) Mausoleum, or "tomb of Mausolus," in the center of Halicarnassus, made by some of the greatest sculptors and artists of Greece—one of the Seven Wonders of the ancient world.[21] Another sister-wife who ruled in her own right after the death of her husband was Ada, sister, wife, and queen of Idrieus until his death in 344/3, after which she ruled alone for three years until deposed by her younger brother Pixodarus. She then withdrew to the fortress of Alinda, where she remained untroubled until the arrival of Alexander the Great in 334. There, she handed Alinda over to him, adopting Alexander as her son, thus ensuring his right of succession as ruler of Caria after her death. As queen of Caria, she commanded her own troops at Halicarnassus alongside Alexander, where she was given the honor of capturing one of the two citadels. She re-mained there until her death before 326 B.C.E.[22]

These sister-wives were to find parallels in Hellenistic Egypt under Macedo-nian rule, where the position of the women of the royal family was strength-ened by marriages between siblings, which kept power and wealth within the dynastic family. Ptolemaic women were also in receipt of divine honors: the first of these, Berenice, niece of Antipater, who married Ptolemy I and became mother of Arsinoe (II) in 316 and of Ptolemy II in 308 B.C.E., was compared to Aphrodite and Isis; a shrine (the Bereniceum) was built in Alexandria in her honor. As well as controlling considerable wealth, these royal women were also noted for their gifts and dedications to sanctuaries. Arsinoe II was granted cities and estates by her husband, Lysimachus, king of Thrace, who renamed Ephesus in her honor. Ptolemaic women came to control far more wealth than any Greek women of earlier times, with the possible exception of Sparta. Fol-lowing Lysimachus's death, Arsinoe returned to Egypt and married her half brother, Ptolemy Ceraunus, and then her full brother, Ptolemy II: the couple were known as the "sibling-lovers" (the *philadelphoi*), reflecting the relation-ship between the goddess Isis and her brother, Osiris. These brother-sister mar-riages were to remain the norm throughout the dynasty. Arsinoe wielded great influence during her brother's reign as "King of Upper and Lower Egypt" and "princess of both lands" in her own right. She was accorded international recognition, equated to Isis during her lifetime and deified after her death—an important move toward the deification of the Ptolemaic dynasty as a whole. Harbors and games were named after her, she appeared on coins wearing the horns of the god Ammon, and the region of Fayum was renamed Arsinoites. She was regarded as a collegial ruler with her husband/brother Ptolemy, and her views on the freedom of the Greeks were recorded at Athens in the Chre-monides decree ("King Ptolemy, in accordance with the policy of his ancestors and his sister, clearly demonstrates his concern for the common freedom of the Greeks . . ."), which created an alliance between Athens, Sparta, and Egypt.[23]

By marrying their brothers, the women of the Ptolemaic dynasty in Egypt, like Arsinoe II, Arsinoe III, Cleopatra II, Cleopatra VI, and Cleopatra VII, ensured that their own children came to power and that they were undeni-ably seen as corulers and colleagues of the reigning kings, their brothers. Arsinoe III, daughter of Ptolemy III and sister-wife of Ptolemy IV, even rode into battle against Antiochus the Great at Raphia in 217 B.C.E. She was in-cluded in the cult of the "father-loving gods" from 216 and was equated with the goddesses Isis and Aphrodite. The fact that she was murdered in 204 B.C.E. after her husband's death, by Agathocles, who took power as guardian of her son, Ptolemy V, suggests there was concern about her political role. Indeed, during the second century, Ptolemaic queens increasingly took power as regents for their sons, even taking precedence over them, while following Cleopatra I (204–176), the women of the royal family typically took the name Cleopatra and married their male relatives.[24]

The first Cleopatra, Cleopatra I, daughter of Antiochus III of Syria, married Ptolemy V (Ephiphanes) in 194/3 B.C.E., reigning jointly with him. The couple were worshipped as gods, and after Ptolemy's death in 180, Cleopatra ruled as regent for their son Ptolemy VI, being named before him in official documents. A priesthood in honor of the two of them was established in 178 or 177 B.C.E. at Ptolemais. Like her predecessors, Arsinoe II, Berenice II, and Arsinoe III, she was deified, with her own cult established: she was also the mother of Ptolemy VIII and Cleopatra II.[25] This younger Cleopatra married her elder brother, Ptolemy VI, probably early in 175, having been given the title of queen (*basilissa*) after the death of their mother the previous year. The royal couple were worshipped as the "mother-loving gods." Their reign was not untroubled; Ptolemy VIII at times reigned with them and seized sole power briefly in 164/3. After the death of Ptolemy VI, Ptolemy VIII married Cleopatra II and reigned for a short period with her, after which he married her daughter, Cleopatra III, in 141 or 140 B.C.E. In 132 civil war broke out between Cleopatra II and her brother, who fled to Cyprus, with Cleopatra proclaiming herself "savior" and ruler. Ptolemy VIII soon returned, and it was Cleopatra's turn to flee from Alexandria; in 124 their co-rulership was reestablished. After his death in 116 B.C.E., Cleopatra may have continued ruling alongside Ptolemy IX (her grandson) and her daughter Cleopatra III.[26]

Ptolemy VIII broke with custom by leaving the kingdom to Cleopatra III as ruler, allowing her to choose which son she wished to govern with her. Cleopatra appears to have wished to reign with her younger son, Ptolemy X, though the citizens of Alexandria insisted on Ptolemy IX taking the throne. However, Cleopatra was officially named before both her sons. Like her royal predecessors, she was identified as Isis and the object of cult and received the title "bringer of victory." From 107 B.C.E. she ruled with her younger son after Ptolemy IX fled to Cyprus, and then in 105 or 104 she deposed Ptolemy X. She prevented Ptolemy IX from returning to Egypt by orchestrating an invasion of Palestine, but she was murdered by Ptolemy X in October of 101 B.C.E. Cleopatra's daughter by Ptolemy VIII, Cleopatra IV, wife of her brother Ptolemy IX, was rejected by her husband (apparently at the instigation of their mother). Cleopatra IV raised an army against him and joined forces with Antiochus IX of Syria, whom she married in 115, but she was killed in 112 B.C.E. on

Antiochus's orders. After Ptolemy IX rejected Cleopatra IV, he married another sister, Cleopatra V (Selene), who, dominated by her mother, Cleopatra III, stayed in Alexandria when Ptolemy IX fled to Cyprus. Her mother married her in 103 to Antiochus VIII to gain his support against her son Ptolemy IX. After Antiochus's death Cleopatra III married her stepson Antiochus X. Another ambitious princess, Cleopatra Berenice III, daughter of Ptolemy IX and Cleopatra IV and the wife of Ptolemy X, married her father and ruled collegially with him after her husband was driven out of Alexandria in 88 B.C.E. She reigned alone for several months after her father-husband's death in 81, after which she was murdered by her son, Ptolemy XI.[27]

POWERFUL WOMEN IN THE ROMAN PERIOD

In the first century B.C.E., Rome came to play an increasingly important role in Egyptian dynastic struggles. When Ptolemy XII, Auletes, was deposed, leaving Alexandria for Rome in 58 B.C.E., Egypt was left in the joint control of his sister-wife Cleopatra VI, Tryphaena, daughter of Ptolemy IX, and their daughter, Berenice IV. Berenice appears to have held the real power, ruling alone after Cleopatra's death in 58 or 57. Not long after her father was reinstated in 55 B.C.E., he had her murdered, evidence that she wielded considerable power.[28] At his death Ptolemy XII left the throne to his remaining daughter, the final and best-known Cleopatra (VII), and her younger brother Ptolemy XIII. At first, in 52 to 51 B.C.E., Cleopatra ruled alone, then shared power with Ptolemy XIII, whom she married. Their relationship was troubled: she was at one point forced out of Alexandria by her brother, with a still younger brother claiming power for a brief period. In 48 B.C.E. her husband-brother Ptolemy XIII had her exiled; she raised troops in Arabia in order to return to power. Julius Caesar intervened in the struggle in 48 B.C.E., requesting that both sides disband their troops and return to joint rule. Cleopatra complied; when Ptolemy XIII resisted, he was killed in battle. Cleopatra was declared sole queen in 47 B.C.E. Her son, Ptolemy XV Caesarion, said to have been the offspring of her liaison with Caesar, was born in June of 47 B.C.E. From 46 to 44, Cleopatra was named co-ruler with her younger brother Ptolemy XIV. In 46 B.C.E. she departed Egypt to organize an alliance with Rome; once there, she was settled in a luxurious villa by Caesar. After his assassination on the Ides of March in 44 B.C.E., she returned to Egypt, where her fleet assisted Caesar's supporters against their senatorial opponents. Ptolemy XIV was murdered, and Ptolemy XV Caesarion was now named pharaoh alongside, but after, his mother Cleopatra.

In 41 B.C.E. Mark Antony gained Cleopatra's support for his planned war against Parthia, granting Egypt considerable concessions in return. It was at this point, when they met at Tarsus, that the famous relationship between the two was said to have commenced. During the next few years, Egypt's gains included part of Cilicia, Phoenicia, regions of Judaea and Arabia, land on Crete, and territory at Cyrene in North Africa. With this additional power and wealth, Cleopatra's rule became more spectacular, and in 34 B.C.E., after Antony's conquest of Armenia, she was named "queen of kings" and a "new Isis." Her children by Antony, the twins Alexander Helios (Sun) and Cleopatra Selene (Moon), and Ptolemy Philadelphus, were granted imposing titles and titular realms. It was with wealth from Egypt that Antony financed the fleet against Caesar's great-nephew, Octavian, at the battle of Actium in September of 31 B.C.E. Reportedly, it was seeing Cleopatra's ship turn and leave the battle that caused Antony to follow and throw away his chance of victory.

Back in Alexandria, Cleopatra negotiated unsuccessfully with Octavian to retain her kingdoms for her children. Following Antony's suicide, she killed herself with a poisonous asp on August 12, 30 B.C.E. As the last Ptolemaic queen, her death brought an end to the Ptolemaic dynasty and the kingdoms of Alexander the Great's successors, resulting in Egypt's annexation by Rome.[29] Cleopatra's children were taken to Italy and paraded in Octavian's triumph. In Rome they were raised by Antony's ex-wife (Octavian's sister) alongside her own children by Antony. Their political status was not entirely valueless to Octavian; Cleopatra Selene II, the last surviving member of the Ptolemaic dynasty after the death of her brothers, was married by Octavian (now Augustus) to the African king Juba II of Numidia with a large dowry. As allies of Rome, they were settled in Mauretania, where they established Caesarea as a new capital in honor of Augustus.[30]

Cleopatra VII was seen by the Romans as the "courtesan queen"—a lady of un-Roman, oriental, and luxurious tendencies—a complete contrast to Antony's earlier wife, Octavia Minor (69–11 B.C.E.), who was portrayed as possessing all Roman feminine virtues. In Republican Rome, women, although financially independent of their husbands and possessing far greater freedom within the household than the citizen women of ancient Athens, were legally required to have a male guardian. Stereotypically, women's epitaphs included the terms "old-fashioned," "domestic," "chaste," "obedient," "charming," "not extravagant or given to ornamentation," "pious," and "devoted to household work." The term *univira* (married to only one man) was especially a point of honor. Octavia Minor, the sister of the first Roman emperor, Augustus (Octavian), and the fourth wife of Mark Antony, was respected and admired for her loyalty to her family and husbands as well as for her commitment to traditional feminine virtues. She attempted to supplicate for the victims of the triumvirate's proscriptions and mediated between her brother and her husband in the Treaty of Tarentum in 37 B.C.E.—honored on coinage. In 35 B.C.E. she tried to provide Antony with troops for his eastern campaigns in Parthia, but he sent her back to Rome, where she maintained his household until their divorce in 32 B.C.E. Despite this, she took charge of his children by his wives Fulvia and Cleopatra after his suicide. As a member of the imperial family, she established libraries in the Porticus Octaviae in Rome. At her death in 11 or 10 B.C.E., she was granted a state funeral and buried beside her son Marcellus.

While Octavia enshrined the ideals of the Republican matron, by the end of the republic, aristocratic women were gaining attention from historians as individuals, worthy of comment or criticism in their own right. For example, Sempronia, an adherent of Catiline, was noted for committing many crimes of "masculine daring," both as an accessory to murder and by repudiating debts on oath.[31] Similarly, Fulvia, daughter of Marcus Fulvius Bambalio, who married three radical politicians, including Mark Antony, supported her husbands in their political aims, clearly foreshadowing the powerful women of the early imperial period. Pilloried for her activities by Cicero, she is depicted as the antithesis of the ideal Roman matron, canvassing politically for Antony, foiling attempts by Cicero to have him proclaimed a public enemy, attending the execution of mutinous soldiers, and raising troops and participating in 41 to 40 B.C.E. in the Perusine War with Antony's brother. Portrayed by her opponents as ambitious, greedy, and cruel, she defended Antony's interests in Rome in his absence, while she may even have furthered the marriage of Antony with Octavian's sister (which took place after her death in 40 B.C.E.).[32] As well as by wives and mothers, influence in political schemes could also be wielded by courtesans in the late republic. A certain Praecia furthered her friends' ambitions and was able to manipulate the awarding of at least one important military command and province.[33]

The other class of women to possess specific power and influence in republican and imperial Rome was that of the six Vestal Virgins, women in service to the goddess Vesta. Their main role was to keep alight the sacred fire of Vesta in her temple in the Roman forum and to guard the "sacred things," including the ancient Palladium (the image of Minerva rescued from Troy when the Greeks sacked it), referred to by Livy as the "pledge of Roman imperium." They also participated at various rites and prepared the *mola salsa* (the grain) for official sacrifices. Of all Roman women of this period, they were the freest from male control; they were the only women to have a permanent physical presence in the forum and permitted to address the Senate. Statues show that their hair was arranged like that of brides on their day of marriage, but they dressed as Roman matrons, that is, as women who were not eligible to be sought as brides. They had to be circumspect in their dress so as not to arouse the sexual interest and attentions of men. In times of crisis they ran the risk of being identified as scapegoats and were sometimes buried alive to avert the wrath of the gods from Rome.[34]

Women in the late republic may not have had any official engagement in public life, but they did share in the social prestige of both their own family and that of their husband. Their unofficial political influence developed in the imperial period into the very real power possessed by women in the Julian and Claudian dynasties. Imperial women had no authority in their own right, but by their association with husbands, brothers, and sons, they could have extensive opportunities for political influence at the center of government—especially as regents for underage sons or as the wives of weak rulers. Even in Augustus's reign, his wife, Livia, and sister, Octavia, were granted extraordinary honors such as the right to manage their financial and legal affairs without a guardian and sacrosanctity such as that possessed by the tribunes. Livia was given the title of Augusta (empress) and made priestess of the Divus Augustus (divine Augustus) on his death, perhaps to strengthen the position of her son Tiberius as Augustus's successor. She was later granted divine status by her grandson, Claudius, in 42 C.E.[35] After this, women of the imperial family were regularly deified after death, appearing on coinage and having important cities and regions named after them. They were remembered in public prayers and sacrifices and in official calendars, had statues erected in their honor, and received public dedications. Many imperial women are seen in the sources as responsible for the accession of their menfolk—Livia, Agrippina the Younger, and Julia Maesa, for example; although this can be meant as an oblique attack on their sons, whom they brought to power, it does not negate the very real influence these women possessed.

Livia clearly had great influence on both her husband, Augustus, during their fifty-two years of marriage, as well as on her son Tiberius. Married to Augustus when she was pregnant with her second son, she is reported to have advised him on his policies and accompanied him on his travels, while still maintaining the stance of the traditional Roman matron in both private and public. As Augustus had no sons, Tiberius came to be his designated successor; the reports of Livia's having eliminated other possible contenders have no evidence to support them. Similarly, there is no foundation for the belief that she also manipulated Augustus's own death. The honors granted to her at this point, with Tiberius also awarding her the right to sit with the Vestals at the theater, denote the special status enjoyed by the emperor's wife or mother, though this was never institutionalized into an official recognition of political influence or power. For example, she played a vital role in the establishment of imperial power (the principate) in Rome, but this was never formally acknowledged or institutionalized in the case of her successors. However, her image served to set the standard for other imperial women regarding the idealization of imperial female virtues, and her public association with Pietas and Concordia (Piety and Concord) was reflected in the representation of her successors in their role as imperial wives and mothers.[36]

A similar impact on the idealized perception of imperial wives was made by Vipsania Agrippina (Agrippina the Elder), a Roman matron in the traditional mold, who helped to establish the concept of the imperial helpmate participating collegially in her husband's official role. Granddaughter of Augustus and wife of the highly popular general Germanicus, Tiberius's adopted son, she traveled with her husband on his official campaigns, on several occasions rallying the troops against defeat, and bore him nine children (fecundity being a highly prized asset of any potential empress). She was also reputed to have possessed "insolent speech and a stubborn spirit," and on his deathbed Germanicus is said to have warned her to "put aside her intractable temper" and avoid conflict in Rome, not least with the emperor Tiberius.[37] However, after she returned Germanicus's ashes to Rome following his death in the East, she continued to promote the rights of her sons. Tiberius, afraid of her popularity with the army and the fact that she wanted her sons to be his successors, first refused to allow her to remarry, then exiled her to the island of Pandateria, where she starved herself to death in 33 C.E. Tiberius had the day of her death declared a holiday. Though she did not live to see it, her youngest son, Gaius, would become emperor, and her oldest daughter, Agrippina the Younger, empress as wife of Claudius and mother of Nero.[38]

Other women in the Julio-Claudian dynasty had a reputation for infamous behavior, as a result of either promiscuity or unrestricted ambition, though the sources have to be read with caution. Messalina, third wife of the emperor Claudius, was an example of the former, according to the ancient sources. Her involvement with politics is understated, and her sexuality is blamed for her crimes. As mother of Octavia and Britannicus, her alleged elimination of rivals was undoubtedly politically motivated by the desire to ensure the succession for her son. A marriage in which she took as another husband Gaius Silius, presumably hoping to transfer power to him, ensured her downfall and execution.[39] Claudius's fourth wife and niece, Agrippina the Younger, whom he married in 49 C.E., was no less ambitious but immeasurably more successful in that she succeeded in persuading Claudius to betroth his daughter Octavia to her own son Nero (by an earlier marriage to Gnaeus Domitius Ahenobarbus), adopt him, and name him his successor. She had already been banished on one occasion in 39 C.E. by her brother Caligula (Gaius). Tacitus records that when soothsayers warned her that she would be murdered by her own son, her response was "Let him kill me, if only he becomes emperor!"[40] On Claudius's death, allegedly at the hand of Agrippina by poison in 54 C.E., because he wished to give his own son Britannicus rank equivalent to that of Nero, she assumed the regency for Nero; the first password of the praetorian guard was *optima mater* (the best mother), implying that it was clear to whom Nero owed his position as emperor. Not long afterward she was forced to leave the imperial palace, and Nero became increasingly emancipated from her control, encouraged by the Senate, which feared that she might wish to assume political leadership. When he eventually had her assassinated in 59 C.E. in the Gulf of Baiae after attempts to poison her and sink her ship failed (he had her stabbed), the Senate merely voted a celebration of thanks for his safety.[41]

After a period of relevant quiescence for imperial women, Julia Domna became one of the more important personages in the empire between 193 and 217 C.E. She married the (later) emperor Septimius Severus in 185 and was the mother of Caracalla and Geta. Between 208 and 211 she accompanied Severus on campaign in Britain and may have been involved in the downfall of the praetorian prefect Fulvius, who had opposed her. To honor her for accompanying Severus on his travels she earned the title *mater castrorum* (mother of the camp), despite enemies who accused her of adultery and treason. When Severus died in 211 C.E., she tried to unite the interests of her two sons who had been left as joint emperors and maintain the stability of the empire. However, when Geta was murdered in her presence by Caracalla's soldiers, she was forced to take on a lesser role as adviser to Caracalla, for which she received various honorary titles. When Caracalla was murdered in 217 C.E. while on campaign against the Parthians, Domna, who had accompanied him, is said to have committed suicide in response. She is particularly well known for her literary interests, and she had surrounded herself with a circle of writers, most notably Philostratus, author of the life of Apollonius of Tyana. Her patronage may well have inspired similar literary ambitions in later empresses.[42] Domna's sister, Julia Maesa, lived at court until the death of Caracalla, when she was banished to the family home at Emesa. There, assisted by the efforts of her daughter, Julia Soaemias, she managed to achieve the proclamation by the army stationed there of her grandson Elagabalus as emperor in 218, supporting the troops in the decisive battle against Macrinus at Antioch. As grandmother of the young emperor, who reigned from 218 to 222 C.E., she wielded a great deal of power but was unsuccessful in her attempts to shape his reign, not least in her attempts to dissuade him from marrying one of the Vestals. His mother, Soaemias, was also influential during his reign and established a court on the Quirinal to examine the behavior of Rome's women. Maesa persuaded Elagabalus to adopt her younger grandson, Severus Alexander, who succeeded Elagabalus when he and his mother were murdered by the praetorian guard in 222. She retained some influence on imperial policy until her death in 226 C.E. Severus Alexander's mother, Julia Mamaea, Maesa's younger daughter, who was involved in the deposition of her nephew, had administered the empire alongside Maesa and continued to do so after her mother's death. Like her sister, she too was murdered with her son, assassinated by mutinous troops in Germany in 235 C.E. These Julias—Domna, Maesa, Soaemias, and Mamaea— held the reigns of power for some forty-two years and were arguably more important than any of their predecessors. Both Domna and Maesa were deified after their deaths, while Soaemias and Mamaea, in contrast, suffered *damnatio memoriae* (condemnation of their memory) for their support of their sons.[43]

In the Near East the power of these empresses was also reflected in the activities of Queen Zenobia of Palmyra in Syria, who came to power in 267 C.E. for her son Vaballathus when her husband, Odaenathus, and his eldest son were assassinated. Claiming descent from Cleopatra, she ruled over a court of philosophers and poets and came into conflict with Rome when her armies took control of Syria, Palestine, and Lebanon in the early years of her reign. Her coinage featured herself and her son as Augusta and Augustus. The emperor Aurelian himself marched east in 272 C.E. to deal with what was seen as an attack on Roman power. She was defeated at both Antioch and Emesa and was later captured with her son after fleeing to the river Euphrates. Sources record either that she was paraded in Aurelian's triumph at Rome and was granted a villa at Tibur by the emperor, or that she died on the journey to Italy, perhaps by self-starvation. The fact that she was apparently succeeded by her father at Palmyra shows that her rule had not been unpopular with her subjects even when she led them directly into confrontation with Rome.[44]

POWERFUL WOMEN IN THE LATE ANTIQUE PERIOD

Imperial women received access to power and status with the advent of Christianity and the accession to the throne of Constantine the Great, the first Christian emperor, who founded a new capital in the East, Constantinople, in 330 C.E.

During the preceding decades, with the empire racked by numerous civil wars and multiple rulers, women appear to have been of use primarily for deployment in marriage alliances that consolidated relationships among the powerful men who shared the empire. With the stability of the Constantinian dynasty, though itself short-lived, the wives and mothers of emperors, and occasionally their sisters too, found a part to play in the political and social arena. In this new Christian milieu, where women and men supposedly shared spiritual equality, women are seen securing their dynasty through the practical exercise of their piety, as evinced through pilgrimages, the foundation of churches, the acquisition of holy relics, and public prayers and vows for the family and empire. That a number of these imperial women were from the lower classes (like Helena, mother of Constantine) or of "barbarian," that is, German or Frankish descent (e.g., Eudoxia, wife of Arcadius), was not allowed to detract from their status or achievements. They played a particularly significant role in times of religious controversy, as well as ruling either collegially with husbands or brothers or as de facto emperors. Helena, for example, worked with her son Constantine in consolidating the spread of Christianity throughout the empire by the foundation of churches in the Holy Land between 326 and 328 C.E., beneficence toward the poor and unfortunate, and her personification of imperial religiosity: the tale that she discovered the True Cross in Jerusalem is not contemporary but was accepted by the end of the century. Constantine refounded and renamed Drepanum in Bithynia as Helenoupolis (city of Helena) in her honor, and from 324 C.E. the coinage bore her portrait, with the legend, "Security of the Republic," while she was given the title of Augusta in the same year.[45]

With the Theodosian dynasty established in 379 C.E., imperial women and eunuchs became strong and powerful players in the government of the empire as a consequence of their access to the weak rulers of the time. One such empress, Eudoxia, daughter of the Frankish general Bauto, easily dominated her husband, Arcadius, promoting an image of collegiality in the capital by her fecundity (five children) and advocacy of orthodoxy. She not only managed to ensure the downfall of the powerful eunuch and ex-consul Eutropius but also turned against the patriarch John Chrysostom when he denounced her as Jezebel and Salome because of her luxurious lifestyle: she had him exiled in 403 and again in 404 C.E. Her death from a miscarriage was popularly believed to have been divine punishment for interfering in church affairs.[46]

Eudoxia's eldest daughter, Pulcheria, inherited her mother's political acumen and determination but in this case dominated—and even ruled for—her younger brother Theodosius II. At the age of fifteen, in 414 C.E., she made her sisters follow her in taking a public vow of perpetual virginity in St. Sophia, after which she was given the title of Augusta and ruled as regent for Theodosius. While at times engaged in an internecine struggle with her sister-in-law, Athenais-Eudokia, Pulcheria was responsible for her brother's scholarly and theological education, a Byzantine campaign against Persia in the early 420s in the guise of a crusade, and legislation against Jews, pagans, and heretics in a drive for religious conformity. She clearly viewed herself as collegially co-ruling with her brother. She even expected to be allowed access to the "Holy of Holies" in St. Sophia to receive communion as if emperor in her own right, and she played the major part in the deposition of the patriarch Nestorius for heresy in 431 C.E. When her brother died from a riding accident in 450, she took charge of the empire, going through a form of marriage with the general Marcian and making him emperor by crowning him in front of the army. One of her greatest achievements was at the Council of Chalcedon in 451, at which orthodoxy was defined and the Chalcedonian Creed formulated to counteract the Eastern heresies that were dividing the church. Pulcheria was present in person at the council and was acclaimed there as a "second Helena." As with Eudoxia, imperial women derived power from their public piety, which was thought to preserve the empire and bring success: Pulcheria established several churches in the capital and organized the reception of the relics of St. Stephen in Constantinople, while her sister-in-law, Eudokia, the wife of Theodosius II, went on pilgrimage to Jerusalem and retired there. Eudokia promoted the foundation of churches and took an interest in theological debate.[47]

Following the pattern by which Pulcheria raised Marcian to the purple, a number of later Byzantine empresses transferred power to a new ruler of their own selection on the death of their husbands or sons. On Zeno's death without children in 491 C.E., his wife, Ariadne, passed over his brother Longinus and chose a public servant, Anastasius, whom she married and made emperor. In 578 C.E. Sophia, when the dementia of her husband, Justin II, prevented him from ruling, chose first Tiberius (II) and then Maurice as his successors, while retaining a firm grip on government for herself: Tiberius's wife and children were forced to live in a separate palace. In the eleventh century Zoe Porphyrogenita, who was the heir to the throne in her own right, legitimated four emperors, including three husbands and an adopted son, and ruled for several weeks with her younger sister Theodora.[48] The regency, however, was the normal role through which empresses controlled government, and a number of them played an important part in government as regents for their sons, not always to the delight of the populace, or indeed the son. Heraclius in 641 C.E. left Martina, his wife and niece, as regent for her stepson,

Heraclius Constantine (Constantine III). The stepson, already of age, and her own underage son, Heraclonas, were to rule jointly. Martina clearly expected to govern the empire. However, the populace objected, and after Heraclius Constantine's death (probably from tuberculosis, though poison was also suspected), she and her son were deposed, mutilated, and exiled. The anger against her was inspired by the fact that she was seen as having tried to keep her stepson and his family from power and by her incestuous relationship with her uncle. The fact that a large number of her children were disabled was seen as divine punishment.[49]

After the death of Leo IV, another regent, Irene, ruled on behalf of their son, Constantine VI. She initially refused to step aside, and after several periods of troubled joint rule, she had him deposed and blinded in 797 c.e.—in the purple chamber of the palace in which she had given birth to him—so that she could rule, specifically as emperor, not empress, without a co-ruler. The one disadvantage of empress-regents was that they could not personally lead an army. There were many emperors in the same position, but it had disastrous consequences in at least one case for an empress ruling as regent for a young son: Irene's reign nearly lost credibility in the face of great Arab successes on the eastern border, and Zoe Karbounopsina's regency for Constantine VII in the early tenth century foundered on inadequate military generalship against the ferocious Bulgarians.[50]

Empress-consorts also had considerable power and influence. Imperial wives were invariably chosen from the empire itself (the practice of marrying foreign princesses came to the fore only in the late eleventh century), and an empress interested in politics was able to interview ministers, clergy, and foreign ambassadors without reference to her husband and to correspond privately with world leaders: the principle of collegiality ensured that in certain cases empresses were seen almost as corulers with their husbands. Theodora, wife of Justinian, despite her background as a hippodrome performer, co-ruled so closely with her husband that she is mentioned numerous times in his legislation, particularly with regard to social issues such as prostitution and the granting of financial support to divorcees and widows. She was publicly linked with him in acts of charity and construction throughout the empire, while her love of power is shown by the fact that she saved the throne by dissuading him from fleeing in the face of riots in the capital in 532 c.e. At the same time she appeared to follow a contrary religious policy to that of Justinian, though it was suspected that the couple were still working in concert to keep everyone in the empire happy. A mosaic at the front gate of the imperial palace depicted Justinian and Theodora together receiving the homage of conquered Western monarchs. Procopius, in his *Secret History*, complained that "neither did any-thing apart from the other to the end of their joint lives!"[51]

Nevertheless, the public life of an empress remained largely separate from that of her husband, especially prior to the eleventh century, and involved the orchestration of a parallel court to that of the emperor, revolving around cer-emonies involving the wives of court officials. It is difficult to gauge the size of the empress's retinue, but Theodora was accompanied by 4,000 attendants when she visited the spa at Pythion across the Sea of Marmara in 529 C.E. While the empress primarily presided over her own ceremonial sphere, with her own duties and functions, she also could be present at court banquets, audiences, and receptions of envoys, as well as take part in processions and services in Hagia Sophia and elsewhere. One of her primary duties was the reception of the wives of foreign rulers and heads of state. Nor were empresses restricted to the capital: Martina notably accompanied Heraclius and the army while he was fighting the Persians, and many of their children were born while they were on campaign.[52]

Byzantine empresses, whether consorts or regents, could command very considerable wealth: a new empress distributed lavish amounts of gold to the patriarch, Senate, and clergy, and imperial women generally possessed great financial resources and patronage. Their status was also signaled by the trap-pings of power and majesty—heavy robes embroidered with gold and jew-els, precious gems, their retinues, and charitable donations. The enjoyment of wealth was not restricted to empresses. Women in Byzantium generally are well documented as owners of property and administrators of their own es-tates, while many wealthy women, in addition to supervising family, servants, and property, ran shops or household workshops that made clothes for sale. In tax registers, widows and other women are frequently named as owners of houses and property and are listed as taxpayers. Danielis, a widow from Patras in Greece in the ninth century, controlled "not a small part of the Pelo-ponnese" and reportedly owned innumerable slaves, 3,000 of whom Leo VI (886–912 C.E.) freed and settled in southern Italy. For her generous financial support of his father, the (later) emperor Basil I, she was given the honorary title of *basileometer*, mother of the emperor.[53]

Empresses who did not remarry, like Irene, or who never married, like Theodora, the last member of the Macedonian house, who died in 1056 C.E., ruled in exactly the same way as emperors: they presided over the court, ap-pointed officials, issued decrees, settled lawsuits, received ambassadors and heads of state, fulfilled the emperor's ceremonial role, and made decisions on matters of financial and foreign policy. These imperial women played a role in government unprecedented in the classical world. Arguably the Byzantine princess Theophano took this skill and experience with her to Germany in 972, when as a young girl she was transported to Western Europe and married to Emperor Otto II of the Holy Roman Empire. Despite the fact that she was not the daughter of a ruling emperor, but rather the niece of John I Tzimiskes (who came to the throne by assassinating his predecessor), she showed great political skill as co-imperatrix during her husband's reign, in which she side-lined his domineering mother, Adelheid. As regent, she defended the empire for her three-year-old son, Otto III, from 983 until 991 C.E. The bishop and chronicler Thietmar of Merseburg eulogized her in terms that would have applied equally appropriately to her Byzantine predecessors and counterparts: "Though Theophanu was of the weak sex she possessed moderation, trustworthiness, and—what is not often found in Greece—good manners. In this way she protected with male vigilance the royal power for her son, friendly with all those who were honest, but with terrifying superiority against rebels."[54] Considering the hatred and opposition toward Theophano in the West, inspired by her Eastern birth and love of luxury (daily baths, silk clothes, and golden forks), this is praise indeed. It should be noted that it was her presence that began the trend for imperial regalia and ceremony in the West; it was after his marriage to her that Otto II proclaimed himself *Romanorum imperator augustus* (august emperor of the Romans), stating clearly that his power was equal to that of the Byzantine Empire itself. Theophano was a proud descendent of a thousand years of powerful imperial women.

CHAPTER EIGHT

Artistic Representation: Survival of the Classical Ideal

SHELBY BROWN

Other authors in this volume have looked at women's bodies and sexuality, roles in and outside the home, and private as opposed to public selves primarily as revealed through texts. My task is to consider how women are depicted in images from 500 B.C.E. to 1000 C.E., and I limit myself to fairly broad generalizations within a narrow range of topics in order to cover this span of time.[1] Scholarly debate about how to interpret women's appearance and behavior in ancient art is ongoing, and discovering what is generally called the "lived experience" of women is problematic. We should not assume that images provide a realistic view of women or even of any one woman's true appearance. Very often, even individualizing portraits or funerary images that are intended to represent a real person idealize or generalize. Even so, we can identify consistently depicted attributes of women that reflect ideal physical and moral or behavioral qualities and then follow these across time. My emphasis will be on beauty, sexuality, and female modesty, with a focus on physical qualities and symbols established in classical art that are traceable through succeeding centuries. The women depicted as establishing the norms are the free and elite, or at least the average citizen (or citizen's wife), while the slave, poor, or working woman is her foil.

This series of volumes on women begins with the art of the fifth century B.C.E. The work of artists of the classical period, especially in Athens, proved to be enormously influential throughout the ancient world and into modern times. It is no longer art historical practice to claim this period as the greatest or the best, and classical art, while not always devalued, has certainly come down off its pedestal as "the standard" and is now seen as reflecting but one century in a small region of the known (Western) world. Nevertheless, classical artists established a powerful image of female beauty, subsequently spread by the conquests of Alexander the Great and then of the Romans, to which future centuries strongly responded. The symbolic representation of female appearance and behavior in the art of the fifth and fourth centuries B.C.E. affected artists so thoroughly—whether they were copying, rejecting, or ignoring a classical style—that images of women often refer in one way or another to classical standards for the next thousand years and beyond.[2]

My goal in the limited context of this chapter is to focus on appearance, actions, and gestures clearly and frequently shown in art, since the difficulties of understanding representations of women can be profound. The same problems that plague us as we seek information about women's lives in literary and textual evidence are present in, and sometimes multiplied by, art and material culture. Often we cannot identify the owners of ancient works of art or even the artworks' original physical location. Images cannot be fully understood when divorced from their function and context, yet material culture is variously preserved based on its medium and environment and often haphazardly discovered, leaving vast holes in our information. Due to damage and loss, the relative frequency of types of surviving images is statistically unreliable. It is appropriate—in fact, essential—from an archaeological perspective to examine representations of women separately from texts and to consider the contexts of the objects and art that survive. Yet given that contexts are very often lacking entirely or poorly preserved, and texts do provide information we need to make sense of many images, there is a tendency to use art to validate and explain texts, and vice versa, rather than to evaluate each independently. Excavation strategies and scholarly research have also emphasized different types of art and physical remains at different times.

The theoretical approaches to and goals of looking at images of women in ancient art have changed dramatically in the past forty years. Influenced by semiotic studies, psychoanalytical theories, and feminist art history, especially in the 1970s, artists and historians began increasingly to question the intended viewers of art and film and to identify, analyze, and undermine assumptions about women and "others," often the nonelite, being viewed by an assumed dominant viewer. Over time the related fields of classics, history, art history, anthropology, and (more slowly) ancient art history and archaeology began to seek greater understanding of the functions, locations, contexts, viewers, buyers, and sponsors/patrons of artworks. Overlapping and evolving approaches within a growing host of disciplines have all contributed variously to new ways of seeing ancient art and material culture.[3] Sometimes, reasonable authors writing about the same images interpret them wildly differently, and one of the fascinating jobs of the classical art historian is to keep up with the latest interpretations of and changing ideas about artistic media, images, and monuments.[4] Multiple interpretations are not just inevitable but desirable, especially if we acknowledge just how little we actually know about antiquity and refrain from seeking a fixed truth.

Feminist theory initially focused on undermining a privileged male gaze and ultimately on understanding "the processes through which images or representations are constructed" and how they relate to the construction of identity.[5] An ultimate goal remains to recast scholarly assumptions and theoretical approaches. The early academic focus of the cultural or ancient art historian interested in the women of past cultures was to find women in the first place, within a textual and artistic tradition that favored male achievements, and then eventually to undermine ideas about what was culturally important and to challenge modern interpretive strategies. Authors writing today identify multiple, evolving stages of feminist research and offer many approaches to engendering texts, material culture, and art. The debate and analysis of the last forty years have effectively resulted in far more nuanced and critical assessment of evidence for women, recreation of a female point of view, and evaluation of women's social roles and status from complex and varied perspectives, even though the feminist contribution to this discourse has sometimes been underestimated. Much work on gender and sexuality has also benefited archaeology and art history in asking how sexuality is socially constructed and how context dictates our interpretations of representations of women.[6] The classical art described in the following pages was created by male artists in the context of institutions established by and for men, although it is possible that women's patronage affected certain types of representations. Greek citizens' mothers, wives, and daughters were not citizens themselves, and they remained under the control of a father, husband, or male guardian for their lifetimes. It is safe to say that the art depicting women reflects a male view, even if women accepted it.

MINOAN AND MYCENAEAN WOMEN

A noteworthy change in depictions of women occurred after the Late Bronze Age (roughly 1600–1200 B.C.E.). Keeping firmly in mind that our evidence is limited and difficult to interpret, women's bodies and clothing as depicted in Minoan and Theran art were not yet as tamed and restrained as they were by the sixth and fifth centuries. Some Bronze Age images represent men and women together at public gatherings or processions, although sometimes separated by seating area.[7] Women shown in frescoes and statuettes have hourglass figures and wear long, brightly colored skirts and tight bodices that expose their breasts. A form of Theran split skirt afforded freedom of movement for the legs.[8] The clothing did not survive into later periods, nor did a plump double chin, but other elements of female appearance did: white skin (probably a convention borrowed from the Egyptians); long, dark hair in ringlets partly tied up with ribbons; curls at the forehead showing under a forehead band; narrow waists; small, straight noses; small "rosebud" mouths; and dark, oval eyes. Visible red makeup emphasized lips and cheeks. A woman on a fresco from Mycenae on the mainland has the Theran body and facial type and the colorful, tight bodice, but her breasts are covered with fabric. Mycenaean women's bodies apparently began to be hidden, some under more shapeless garments.[9] Despite a tendency to draw conclusions about women's freedom based largely on their clothing and participation in public events, and to assume that martial Mycenaeans constrained their women, we know little about the circumstances or ways in which women may have participated in their communities or dressed in the elegant and revealing garments that cannot possibly reflect daily wear. However, with the end of the Bronze Age came the end of the bare breast as a fashion statement.

CLASSICAL WOMEN: IDEALS OF BEAUTY
AND BEHAVIOR

Between the Bronze Age and the classical period, enormous cultural, political, and artistic changes are reflected in images of women. In the fifth century B.C.E. and into the fourth, surviving red-figure vases, especially by Athenian makers, provide our main evidence from the private sphere for mythological scenes and events of daily life. The vases were exported widely, and many questions remain about their relative cost, their artistic influence, the accuracy of their representation of Greek social behavior, and the degree to which market forces (local patrons versus foreign buyers) affected artists' thematic choices.[10] Many of the vases for holding, pouring, and drinking wine were intended for male dinner parties and symposia from which citizens' wives and daughters were excluded, although female entertainers and sexually available women—courtesan *hetairai* (courtesans) or lower-status *pornai* (prostitutes)—did attend. Other vessels, such as those designed to carry water for ritual washing before a wedding, are more likely to have been used by women. Utilitarian and decorative objects for private use, such as ceramic *pyxides* (rounded containers), bronze mirrors, and metal and ivory attachments, also depicted goddesses and women. Greek women were rarely represented in classical public art except occasionally in religious contexts, as in the Parthenon frieze showing the preparations for and procession of the Panathenaia,[11] and on funerary monuments. The stone statues of *korai* dedicated in temples—fully dressed maidens who stood with their legs together, arms close to their sides, in comparison with nude males with their legs apart—did not last into the fifth century.[12]

Goddesses and mythological women, whose stories were narrated in stone on temple metopes, friezes, and pediments, offer models of desirable appearance and qualities. In the fifth century B.C.E., images of women and men reflected standards of proportion and beauty that crossed the boundaries of public and private art. Both genders have an oval face, straight nose, small lips, smooth cheeks, and rounded chin. Like the Egyptians and Bronze Age Greeks, classical Greeks emphasized women's pale skin, sometimes shown by an added white slip in vase painting or by the background white that serves as female skin color on white-ground *lekythoi* (oil containers).[13] Although artists sometimes depicted old age, body fat, or physical damage, the default human body was youthful and slender. Women in the archaic and very early classical periods often appear to have been created from a male model, presumably because artists had far greater opportunity to observe men during nude exercise. Vase paintings in particular often show women who resemble men with breasts added on. In the tondo of a red-figure *kylix* (drinking cup) of just before 500 B.C.E., shown in Figure 8.1, a naked young man with a cloak draped over his left shoulder steps in a dance as he plays the double flute; a girl playing the castanets dances next to him. Their bodies are almost interchangeable, except that hers has pointed, sideways breasts added to the upper chest. She wears a fawn skin over an almost invisible garment that leaves her breasts and much of her body exposed. By the mid-fifth century B.C.E., artists were representing distinctively feminine, plumper female bodies with curving, more realistic breasts; mature goddesses, as on the east pediment of the Parthenon, are even shown as quite voluptuous.[14] Both male and female bodies often turn in three dimensions to offer the viewer, even in two-dimensional art, a three-quarter view of the subject's rounded limbs and curving face.

FIGURE 8.1: Interior tondo of a red-figure *kylix*. Showing a dancing girl and male flute player, from the late sixth century B.C.E. The female body is not yet clearly distinguishable from the male. British Museum no. 1843,1103.9. © The Trustees of the British Museum.

Idealized classical faces cannot always easily be distinguished by gender, aside from a heavier chin on men, and mortals cannot easily be distinguished from gods. Faces were consistently smooth and calm, with no expression except under extreme conditions, such as the pain incurred in combat. A faint downturn to the mouth, a forehead wrinkle, and slightly parted lips could indicate men's fear, pain, or emotion, while women's faces generally remained blank, their emotion expressed by gestures. On the west pediment of the temple of Zeus at Olympia, in the combat of Lapiths and centaurs at the wedding of Perithoos, the bestial centaurs show more feeling than the humans, wrinkling their foreheads and grimacing; the Lapith males show little facial expression, and the women, although fighting off half-human attackers trying to abduct them, remain completely expressionless.[15]

A Greek woman's *peplos* or *chiton*, essentially a dress made from a big rectangle of wool or linen, was designed to cover her body from neck to feet.

The type and fineness of the fabric and different methods of sewing or pin-ning the shoulders, folding the cloth over and bunching it, and tying on belts of variable thickness created a more or less elegant effect. Female clothing in early fifth-century B.C.E. art stayed relatively rectangular in shape as it fell from shoulders to feet. Soon, however, artists emphasized the body under the fabric. Garments were designed to drape and lie in decorative patterns, and both men and women were often posed for aesthetic effect within symmetrical compositions that reinforced elegant patterns. Women's clothing, however, of-fered the most scope for design. Curving, flowing folds that billow with the movement of the body and enhance its three-dimensional design, along with more clinging folds emphasizing breasts and belly, became a standard of sexu-alized beauty maintained for centuries. In contrast, women's posture, gaze, and gestures showed a self-restraint that counteracted the clinging, body-enhancing garments. In Figure 8.2, a respectable mother (the deceased) on a late fifth-century B.C.E. funerary monument sits attended by a slave holding the baby. The young mother holds a box on her lap, a symbol of appropriate feminine concern with ornament and self-decoration. The fall of drapery over her right breast exposes and enhances its rounded shape, although her garment fully covers her body. Her covered head, solemn face, and downward glance pro-claim that she is modest. Because they are deceased, women in funerary art are especially restrained, but mothers in general refrain from showing enjoyment even when admiring their babies.[16]

Female interest in ornamentation and primping is referenced in art by deco-rative patterns on clothing, delicate buttons and pins, elaborately belted and tied hair and garments, and jewelry (earrings, necklaces, and bracelets), as well as by scenes of women seated with their slaves, holding mirrors, jewelry boxes, and small pots for perfume or makeup. Female hair had to be coiffed and bound up; like bodies, hair was enticing and needed to be controlled. Respect-able women had long hair, while slaves' hair was cut short. In art, long hair is carefully tied back with decorative fillets and cloth or covered by a mantle. Women also veil themselves—envelope themselves in a cloak or shawl and cover their heads (and thus their hair) and sometimes part of their faces—and look downward in varied interactions with men, including wedding scenes.[17] Whether veiled or not, they restrain their limbs, gestures, and expressions un-less there is an acceptable context, such as pleading, fleeing, fighting off attack, mourning, or experiencing (maenadic) ecstasy.

Mythological scenes depict women with a breast exposed being chased or resisting abduction or rape, like the Lapith woman on the west pediment of the temple of Zeus at Olympia, or Cassandra on red-figure vases, clinging in full

FIGURE 8.2: Marble tombstone of an unknown woman, holding an open box on her lap as a slave stands nearby holding
her baby. The mother sits in a slightly curving pose that emphasizes her downward gaze; this was the posture of a respectable
female, here also serving as a sign of sadness. British Museum
no. 1894,0616.1. © The Trustees of the British Museum.

frontal nudity to the statue of Athena at Troy with her arm raised in pleading
gesture; Ajax, with his sword aimed at her, prepares to snatch her away from
Athena's sanctuary. Only very rarely does a female pursue a man, sometimes in
a humorous way, as when the goddess Eos on a red-figure vase fragment chases
Tithonos, or Cassandra chases Ajax in a reversal of the usual story.[18] Truly
frightening female pursuers in art are hybrid monsters like gorgons, harpies,

and sirens (although sirens lure more than pursue). The gorgon is especially representative of femininity gone wrong. The archaic gorgon had a large, flat, masklike face with a trilobed nose, huge eyes, a large mouth with feline fangs and lolling tongue, and snaky hair. In the fifth century Medusa's face became beautiful, although still deadly; she could even be shown as pitiful, with the bared breast(s) of the attacked woman. Greek hybrid beings generally possessed either too many or too few body parts, which sometimes functioned inappropriately; the sphinx used her mouth/voice to ask deadly riddles; the siren used hers to sing men to their deaths. Medusa had not only snaky hair and, initially, a monstrous face but also a deadly gaze, since unlike respectable women she looked directly at men and turned them to stone. Even after Perseus had killed her, the eyes in her severed head (the *gorgoneion*) retained their power. Her gorgon siblings, equally ugly, had no ability to cause death by their inappropriate looking; they merely pursued Perseus after he had killed their sister. The *gorgoneion* lasted far longer in art than the whole woman; first masklike and then beautiful, it served as an apotropaic device, useful on shields and temples alike to ward off enemies, and the gorgon image's protective function survived under Christianity.[19]

Images of women letting their hair down during mourning—and then disheveling, pulling, and tearing it as well as their clothing to symbolize appropriate grief—offer a rare glimpse of an acceptable inversion of contained and calm femininity.[20] Less acceptable inversions show, for example, maenads dancing wildly, playing rhythmic instruments like tambourines, and (transported by Dionysos) throwing their heads back, letting their hair fly, opening their mouths, and crying out. Maenads' loss of self-control leaves them vulnerable to sexual molestation and attack, and their attempts to fend off satyrs are frequently depicted in art. They are molested whether sleeping or awake, even when not under the influence of the god.[21]

Male nudity or seminudity, originally signifying a context of athletic exercise or competition, came to symbolize moral as well as physical virtue[22] and was eventually incorporated in art even into scenes of real life. Male bodies were almost universally toned and slender, with visible musculature. The bodies of heavy athletes such as pankratiasts and boxers were bulkier, although muscular, and occasionally even humorously big-bellied. The costumed, disproportionate bodies of comic actors in vase painting, along with an occasional fat, nonathletic male, also reflect a humorous contrast with the athletic norm.[23] Women, even goddesses, were on the contrary not shown nude or seminude except under special circumstances, since artists needed a reason to undress or expose them. The breast of a flying goddess, for example, might "accidentally" be revealed. Other females' nudity generally showed vulnerability and implied titillation. On vases women's bodies were sometimes exposed while bathing; the pots may have been women's vases showing female activities, or perhaps the women are assumed to be unaware of a watcher or willing to be seen (implying sexual availability).[24]

Entertainers and prostitutes, whether higher-status *hetairai* or lower-status *pornai*, were also represented partially undressed or fully naked, generally in scenes of symposium sex. Couples are often shown having sex in the presence of one another on dining couches.[25] A red-figure *kylix* of the late sixth century B.C.E. showcases female slaves with short hair, their faces contorted in performing oral sex. Older and bulkier than the slender ideal, they twist their bodies, penetrated in multiple orifices by multiple partners, who do not seem gentle.[26] There is no reason to believe that it was feasible to protect women from such scenes of sexual activity, and women could hardly avoid the images of naked men commonly found in both private and public art; however, symposium vases were designed for men whose mothers, wives, and daughters were elsewhere during the parties.

While *hetairai* and prostitutes were sexually active on vases, sexuality was denied respectable women, and wives were not shown even in bed with legitimate husbands. A fascinating red-figure exception, a *lekythos* of the fifth century, depicts Theseus's imminent abandonment of Ariadne, who is lying in bed with him. A small figure flying away may represent her virginity. Ariadne twists slightly away from Theseus and turns her body and calm, contented face toward us in peaceful sleep (a miniature personified Hypnos ensures that she will stay asleep).[27] Behind her lies Theseus, starting to rise at the urging of Athena, who seems to shush him as he makes a surprised or possibly pleading gesture. Ariadne is treated as a bride, and her clothing and body language are wholly respectable. She is fully dressed with her hair neatly tied up, her legs pressed together, and her hands clasped at her breast.

The Etruscans in northern Italy in the late sixth, fifth, and fourth centuries owe much of their iconography to the Greeks, borrowing many stylistic attributes and narrative motifs from Greek art; however, there are notable differences in the contexts in which women are depicted. Like Bronze Age Greek women, Etruscan women are shown participating in public events with men, and women of high status, not just prostitutes or flute girls, attend dinner parties. Husbands and wives are shown reclining together on dining couches in tomb paintings and on cinerary urns and sarcophagus lids; they are even shown in the marital bed together, under the covers. One especially intimate scene on a sarcophagus lid from the Ponte Rotto necropolis in Vulci, from the second half of the fourth century B.C.E., represents a couple facing one another, eyes locked, as they embrace under a coverlet. Their arms partly hide their nude upper bodies. A more conventional funerary couple from the same necropolis, dressed and bejeweled, is largely hidden by their coverlet.[28] In general, although they have more freedom in public and in their funerary intimacy with their husbands, Etruscan women's images reflect ideal Greek femininity: pale skin; slender bodies; controlled gestures; oval, smooth, calm faces with small rosebud lips and straight noses; carefully arranged drapery; and symmetrically coiffed hair. While men show the effects of age and weight gain, women barely do. A later, Hellenistic (second-century B.C.E.) Etruscan funerary "portrait" on the sarcophagus of a woman whose preserved body permitted comparison with her image offers a salutary reminder of the difference between representation and genuine human remains; although the funerary statue has a slight double chin, the actual woman had a deformed jaw and other problems that were well disguised in her typically Greek funerary image.[29]

HELLENISTIC WOMEN

Hellenistic art from the death of Alexander to Augustus's principate introduced a vast expansion of the meaning of "Greek" and included the spread of Greek ideas and ideals into the eastern Mediterranean, the breakup of Alexander's world into separate kingdoms, and the conquests by the Romans in the late republic. This period is variously defined by art historians[30] and is difficult to mine for uniform images of women. Marble grave statues and honorific statues occur in a variety of poses and types along with smaller terra-cotta figurines. Women are honored alone or in family groups, largely in sanctuaries. Although artists commemorated men with individualized portraits, women's faces remain generic, harking back to the classical, and their drapery is also reminiscent of the earlier style, now with a finer outer wrap or mantle clinging to the garment beneath (rather than with a thicker wrap over a thin dress). There are many small variations of stance and pose. Often, although the body is completely enveloped, feminine curves are still clearly visible, and both clothing and stance emphasize a restrained sexuality. In one common variation the woman crosses one arm over her body below her breasts, pulling her mantle tightly over her belly; she raises her other arm and holds her hand to her face or veil in a gesture associated with modesty.[31]

Smaller figurines, especially those called Tanagra from a famous find spot, offer a more informal look at women who may be of a lower social class: they stand, sit, dance, and pose alone or in pairs in brightly colored garments whose pinks, blues, and whites are better preserved than the colors on marble statues of larger size. Color was significant to the final effect of statues, statuettes, and other painted artworks, whose surfaces have faded so greatly that reconstructed polychromatic surfaces can be shocking.[32] Women's clothing and ornamentation in all periods could be rich and colorful, contributing to the beauty of an attractive woman. The figurines are intended to showcase women's figures, elegant poses, and beautiful movements. In Figure 8.3, two seated women lean together, creating a triangle composition, faces close as they talk intimately with typical calm expressions; one holds her breast, since her garment has slipped down. Such figurines supposedly allow us a glimpse of a private female world, one that nevertheless reinforces standards of beauty and feminine behavior.

Along with modestly dressed statues of women, nude statues of Aphrodite proliferated in the Hellenistic period, after the sculptor Praxiteles created a shocking, entirely naked cult statue of Aphrodite in the late fourth century B.C.E.

FIGURE 8.3: Terra-cotta Tanagra figurine. Two women speaking intimately; the bright color of their clothing is largely preserved. British Museum no. 1885.3–16.1. © The Trustees of the British Museum.

The goddess has been caught either undressing for a bath or starting to cover herself after one; she attempts to hide her genitals with one hand, thereby showing appropriate modesty and also drawing attention to her sexuality. The people of Kos rejected the statue, accepting a clothed Aphrodite instead, while the people of Knidos took the naked version, which greatly improved tourism to the island. This statue was enormously influential in defining female beauty and sexual appeal, and many varieties of naked Aphrodite statues and statuettes followed, intended for sanctuary dedication and home enjoyment, some more voluptuous and unaware of a voyeur than others. Famous original statues were copied and modified in larger or smaller versions for centuries. Most are standing goddesses who attempt to cover their breasts as well as genitals, but some crouch naked.[33] These statues seem especially lifelike and immediate because of a fourth-century B.C.E. sculptural technique whereby a figure's weight was distributed more on one leg than the other, and the body was thereby shown in realistic, slightly unbalanced motion (a *contrapposto* position).

In the fourth and later centuries, the impact of narrative scenes was enhanced by dynamic facial expressions showing fear, pain, and other emotions, and bodies were displayed against a backdrop of dramatic, clinging garments. Even so, the standards of feminine restraint held true for both goddesses and women, even in highly charged situations. On the mid-fourth-century B.C.E. red-figure vase shown in Figure 8.5, Lycurgus, who attacked and killed his family when maddened by Dionysos, has stabbed his wife and drags her by the hair, which is falling down. Above one exposed breast her wound bleeds; her face, however, remains serious as she tries to push him away. Similarly, in the combat of gods and giants on the north frieze of the Pergamon Altar, from the second century B.C.E., a victorious and powerful goddess (Nyx?) in swirling drapery, holding a pot of snakes aloft, has the elegant pose and calm face of her classical predecessors.[34] In complete contrast, yet reinforcing the ideal, are images of old, drunk, or emaciated women whose bodies sag and droop and whose clothing exposes not a titillating glimpse of plump flesh but the opposite of a desirable feminine form.[35] A terra-cotta figurine now in the Metropolitan Museum in New York shows an emaciated old woman, her hair arranged in a youthful hairdo with ringlets, the downward gaze of her wrinkled face with its big nose mimicking that of a modest classical woman. Her garment falls off her right shoulder, exposing a painfully bony chest, and through the fabric we see that her breasts have fallen to her waist and that her curving belly is distended from starvation.[36] A larger stone figure of another woman in the Metropolitan Museum, nicknamed the "Old Market Woman," probably a copy of an earlier original, wears what could be expensive, formal clothing, belted with careful

FIGURE 8.4: Capitoline Venus or Hellenistic Aphrodite. Roman
marble copy (second century C.E.?), from a villa at Campo
Lemini in Latium, of a Hellenistic Aphrodite in the style called
Capitoline. The goddess has been surprised while bathing and
protectively covers her breasts and pubic area with her hands.
British Museum no. 1834,0301.1. © The Trustees of the British
Museum.

folds at the waist and hips, but the effect is ruined as the woman stoops, her
sagging neckline exposing her full but drooping breasts and an expanse of
bony collarbone. Her face and neck are deeply wrinkled.[37] These figures illustrate everything women should not be; they emphasize the expectation of
classical standards of female beauty and modesty in art by representing their
opposite.

FIGURE 8.5: Red-figure calyx crater. Of the mid-fourth century B.C.E., attributed to the Lycurgus Painter, named after the scene of Lycurgus killing his wife. British Museum no. 1849,0623.48. © The Trustees of the British Museum.

ROMAN WOMEN

In the late second and first centuries B.C.E., as the Romans expanded into the eastern Mediterranean and conquered the Greek world, they began to bring original Greek statues home to Rome and Italy and, eventually, to copy them.[38] Despite some suspicion of nudity as symbolic of weakness and licentiousness, Romans nevertheless copied sculptures of athletes and bathing Aphrodites and placed them in their private baths and gardens to bring a veneer of Hellenizing culture to their homes. Artists borrowed from both the earlier classical and the newer Hellenistic styles. In particular, statues of respectable Roman women spread throughout the empire, modeled on those of modest Greek women enveloped in their mantles. Roman women, however, could choose to attach individualized heads, rather than generic ones, to the standardized bodies. The heads were inserted into a sort of body-costume that signified attractive, appropriate dignity. Two similar types, called the "Large Herculaneum Woman" and "Small Herculaneum Woman" after their find spot and size, were especially common, lasting into the third century C.E. Under the Roman Empire, individualizing portraits became important for imperial family members who needed to be widely recognized. A second-century C.E. bust probably representing Faustina the Elder, wife of the emperor Antoninus Pius, reflects the type of portrait head that could be inserted into a standard body type; she was herself represented as a Large Herculaneum Woman, as can be seen in Figure 8.6.[39] Faustina's slightly large nose, thin lips, and distinctive hairstyle individualize her, yet her skin is smooth and youthful and her expression calm in the manner of a classical Greek original.

FIGURE 8.6: Marble portrait bust of Faustina the Elder. Mid-second century C.E. Her smooth face harks back to Greek sculpture, but her distinctive hairstyle, nose, and lips identify her as an individual. British Museum no. 1889,0812.1. © The Trustees of the British Museum.

In the late first century C.E., a startling innovation emerged alongside the usual imagery of a somewhat classicizing, decorous woman with either a standardized or a personalized head. Portrait heads began to be placed on the nude statue bodies of Jupiter and Venus, especially in funerary contexts in which the deceased might be shown in the costume of other gods as well.[40] The naked, realistically fleshy sculpture of a goddess looks particularly silly to us with a human female head stuck on top, yet these were serious images that would presumably not have occasioned laughter in their time. The nude goddess had ceased in this context to be seen as a naked woman (perhaps in the same way an erect penis ceased to be just an erection in its context as an apotropaic symbol). At the same time, Aphrodite statuettes with classical heads continued to serve both as serious votive objects and as decorations for the home, while statuettes of other naked females—such as semidivine nymphs fighting off satyrs—seem to have been intended to amuse and titillate.

Romans had a somewhat different attitude toward sex from the Greeks. Red-figure pottery provides our primary evidence for Greek sexual behavior, and overt sexuality is most freely expressed on vases intended for symposia, showing men partying with courtesans or slaves and *erastes* (adult male "lovers") courting elite *eromenoi* (younger male "beloveds"). Respectable women are completely left out of these scenes. On the contrary, Roman ceramic vessels, medallions, lamps, wall paintings, and other functional and decorative objects show a full range of sex acts between women and men, women and women, men and men, and men and boys. Distinguishing inappropriate from respectable women in art is not as easy as it sounds in texts. Additionally, far more variation in behavior is documented in art than is implied by sexual terminology stressing the importance to men of being the penetrating, active partner. Sexual imagery abounds in portable media, and more permanent paintings of sexual acts also appear on the walls of Roman houses in areas that would seem to us to be quite visible and well trafficked. Women's bodies generally reflect the influence of Greek nudes, with rounded curves; small, firm breasts; pale skin; and calm faces. A respectable woman could apparently be included in sexual activities, and a sequence of two paintings from the Villa under the Farnesina in Rome may even possibly depict the first sexual encounter of a new bride; in the first scene she is veiled and seems withdrawn, while in the second, still dressed but with her veil off, she passionately but seemingly inexpertly kisses her new husband.[41]

In a different context, nudity signified shame and public humiliation. The public solicitations and self-exposure of street prostitutes were associated with their vile status, and enforced public nudity was used by the Romans to revile and punish. Female criminals condemned to the beasts, *ad bestias*, or to deadly mythological reenactments were sometimes exposed naked or partially naked during their torment. One scene on molded terra-cotta lamps of the first and perhaps later centuries C.E. probably depicted the reenactment in the arena of a lover's tryst between a woman and a donkey, as described in Apuleius in the *Metamorphoses*.[42] The legendary Thecla of the *Acts of Paul and Thecla* is shown with bared breasts in some images of her exposure to the beasts on *ampullae* (small, two-handled flasks for holy water) and pilgrim flasks. Thecla, who in stories gave up many attributes of womanhood, including her hair, is emphasized as feminine in art by her clothing and hair or by her naked breasts. Christian images empower her by placing her as the central focus and dominant figure, in comparison with Roman images of *damnati* that emphasize the beasts as much as the human victims and reference the sponsor of the games and the entertainment provided by the event.[43]

Roman magistrates attached great importance to being publicly witnessed as powerful and beneficent in the arena. While the bravery of victims was often appreciated by the crowd, *damnati* were expected to die, ideally in an interesting way. For a martyred woman to remain dignified, unengaged, and as modest and gender-appropriate as circumstances permitted was to subvert the system. The Christian martyrs Perpetua and Felicitas, who were brought naked into the arena at Carthage in the early third century C.E. before being exposed to beasts, were sent back to be dressed when the crowd was offended by the display of a naked, lactating new mother and her young slave (who had also recently given birth). Concerned with her dignity during the *damnatio*, and not wanting to look like a woman in mourning with unkempt hair, Perpetua even pinned it up after being gored by a heifer.[44] Maintaining control over clothing, hair, and emotion in public not only honored the Christian savior but also represented a proper, elite feminine dignity and worthiness.

In early catacomb art, as Christians began to represent stories of interest to them in a popular, simple style, we lose the connection with the conventions of beauty and behavior of women seen in public art. Images of miracles were symbols of hope and salvation in wall painting, and the focus was not on detailed representation of the body or clothing; respectable women wore simple, long garments, modestly covering the body, with their hair tied up and often hidden by a mantle. Identifying real rather than biblical or New Testament women in these early Christian narratives is a formidable task.[45] Meanwhile, surviving funerary images such as Egyptian mummy portraits—although spanning many centuries and varied contexts—reveal even in individualizing portraits the enduring importance in private life of female ornament and beautification. Some images are highly realistic and personal, but many still reflect an underlying Greco-Roman standard of a pale, oval face, dark eyes, red mouth, coiffed hair, and elaborate jewelry. The young woman of the second century c.e. in Figure 8.7 is richly gowned; her hair is beautifully waved, and she wears jewelry of gold, pearls, and semiprecious stones.

FIGURE 8.7: Mummy portrait, second century c.e. Showing a richly gowned and bejeweled young woman with carefully waved hair. British Museum no. 1939,0324.211. © The Trustees of the British Museum.

LATE ANTIQUE AND EARLY BYZANTINE WOMEN

As Jas Elsner has pointed out, the "quest for the first moment of decline" has dominated research on late Roman art.[46] In the public art of the third and fourth centuries, we find many simplified versions of earlier graceful, posed bodies with swirling drapery. Art historians have indeed sometimes considered this imagery to be of lesser quality. There had been all along, however, a popular art of graffiti, shop signs, and inexpensive figurines and other ceramic objects, on which bodies were depicted more sketchily, with little direct focus on traditional traits of Greek beauty and more on practical details of narrative or scene identification. A simpler style of this sort now began to dominate public art, although it did not replace classically influenced imagery: the designer of the Arch of Constantine even included earlier emperors' classicizing works with new reliefs. Relationships of power are now expressed via axially symmetrical design and by the central placement and increased size of important people; these visual symbols strongly influence early Christian art. However, it is noticeable that even two-dimensional, simplified bodies and garments continue to reflect older classical ideals. In reliefs and mosaics, the pull of a garment against a rounded thigh or belly now was indicated by lines and circles or ovals, but the classical impulse to show the body in a graceful stance is still in effect.

As Christian art slowly began to identify women as "good" or "bad" in the third century C.E., naked Aphrodite served as a model for Eve with her tempting and tempted body. Sometimes the crudity of the image fails to illustrate her classical roots, but often her rounded hips, her standing pose with slightly bent leg, and her gesture of covering her genitals recall rather than reject the intentional voyeurism usually implied by the naked female. Naked Eve together with Adam in funerary art can symbolize more than just the "bad feminine"; she also seems to signify marital attraction as well as redemption after the fall. On a sarcophagus of the late third or early fourth century, within images strewn across the available field, Eve stands facing partly forward, turning toward Adam. One leg is slightly bent, and she covers her pubic area with her hand in a pose that echoes a standing nude Aphrodite; her other hand holds Adam's in a gesture reminiscent of the Roman marriage handshake, the *dextrarum iunctio*.[47] The nudity of Aphrodite seems to be a source of happiness and marital symbolism. However, on the mid-fourth-century marble sarcophagus of Junius Bassus, carved in a more traditional style that clearly evokes a classical past, Adam and Eve face away from one another, avoiding eye contact, covering themselves, apparently ashamed.

In the fourth century C.E., the rounded feminine body can sometimes still be found even beneath the increasingly shapeless garments of "good" women. As the body is increasingly deemphasized, however, jewelry and colorful or patterned clothing serve increasingly as symbols of attractive public femininity. A cross of Galla Placidia of the early fifth century C.E. shows the imperial mother and her children within a portrait oval; her complex hairstyle, pearl earrings and necklace, and richly embroidered mantle attest to her wealth and status, recalling older portraits of noble and wealthy pagan women. Her daughter has a less elaborate but still carefully designed series of waves in her pulled-back hair, although the style is far less elaborate. She wears earrings and a necklace but is gowned in simpler, colored clothing.[48] The face of each family member is individualized. Another portrait, of a Christian couple on a late fourth-century or later wedding casket from the Esquiline Treasure, reveals a comparable interest in ornamental clothing and hair, although the man and woman are not as clearly identifiable as individuals. However, the silver casket also features a naked Venus looking in the mirror; the bride, Projecta, primps (fully dressed) in a parallel scene in front of a mirror held by a servant.[49] Again, the nudity of Aphrodite/Venus and the concern for appearance signify a bride and her appropriate feminine concerns, and the classical ideal of a modest but sexually attractive, self-ornamenting woman is maintained within an elite Christian context.

An ivory diptych of the Symmachi and Nicomachi of the fourth or fifth century C.E. may be a wedding gift for a pagan wedding. Its classicizing representations of two priestesses of pagan cults may offer a nostalgic reference to the classical past rather than a genuine commemoration of the women's current duties.[50] On one panel, labeled "of the Symmachi," a woman stands at a pagan altar below an oak tree. Since she is wearing an ivy wreath, she is symbolically associated with the worship of Jupiter and Mercury. She reflects ideal classical beauty and appropriateness. Her slender body faces the altar, and she bends her calm face down toward her task, her delicate fingers taking up incense. Her hair is tied up, her body enveloped in a mantle with loose zigzag folds running down the front. Her left buttock and the swell of her calf are indicated by the pull of her drapery as she rests her weight on her right, forward leg and bends her left knee in a gentle *contrapposto* pose. She meets all the requirements of an attractive, elegant, but respectable woman. The other panel, labeled "of the Nicomachi," shows the explicitly sexualized body of a priestess; standing a little slumped, as if tired (perhaps from dancing), she holds two still-lit torches angled downward; her mantle is bunched below her belly, which shows through the thin fabric of her dress, belted below her breasts. The garment has fallen down from her right breast and hangs in draped concentric folds below, reinforcing the round shape, and the fabric pulls so tightly over her left side that the breast and nipple clearly show through. Her hairstyle has not been preserved, since her face is damaged, but her slightly disheveled hair hangs on her neck. Cymbals hang above her in a tree loaded with pinecones; the cymbals and cones may reference Cybele and Ceres. Here are two opposing reflections of womanhood, one wilder, one restrained, together reflecting a wholly classical image of female beauty and sexuality worthy of exquisite craftsmanship and expensive materials.

In the sixth century, a mosaic from the apse of the Basilica of San Vitale in Ravenna of 547 represents Theodora, the wife of Justinian I, and her ladies, as shown in Figure 8.8. The ladies are slender, with pale skin, delicate fingers, and big eyes. Their hair is covered with beautiful caps, and they wear elaborate jewelry. Their faces, although not exactly the same, cannot easily be distinguished; they are instead individualized by their spectacularly embroidered, colorful garments. The women are lined up in a row beside the central figure of Theodora, their bodies flattened and two-dimensional despite an indication of folds in their clothing. Their frontal poses and the symmetry of the composition had already been appropriate in public imperial art for centuries, and the attributes of femininity recall standards a thousand years old. Their bodies, however, are visibly ignored, covered over and decorated, despite visible folds in their drapery that could have enhanced the body beneath. In contrast, a smaller-scale, more private image from the sixth-century Vienna Genesis illuminated manuscript, shown in Figure 8.9, provides an example of the intersection of sexuality and restraint still to be found in Christian art. In a scene of Rebekah drawing water for Eliezer at the well (which also serves as the trough for his camels), Rebekah's head is covered, and her sleeves and skirt are long and modest; but the fabric pulls against her right thigh and slightly bent knee in a manner reminiscent of classical drapery. To make the effect logical, the artist decided to step her left leg up onto the rim of the well/trough to create a *contrapposto* pose. A highly seductive, white-skinned, barely draped river goddess reclines by a stream flowing to the well, leaning in the style of Roman male river gods on a large water jar from which water pours into the stream. She twists, breasts fully exposed and pubic triangle indicated by the fall of her purple drapery, to observe Rebekah and Eliezer. To complicate matters, she also raises her hand to her chin in a traditional *pudicitia* gesture. Here, a naked bathing Aphrodite making a dressed woman's modesty gesture has been merged with a male water god to create a sexualized and romantic context for Rebekah's wholly appropriate meeting with her future husband's emissary.

FIGURE 8.8: Ladies attending the empress Theodora, wife of Justinian I. Mosaic from the apse, south wall, of the Basilica of San Vitale in Ravenna, from 547 C.E. Photograph courtesy of Art Resource [ART423351].

In this one wonderful image a thousand years of symbolism merge and morph in a new narrative context.

The attractive marriageable or married woman is at one end of the spectrum; the lifelong virgin, especially the Virgin Mary, is at the other. With eternal virginity seen as a blessing and a choice (rather than a disastrous loss of husband and children), the Virgin can sometimes safely have a strong physical presence without an overtone of sexuality. In a miniature scene of the ascension in the sixth-century C.E. illuminated Rabulla Gospel manuscript, Mary is a powerful figure positioned centrally below the ascending Jesus; she has

FIGURE 8.9: A scene of Rebekah at the well with Eliezer. Rebekah is
shown twice, approaching the personified source of the water on the
left and standing at the well on the right. Vienna Genesis vellum Gr. 31
f. 7r, sixth century C.E., Byzantine School. Österreichische National-
bibliothek, Vienna, Austria. The Bridgeman Art Library.

a three-dimensional body and noticeably rounded breasts.[51] In the sixth and
seventh centuries C.E., however, Mary's feminine body is diminished. In a late
sixth- or early seventh-century icon of Mary flanked by saints Theodore and
George, of encaustic on wood from the Monastery of St. Catherine's in Egypt,
Mary stands below the hand of God, with baby Jesus on her lap, a saint on either
side, and two angels behind them glancing up and sideways at the hand. While
Mary's body has been simplified and flattened, she, like the angels, has been
personalized by her sideways glance and the three-dimensionality of her face.

Her cheeks are rounded, and the left one still bears traces of red color shadowing the cheekbone. Her lips are full and pink, her eyes large and dark, her pale face emphasized by the dark cloth covering her. While a consciously designed and idealized physicality is still reflected in Mary's face, her body is disguised by her garment (and her child), and no ornamentation of dress or jewelry emphasizes her physical charms.[52] After the Byzantine iconoclastic debates of the eighth century, another image of the Virgin, in the ninth-century Hagia Sophia mosaic apse, has depth and dignity provided by the three-dimensionality of her throne and by her size; however, as Figure 8.10 shows, her body too is concealed behind the large expanses of her drapery.[53] Not requiring marriage

FIGURE 8.10: Mosaic showing the Virgin and Child. From the apse of the Hagia Sophia, late ninth century C.E. (Photo credit: Dick Osseman.)

to provide a proper context to end her virginity, and with her motherhood a symbol of that virginity rather than of a matron's sexual experience, Mary did not fit the classical model of womanhood or suit the artistic conventions that emphasized a decorated three-dimensional female body.

CONCLUSION

The ideal of classical femininity established in fifth- and fourth-century B.C.E. representations of clothed and nude women was so thoroughly incorporated into Roman and then Christian imagery that its influence was pervasive throughout the succeeding millennium. The proper female in art was the virtuous yet sexually attractive bride or matron who controlled her desires and behavior but showed a proper interest in beauty and self-decoration. To counteract her attractive appearance, she modestly wrapped her body, restrained her gestures, and controlled her gaze and facial expression. The features of a classical face became highly identifiable attributes of a prized, symbolic beauty, and classical artists' use of *contrapposto*, their focus on perfected poses and flowing drapery over an idealized body, and their visual expression of female sexuality held in check by modesty, all combined with this perfect face to create a desirable woman of compelling interest. Many aspects of beauty emphasized by the Greeks are equally desirable today; Western advertising and research on beauty point out our attraction to symmetrical, young faces and show that standardized normative features not only are attractive to mates but also result in financial and other rewards.[54]

Despite the enduring appeal of classical beauty, by the end of the first millennium C.E. new ideals of celibacy and chastity influenced conceptions of feminine beauty. Modesty became separated from overt physicality, as exemplified by images of the Virgin Mary. While her pale, oval face and large eyes, her calm expression, the delicacy of her hands, and her maternal state recalled praiseworthy visual attributes of classical womanhood, the Virgin's transcendence of sexuality and vanity, shown by her covered and unadorned body, elevated her above the desirable physical traits and self-decoration of ordinary women. For the Holy Virgin and ordinary women alike, symmetrical patterns and flat, curving drapery folds now veiled a respectable feminine body whose slenderness was its only link to an original classical ideal.

NOTES

Introduction

1. Elizabeth A. Castelli as quoted in L. Stephanie Cobb, "Real Women or Objects of Discourse? The Search for Early Christian Women," *Religion Compass* 3 (2009): 379–94, at p. 392n7. See E. A. Castelli, "Gender, Theory and The Rise of Christianity: A Response to Rodney Stark," *Journal of Early Christian Studies* 6 (2) (1998): 227–57.
2. Elizabeth A. Castelli as quoted in Cobb, "Real Women," p. 392n7.
3. As a contrast to cultural history, I chose the term *political* rather than *intellectual* quite deliberately. To suggest that cultural history is not also a form of intellectual history is simply incorrect.
4. This summary of cultural history as a discipline owes its existence to two main authors: Peter Burke, *What Is Cultural History?* 2nd ed. (Malden, MA: Polity, 2008); and Anna Green, *Cultural History* (New York: Palgrave Macmillan, 2008). The quotation is from Burke, *What Is Cultural History?* p. 42.
5. Joan Kelly-Gadol, an American scholar of the history of women, first published her chapter "Did Women Have a Renaissance?" in *Becoming Visible: Women in European History*, ed. Renate Bridenthal and Claudia Koonz (Boston: Houghton-Mifflin Boston, 1977), pp. 137–64.
6. Sarah B. Pomeroy, *Goddesses, Whores, Wives, and Slaves: Women in Classical Antiquity* (New York: Schocken Books, 1975), pp. x, xii.
7. See, for example, Edward W. Said, *Orientalism* (New York: Vintage Books, 1978) and *Culture and Imperialism* (New York: Knopf, 1993); and Gayatri Chakravorty Spivak, *In Other Worlds: Essays in Cultural Politics* (New York: Methuen, 1987) and *The Post-Colonial Critic: Interviews, Strategies, Dialogues* (New York: Routledge, 1990).

8. Euripides (ca. 480–406 B.C.E.), for example, frequently refers to "the race of women" and "the male race" in his plays, as does Virgil 400 years later in the *Aeneid*.

9. Summaries of contributions to the field can be found in Helene P. Foley *Reflections of Women in Antiquity* (New York: Gordon and Breach, 1981); Averil Cameron and Amélie Kuhrt, eds., *Images of Women in Antiquity* (London: Croom Helm, 1983); John Peradotto and J.P. Sullivan, eds., *Women in the Ancient World: The Arethusa Papers* (Albany: State University of New York Press, 1984); Sarah B. Pomeroy, *Women's History and Ancient History* (Chapel Hill: University of North Carolina Press, 1991); Georges Duby, Michelle Perrot, Christiane Klapisch-Zuber, and Pauline Schmitt Pantel, *A History of Women in the West* (Cambridge, MA: Belknap Press, 1992); Elaine Fantham, Helene Peet Foley, Natalie Boymel Kampen, Sarah B. Pomeroy, and H. Alan Shapiro, *Women in the Classical World: Image and Text* (New York, Oxford: Oxford University Press, 1994); Laura K. McClure, ed., *Sexuality and Gender in the Classical World* (Oxford and Malden, MA: Blackwell, 2002); and Bella Vivante, *Daughters of Gaia: Women in the Ancient Mediterranean World* (Westport, CT: Praeger, 2007). The last book also includes sections on ancient women in Egypt and Mesopotamia.

10. Ross Shepard Kraemer, *Unreliable Witnesses: Religion, Gender, and History in the Greco-Roman Mediterranean* (Oxford and New York: Oxford University Press, 2011), p. 245.

11. See, for example, Kate Cooper, *The Virgin and the Bride: Idealized Womanhood in Late Antiquity* (Cambridge, MA: Harvard University Press, 1996). See also Mary Daly's classic text on this topic: *Beyond God the Father: Toward a Philosophy of Women's Liberation* (Boston: Beacon, 1973).

12. Cobb, "Real Women," p. 385.

13. See note 10.

14. A *method* is a technique or process that is used to unlock the internal logic (cultural assumptions or values) of a set of data. A *theory* is a supposition or hypothesis that can help explain the data.

15. Pomeroy, *Goddesses*, p. x.

16. For collections translated into English see Ellen Greene, ed., *Women Poets in Ancient Greece and Rome* (Norman: University of Oklahoma Press, 2005); Ian Michael Grant, ed., *Women Writers of Ancient Greece and Rome: An Anthology* (Norman: University of Oklahoma Press, 2004); and Jane McIntosh Snyder, *The Woman and the Lyre: Women Writers in Classical Greece and Rome* (Carbondale: Southern Illinois University Press, 1989).

17. Two of the better-known examples are Jim Powell, trans., *The Poetry of Sappho* (Oxford and New York: Oxford University Press, 2007); and Patricia Wilson-Kastner, *A Lost Tradition: Women Writers in the Early Church* (Washington, DC: University Press of America, 1981) for "Proba's Cento," a Virgilian-like cento traditionally associated with a fourth-century Roman aristocratic woman.

18. See Joyce E. Salisbury, *Perpetua's Passion: The Death and Memory of a Young Roman Woman* (New York: Routledge, 1997).

19. See Carolyn L. Connor, *Women of Byzantium* (New Haven, CT: Yale University Press, 2004); and Wilson-Kastner et al., *A Lost Tradition*, for "Egeria: Account of Her Pilgrimage" (date uncertain—seventh century?).
20. For example, *The Gospel of Mary Magdalene* and *The Acts of Paul and Thecla*. English translations and scholarly discussion of these texts can be found at http://www.earlychristianwritings.com/.
21. For questions about authorship in Greek and Roman texts attributed to women, see references in note 16; for early Christian writings, see Kraemer, *Unreliable Witnesses*; and Hagith Silvan, "Anician Women, the Cento of Proba and Aristocratic Conversion in the Fourth Century," *Vigiliae Christianae* 47 (2) (1993): 140–57. For further bibliography and dating of Egeria's text, see Hagith Silvan, "Piety and Pilgrimage in the Age of Gratian," *Harvard Theological Review* 81 (1) (1988): 59–72.
22. Pliny the Elder, *Natural History* 35.147.
23. Bernadette J. Brooten, "Early Christian Women and Their Cultural Context: Issues of Method in Historical Reconstruction," in *Feminist Perspectives on Biblical Scholarship*, ed. Adela Yarbo Collins (Chico, CA: Scholars Press, 1985), pp. 65–91.
24. In contrast to other Greek city-states, Sparta maintained a type of constitutional monarchy after the introduction of some democratic practices in the fifth century B.C.E.

Chapter 1

1. I want to thank Professor Ray Laurence for his valuable comments on this chapter. For the *life course* approach, see Mary Harlow and Ray Laurence, *Growing Up and Growing Old in Ancient Rome: A Life Course Approach* (London: Routledge, 2002), pp. 1–6.
2. See, e.g., Elaine Fantham, *Julia Augusti: The Emperor's Daughter* (London and New York: Routledge, 2006); Debra Hamel, *Trying Neaira: The True Story of a Courtesan's Scandalous Life in Ancient Greece* (New Haven, CT: Yale University Press, 2003); and Sarah B. Pomeroy, *Goddesses, Whores, Wives, and Slaves: Women in Classical Antiquity* (New York: Schocken Books, 1975).
3. Harlow and Laurence, *Growing Up*, p. 56.
4. Aristotle, *Politics* 7.1335b; and Solon, *Fragmenta* 27.
5. See, e.g., Horace, *Epistulae* 2.2.187–89. For the astrological assumptions and genius, see Jane Chance Nitzsche, *The Genius Figure in Antiquity and the Middle Ages* (New York: Columbia University Press, 1975), pp. 7–41.
6. Mark Golden, *Children and Childhood in Classical Athens* (Baltimore: Johns Hopkins University Press, 1990); and Lena Larsson Lovén and Agneta Strömberg, "Economy," in *A Cultural History of Childhood and Family: Antiquity*, ed. R. Laurence and M. Harlow (London and New York: Berg, 2010), vol. 1, pp. 45–60.
7. Elaine Fantham, Helene Peet Foley, Natalie Boymel Kampen, Sarah B. Pomeroy, and H. Alan Shapiro, *Women in the Classical World: Image and Text* (New York

and Oxford: Oxford University Press, 1994), p. 59; Ville Vuolanto, "Infant Abandonment and the Christianization of Europa," and Judith Evans Grubbs, "The
Dynamics of Infant Abandonment: Motives, Attitudes and (Unintended) Consequences," both in *The Dark Side of Childhood in Late Antiquity and the Middle
Ages*, ed. Katariina Mustakallio and Christian Laes (Oxford: Oxbow Books, forth-
coming). See Ray Laurence, "Community," in *A Cultural History of Childhood
and Family in Antiquity*, ed. R. Laurence and M. Harlow (London: Berg, 2010),
vol. 1, pp. 38–39.

8. R.M. Ogilvie, *The Romans and Their Gods* (London: Hogarth, 1986; originally
published in 1968), pp. 102–3; and Marja-Leena Hänninen, "From Womb to Family: Rituals and Social Conventions Connected to Roman Birth," in *Hoping for
Continuity: Childhood, Education and Death in Antiquity and the Middle Ages*,
ed. Katariina Mustakallio, Jussi Hanska, Hanna-Leena Sainio and Ville Vuolanto,
ACTA IRF 33 (Rome: Institutum Romanum Finlandiae, 2005), pp. 49–59.

9. B. Shaw, "Raising and Killing Children: Two Roman Myths," *Mnemosyne* 54 (2001):
31–77. Against this view, see T. Köves-Zulauf, *Römische Geburtsriten*, Zetemata
87 (Munich, Germany: Beck, 1990), p. 183.

10. See, e.g., Golden, *Children and Childhood*, p. 23.

11. On average life expectancy and mortality rates, see Beryl Rawson, *Children and
Childhood in Roman Italy* (Oxford: Oxford University Press, 2003), p. 341; see
also Véronique Dasen, ed., *Naissance et petite enfance dans l'Antiquité. Actes
du colloque de Fribourg, 28 novembre–1er décembre 2001*, Orbis Biblicus et
Orientalis 203 (Fribourg: Academie Press, 2004). There is, of course, great difficulty in determining child mortality rates in antiquity; see Harlow and Laurence,
Growing Up, pp. 10–11.

12. Ogilvie, *Romans and Their Gods*, pp. 102–3.

13. Plutarch, *vita Romuli* 20. See also Hänninen, "From Womb to Family," p. 57. On
different customs of using amulets and pendants, see Mario Torelli, *Lavinio e Roma.
Riti initiatici e matrimonio tra archeologia e storia* (Rome: Quasar, 1984), pp. 23–31.
An amulet can be seen around the neck of a girl wearing a toga and holding a
woman's hand on the north side procession of the *Ara Pacis* in Rome. There are also
little boys of the imperial family with *bullae* on the same panel of the *Ara Pacis*.

14. Cornelia B. Horne, *"Let the Little Children Come to Me": Childhood and Children in Early Christianity* (Washington, DC: Catholic University Press, 2009),
p. 300.

15. D. Schaps, "The Woman Least Mentioned: Etiquette and Women's Names," *Classical Quarterly* 27 (1977): 323–30.

16. Sue Blundell, *Women in Ancient Greece* (Cambridge, MA: Harvard University
Press, 1995), p. 131.

17. I want to thank professor Mika Kajava for his comments on names. For women's
names in Rome in general, see Mika Kajava, *Roman Female Praenomina: Studies
in the Nomenclatura of Roman Women*, ACTA IRF 14 (Rome: Institutum Romanum Finlandiae, 1994); and Eva Cantarella, *Passato prossimo. Donne romane da
Tacita a Sulpicia* (Milan, Italy: Feltrinelli, 1996), p. 34.

18. Plutarch, *The Roman Questions* 2; and Hänninen, "From Womb to Family," p. 57.

19. Keith Bradley, "Wet-Nursing at Rome: A Study of Social Relations," in *The Family in Ancient Rome: New Perspectives*, ed. Beryl Rawson (New York: Cornell University Press, 1986), p. 202.

20. See, e.g., Sandra Joshel, "Nurturing the Master's Child: Slavery and the Roman Child Nurse," *Signs* 12 (1986): 3–22.

21. Golden, *Children and Childhood*, p. 131.

22. Marjatta Nielsen, "Fit for Fight, Fit for Marriage: Fighting Couples in Nuptial and Funerary Iconography in Late Classical and Early Hellenistic Periods," in *Gender, Cult, and Culture in the Ancient World from Mycenae to Byzantium*, ed. Lena Larsson Lovén and Agneta Strömberg (Sävedalen, Sweden: Paul Åhströms, 2003), pp. 38–53, esp. p. 40. It seems that some women used *strigils* even in Pompeii; see Ria Berg, "Il mundus muliebrus nelle fonti latine e nei contesti pompeiani" (PhD diss., University of Helsinki, Faculty of Humanities, 2010), p. 94.

23. See, for example, Harlow and Laurence, *Growing Up*, p. 48. On children in visual art, see J. Huskinson, *Roman Children's Sarcophagi: Their Decoration and Its Social Significance* (Oxford: Oxford University Press, 1996).

24. For *paides amphithaleis*, see Golden, *Children and Childhood*, p. 30. For *patrimi matrimi*, see Cicero, *De haruspicum responso.* 11; Livy, *Ab Urbe Condita* 37.3; Gellius, *Noctium Atticarum* 1.12; Tacitus, *Historiae* 4.53; Macrobius, *Saturnalia* 1.6; and Dionysius Halicarnasseus, *Antiquitates Romanae* 2.22.

25. I. C. Mantle, "The Roles of Children in Roman Religion," *Greece and Rome*, 2nd ser., 49 (2002): 85–106, esp. pp. 103–4.

26. Laurence, "Community," p. 40.

27. See, e.g., Louise Bruit Zaidman, "Pandora's Daughters and Rituals in Grecian Cities," in *History of Women I: From Ancient Goddesses to Christian Saints*, ed. Pauline Schmitt Pantel (Cambridge, MA: Harvard University Press, 1992), p. 348.

28. Ross Shepard Kraemer, *Her Share of the Blessings: Women's Religions among Pagans, Jews, and Christians in the Greco-Roman World* (New York: Oxford University Press, 1993), p. 23; and Susan Guettel Cole, "The Social Function of Rituals of Maturation: The Koureion and the Arkteia," *Zeitschrift für Papyrologie und Epigraphik* 55 (1984): 233–44.

29. Arnobius, *Adversus Gentes* 5, 2, 67, 407.

30. Blundell, *Women in Ancient Greece*, pp. 132–33. On literacy in general, see William V. Harris, *Ancient Literacy* (Cambridge, MA: Harvard University Press, 1989); and Mary Beard, Alan K. Bowman, Mireille Corbier, Tim Cornell, James L. Franklin Jr., Ann Hanson, Keith Hopkins, and Nicholas Horsfall, *Literacy in the Roman World* (*Journal of Roman Archaeology* suppl. 3, 1991). On girls' education, see chapter 6 in this volume.

31. Fantham et al., *Women in the Classical World*, p. 59; Rawson, *Children and Childhood*, p. 195; and Susan Guettel Cole, "Could Greek Women Read and Write," in *Reflections of Women in Antiquity*, ed. Helene P. Foley (New York: Gordon and Breach, 1981), pp. 219–45. See, e.g., Pliny the Younger, *Epistulae* 60 to his wife, Calpurnia.

32. For the celebrations of women outside their homes, see Lucia Nixon, "The Cults of Demeter and Kore," and Lin Foxall, "Women's Ritual and Men's Work in

Ancient Athens," in *Women in Antiquity: New Assessments*, ed. Richard Hawley and Barbara Levick (London and New York: Routledge, 1995), pp. 75–96, 97–110; and Sarolta A. Takács, *Vestal Virgins, Sibyls, and Matrons: Women in Roman Religion* (Austin: University of Texas Press, 2008), pp. 25–59. For women's activity as patronesses, see Emily A. Hemelrijk, "Women's Participation in Civic Life: Patronage and 'Motherhood' of Roman Associations," in *De Amicitia: Friendship and Social Networks in Antiquity and the Middle Ages*, ed. Katariina Mustakallio and Christian Krötzl, ACTA IRF 36 (Rome: Edizione Quasar, 2010), pp. 49–62.

33. On women and textiles, see, e.g., Elizabeth Wayland Barber, *Women's Work: The First 20,000 Years* (New York and London: W. W. Norton, 1994), pp. 29–40.

34. See, e.g., A. Cameron and A. Kuhrt, eds., *Images of Women in Antiquity* (London: Croom Helm, 1983).

35. On Rome communal family meals, see Suetonius, *Caligula* 24: Caligula forbade anyone from eating with their parents, wife, or children during the period of public mourning. Youngsters had their places on the lowest couch: Suetonius, *Augustus* 64 (echoed by Plutarch, *Moralia* 619d); sitting at the ends of the couches: Suetonius, *Claudius* 32; or sitting at a separate table: Tacitus, *Annales* 13.16. Suzanne Dixon, *The Roman Family* (Baltimore: John Hopkins University Press, 1992) pp. 101–102. On the feast for the assumption of the *toga virilis*, see Pliny the Younger, *Epistulae* 10.16; and Cicero, *Epistulae ad Atticum* 9.6. On the wedding feast (*cena nuptialis*), see Catullus, *Carmina* 62.3.

36. Véronique Dasen, "Blessing or Portent: Multiple Births in Ancient Rome," in Mustakallio et al., *Hoping for Continuity*, p. 61.

37. Ville Vuolanto, "Selling and Pawning of Children in Roman Empire," paper presented at the Darker Sides of Childhood II conference of the Institutum Romanum Finlandiae, Rome, March 15, 2010.

38. For the milkbrothers (*collactaneus*), see Mireille Corbier, "La petite enfance à Rome. Lois, normes, pratiques individuelles et collectives," *Annales. Economies, Sociétés, Civilisations* 54 (1990): 1257–90. Scipio Africanus Maior had a sexual relationship with his slave woman, who gave a birth to a child. Happily, his legal wife, Aemilia, took care of the mother and child after the death of Scipio Africanus and even freed them; see Valerius Maximus, *Memorable Words and Deed* 6.7.1.

39. See, e.g., Rosanna Friggeri, *The Epigraphic Collection of the Museo Nazionale of the Baths of Diocletian* (Rome: Electa, 2001), pp. 97, 145. One example is the epitaph of Flavia Ionica, daughter of the emperor's freedman, who died when she was 15 (*Corpus Inscriptionum Latinarum* X, 6609), and another is the funerary tablet of Cornelia Frontina, daughter of Marcus Ulpius Callistus, freedman of Trajan (*Corpus Inscriptionum Latinarum* VI, 10164).

40. Menandros, *Perikeiromene* 894–95, Francis G. Allison, trans., *Menander, the Principal Fragments* (Cambridge, MA: Harvard University Press, 1964), pp. 278–79.

41. Concerning Spartans, see, e.g., Xenophon, *Lakedaimoniōn politeia* (Constitution of the Lacedaemonians) 1.2–10 (fourth century B.C.E.), available at: http://www.stoa.org/diotima/anthology/wlgr/wlgr-greeklegal97.shtml (accessed April 15, 2010).

42. Susan Treggiari, *Roman Marriage: Iusti Coniuges from the Time of Cicero to the Time of Ulpian* (Oxford: Clarendon, 1991), Part II *Sponsi* 3 Choosing a *Coniunx*, pp. 83–124.

43. On the role of Athena Apatouria in the life of an Athenian woman, see, e.g., Pauline Schmitt "Athena Apatouria et la ceinture: les aspects féminins des Apatouries à Athénes," *Annales: Economies, Sociétés, Civilizations* 32 (1977): 1059–73.

44. See Aphrodite Avagianou, *Sacred Marriage in the Rituals of Greek Religion* (Bern: Peter Lang, 1991); and Jana Shopkorn, *"Til Death Do Us Part": Marriage and Funeral Rites in Classical Athens*, note 1, available at: http://old.perseus.tufts.edu/classes/JSp.html (accessed April 15, 2010).

45. See Blundell, *Women in Ancient Greece*, pp. 122–23; Harlow and Laurence, *Growing Up*, pp. 8–60; and Mary Harlow and Ray Laurence, "Betrothal, Mid-Late Childhood and the Life Course," in *Ancient Marriage in Myth and Reality*, ed. Lena Larsson Lovén and Agneta Strömberg (Cambridge: Cambridge Scholars Publishing, 2010), pp. 56–77.

46. See, e.g., Roger Just, *Women in Athenian Law and Life* (London and New York: Routledge, 1989), pp. 47–50.

47. See, e.g., Larsson Lovén and Strömberg, "Daughters, Dowries and Family Status" in the chapter "Economy," pp. 48–49.

48. Treggiari, *Roman Marriage*, pp. 16–18; and Harlow and Laurence, *Growing Up*, pp. 56–64.

49. Harlow and Laurence, *Growing Up*, p. 86.

50. For *confarreatio*, *coemptio*, and *usus*, see Eva Cantarella, *Pandora's Daughters: The Role and Status of Women in Greek and Roman Antiquity*, trans. Maureen B. Fant (Baltimore: Johns Hopkins University Press, 1987), pp. 116–18; and Pierre Grimal, *Love in Ancient Rome*, trans. Arthur Train Jr. (Norman: University of Oklahoma Press, 1986), pp. 57–62.

51. Treggiari, *Roman Marriage*, pp. 21–24.

52. Gellius, *Noctes Atticae* 10.15.23. On Flamen and Flaminica Dialis, see Katariina Mustakallio, "Creating Roman Identity: Exemplary Marriages," in Larsson Lovén and Strömberg, *Ancient Marriage*, pp. 15–16; on *diffarreatio* (ritual form used to dissolve *confarreatio* marriage), see Treggiari, *Roman Marriage*, p. 24.

53. Cantarella, *Pandora's Daughters*, p. 117.

54. Treggiari, *Roman Marriage*, pp. 16–21.

55. See Gaius, *Institutiones* 1.111.

56. Treggiari, *Roman Marriage*, pp. 13–49; and Jane F. Gardner, *Women in Roman Law and Society* (London and New York: Routledge, 1990), pp. 31–66.

57. Treggiari, *Roman Marriage*, pp. 229–61.

58. Gardner, *Women in Roman Law*, pp. 77–78.

59. *Codex Justinianus* 5.24.1, cited in Judith Evans Grubbs, "Children and Divorce in Roman Law," in Mustakallio et al., *Hoping for Continuity*, pp. 33–47, esp. p. 36.

60. See, e.g., Eva Cantarella, *Secondo natura. La bisessualità nel mondo antico* (Milan, Italy: Rizzoli, 1995), pp. 269–81. For the visual evidence, see Natalie Kampen, *Sexuality in Ancient Art* (Cambridge: Cambridge University Press, 1996).

61. Demosthenes 59.18–122; Treggiari, *Roman Marriage*, pp. 199–201, 262–319.

62. Epictetus, *Enchiridion* 40.

63. Livy, *Ab Urbe Condita* 4.2.5–11. For the discussion on intermarriage, see M. Panciera, "Livy, Conubium and Plebeians' Access to the Consulship," in *Augusta Augurio, Rerum humanarum et Livinarum commentationes in honorem Jerzy Linderski*, ed. C. F. Kondrad (Wiesbaden, Germany: Franz Steiner, 2004), p. 90.

64. See Apuleius, *Apologia* 69; and Elaine Fantham, "Aemilia Pudencilla: Or the Wealthy Widow's Choice," in *Women in Antiquity: New Assessments*, ed. Richard Hawley and Barbara Levick (London and New York: Routledge, 1995), pp. 220–32, esp. p. 225.

65. Rawson, *Children and Childhood*, pp. 96–97; and Pliny the Younger, *Epistulae* 4.21.1–3.

66. Rawson, *Children and Childhood*, p. 96.

67. Plutarch, *vitae Lycurgus et Numa* 3.1; see Eva Cantarella, "Marriage and Sexuality in Republican Rome: A Roman Conjugal Love Story," in *The Sleep of Reason: Erotic Experience and Sexual Ethics in Ancient Greece and Rome*, ed. Martha C. Nussbaum and Juha Sihvola (Chicago: University of Chicago Press, 2002), pp. 269–82, esp. pp. 276–77.

68. Hyperides, Fragment 205, ed. Blass.

69. Horace, *Satire* 1.8; Horace, *Epode* 5; K. Cokayne, *Experiencing Old Age in Ancient Rome* (London: Routledge, 2003), pp. 134–35, 150–51; and Laura Cherubini, *Strix. La strega nella cultura romana* (Druento, Italy: UTET Libreria, 2010), pp. 146–51.

70. See, e.g., Tim G. Parkin, *Old Age in the Roman World* (Baltimore: Johns Hopkins University Press, 2003), pp. 243–46.

71. See Katariina Mustakallio, "Representing Older Women: Hersilia, Veturia, *Virgo Vestalis Maxima*," in *On Old Age: Approaching Death in Antiquity and the Middle Ages*, ed. Christian Krötzl and Katariina Mustakallio (Turnhout, Belgium: Brepols, 2012), pp. 41–56.

72. For the representations of older women see Suzanne Dixon, *Cornelia, Mother of Gracchi* (London: Routledge, 2006); Diana E. E. Kleiner and Susan B. Matheson, eds., *I Claudia II: Women in Roman Art and Society* (Austin: University of Texas Press, 2000); and J. Ginsburg, *Representing Agrippina: Construction of Female Power in the Early Roman Empire* (Oxford: Oxford University Press, 2006).

73. Katariina Mustakallio, "Roman Funerals: Identity, Gender and Participation," in Mustakallio et al., *Hoping for Continuity*, p. 187.

Chapter 2

1. First published in 1984. Published in English in 1985 and 1986.

2. For the exact significance of *sôphrosunê* for male virtue, see Helen F. North, *Sophrosyne: Self-Knowledge and Self-Restraint in Greek Literature*, Cornell Studies in Classical Philology 35 (Ithaca, NY: Cornell University Press, 1966).

3. For a full discussion of the meaning of female *sôphrosunê*, see Helen F. North, "The Mare, the Vixen and the Bee: Sophrosyne as the Virtue of Women in Antiquity," *Illinois Classical Studies* 2 (1977): 35–48.

4. On *pudicitia* see Rebecca Langlands, *Sexual Morality in Ancient Rome* (Cambridge: Cambridge University Press, 2006).

5. Hesiod, *Theogonia* 126–38; *Homeric Hymn to Gaia* 1–4.

6. On the female body as the "body politic" under Augustus, see J.L. Sebesta, "Women's Costume and Feminine Civic Morality in Augustan Rome," in *Gender and the Body in the Ancient Mediterranean*, ed. Maria Wyke (Oxford: Blackwell, 1998), pp. 106–7 and fig. 1 on p. 106.

7. *Dyskolos* 842–44; *Perikeiromenê* 1013–14; *Samia* 727. Unless otherwise indicated, all translations are the authors' own.

8. *Coniugalia praecepta* 144a–b. See further, Page duBois, *Sowing the Body: Psychoanalysis and Ancient Representations of Women* (Chicago: University of Chicago Press, 1988), pp. 39–43, 67–69.

9. Plautus, *Asinaria* 874, *Truculentus* 149; Lucilius 278, 330. See further J.N. Adams, *The Latin Sexual Vocabulary* (London: Duckworth, 1982), pp. 154–55.

10. Sappho Fragment 105a; *Homeric Hymn to Demeter* 15–20; Catullus 61.184–88 and 62.39–45.

11. Lucretius 4.1272; Virgil, *Georgics* 3.136; Sophocles, *Antigone* 569. See Adams, *Latin Sexual Vocabulary*, pp. 83–84.

12. Hesiod, *Opera et Dies* 67, *Theogonia* 590–99, *Opera et Dies* 65–68.

13. Aristophanes, *Lysistrata* 1–240.

14. Cicero, *Pro Caelio* 15; Juvenal 6.82–110 and 6.115–32; Seneca, *De Beneficiis* 6.32.1. On the invective aspect of these passages see Thomas A.J. McGinn, *Prostitution, Sexuality, and the Law in Ancient Rome* (New York: Oxford University Press, 1998), pp. 168–70.

15. See Anne Carson, "Putting Her in Her Place: Woman, Dirt and Desire," in *Before Sexuality: The Construction of Erotic Experience in the Ancient Greek World*, ed. David M. Halperin, John J. Winkler, and Froma Zeitlin (Princeton, NJ: Princeton University Press, 1990).

16. [Demosthenes] 59.22 and 33.

17. Firmicus 6.11.6.

18. Martial 2.39, 10.52; Juvenal 2.68–70. On adulterous women see McGinn, *Prostitution*, pp. 156–94; and Kelly Olson, *Dress and the Roman Woman: Self-Presentation and Society* (New York: Routledge, 2008), pp. 47–50, on the figurative meaning of *togate*.

19. Xenophon, *Oeconomicus* 7.11; Lysias 1.6; Demosthenes 44.49.

20. Cynthia B. Patterson, *The Family in Greek History* (Cambridge, MA: Harvard University Press, 1998), pp. 121–25. Patterson emphasizes that the wife is also punished and therefore is not considered completely passive in the crime. But other crimes also attach blame to individuals, like boys, not considered responsible for the crime itself, such as being pimped in their youth (Aeschines 1.19–20; Demosthenes 22.30; Andocides 1.100).

21. Holt N. Parker, "The Teratogenic Grid," in *Roman Sexualities*, ed. Judith P. Hallett and Marilyn B. Skinner (Princeton, NJ: Princeton University Press, 1997), pp. 48–49.

22. See Susan Guettel Cole, "*Gynaiki ou Themis*: Gender Difference in the *Leges Sacrae*," *Helios* 19 (1992): 104–22; Carson, "Putting Her in Her Place,"

pp. 134–69; and Robert Parker, *Miasma: Pollution and Purification in Early Greek Religion* (Oxford: Oxford University Press, 1983).

23. Hesiod, *Opera et Dies* 753–55.

24. Pliny, *Naturalis Historia* 7.64, 28.44, 82–86. See also Columella, *De Re Rustica* 11.3.38 and 10.337–68. See further Amy Richlin, "Pliny's Brassiere," in Hallett and Skinner, *Roman Sexualities*, pp. 201–4.

25. Pliny, *Naturalis Historia* 28.73; and Richlin, "Pliny's Brassiere," p. 205.

26. On gender and the Greek house see Lisa C. Nevett, "Gender Relations in the Classical Greek Household," *Annual of the British School at Athens* 90 (1995): 363–81.

27. On veiling practices see Lloyd Llewellyn-Jones, *Aphrodite's Tortoise: The Veiled Woman of Ancient Greece* (Swansea: Classical Press of Wales, 2003).

28. See ibid., pp. 46–66, for images of veils.

29. Euripides, *Hippolytus* 201–2.

30. Plutarch, *Lycurgus* 14–15. On Spartan women see Sarah B. Pomeroy, *Spartan Women* (Oxford: Oxford University Press, 2002).

31. Livy 1.57–58 and Valerius Maximus 6.1.1.

32. See Langlands, *Sexual Morality*, pp. 80–96, 142–44.

33. On women's participation in the cult of Pudicitia and special public honors for virtuous women, with discussion of how the public display of female virtue was problematic, see ibid., pp. 37–77.

34. For the *stola* see Olson, *Dress and the Roman Woman*, pp. 27–33, and Jonathan Edmondson, "Public Dress and Social Control in Late Republican and Early Imperial Rome," in *Roman Dress and the Fabrics of Roman Culture*, ed. Jonathan Edmondson and Alison Keith (Toronto: University of Toronto Press, 2008), pp. 22–26. For *vittae* see Olson, *Dress and the Roman Woman*, pp. 36–39; and Elaine Fantham, "Covering the Head at Rome: Ritual and Gender," in *Roman Dress and the Fabrics of Roman Culture*, pp. 163–68. See also Sebesta, "Women's Costume," pp. 111–13.

35. On the *palla* see Olson, *Dress and the Roman Woman*, pp. 33–36.

36. Seneca, *Controversiae* 2.7.6; Valerius Maximus 6.3.10. See Olson, *Dress and the Roman Woman*, p. 34. Contra A. T. Croom, *Roman Clothing and Fashion* (Stroud, UK: Tempus, 2002), p. 89; J. L. Sebesta, "Symbolism in the Costume of the Roman Woman," in *The World of Roman Costume*, ed. J. L. Sebesta and L. Bonafonte (Madison: University of Wisconsin Press, 1994), pp. 48–49; and Sebesta, "Women's Costume," pp. 111–13.

37. Olson, *Dress and the Roman Woman*, p. 36.

38. On status and adornment see ibid., pp. 97–99, 101–3, 116.

39. Ibid., p. 104.

40. See Allison Glazebrook, "Cosmetics and *Sôphrosunê*: Ischomachos's Wife in Xenophon's *Oikonomikos*," *Classical World* 102 (3) (2009): 244–47; and Olson, *Dress and the Roman Woman*, pp. 80–89.

41. Hesiod, *Theogonia* 590–99, 585; Xenophon, *Oeconomicus* 10.2–8. On the anticosmetic tradition in particular, see Glazebrook, "Cosmetics and *Sôphrosunê*," pp. 244–47; Olson, *Dress and the Roman Woman*, p. 59; and Bernard Grillet, *Les*

femmes et les fards dans l'antiquité grecque (Lyon, France: Centre national de la recherche scientifique, 1975), pp. 97–114.

42. See Richard Hawley, "The Dynamics of Beauty in Classical Greece," in *Changing Bodies, Changing Meanings: Studies on the Human Body in Antiquity*, ed. Dominic Montserrat (New York: Routledge, 1998), pp. 42–43: There is an increasing tendency over the fifth century B.C.E. to view "contrived or self-obsessed beauty as a hallmark of the disreputable prostitute in contemporary comedy and prose literature." For Roman women see Olson, *Dress and the Roman Woman*, p. 95.

43. Xenophon, *Oeconomicus* 10.13.

44. See Luc. *Am.* 39; Achilles Tatius 2.38; Martial, *Epigrammata* 3.55; and Ovid, *Ars Amatoria* 3.159–60, 206–8, 257–58. For discussion see Olson, *Dress and the Roman Woman*.

45. Lucilius 534–35. See also Juvenal. 6.508–10.

46. Juvenal 6.457–59.

47. See M. Wyke, "Woman in the Mirror: The Rhetoric of Adornment in the Roman World," in *Women in Ancient Societies: An Illusion of the Night*, ed. L. J. Archer, S. Fischer, and M. Wyke (London: Routledge, 1994), pp. 134–51. For ancient examples see Seneca, *Controversiae* 2.7 exc. and Valerius Maximus 9.1.3.

48. For recent discussions of ancient women and cosmetics, see Glazebrook, "Cosmetics and *Sôphrosunê*," pp. 234–38, 244–48; and Olson, *Dress and the Roman Woman*, pp. 60–66.

49. See B. Thomas, "Constraints and Contradictions: Whiteness and Femininity in Ancient Greece," in *Women's Dress in the Ancient Greek World*, ed. Lloyd Llewellyn-Jones (London: Classical Press of Wales, 2002), pp. 3–5.

50. Euripides, *Alcesits* 159 and *Medea* 923; Sophocles, *Antigone* 1239 and *Electra* 1023. See Thomas, "Constraints and Contradictions," p. 7.

51. Aristophanes, *Ecclesiazusae* 928; Pliny, *Naturalis Historia.* 26.103; Plautus, *Truculentus* 294; and Ovid, *Ars Amatoria* 3.211–12.

52. Olson, *Dress and the Roman Woman*, pp. 62, 80, 89–92, 94–95.

53. On the dress and adornment of prostitutes, see Andrew Dalby, "Levels of Concealment: The Dress of Hetairai and Pornai in Greek Texts," in Llewellyn-Jones, *Women's Dress*, pp. 111–24; and Olson, *Dress and the Roman Woman*, pp. 47–51.

54. Athenaeus 13.568f, 569a–b, e. Note, for example, a drinking cup by the Tarquinia Painter, Antikenmuseum Basel und Sammlung Ludwig, Kä 415 (ca. 470–460 B.C.E.). See further Ellen D. Reeder, "Representing Women," in *Pandora: Women in Classical Greece*, ed. Ellen D. Reeder (Baltimore: Trustees of the Walters Art Gallery, 1995), pp. 123–26, esp. pp. 124, 183–92.

55. Seneca, *Controversiae* 1.2.5 and 1.2.2; Ovid, *Ars Amatoria* 1.15.18, 1.2.5, 1.2.21; and Martial 12.97.8. See also Olson, *Dress and the Roman Woman*, pp. 94–95.

56. Athenaeus 13.557f and 568b–c. Prostitutes of course also wear *psimuthion* and some sort of blush. Euboulos mentions *sukaminos* (mulberry juice) on the lips

(Athenaeus 13.557f). Alexis provides a full description of their possible adornment (Athenaeus 13.568a–d).

57. Plutarch, *Alcibiades* 39. The actual verb is *hupographein.*

58. Xenophon, *Memorabilia* 2.1.22. See Gloria Ferrari, "Figures of Speech: The Picture of *Aidos*," *Metis* 5 (1990): 189, on this passage: "Although Virtue's gaze is not described in terms as explicit, the pointed contrast of corresponding features implies that hers is the opposite of Vice's impudent stare. Steady and without guile, with eyelids modestly lowered, Virtue's eyes are just kept to herself."

59. Athenaeus 13.568b–c.

60. In contrast, note Plutarch, *Lycurgus* 15 on Sparta and the sharing of wives for procreation.

61. Daughters inherited through the dowry system, but such an inheritance was commonly movable property only.

62. Homer, *Odyssey* 1.214–16.

63. In contrast, note David Cohen, *Law, Sexuality, and Society: The Enforcement of Morals in Classical Athens* (Cambridge: Cambridge University Press, 1991), pp. 100–109.

64. Aeschines 1.183; [Demosthenes] 59.85–87.

65. See Allison Glazebrook, "Prostituting Female Kin (Plut. *Sol.* 23.1–2)," *Dike: Rivista Di Storia Del Diritto Greco Ed Ellenistico* 8 (2005): 33–53.

66. On adultery laws see Eva Cantarella, "Homicides of Honor: The Development of Italian Adultery Law over Two Millennia," in *The Family in Italy: From Antiquity to the Present*, ed. David I. Kertzer and Richard P. Saller (New Haven, CT: Yale University Press, 1991), pp. 229–35; and Susan Treggiari, *Roman Marriage: Iusti Coniuges from the Time of Cicero to the Time of Ulpian* (Oxford: Clarendon, 1991), pp. 264–98.

67. See Horace, *Satirae* 1.2.63; Martial 2.39; and Juvenal 2.68–70. For discussion see McGinn, *Prostitution*, pp. 156–94 (in particular pp. 156–70); and Jane Gardner, *Women in Roman Law and Society* (Bloomington: Indiana University Press, 1986), pp. 127–32. Note Kelly Olson, "Matrona and Whore: Clothing and Definition in Roman Antiquity," in *Prostitutes and Courtesans in the Ancient World*, ed. Christopher A. Faraone and Laura K. McClure (Madison: University of Wisconsin Press, 2006), pp. 192–96; and Olson, *Dress and the Roman Woman*, pp. 47–49, on the questionable ubiquity of the practice.

68. For Greece, see Allison Glazebrook, "The Bad Girls of Athens: The Image and Function of *Hetairai* in Judicial Oratory," in Faraone and McClure, *Prostitutes and Courtesans in the Ancient World*, pp. 125–38. For Rome, see McGinn, *Prostitution*, pp. 140–215; and Catharine Edwards, "Unspeakable Professions: Public Performance and Prostitution in Ancient Rome," in Hallett and Skinner, *Roman Sexualities*, p. 81.

69. See Glazebrook, "Bad Girls of Athens"; and Virginia J. Hunter, *Policing Athens: Social Control in the Attic Lawsuits, 420–320 B.C.* (Princeton, NJ: Princeton University Press, 1994), pp. 113–16.

70. [Demosthenes] 59.122.

71. Glazebrook, "Bad Girls of Athens," pp. 125–38. On the excess of prostitutes after the classical period, see Hans Herter, "The Sociology of Prostitution in Antiquity in the Context of Pagan and Christian Writings," trans. Linwood DeLong, in *Sex and Difference in Ancient Greece and Rome*, ed. Mark Golden and Peter Toohey (Edinburgh: Edinburgh University Press, 2003), p. 99.

72. See McGinn, *Prostitution*, pp. 168–70, for other examples.

73. On Clodia and the representations of her in Latin literature in general, see Marilyn B. Skinner, "Clodia Metelli," *Transactions of the American Philological Association* 113 (1983): 273–87.

74. Cicero openly calls Clodia a *meretrix* at 38. He indirectly alludes to her as one at 1, 37, 49 and associates her with the life and habits of a *meretrix* at 49, 50, 57. On Cicero's attack against Clodia and her portrait as a prostitute, see Tom Hillard, "On the Stage, behind the Curtain: Images of Politically Active Women in the Late Roman Republic," in *Stereotypes of Women in Power: Historical Perspectives and Revisionist Views*, ed. Barbara Garlick, Suzanne Dixon, and Pauline Allen (London: Greenwood, 1992), pp. 37–64; and Katherine A. Geffcken, *Comedy in the Pro Caelio, with an appendix on the* In Clodium et Curionem (Leiden: Brill, 1973), pp. 31–34, 37.

75. See, for example, Sappho 94 and Sulpicia 1 ([Tib.] 3.13). On Sappho see Ellen Greene, "Apostrophe and Women's Erotics in the Poetry of Sappho," in *Reading Sappho: Contemporary Approaches*, ed. Ellen Greene (Berkeley: University of California Press, 1996), pp. 233–47. On Sulpicia see Alison Keith, "*Tandem venit amor*: A Roman Woman Speaks of Love," in Hallett and Skinner, *Roman Sexualities*, pp. 295–310.

76. See the section "Imagining the Female Body" earlier in the chapter.

77. For discussion and examples, see Lesley A. Dean-Jones, "The Politics of Pleasure: Female Sexual Appetite in the Hippocratic Corpus," *Helios* 19 (1992): 72–81, esp. pp. 76–79.

78. Carson, "Putting Her in Her Place," pp. 140–42.

79. Homer, *Odyssey* 10.274–301, 466–74; Hesiod, *Opera et Dies* 582–88; and Euripides, *Medea*.

80. Virgil, *Aeneid* 4. See also Catullus 11 and 51.

81. Propertius 1.1.1–4; Tibullus 1.5.61–66, 1.6.37–38; and Ovid, *Ars Amatoria* 2.199–216. On the elegiac poets see M. Wyke, "Taking the Woman's Part: Engendering Roman Love Elegy," *Hermes* 23 (1994): 110–28.

82. See Robert F. Sutton, "Pornography and Persuasion on Attic Pottery," in *Pornography and Representation in Greece and Rome*, ed. Amy Richlin (Oxford: Oxford University Press, 1992), pp. 24–32.

83. Xenophon, *Oeconomicus* 10.12.

84. See chapter 4, "Medicine and Disease," in this volume.

85. Catullus 61.22. See also 61.165–72 in *Sexuality in Greek and Roman Society and Literature: A Sourcebook*, ed. and trans. Marguerite Johnson and Terry Ryan (New York: Routledge, 2005), pp. 74, 77.39.

86. Pliny, *Ep. Epistulae* 7.5.

87. Plato, *Symposium* 191D–E.

88. See, for example, Eva Cantarella, *Bisexuality in the Ancient World*, trans. Cormac Ó Cuilleanáin (New Haven, CT: Yale University Press, 1992), p. 78.

89. Sappho 1 and 94.

90. See Marilyn B. Skinner, *Sexuality in Greek and Roman Culture* (Malden, MA: Blackwell, 2005), p. 75; and Cantarella, *Bisexuality*, p. 79. Contra Holt N. Parker, "Sappho Schoolmistress," *Transactions of the American Philological Association* 123 (1993): 309–51; and Lyn Hatherly Wilson, *Sappho's Sweet Bitter Songs: Configurations of Male and Female in Ancient Greek Lyric* (New York: Routledge, 1996), pp. 68–86.

91. Poem 94. See Wilson, *Sappho's Sweet Bitter Songs*, pp. 43–67.

92. For a summary of scholarship on these choruses, see Skinner, *Sexuality*, pp. 72–74. For scholars who see the poems as an expression of the erotic feelings of the chorus, see Pomeroy, *Spartan Women*, pp. 143–45; and C. Calame, *Les choeurs de juenes filles in Grèce archaïque, I: Morphologie, fonction religieuse et sociale* (Rome: Edizioni dell"Ateneo and Bizzarri, 1977), pp. 32–40. See also E. Stehle, *Performance and Gender in Ancient Greece: Nondramatic Poetry in Its Setting* (Princeton, NJ: Princeton University Press, 1997), pp. 30–39, 73–93, who concludes the choruses are objects of desire only.

93. Alcman, *Partheneion,* 1.64–77.

94. Plutarch, *Lycurgus* 14Z.3. See Skinner, *Sexuality*, p. 75; and Stehle, *Performance and Gender*, pp. 31–32.

95. Alcman, *Partheneion* 1.77. The verb *teirein* is associated with the effects of Eros in Hesiod, Fragment 105: *min eteiren eros* (desire kept weakening him/her) and Telestes. 1.6: *nin erōs eteiren* (desire kept weakening him/her). See also Alcman's third *Partheneion* referring to *lusimelēs*, limb-loosening. Refer to Skinner, *Sexuality*, pp. 73–74, on the erotic connotations of this term.

96. Calame, *Les Choeurs*, pp. 400–420. For a concise summary of Calame's controversial argument with discussion of counterarguments and models, see Skinner, *Sexuality*, pp. 74–76.

97. Asclepiades 7.

98. See Judith P. Hallett, "Female Homoeroticism and the Denial of Roman Reality in Latin Literature," in Hallet and Skinner, *Roman Sexualities*, pp. 255–73. Note Phaedrus *Fabulae* 4.16.

99. Ovid, *Metamorphoses* 9.727. For the full account see 9.666–797.

100. Martial 1.90, 7.67, 7.70.

101. See Hallett, "Female Homoeroticism," p. 259.

102. Seneca, *Controversiae* 1.2.23; and Martial 7.67, 7.70.

103. Peter Brown, *The Body and Society: Men, Women, and Sexual Renunciation in Early Christianity* (New York: Columbia University Press, 1988).

104. Tertullian, *On the Dress of Women* 1.1; and Jerome, *Letter* 38.4.

105. Gregory of Nyssa, "Life of Macrina" 992, trans. W. K. Lowther Clarke, available at: http://www.ccel.org/ccel/pearse/morefathers/files/gregory_macrina_1_life.htm (accessed March 2010).

106. Augustine, *On the Good of Marriage* 21.

107. On the question of Christian men's sexual activity with their slaves, see Carolyn Osiek, "Female Slaves, Porneia, and the Limits of Obedience," in *Early Christian*

Families in Context: An Interdisciplinary Dialogue, ed. David L. Balch and Carolyn Osiek (Grand Rapids, MI: Eerdmans, 2003), pp. 270–74.

108. Clement of Alexandria, *The Instructor* 2.114.1–4, 2.116.1–27.3, 3.68.1–3, 3.69.3–70.4.

109. Palladius, *The Lausiac History* 5.2, trans. Robert Meyer (New York: Newman Press, 1965), pp. 36–37.

110. John Chrysostom, "Homily 17.2," trans. G. Prevost, available at: http://www.ccel.org/ccel/schaff/npnf110.iii.XVII.html (accessed March 2010); Elizabeth A. Clark, "John Chrysostom and the 'Subintroductae'," *Church History* 46 (2) (1977): 171–85; and Jerome, *Letter* 22.14. The councils of Elvira (306 C.E., Canon 27), Ancyra (314 C.E., Canon 19), and Nicaea (325 C.E., Canon 3) condemned the practice.

111. The major work on this topic is Bernadette J. Brooten, *Love between Women: Early Christian Responses to Female Homoeroticism* (Chicago: University of Chicago Press, 1996).

112. Augustine, *Letter* 211.14, trans. J. G. Cunningham, available at: http://www.ccel.org/ccel/schaff/npnf101.vii.1.CCXI.html#vii.1.CCXI-Page_564 (accessed March 2010).

113. Following Leviticus 15:19. Jerome, *In Zach.* 3.13; *Comm. in Ezech.* 6.18; and Augustine, *Literal Commentary on Genesis* 11.42, quoted in Elizabeth A. Clark, *Women in the Early Church* (Wilmington, DE: Michael Glazier, 1983), p. 40.

114. Gillian Cloke, *This Female Man of God: Women and Spiritual Power in the Patristic Age, A.D. 350–450* (London and New York: Routledge, 1995), p. 213; and Lynda L. Coon, *Sacred Fictions: Holy Women and Hagiography in Late Antiquity* (Philadelphia: University of Pennsylvania Press, 1997), p. xxiii.

115. Eusebius, *Church History* 5.1.18, trans. A. Cushman McGiffert, available at: http://www.ccel.org/ccel/schaff/npnf201.iii.x.ii.html (accessed March 2010). See also *The Passion of Saints Perpetua and Felicitas* 21, trans. R. E. Wallis, available at: http://www.ccel.org/ccel/schaff/anf03.vi.vi.i.html (accessed March 2010).

116. *The Passion of Saints Perpetua and Felicitas* 6.3.

117. Jerome, *Letter* 45.3, trans. W. H. Fremantle, available at: http://www.ccel.org/ccel/schaff/npnf206.v.XLV.html (accessed March 2010).

118. John Anson, "The Female Transvestite in Early Monasticism: The Origin and Development of a Motif," *Viator* 5 (1974): 1–32.

119. *Acts of Paul and Thecla* 25.

120. *Canons of the Council of Gangra* (fourth century), Canon 13.

121. Jerome, *Letter* 22. 27, trans. W. H. Fremantle, available at: http://www.ccel.org/ccel/schaff/npnf206.v.XXII.html (accessed March 2010).

122. David Hunter, *Marriage, Celibacy, and Heresy in Ancient Christianity* (Oxford: Oxford University Press, 2007).

123. On New Testament roots, see Mark 8:34; Luke 9:1–6; 1 Cor. 7. On the changes in opportunity and the emphasis on virginity in Frankish holy women, see Suzanne F. Wemple, *Women in Frankish Society: Marriage and the Cloister, 500 to 900* (Philadelphia: University of Pennsylvania Press, 1981), pp. 152–53.

124. Ambrose, *De institutione virginis* 6.41–52.

125. Prudentius, *Peristephanon*, Hymns 3 (Eulalia), 4 (Encratis), 12 (Paul), 14 (Agnes); and 1 Cor. 7:1–9.

126. Hippocratic authors, *On the Nature of the Child* (20, vii 508, 6–7); Soranus, *Gynecology* 1.3.7; 1.16; and Ann Ellis Hanson, "The Medical Writers' Woman," in *Before Sexuality: The Construction of Erotic Experience in the Ancient Greek World*, ed. David M. Halperin, John J. Winkler, and Froma I. Zeitlin (Princeton, NJ: Princeton University Press, 1990). In Christian texts see particularly Ambrose, *Exhort. Virg* 6.35 and *Acts of Paul and Thecla* 5–6.

127. On the necessity of virginal body and spirit, see Jerome, *Against Helvidius* 22.6; and Ambrose, *De virginibus* 2.2.24.

128. Ambrose, *De institutione virginis* 52; translation given in Giulia Sissa, "Maidenhood without Maidenhead," in Halperin, Winkler, and Zeitlin, *Before Sexuality*, p. 361.

129. Ambrose, *De institutione virginis* 109, 112. The "fountain sealed": Jerome, *Letter* 22.25.

130. Jerome, *Letter* 107.7.

131. Prudentius, *Peristephanon*, trans. H. J. Thomson (London: Heinemann, 1953), pp. 339–41, ll. 31–37.

132. Ibid., ll. 69–80. On the sexual nature of the penetrating sword, see Adams, *Latin Sexual Vocabulary*, pp. 20, 21, 219.

133. Patricia Cox Miller, "The Blazing Body: Ascetic Desire in Jerome's Letter to Eustochium," *Journal of Early Christian Studies* 1 (1993): 21–45.

134. Elizabeth A. Clark, *Ascetic Piety and Women's Faith: Essays on Late Ancient Christianity* (New York: Edwin Mellen, 1986); and Joyce Salisbury, *Church Fathers, Independent Virgins* (London and New York: Verso, 1992).

135. Ambrose, *De virginitate* 1.11.63–65.

136. Gerontius, *Life of Melania* 1.

137. Augustine, *Letter* 262.1–2.

138. Kate Cooper, *The Virgin and the Bride: Idealized Womanhood in Late Antiquity* (Cambridge, MA: Harvard University Press, 1996).

139. Canon 3 of the Council of Carthage (390); Canons 5 and 38 of the Acts of the Council of Hippo (393); Jerome, *Letter* 24.2; René Metz, *La consecration des vierges dans l'Église romaine* (Paris: Presses universitaires de France, 1959).

Chapter 3

1. Deborah Lyons, "The Scandal of Women's Ritual," in *Finding Persephone: Women's Rituals in the Ancient Mediterranean*, ed. Maryline Parca and Angeliki Tzanetou (Bloomington: Indiana University Press, 2007), pp. 29–51.

2. Epiphanius, *Medicine Box* 79.

3. Andreas Bendlin, "Purity and Pollution," in *A Companion to Greek Religion*, ed. Daniel Ogden (Oxford: Blackwell, 2007), pp. 178–89.

4. Robert Parker, *Miasma: Pollution and Purification in Early Greek Religion* (Oxford: Clarendon, 1983).

5. While Walter Burkert maintains that Demeter's priestesses had to be unmarried, Joan Connelly provides archaeological evidence that some of Demeter's priestesses

were married with children. See relevant discussions in Walter Burkert, *Greek Religion: Archaic and Classical*, trans. John Raffan (Oxford: Basil Blackwell, 1985); and Joan Breton Connelly, *Portrait of a Priestess: Women and Ritual in Ancient Greece* (Princeton, NJ: Princeton University Press, 2007).

6. Maurice Olender, "Baubo," in *Encyclopedia of Religion*, vol. 2, ed. Lindsay Jones, 2nd ed. (Detroit: Macmillan Reference USA, 2005), pp. 803–4.

7. Joan R. Branham, "Blood in Flux, Sanctity at Issue," *RES: Anthropology and Aesthetics* 31 (1997): pp. 53–70.

8. Bendlin, "Purity and Pollution," p. 182.

9. Bella Vivante, *Daughters of Gaia: Women in the Ancient Mediterranean World* (Westport, CT: Praeger, 2007).

10. Celia E. Schultz, "Sanctissima Femina: Social Categorization and Women's Religious Experience in the Roman Republic," in Parca and Tzanetou, *Finding Persephone*, pp. 92–113.

11. Ibid., p. 93.

12. Joan R. Branham, "Bloody Women and Bloody Spaces: Menses and the Eucharist in Late Antiquity and the Early Middle Ages," *Harvard Divinity Bulletin* 30 (4) (2002), available at: http://www.hds.harvard.edu/news/bulletin/articles/branham. html (accessed January 17, 2011).

13. Ibid.

14. Branham, "Blood in Flux," p. 53.

15. Ibid., p. 69.

16. Shaye J.D. Cohen, "Menstruants and the Sacred in Judaism and Christianity," in *Women's History and Ancient History*, ed. Sarah B. Pomeroy (Chapel Hill: University of North Carolina Press, 1991), pp. 273–99. As with early Christian churches, it is unlikely that this proscription against menstruants was practiced in all or even most synagogues. See, for example, Susannah Heschel, "Gender and Agency in the Feminist Historiography of Jewish Identity," *Journal of Religion* 84 (4) (2004): 580–91.

17. Branham, "Bloody Women."

18. Cohen, "Menstruants," pp. 288–89.

19. For example, see Paul's comments on the subject of head coverings in his first letter to the Corinthians, verses 11:2–16. Should anyone disagree with his pronouncement, Paul states, "We have no such custom, nor do the churches of God." Since 1 Corinthians is one of the earliest letters in the Pauline corpus, it is more likely that very few customs were shared consistently by the nascent Christian communities spread over hundreds of kilometers and evangelized by different missionaries with inconsistent views on worship.

20. See also Gen. 5:1–2. For an excellent discussion on the difference between early Christian and early Judaism exegeses on these verses, see Daniel Boyarin, "Gender," in *Critical Terms for Religious Studies*, ed. Mark C. Taylor (Chicago: University of Chicago Press, 1998), pp. 117–35.

21. Tertullian, *On the Dress of Women* 1.1.1–1.1.2.

22. Janett Morgan, "Women, Religion, and the Home," in Ogden, *Companion to Greek Religion*, pp. 297–310.

23. Achilles Tatius, *Leucippe and Clitophon* 7.13.

24. Connelly, *Portrait*, pp. 32–33.

25. Burkert, *Greek Religion*, p. 243.
26. Morgan, "Women, Religion, and the Home," p. 304.
27. Ibid., p. 305.
28. Burkert, *Greek Religion*, pp. 176–77.
29. A. Henrichs, trans., "Rules of Ritual," Miletus, 276/5 B.C.E., in *Women's Life in Greece and Rome: A Sourcebook in Translation*, ed. Mary R. Lefkowitz and Maureen B. Fant (Baltimore: Johns Hopkins University Press, 2005), pp. 273–74.
30. A. Henrichs, trans., "Epitaph of Alcmeonis, a Priestess of Dionysos," in *Women's Religions in the Greco-Roman World: A Sourcebook*, ed. Ross Shepard Kraemer (New York: Oxford University Press, 2004), p. 21.
31. Schultz, "Sanctissima Femina," p. 97.
32. Ovid, *Fasti* 4.494.
33. Schultz, "Sanctissima Femina," p. 97.
34. Ovid, *Fasti* 6.551–68.
35. Ovid, *Fasti* 6.295–301.
36. Mika Kajava, "Hestia: Hearth, Goddess, and Cult," *Harvard Studies in Classical Philology* 102 (2004): 1–20.
37. C.M.C. Green, *Roman Religions and the Cult of Diana at Aricia* (New York: Cambridge University Press, 2007).
38. W. Warde Fowler, *The Roman Festivals of the Period of the Republic* (London: Macmillan, 1908).
39. Green, *Roman Religions*, p. 138.
40. Statius, *Silvae* 3.1.55–60.
41. Ovid, *Fasti* 5.153–54.
42. In a letter to his friend, Cicero tells us about a man dressed in women's clothing who infiltrated the women-only rites when they were held in Julius Caesar's house. At the time, Caesar was a *praetor* (a type of Roman magistrate). Cicero, *Epistulae ad Atticum* 1.13.3.
43. *Tractate Megillah* 22b.
44. John Chrysostom, *Against Judaizing Christians* 2.3.3–6; 4.7.3. See also Ross Shepard Kraemer, *Her Share of the Blessings: Women's Religions among Pagans, Jews and Christians in the Greco-Roman World* (Oxford: Oxford University Press, 1992). Kraemer suggests the "Feast of Trumpets" festival was probably Rosh Hashanah (p. 108).
45. Kraemer, *Her Share*, p. 108.
46. Bishop Damasus (r. 366–384 C.E.) was known as *auris-cal-pius matronarum*, or "the ear-tickler of noble ladies," according to Peter Brown in *The Cult of Saints* (Chicago: University of Chicago Press, 1981), for his ability to separate wealthy women from their money, which he used to finance the identification and expansion of martyrs' shrines in the Roman catacombs.
47. Michele Renee Salzman, *On Roman Time: The Codex-Calendar of 354 and the Rhythms of Urban Life in Late Antiquity* (Berkeley: University of California Press, 1990).
48. Epiphanius, *Medicine Box* 79.1.

49. J.E. Bickersteth, "Unedited Greek Homilies (Acephalous, Anonymous or Attributed to John Chrysostom) for Festivals of the Virgin Mary," *Orientalia Christiana Periodica* 46 (2) (1980): 474–80.

50. "Delphic Oracle," in *The Concise Oxford Companion to Classical Literature*, ed. M.C. Howatson and Ian Chilvers (Oxford University Press, 1996), Oxford Reference Online, available at: http://www.oxfordreference.com/views/ENTRY. html?subview=Mainandentry=t9.e887 (accessed June 10, 2010).

51. Connelly, *Portrait*, p. 75.

52. Ibid., p. 75.

53. Ibid., p. 9.

54. See ibid., "Index of Priestesses," pp. 393–97.

55. "The Priestess Alexandria, Rome, 2nd Cent, AD (?)," in Lefkowitz and Fant, *Women's Life*, p. 302.

56. "Tata, Aphrodisias, 2nd Cent. AD," in Lefkowitz and Fant, *Women's Life*, pp. 302–3.

57. Schultz, "Sanctissima Femina," pp. 97–100.

58. Ibid., p. 101.

59. Steven J. Friesen, "Asiarchs," *Zeitschrift für Papyrologie und Epigraphik* 126 (1999): 275–90.

60. Ibid., tables 2a and 2b, p. 283.

61. Of the thirty-five males who claimed the throne of Rome between 200 and 251 C.E., only one was not murdered, executed, or killed in battle: Septimius Severus (r. 193–211 C.E.).

62. "Epitaph Set Up by Rufina, Head of Synagogue," in Kraemer, *Women's Religions*, p. 251.

63. Ibid., p. 374.

64. Ibid., pp. 373–75.

65. Kraemer, *Women's Religions*, 88G, p. 254. For a discussion of this term and its meaning see Ross Shepard Kraemer, "A New Inscription from Malta and the Question of Women Elders in Diaspora Jewish Communities," *Harvard Theological Review* 78 (3–4) (1985): 431–38.

66. Jack N. Lightstone, "Roman Diaspora Judaism," in *A Companion to Roman Religion*, ed. Jörg Rüpke (Oxford: Blackwell, 2007), p. 374.

67. Ross Shepard Kraemer, trans., "Ten Inscriptions from a Synagogue Commemorating Contributions from Women for the Paving of a Mosaic Floor," in Kraemer, *Women's Religions*, p. 165.

68. Lee I. Levine, *The Ancient Synagogue: The First Thousand Years*, 2nd ed. (New Haven, CT: Yale University Press, 2005). See especially pp. 511–18.

69. Luke 8:2–3.

70. Hippolytus of Rome (ca. 170–ca. 240) first gives Mary Magdalene this title in his *Commentary on the "Song of Songs."*

71. See Phil. 4:2, Col. 4:15, and Rom. 16.

72. Kevin Madigan and Carolyn Osiek, eds., *Ordained Women in the Early Church: A Documentary History* (Baltimore: Johns Hopkins University Press, 2005).

73. Madigan and Osiek, "Index of Deaconesses, Presbyters, and Episcopa," in ibid., pp. 217–18.

74. Madigan and Osiek, *Ordained Women*, p. 9.
75. For the full story of Hilda and other royal nuns in England's early history, see Bede, *The Ecclesiastical History of the English Church and People* (Oxford: Oxford University Press, 1996).
76. Kimberly B. Stratton, *Naming the Witch: Magic, Ideology and Stereotype in the Ancient World* (New York: Columbia University Press, 2007).
77. See Stephen Benko, *Pagan Rome and the Early Christians* (Bloomington: Indiana University Press, 1984); and Margaret Y. MacDonald, *Early Christian Women and Pagan Opinion: The Power of the Hysterical Woman* (Cambridge: Cambridge University Press, 1996).
78. Stratton, *Naming the Witch*, pp. 17–18.
79. Ibid., p. 22.
80. On this practice and the types of curses that deceased children were entreated to activate, see Eve D'Ambra, "Racing with Death: Circus Sarcophagi and the Commemoration of Children in Roman Italy," in *Constructions of Childhood in Ancient Greece and Italy*, ed. Ada Cohen and Jeremy B. Rutter (Princeton, NJ: American School of Classical Studies at Athens, 2007), pp. 339–51.
81. Ibid., p. 349n46.
82. Neil Brodie, "Aramaic Incantation Bowls," in *Cultural Heritage Resource* (Palo Alto: Stanford Archaeological Center, 2008), available at: http://www.stanford.edu/group/chr/drupal/ref/aramaic-incantation-bowls (accessed March 11, 2011).
83. Erica C.D. Hunter, "Manipulating Incantation Texts: Excursions in Refrain 'A,'" *Iraq* 64 (2002): 259–73; and Stratton, *Naming the Witch*, p. 156.
84. Aramaic inscription is written in a spiral from the center outward. Translation: (1) Accursed. Overturned overturned overturned overturned overturned overturned (2) overturned. Overturned be the earth and the heavens, overturned be the stars and the planets, (3) overturned be markets and streets, overturned be the hour of all humankind, overturned be (4) the curse of the mother and her daughter, of the daughter-in-law and her mother-in-law, of men and women who stand in the field (5) and in the town and in the mountain and temple and synagogue. Bound and sealed be the curse that she cursed. In the name of (6) Betiel and Yequtiel and in the name of the great YYY the angel that has eleven names SSKB' KBB' KNYBR' SRY' (7) SYR'DY' MRYRY' 'NNY' BTWQP' 'NQP' 'NS PSPS scorched in fire. Whoever transgresses against those names, (8) these angels—Bound and sealed are all demons and bands (of spirits), and all that is of the earth calls and all that is of the heavens hearkens. I heard the voice of the earth (9) DQYQYH is its name, receiving all souls from this world. I heard the voice of the woman who cursed and I sent against her angels, NKYR (10) NKYR NKYR NKYR, YY, take the vengeance of YY. We shall rejoice and we shall rejoice, YY, and SS ??? ?YMW, the woman who cursed. And they sent and injured her from clouds of hail that she may neither (11) avenge nor curse. Translation after J.B. Segal, *Catalogue of Aramaic and Mandaic Incantation Bowls in the British Museum*, with a contribution by Erica C.D. Hunter (London: Trustees of the British Museum, 2000).
85. Shadi Bartsch, *The Mirror of the Self: Sexuality, Self-Knowledge, and the Gaze in the Early Roman Empire* (Chicago: University of Chicago Press, 2006).

86. Elizabeth A. Castelli, *Martyrdom and Memory: Early Christian Culture Making* (New York: Columbia University Press, 2004). See especially "Christian Polemics against Spectacle," pp. 112–17.

87. Due to the popularity of the Christian cult of saints in the fourth century and the early view of martyrs' relics as holy, early Christians held a mixed view toward the idea of death pollution.

Chapter 4

1. Vivian Nutton, "Healers in the Medical Market Place: Towards a Social History of Graeco-Roman Medicine," in *Medicine in Society: Historical Essays*, ed. Andrew Wear (Cambridge: Cambridge University Press, 1992), pp. 15–58, at pp. 52 and 56.

2. On this, also see Raymond Van Dam, *Saints and Their Miracles in Late Antique Gaul* (Princeton, NJ: Princeton University Press, 1993), pp. 95–96; and Jane Rowlandson, ed., *Women and Society in Greek and Roman Egypt: A Sourcebook* (Cambridge: Cambridge University Press), pp. 281–82.

3. On the socially constructed concepts of "disease" and "illness" in Greek society, see Geoffrey E. R. Lloyd, *In the Grip of Disease: Studies in the Greek Imagination* (Oxford: Oxford University Press, 2003), pp. 1–13.

4. See Helen King, *Hippocrates' Woman: Reading the Female Body in Ancient Greece* (London and New York: Routledge, 1998), pp. 157–71, for a warning against assuming women took on nursing roles in the ancient world.

5. One interpretation for this image is that the woman (probably a wealthy woman) is reading poetry, and her servant is handing her some perfume (typical activities for elite women). However, it is not impossible that women read medical texts, and medical texts on perfumed ointments have been attributed to women.

6. See, for instance, King, *Hippocrates' Woman*, pp. 99–113; Vivian Nutton, *Ancient Medicine* (London and New York: Routledge, 2004), pp. 32–34, 53–57; and Heinrich von Staden, "Women and Dirt," *Helios* 19 (1992): 7–30.

7. This issue is often called "nested identity" or group/dyadic personality; see Bruce J. Malina and Jerome H. Neyrey, *Portraits of Paul: An Archaeology of Ancient Personality* (Louisville, KY: Westminster John Knox, 1996), pp. 152–201. The cases of women being named after the male of the household, and of the woman's fertility having consequences for the household (discussed later on), demonstrate the social nature of women's identity.

8. For a definition of authority figures, see Geoffrey E. R. Lloyd, *Adversaries and Authorities: Investigations into Ancient Greek and Chinese Science* (Cambridge: Cambridge University Press, 1996), p. 20.

9. *Diseases of Women* 1.62 (8.126.7–14 Littré). It is conventional to refer to Hippocratic texts by giving the name of the editor (here Littré), the volume in which the text is to be found (here 8), the page at which the passage is to be found (here 126), and, when needed, the lines of the passage (here 7–14). On this passage, see Ann Ellis Hanson, "The Medical Writer's Woman," in *Before Sexuality: The Construction of Erotic Experience in the Ancient Greek World*, ed. David M. Halperin, John J. Winkler, and Froma I. Zeitlin (Princeton, NJ: Princeton

University Press, 1990), pp. 309–38, at p. 310; King, *Hippocrates' Woman*, p. 48; and Laurence M. V. Totelin, *Hippocratic Recipes: Oral and Written Transmission of Pharmacological Knowledge in Fifth- and Fourth-Century Greece* (Leiden: Brill, 2009), pp. 114–16.

10. *Diseases of Women* 1.40 (8.96–98 Littré).

11. *Epidemics* 1.8 (2.646 Littré), 1.13.5 (2.694 Littré), 7.6 (306 Smith), 3.1.10 (3.60 Littré). On these stories, see Nancy Demand, *Birth, Death, and Motherhood in Classical Greece* (Baltimore and London: Johns Hopkins University Press, 1994), pp. 48–70.

12. *Epidemics* 1.13.13 (2.712 Littré).

13. *Diseases of Women* 1.1 (8.12 Littré).

14. On the Hippocratic female body see, e.g., Lesley A. Dean-Jones, *Women's Bodies in Classical Greek Science* (Oxford: Oxford University Press, 1994); Hanson, "Medical Writer's Woman"; and King, *Hippocrates' Woman*, pp. 21–39. Not all Hippocratic authors saw women as completely different from men; some suggested that sexuality existed on a "sliding scale" from male to female. See King, *Hippocrates' Woman*, pp. 9–10. No Hippocratic author saw women as inverted men, on which see Thomas W. Laqueur, *Making Sex: Body and Gender from the Greeks to Freud* (Cambridge, MA: Harvard University Press, 1990).

15. On this *hodos*, see King, *Hippocrates' Woman*, p. 28; Paula Manuli, "Fisiologia e patologia del femminile negli scritti ippocratici dell' antica ginecologia greca," in *Hippocratica: actes du Colloque hippocratique de Paris, 4–9 septembre 1978*, ed. Mirko D. Grmek and F. Robert (Paris: Éditions du Centre national de la recherche scientifique, 1980), pp. 393–408, at p. 399; and Giulia Sissa, *Greek Virginity*, trans. Arthur Goldhammer (Cambridge, MA: Harvard University Press), p. 53.

16. Plato, *Timaeus* 91c–d.

17. The seminal articles here were Manuli, "Fisiologia e patologia del femminile"; and Aline Rousselle, "Images médicales du corps: observation féminine et idéologie masculine. Le corps de la femme d'après les médecins grecs," *Annales: Economies, Sociétés, Civilisations* 35 (1980): 1089–115. These works were shortly followed by that of Geoffrey E. R. Lloyd, *Science, Folklore and Ideology: Studies in the Life Sciences in Ancient Greece* (Cambridge: Cambridge University Press, 1983), pp. 112–200. For a description of the literature after 1983, see Totelin, *Hippocratic Recipes*, pp. 111–14.

18. On the gynecological therapies of the Hippocratic corpus, see Totelin, *Hippocratic Recipes*.

19. *Diseases of Women* 2.134 (8.302–4 Littré)

20. *Diseases of Women* 1.62 (8.126 Littré).

21. The medical writer Soranus (see later on) summarizes the debate at *Gynecology* 3.1.

22. Aristotle, *Generation of Animals* 2.3 (737a). On the female body in Aristotle, see Robert Mayhew, *The Female in Aristotle's Biology: Reason or Rationalization* (Chicago and London: University of Chicago Press, 2004).

23. Herophilus fragments 61, 106, and 193. On Herophilus's gynecology, see Heinrich von Staden, *Herophilus: The Art of Medicine in Early Alexandria* (Cambridge: Cambridge University Press, 1989), pp. 296–99.

24. Herophilus fragment 114 (von Staden).

25. See Aretaeus, *On Acute Diseases* 2.11; Celsus, *On Medicine* 4.27.1; and Soranus, *Gynecology* 1.8. For the amulets, see Christopher Faraone, "New Light on Ancient Greek Exorcisms of the Wandering Womb," *Zeitschrift für Papyrologie und Epigraphik* 144 (2003): 189–97. See later on for more information on amulets.

26. Soranus, *Gynecology* 4.14.

27. Soranus, *Gynecology* 1.42, 3.5, 4.7.

28. On the history of Soranus's text, see Rebecca Flemming, *Medicine and the Making of Roman Women: Gender, Nature, and Authority from Celsus to Galen* (Oxford: Oxford University Press, 2000), pp. 228–46; Ann E. Hanson and Monica H. Green, "Soranus of Ephesus: *Methodicorum Princeps*," in *Aufstieg und Niedergang der römischen Welt. Geschichte und Kultur Roms im Spiegel der neueren Forschung. Teil II. Principat. Band 37: Philosophie, Wissenschaften, Technik. 2 Teilband: Wissenschaften (Medizin und Biologie)*, ed. Wolfgang Hasse (Berlin and New York: Walter de Gruyter, 1994), pp. 968–1075; and Nutton, *Ancient Medicine*, chap. 13.

29. On Galen's female patients, see Susan P. Mattern, *Galen and the Rhetoric of Healing* (Baltimore: Johns Hopkins University Press, 2008), especially pp. 112–14. On Arria, see Galen, *Theriac to Piso* 11 (14.218–19 Kühn). On the wife of Boethus, see Galen, *On Prognosis* 8 (110–13 Nutton). On coquetry, see Galen, *Composition of Remedies according to Places* 1.2 (12.434–35 Kühn). It is conventional to refer to Galenic texts in the same way as to Hippocratic texts (see note 9).

30. Galen, *On the Use of Parts* 14.6 (296–310 Helmreich), *On the Dissection of the Uterus* (edition Nickel), and *On the Affected Parts* 6.5 (8.420–24 Kühn).

31. Philip A. Harland, *Associations, Synagogues and Congregations: Claiming a Place in Ancient Mediterranean Society* (Minneapolis: Fortress, 2003), p. 61.

32. For examples of women's healing through incubation, see Emma J. Edelstein and Ludwig Edelstein, *Asclepius: A Collection and Interpretation of the Testimonies*, vol. 1 (Baltimore: Johns Hopkins University Press, 1998 [1945]), at T. 423, nos. 1, 2, 4, 23, 25, 31, 34, 39, 41, and 42. These are also discussed in Lynn R. LiDonnici, *The Epidaurian Miracle Inscriptions: Text, Translation, and Commentary* (Atlanta, GA: Scholars Press, 1995).

33. See Robin Osborne, "Hoards, Votives, Offerings: The Archaeology of the Dedicated Object," *World Archaeology* 36 (2004): 1–10.

34. The reader should look to modern practices of lighting votive candles in cathedrals to shed light on the process of such offerings. There, the element of choice and intention is evident: A person selects an object, dedicates it ritually, and leaves with the expectation that the power of that action will continue. A woman offering an ex-voto is doing something that she felt would help cure her.

35. Mark 5:25–34; Matthew 9:20–22; and Luke 8:43–48. See Charlotte Fronrobert, "The Woman with a Blood-Flow (Mark 5.24–34) Revisited: Menstrual Laws

and Jewish Culture in Christian Feminist Hermeneutics," in *Early Christian Interpretation of the Scriptures of Israel: Investigations and Proposals*, ed. Craig E. Evans and James A. Sanders (Sheffield: Sheffield University Press, 1997), pp. 121–40; Mary Jean Selvidge, *Woman, Cult and Miracle Recital: A Redactional Critical Investigation on Mark 5:24–34* (London: Associated University Presses, 1990); and Elaine E. Wainwright, *Women Healing/Healing Women: The Genderization of Healing in Early Christianity* (London: Equinox, 2006), pp. 112–23.

36. Mark 5:25–34. Note that in later (Patristic) commentary and sermons, this woman is portrayed as an authority or exemplar of great faith (Ephrem the Syrian, Jerome, Peter Chrysologus; see Thomas C. Oden and Christopher A. Hall, eds., *Ancient Christian Commentary on Scripture, New Testament 2 (Mark)* [Downers Grove, IL: Intervarsity Press, 1998], pp. 73–74).

37. William E. Klingshirn, *Caesarius of Arles: The Making of a Christian Community in Late Antique Gaul* (Cambridge: Cambridge University Press, 1994).

38. A woman approaches the bishop during vespers and cries out forcefully for Caesarius to heal her, which he does (2.16).

39. Raymond Van Dam, "Images of Saint Martin in Late Roman and Early Merovingian Gaul," *Viator* 19 (1988): 1–27; and Van Dam, *Saints and Their Miracles*, pp. 94–102, 216–95.

40. Bella, a blind woman, became convinced that she would be healed by going to his shrine. She arranged to travel there, was cured, and brought other blind people there subsequently (VM 1.19). A woman with a flow of blood took lodgings near the shrine. She touched the tomb and then her body. She was cured (VM 2.10). A lame woman, Remigia, came to the shrine and was cured. Every year she returned and brought food for the monks. A mute woman had great faith that she would be cured. She traveled to the shrine and was cured (VM 2.30). One instance points out the role played by the patient in achieving her own healing. A lame and blind woman has healing in two stages. First, her lameness is cured, and then she declares that she will not depart until her sight also is restored. This also happened (VM 3.39). These are all in Van Dam, *Saints and Their Miracles*.

41. Brian E. Daley, *Gregory of Nazianzus* (London: Routledge, 2006); Tomas Hägg, "Playing with Expectations: Gregory's Funeral Orations on His Brother, Sister and Father," in *Gregory of Nazianzus: Images and Reflections*, ed. Jostein Børtnes and Tomas Hägg (Copenhagen: University Press, 2006), pp. 133–51; John A. McGuckin, *St. Gregory of Nazianzus: An Intellectual Biography* (Crestwood, NY: St. Vladimir's Seminary Press, 2001); Hebert Thurston, "The Early Cultus of the Reserved Eucharist," *Journal of Theological Studies* 11 (1910): 275–79; and Frans Van de Paverd, "A Text of Gregory of Nazianzus Misinterpreted by F. E. Brightman," *Orientalia Christiana Periodica* 42 (1976): 197–206.

42. Gregory of Nazianzus, *Oration* 8.18. See also Leo P. McCauley, John J. Sullivan, Martin R.P. McGuire, and Roy J. Deferrari, *Funeral Orations by Saint Gregory Nazianzen and Saint Ambrose* (Washington, DC: Catholic University of America Press, 1953); and Patricia Cox Miller, *Women in Early Christianity: Translations from Greek Texts* (Washington, DC: Catholic University of America Press, 2005), pp. 280–81.

43. See Betz, *Greek Magic Papyri* vol. 1, PGM 7.208–9; PDM 14:953–55, 956–60, 961–65, 970–84.

44. British Museum OA.9861. On gynecological amulets, see Faraone, "New Light"; Ann E. Hanson, "Uterine Amulets and Greek Uterine Medicine," *Medicina nei Secoli 7* (1995): 281–99; and Ann E. Hanson, "A Long-Lived 'Quick-Birther' (*Okytokion*)," in *Naissance et petite enfance dans l'antiquité*, ed. Véronique Dasen (Fribourg and Göttingen: Vandehoeck and Ruprecht, 2004), pp. 265–80.

45. Klingshirn, *Caesarius of Arles: The Making*, pp. 162, 167; and Stephen Wilson, ed., *Saints and Their Cults: Studies in Religious Sociology, Folklore and History* (Cambridge: Cambridge University Press, 1983), pp. 18–25.

46. Matt. 9:20.

47. *Life of Caesarius* 2.13–15. For other cases, see 1.51, 2.12. A lame woman arranges to be brought to the horse of the bishop, touches the saddle, and is cured (2.25). Young boys and girls were sent to the church (likely by their parents) to obtain vessels of sacred oil or water that the bishop had blessed (2.17), which would then be used in the household when someone fell ill. See also 2.38–42. See Charles Harris, "Visitation of the Sick," in *Liturgy and Worship*, ed. W.K. Lowther Clarke and Charles Harris (London: SPCK, 1932), pp. 475–78, at pp. 483–85, for a discussion of the self-administered oil. In the case of Martin of Gaul, a woman had been ill. She takes a piece of consecrated bread and is cured (VM 4.21).

48. Sermon 13.3. Sr. Mary Magdeleine Mueller, Saint Caesarius of Arles: *Sermons* I (New York: Fathers of the Church, 1956), *Sermons* II (1964).

49. Klingshirn, *Caesarius of Arles: The Making*, pp. 171ff.

50. Caesarius of Arles, *Sermons* I, 13.5; see also 50.1.

51. Caesarius of Arles, *Sermons* II, 51.4; see also 52.4.

52. See similar passage in II 54.1, 3. See also Sermon II 184.4–5.

53. Soranus, *Gynecology* 1.63 and 3.42.

54. National Archaeological Museum, Athens, inv. 993. For the inscription, see Évelyne Samama, *Les médecins dans le monde grec: sources épigraphiques sur la naissance d'un corpus médical* (Geneva: Librairie Droz, 2003), pp. 109–10 (no. 2). See Demand, *Birth, Death, and Motherhood*, pp. 132 and 166; and Nancy Demand, "Monuments, Midwives and Gynecology," in *Ancient Medicine in Its Socio-Cultural Context*, ed. Philip J. van der Eijk, H.F.J. Horstmanshoff, and P.H. Schrijvers (Amsterdam: Rodopi, 1995), pp. 275–90, at p. 287.

55. See Demand, "Monuments, Midwives and Gynecology"; Flemming, *Medicine and the Making of Roman Women*, pp. 383–91; and Samama, *Médecins dans le monde grec*, pp. 15–16.

56. See Rebecca Flemming, "Women, Writing, and Medicine in the Classical World," *Classical Quarterly 57* (2007): 257–79, at p. 259.

57. Ostia, Antiquarium, inv., 5203. Isola Sacra, necropolis of Portis, tomb 100. Description of childbirth: Soranus, *Gynecology* 2.3.

58. Samama, *Médecins dans le monde grec*, pp. 389–90 (no. 280).

59. Galen, *Composition of Remedies according to Places* 9.2 (13.250 Kühn), 10.2 (13.341 Kühn). For Antiochis as the dedicatee, see Heraclides fragments 1–5. The fragments of Heraclides are edited by Alessia Guardasole, *Eraclide di Taranto: Frammenti* (Naples, Italy: M. D'Auria, 1998).

60. Flemming, "Women, Writing, and Medicine," pp. 265–66, notes that there is "nothing that explicitly links the three Antiochis" (statue, Heraclides, remedies). Nutton, *Ancient Medicine*, p. 196, equates Antiochis the dedicatee of Heraclides with Antiochis of Tlos.

61. *Diseases of Women* 1.46 (8.106 Littré): cutter of the umbilical cord; 1.68 (8.144 Littré): healing woman; *Flesh* 19 (8.614 Littré): female healer.

62. See, for instance, *Excision of the Fetus* 4 (8.514.15 and 17; 516.4 and 5 Littré). See Ann E. Hanson, "Phaenarete: Mother and *Maia*," in *Hippokratische Medizin und antike Philosophie*, ed. Renate Wittern and Pierre Pellegrin (Hildesheim, Germany: Olms, 1996), pp. 159–81, at p. 171.

63. See Hanson, "Phaenarete," p. 170.

64. See Dean-Jones, *Women's Bodies*, p. 212.

65. Demand, "Monuments, Midwives and Gynecology," p. 267. On ancient birth, see also Demand, *Birth, Death, and Motherhood*, especially p. 66; Ann E. Hanson, "A Division of Labor: Roles for Men in Greek and Roman Births," *Thamyris* 1 (1994): 157–202; and King, *Hippocrates' Woman*, especially p. 180.

66. Hyginus, *Fabula* 274. See Helen King, "Agnodike and the Profession of Medicine," *Proceedings of the Cambridge Philological Society* 32 (1986): 53–77; and King, *Hippocrates' Woman*, p. 181.

67. Plato, *Thaetetus* 149b–e, 157c–d.

68. Demand, *Birth, Death, and Motherhood*, p. 66, argues these treatises were addressed to women.

69. See von Staden, *Herophilus*, pp. 296–99.

70. Soranus, *Gynecology* 1.3.

71. Muscio, *Gynaecia*, prologum (3 Rose).

72. Flemming, "Women, Writing, and Medicine," p. 261.

73. Galen, *On Prognosis* 8 (110 Nutton).

74. Eunapius, *Vitae Sophistarum* 6.3.

75. One example is the case of Arata, a woman of Lacedaemon, who has dropsy. She remains in that city, while her mother goes to the temple of Asclepius at Epidaurus and sleeps there. The mother has a dream-vision of the god "operating" on her daughter. The mother returns to Lacedaemon, where she finds her daughter in good health. Edelstein and Edelstein, *Asclepius*, T. 423, p. 233.

76. Ibid., T. 331, p. 174.

77. Herondas, *The Women Sacrificing to Asclepius*.

78. Philostratus, *The Life of Apollonius of Tyana*, book 3.38. See also the case of the man who asked on behalf of his wife, who suffered from difficult labor (book 3.39).

79. Mark 7:24–30; Matt. 15:22–28. See Wainwright, *Women Healing*, pp. 122–30. See also Bonnie Thurston, *Women in the New Testament: Questions and Commentary* (New York: Crossroad, 1998), pp. 72–73. Later Christian writers (Chrysostom, Tertullian) commend the strength and tenacity of this woman. See *Ancient Christian Commentary on Scripture, New Testament 2 (Mark)*, pp. 100–102.

80. A widow came to see the bishop and pleaded earnestly for the healing of her son. The prayers of the bishop accomplished this healing. See William Klingshirn, *Caesarius of Arles: Life, Testament, Letters* (Liverpool: Liverpool University Press,

1994), pp. 39–40. A woman named Eucryia begs Caesarius to heal her slave girl, and he does (2.18); this is found in Klingshirn, *Caesarius of Arles: Life.*

81. A mother has a vision in which she should take her daughter to the shrine. She does so, and the girl is cured (VM 2.38). The woman Remigia (mentioned earlier) also intervened to heal her ill servant. She visited the shrine and requested a healing, and this happened (VM 2.22).

82. See Wainwright, *Women Healing*, pp. 164–72.

83. This text parallels the earlier description of Jesus sending out the twelve disciples (Luke 9:1–6; also in Mark 6:6b–13; Matt. 10:1, 7–11, 14).

84. John Dominic Crossan, *The Historical Jesus: The Life of a Mediterranean Jewish Peasant* (San Francisco: Harper Collins, 1992), p. 334. See also Wainwright, *Women Healing*, pp. 164–72.

85. 1 Cor. 9:5, discussed in Crossan, *Historical Jesus*, p. 35. When we look at the female deacons in the next section, we see exactly this scenario—women visiting and ministering to women in their homes.

86. 1 Cor. 12:28–29.

87. An excellent example is the votive bas-relief of the third century B.C.E. from the Asclepieion of Piraeus. See Gerald D. Hart, *Asclepius, the God of Medicine* (London: Royal Society of Medicine Press, 2002), p. 103, fig. 47; see also p. 32, fig. 15. Many examples are in Karl Kerényi, *Asklepios: Archetypal Image of the Physician's Existence*, trans. Ralph Manheim (New York: Bolligen/Pantheon Books, 1959). See discussion in Edelstein and Edelstein, *Asclepius*, vol. 2, pp. 86–91; Hart, *Asclepius*, pp. 28–40; Jennifer Larson, *Greek Heroine Cults* (Madison: University of Wisconsin Press, 1995), pp. 62–64; and M. Compton, "The Association of Hygieia with Asklepios in Graeco-Roman Asklepieion Medicine," *Journal of the History of Medicine* 57 (2002): 312–29.

88. Edelstein and Edelstein, *Asclepius,* vol. 1, T. 553–55, 628, 631, 670, 742. On the family of Asclepius, see Compton, "Association of Hygieia," pp. 312–29; Edelstein and Edelstein, *Asclepius*, vol. 2 pp. 85–91; Hart, *Asclepius*, pp. 28–40; and Larson, *Greek Heroine Cults*, pp. 62–64.

89. Suggested by Compton, "Association of Hygieia," pp. 332–33.

90. See R.J.S. Barrett-Lennard, *Christian Healing after the New Testament: Some Approaches to Illness in the Second, Third, and Fourth Centuries* (Lanham, MD: University Press of America, 1994); and Amanda Porterfield, *Healing in the History of Christianity* (Oxford: Oxford University Press, 2005), pp. 44, 50.

91. See Paul F. Bradshaw, Maxwell E. Johnson, L. Edward Phillips, and Harold W. Attridge, *The Apostolic Tradition: A Commentary* (Minneapolis: Fortress, 2002); R. Hugh Connolly, *Didascalia Apostolorum: With Introduction and Notes* (Oxford: Clarendon, 1929); Jean Daniélou, *The Ministry of Women in the Early Church*, trans. G. Simon (Westminster, MD: Faith Press, 1974); J. G. Davies, "Deacons, Deaconesses and the Minor Orders in the Patristic Period," in *Church Ministry and Organization in the Early Church Era*, ed. Everett Ferguson (New York: Garland, 1993); and Roger Gryson, *The Ministry of Women in the Early Church*, trans. Jean Laporte and Mary Louise Hall (Collegeville, MN: Liturgical Press, 1976).

92. See Connolly, *Didascalia Apostolorum* 16.3.12.6–7, p. 149. See also Alistair Stewart-Sykes, *The Didascalia Apostolorum* (Turnhout, Belgium: Brepols, 2009), p. 194. A similar passage is found in Epiphanius. See Frank Williams, trans., *The Panarion of Epiphanius of Salamis* (Leiden: Brill, 1994), 3.2.79, p. 623. See discussion in Davies, "Deacons," p. 239; Gryson, *Ministry*, pp. 42–43, 44–46; and Aime Georges Martimort, *Deaconnesses: An Historical Study* (San Francisco: Ignatius Press), pp. 38–42, 112.

93. The charismatic healing mentioned by Paul in 1 Corinthians continued in the patristic era; see *Apostolic Tradition,* section 14 (Bradshaw et al., *Apostolic Tradition*, pp. 80–81); Gregory Dix, *The Treatise on the Apostolic Tradition of St. Hippolytus of Rome, Bishop and Martyr* (London: Society for Promoting Christian Knowledge, 1937), pp. 22; Irenaeus, *Against Heresies* 2.32.4–5, 2.31.2; and Justin Martyr, *Dialogue with Trypho* 39. See discussion in Harris, "Visitation," p. 475.

94. See Connolly, *Didascalia Apostolorum*, pp. xliv, 138, 140 (translation of 3.8); and Stewart-Sykes, *Didascalia Apostolorum*, pp. 188–89.

95. Tertullian, *Prescription against Heretics* 41 (translation and glosses by Steven Muir).

96. Gregory of Nazianzus, *Oration* 18.30. See especially the translation by Miller in *Women in Early Christianity*, p. 284.

97. In Gregory of Tours, *Vita Patrum: Life of the Fathers*, trans. and ed. by Fr. Seraphim Rose (Platina, CA: St. Herman of Alaska Brotherhood, 1988). See also accounts of the late sixth-century female saint Radegund, discussed in Gieselle De Nie, "Fatherly and Motherly Curing in Sixth-Century Gaul: Saint Radegund's Mysterium," in *Women and Miracle Stories: A Multidisciplinary Exploration*, ed. Anne-Marie Corte (Leiden: Brill, 2003), pp. 53–86.

98. VP Monegunde 3.

99. See Mary Beard, John North, and Simon Price, *Religions of Rome*, vols. 1–2 (Cambridge: Cambridge University Press, 1998), vol. 2, pp. 260–68; Naomi Janowitz, *Magic in the Roman World: Pagans, Jews and Christians* (London: Routledge, 2001); G. Luck, *Arcana Mundi: Magic and the Occult in the Greek and Roman World* (Baltimore: Johns Hopkins University Press, 1985); and M. Meyer and P. Mirecki, eds., *Ancient Magic and Ritual Power* (Leiden: Brill, 1995).

100. Homer, *Odyssey* 4.219ff., 10.213; Sophocles frs. 491–93 (Nauck).

101. See, for instance, Aristophanes, *Women at the Thesmophoria* 561.

102. See Flemming, "Women, Writing, and Medicine," p. 257.

103. Scribonius Largus, *Composite Remedies* 122.

104. Scribonius Largus, *Composite Remedies* 16.

105. *Greek Magical Papyri* 20.4–12.

106. See, for instance, Galen, *Mixing and Powers of Simple Drugs* 10.23 (12.300–301 Kühn).

107. The cases of Cleopatra, Elephantis, and Lais are discussed later on. The reader can find more information on the other women in Flemming, *Medicine and the Making of Roman Women*, pp. 39–42; Flemming, "Women, Writing, and Medicine"; relevant articles in Paul T. Keyser and Georgia L. Irby-Massie,

eds., *The Encyclopedia of Ancient Natural Scientists: The Greek Tradition and Its Many Heirs* (London: Routledge, 2008); Holt N. Parker, "Women Doctors in Greece, Rome, and the Byzantine Empire," in *Women Healers and Physicians: Climbing a Long Hill*, ed. Lilian R. Furst (Lexington, KY: University Press of Kentucky, 1997), pp. 131–50; and relevant articles in I. M. Plant, ed., *Women Writers of Ancient Greece and Rome: An Anthology* (London: Equinox, 2004).

108. See Parker, "Women Doctors"; and Plant, *Women Writers*.

109. Flemming, *Medicine and the Making of Roman Women*, p. 41.

110. Pliny, *Natural History* 28.81, 28.82.

111. Pliny, *Natural History* 28.38, 28.66, 28.82, 28.262, 32.135, 32.140.

112. Athenaeus, *Deipnosophists* 322a.

113. See David Bain, "Salpe's *ΠΑΙΓΝΙΑ*: Athenaeus 322A and Pliny. *H.N.* 28.38," *Classical Quarterly* 48 (1997): 262–68; and James N. Davidson, "Don't Try This at Home: Pliny's Salpe, Salpe's *Paignia* and Magic," *Classical Quarterly* 45 (1995): 590–92.

114. On the association between courtesans and fish in the Greek world, see James N. Davidson, *Courtesans and Fishcakes: The Consuming Passions of Classical Athens* (New York: St. Martin's, 1997).

115. Pliny, *Natural History* 28.81; Galen, *Composition of Remedies according to Places* 1.2 (12.416 Kühn); Martial 12.43.4; and Suetonius, *Tiberius* 43.2.

116. On Cleopatra, see Flemming, "Women, Writing, and Medicine," pp. 276–78.

117. Galen, *Composition of Remedies according to Places* 1.1 (12.403–4 Kühn): eight remedies against alopecia; Galen, ibid. 1.2 (12.432–34 Kühn): seven recipes to make the hair grow; Galen, ibid. 1.8 (12.492–93 Kühn): eight recipes against dandruff; Paul of Aegina 3.2.1: four recipes to dye the hair.

118. Aetius 8.6.

119. Metrodora 6. The *editio princeps* of this text is by A. P. Kousis, "Metrodora's Work 'On the Feminine Diseases of the Womb' according to the Greek Codex 75,3 of the Laurentian Library," *Praktika tēs Akadēmias Athēnōn* 20 (1945): 46–69. The passage examined here is at p. 57, ll. 14–16.

120. See Monica Green, "Medieval Gynaecological Texts: A Handlist," in *Women's Healthcare in the Medieval West: Texts and Contexts*, ed. Monica Green (Aldershot, UK: Ashgate, 2000), pp. 1–36, at pp. 8–10. Neither text has ever been edited according to modern standards.

121. See Hanson and Green, "Soranus of Ephesus," 987 (full reference in note 28).

122. Pliny mentions remedies by Olympias of Thebes in *Natural History* (20.226, 28.246, 28.253).

123. See Manfred Ullmann, *Die Medizin im Islam* (Leiden: Brill, 1970), pp. 127–28, for references to manuscripts.

124. Florence, Biblioteca Laurenziana, Pluteus 75.3, 4v–19r.

125. On this treatise, see most recently Marie-Hélène Congourdeau, " 'Metrodora' et son œuvre," in *Maladie et société à Byzance: Études présentées au 17e congrès international des sciences historiques (Madrid, 1990)*, ed. Evelyne Patlagean (Spoleto, Italy: Centro italiano di studi sull'Alto medioevo, 1993), pp. 57–96;

Flemming, "Women, Writing, and Medicine," pp. 276–79; and Holt N. Parker, "Metrodora," in Keyser and Irby-Massie, *Encyclopedia of Ancient Natural Scientists*, pp. 552–53.
126. Flemming, "Women, Writing, and Medicine," p. 275.
127. Gorgonia and Nonna, discussed in the previous section.
128. See Fronrobert, "Women with a Blood-Flow," pp. 127–28; and Selvidge, *Woman, Cult and Miracle Recital*, p. 20. On the statue, Eusebius, *Church History* 7.18; Sozomen, quoted in Eusebius H.E. 5.21; and Philostorgus in Amidon 7:3a (p. 91). Also Athanasius, *Vita St. Antonii* (NPNF 4:188–93).

chapter 5

1. Marilyn Arthur, "The Divided World of Iliad VI," in *Reflections of Women in Antiquity*, ed. Helene Foley (New York: Gordon and Breach, 1981), pp. 19–44.
2. Thucydides, *Peloponnesian War* 2.46.
3. Cicero, *de Re Publica* 5 (= Lactantius, *Epitome of the Divine Institutes* 33.5).
4. Herodotus, *Histories* 7.239.
5. Lisa C. Nevett, *House and Society in the Ancient Greek World* (Cambridge and New York: Cambridge University Press, 1999), pp. 53–79.
6. Lysias 1.9–10; translation in Nevett, *House and Society*, p. 18.
7. Susan Walker, "Women and Housing in Classical Greece: The Archaeological Evidence," in *Images of Women in Antiquity*, ed. Averil Cameron and Amélie Kuhrt (London: Croom Helm, 1983), pp. 81–91.
8. For example, Michael H. Jameson, "Domestic Space in the Greek City-State," in *Domestic Architecture and the Use of Space*, ed. Susan Kent (Cambridge and New York: Cambridge University Press, 1990), pp. 92–113.
9. David Cohen, "Seclusion, Separation, and the Status of Women in Classical Athens," in *Women in Antiquity*, ed. Ian McAuslan and Peter Walcot (Oxford and New York: Oxford University Press, 1996), pp. 134–45.
10. Lloyd Llewellyn-Jones, *Aphrodite's Tortoise: The Veiled Woman of Ancient Greece* (Swansea: Classical Press of Wales, 2003), p. 193.
11. Theognis of Megara 579–80; and Llewellyn-Jones, *Aphrodite's Tortoise*, p. 201.
12. Llewellyn-Jones, *Aphrodite's Tortoise*, pp. 199–200.
13. Riet Van Bremen, *The Limits of Participation: Women and Civic Life in the Greek East in the Hellenistic and Roman Periods* (Amsterdam: J. C. Gieben, 1996).
14. Plato, *Republic* 455d.
15. Plato, *Laws* 781a.
16. Xenophon, *Oeconomicus* 7.17–28.
17. Xenophon, *Oeconomicus* 9.15.
18. Froma I. Zeitlin, *Playing the Other: Gender and Society in Classical Greek Literature* (Chicago: University of Chicago Press, 1996), p. 353.
19. Ibid., p. 354.
20. Sophocles, *Antigone* 18–19.
21. M. W. Blundell, *Sophocles' Antigone* (Newburyport, MA: Focus Classical Library, 1998), p. 76.

22. Sophocles, *Antigone* 579.
23. Helene P. Foley, *Female Acts in Greek Tragedy* (Princeton, NJ: Princeton University Press, 2001), pp. 243–71.
24. Euripides, *Phoenissae* 88–102.
25. E. Craik, trans., *Euripides: Phoenecian Women* (Warminster, UK: Aris and Phillips, 1988), p. 133.
26. Arlene Saxonhouse, "Another Antigone: The Emergence of the Female Political Actor in Euripides' *Phoenician Women*," *Political Theory* 33 (4) (2005): 489.
27. Matthew Dillon, *Girls and Women in Classical Greek Religion* (London and New York: Routledge, 2002), pp. 37–72.
28. Ibid., pp. 109–20.
29. For a different view of this festival, see Tulloch's chapter on religion in this volume.
30. Van Bremen, *Limits of Participation*, pp. 11–81.
31. Livy, *Ab Urbe Condita* 1.9.1. On the different sources and explanations for the myth, see Gary B. Miles, *Livy: Reconstructing Early Rome* (Ithaca, NY: Cornell University Press, 1995), pp. 184–90.
32. Livy, *Ab Urbe Condita* 1.13.3.
33. Sallust, *Bellum Catilinae* 25.
34. Barbara W. Boyd, "*Virtus Effeminata* and Sallust's Sempronia," *Transactions of the American Philological Association* 117 (1987): 183–201.
35. Cornelius Nepos, *de Viris Illustribus* fr. 1.1.
36. Cicero, *Brutus* 211.
37. *Laudatio Turiae* 1.30.
38. Asconius, *On Cicero's Pro Milone* 32.
39. Appian, *Bellum Civile* 51.
40. Cicero, *Epistulae ad Brutum* 24.1.
41. Cicero, *Epistulae ad Atticum* 15.11.
42. Andrew Wallace-Hadrill, *Houses and Society in Pompeii and Herculaneum* (Princeton, NJ: Princeton University Press, 1994), pp. 8–14.
43. Vitruvius, *de Architectura* 6.5.1.
44. Suzanne Dixon, "A Family Business: Women's Role in Patronage and Politics at Rome 80–44 BC," *Classica et Mediaevalia* 34 (1983): 91–112.
45. Susan Treggiari, *Terentia, Tullia and Publilia: The Women of Cicero's Family* (London and New York: Routledge, 2007), pp. 87–96.
46. Cicero, *Pro Roscio Amerino* 27.
47. Cicero, *Epistulae ad Atticum* 12.51.3.
48. *Corpus Inscriptionum Latinarum* 10.810.
49. *Corpus Inscriptionum Latinarum* 4.1136; Ramsay MacMullen, "Women in Public in the Roman Empire," *Historia: Zeitschrift für Alte Geschichte* 29 (2) (1980): 210.
50. Quintilian, *Institutio Oratoria* 1.1.6.
51. Appian, *Bellum Civile* 4.32.
52. A. J. Marshall, "Ladies at Law: The Role of Women in the Roman Civil Law Courts," in *Studies in Latin Literature and Roman History*, vol. 5, ed. Carl Deroux (Brussels: Collection Latomus, 1989), pp. 35–54.

53. Jane F. Gardner, *Women in Roman Law and Society* (Bloomington: Indiana University Press, 1986), pp. 233–37.

54. Valerius Maximus, *Memorable Words and Deeds* 8.2.2.

55. *Digest of Roman Law* 2.13.4, 10.

56. *Corpus Inscriptionum Latinarum* 4.4528, 8203, 8204.

57. Galen, *On Prognosis* 8.8.

58. Ausonius, *Parentalia* 6.6.

59. Gardner, *Women in Roman Law*, pp. 130, 132–33.

60. *Digest of Roman Law* 23.2.43.1.

61. *Digest of Roman Law* 23.2.43.9.

62. *Codex Justinianus* 9.9.28.

63. Natalie B. Kampen, "Social Status and Gender in Roman Art: The Case of the Saleswoman," in *Feminism and Art History*, ed. Norma Broude and Mary D. Garrard (New York: Harper and Row, 1982), pp. 63–78.

64. *Corpus Inscriptionum Latinarum* 1.1011.

65. Tom Hillard, "On the Stage, behind the Curtain: Images of Politically Active Women in the Late Roman Republic," in *Stereotypes of Women in Power: Historical Perspectives and Revisionist Views*, ed. Barbara Garlick, Suzanne Dixon, and Pauline Allen, Contributions in Women's Studies 125 (London: Greenwood, 1992), pp. 37–64.

66. For a different view of women's roles in the early house church, see Tulloch's chapter on religion in this volume. See also Carolyn Osiek and Margaret Y. Macdonald, with Janet H. Tulloch, *A Woman's Place: House Churches in Earliest Christianity* (Minneapolis: Fortress, 2006).

67. Suetonius, *Divus Augustus* 84.

68. M.B. Flory, "*Sic exempla parantur*: Livia's Shrine to Concordia and the Porticus Liviae," *Historia* 33 (1984): 309–30; and Nicholas Purcell, "Livia and the Womanhood of Rome," *Proceedings of the Cambridge Philological Society* 32 (1986): 78–105.

69. Mireille Corbier, "Male Power and Legitimacy through Women: The Domus Augusta under the Julio-Claudians," in *Women in Antiquity: New Assessments*, ed. Richard Hawley and Barbara Levick (London and New York: Routledge, 1995), pp. 178–93.

70. Elaine Fantham, Helene Peet Foley, Natalie Boymel Kampen, Sarah B. Pomeroy, and H. Alan Shapiro, "Women of the High and Later Empire: Conformity and Diversity," in *Women in the Classical World: Image and Text* (New York and Oxford: Oxford University Press, 1994), pp. 345–94.

71. Eusebius, *Life of Constantine* 2.44.

72. Carolyn L. Connor, *Women of Byzantium* (New Haven, CT: Yale University Press, 2004).

Chapter 6

1. Aristotle, *Politics* 1253b1.

2. Keith Bradley, *Slavery and Society at Rome* (Cambridge: Cambridge University Press, 1994), pp. 145–53.

3. Although female slaves were not used overtly for breeding purposes; Jane F. Gardner, *Women in Roman Law and Society* (London: Croom Helm, 1986), pp. 206–9.

4. Siegfried Jaekel, ed., *Menandri Sententiae* (Leipzig, Germany: Teubner, 1964), *Synkrisis* 1.209–10.

5. William V. Harris, *Ancient Literacy* (Cambridge, MA: Harvard University Press, 1989), p. 114.

6. Susan Guettel Cole, "Could Greek Women Read and Write?" in *Reflections of Women in Antiquity*, ed. Helene P. Foley (New York: Gordon and Breach, 1981), p. 219; and Harris, *Ancient Literacy*, pp. 3–24.

7. Harris, *Ancient Literacy*, p. 114 (Attica), p. 141 (Hellenistic cities), and p. 267 (Italy).

8. For girls, Teos but also possibly Pergamum. See Raffaella Cribiore, *Gymnastics of the Mind: Greek Education in Hellenistic and Roman Egypt* (Princeton, NJ, and Oxford: Princeton University Press, 2001), pp. 83–85; and Sarah B. Pomeroy, "*Technikai kai Mousikai*: The Education of Women in the Fourth Century and in the Hellenistic Age," *American Journal of Ancient History* 2 (1977): 51–68.

9. George Kennedy, "The History of Latin Education," in "Latinitas: The Tradition and Teaching of Latin," ed. M. Santirocco, special issue, *Helios* 14 (2) (1987): 7–8.

10. Cribiore, *Gymnastics of the Mind*, p. 75.

11. Harris, *Ancient Literacy*, p. 136.

12. Teresa Morgan, *Literate Education in the Hellenistic and Roman Worlds* (Cambridge: Cambridge University Press, 1998), pp. 3–4.

13. Jaekel, *Menandri Sententiae* 171, 203. The three epigraphs in this chapter are examples of Menandrian *gnomai*. See Morgan, *Literate Education*, pp. 135–38; and Heather I. Waddell Gruber, "The Women of Greek Declamation and the Reception of Comic Stereotypes" (PhD diss., University of Iowa, 2008).

14. Elite Roman women married younger than those of the middle classes, in their early to mid-teens as opposed to the mid- to late teens, with twelve being the minimum legal age for marriage.

15. Harris, *Ancient Literacy*, pp. 113–14. See also Sarah B. Pomeroy, *Spartan Women* (Oxford: Oxford University Press, 2002), p. 5.

16. Pomeroy, *Spartan Women*, p. 8.

17. Elaine Fantham, Helene Peet Foley, Natalie Boymel Kampen, Sarah B. Pomeroy, and H. Alan Shapiro, *Women in the Classical World: Image and Text* (New York and Oxford: Oxford University Press, 1994), p. 60.

18. In the *Republic* (5.452a, 456b–c) just the guardians, extended to all women in the *Laws* (7.804d, 7.806a).

19. Aristotle, *Politics* 1260b.

20. Sarah B. Pomeroy, *Goddesses, Whores, Wives, and Slaves: Women in Classical Antiquity.* New York: Schocken Books, 1975), p. 131, citing Stobaeus 16.30.

21. Quintilian, *Institutio Oratoria* 1.1.6.

22. Mary R. Lefkowitz and Maureen B. Fant, eds., *Women's Life in Greece and Rome: A Source Book in Translation*, 2nd ed. (Baltimore: Johns Hopkins University Press, 1992), pp. 50–54.

23. Cribiore, *Gymnastics of the Mind*, p. 76.

24. Ibid., p. 76.

25. See Roger S. Bagnall and Raffaella Cribiore, eds., *Women's Letters from Ancient Egypt: 300 B.C.–A.D. 800* (Ann Arbor: University of Michigan Press, 2006); and Jane Rowlandson, ed., *Women and Society in Greek and Roman Egypt: A Sourcebook* (Cambridge: Cambridge University Press, 1998).

26. *Vindolanda Tablet* 2.291. This letter and two others (*Vindolanda Tablet* 2.292, 3.663) are the earliest known examples of handwriting in Latin by a woman. See also Judith Hallett, "The Vindolanda Letters from Claudia Severa," in *Women Writing Latin in Roman Antiquity, Late Antiquity, and the Early Christian Era*, ed. Laurie J. Churchill, Phyllis R. Brown, and Jane E. Jeffrey (New York and London: Routledge, 2002), pp. 93–99. Photographs and texts are available at Vindolanda Tablets Online: http://vindolanda.csad.ox.ac.uk/.

27. Alan K. Bowman, *Life and Letters on the Roman Frontier: Vindolanda and Its People* (London: British Museum Press, 2003), pp. 79–96.

28. I. M. Plant, ed., *Women Writers of Ancient Greece and Rome: An Anthology* (London: Equinox, 2004), p. 1.

29. Ibid., p. 2.

30. Ibid., p. 7n1.

31. See Emily Hemelrijk, *Matrona Docta: Educated Women in the Roman Elite from Cornelia to Julia Domna* (London and New York: Routledge, 1999).

32. Ibid., p. 56.

33. See Raymond Starr, "The Circulation of Literary Texts in the Roman World," *Classical Quarterly* 37 (1987): 213–23; and L. D. Reynolds and N. G. Wilson, *Scribes and Scholars: A Guide to the Transmission of Greek and Latin Literature*, 3rd ed. (Oxford: Clarendon, 1991).

34. Plant, *Women Writers*. On women's philosophical writings, see also Bella Vivante, *Daughters of Gaia: Women in the Ancient Mediterranean World* (Westport, CT: Praeger, 2007), pp. 155–73.

35. Gillian Clark, *Women in Late Antiquity: Pagan and Christian Life-Styles* (Oxford: Oxford University Press, 1993), p. 130.

36. Plant, *Women Writers*, pp. 164–68.

37. Ibid., pp. 170–88.

38. Ibid., pp. 198–209. Many of her other works also are extant.

39. Clark, *Women in Late Antiquity*, p. 130.

40. Her scholarly work survives only in summary form. See Jane McIntosh Snyder, *The Woman and the Lyre: Women Writers in Classical Greece and Rome* (Carbondale: Southern Illinois University Press, 1989), pp. 113–20.

41. Plant, *Women Writers*, pp. 189–97; and Snyder, *Woman and the Lyre*, pp. 141–51.

42. See Barbara K. Gold, "Hrotswitha Writes Herself: *Clamor Validus Gandeshemensis*," in *Sex and Gender in Medieval and Renaissance Texts: The Latin Tradition*, ed. Barbara K. Gold, Paul Allen Miller, and Charles Platter (Albany: State University of New York Press, 1997), pp. 41–70; and Peter Dronke, *Women Writers of the Middle Ages* (Cambridge: Cambridge University Press, 1984), pp. 55–83.

43. Jaekel, *Menandri Sententiae* 363.

44. Richard Saller, "Household and Gender," in *The Cambridge Economic History of the Greco-Roman World*, vol. 1, ed. Walter Scheidel, Ian Morris, and Richard Saller (Cambridge: Cambridge University Press, 2007), pp. 92–94.

45. Ibid., p. 87.

46. Xenophon, *Oeconomicus* 7.18ff.

47. Susan Treggiari, "Lower-Class Women in the Roman Economy," *Florilegium* 1 (1979): 78. Sandra Joshel reaches similar conclusions in *Work, Identity, and Legal Status at Rome: A Study of Occupational Inscriptions* (Norman: University of Oklahoma Press, 1992), p. 69.

48. Treggiari, "Lower-Class Women," pp. 78–79.

49. Jon-Christian Billigmeier and Judy A. Turner, "The Socio-Economic Roles of Women in Mycenaean Greece: A Brief Survey from Evidence of the Linear B Tablets," in Foley, *Reflections of Women*, pp. 1–18.

50. Suetonius, *Divus Augustus* 63, 64.

51. Homer, *Odyssey* 5.61–62 and 10.220–23.

52. Quintilian, *Institutio Oratoria* 1.1.4–5; Soranus, *Gynecology* 2.17.

53. Vivante, *Daughters of Gaia*, pp. 99–103.

54. Saller, "Household and Gender," p. 104. See also Sarah B. Pomeroy, *Women in Hellenistic Egypt: From Alexander to Cleopatra* (New York: Schocken Books, 1984), pp. 125–73.

55. Susan Treggiari, "Jobs for Women," *American Journal of Ancient History* 1 (1976): 91.

56. Ibid., pp. 93–98.

57. Cribiore, *Gymnastics of the Mind*, p. 77.

58. 1 Tim. 2:12; Cribiore, *Gymnastics of the Mind*, p. 81; and Clark, *Women in Late Antiquity*, p. 128. For women's leadership roles in early house churches, see Carolyn Osiek and Margaret Y. Macdonald, with Janet H. Tulloch, *A Woman's Place: House Churches in Earliest Christianity* (Minneapolis: Fortress, 2006).

59. Lefkowitz and Fant, *Women's Life*, pp. 213–15.

60. Jaekel, *Menandri Sententiae* 584. The point is that both orators and prostitutes practice dissimulation.

61. Plutarch, *Solon* 23.

62. See Stephanie L. Budin, "Sacred Prostitution in the First Person," in *Prostitutes and Courtesans in the Ancient World*, ed. Christopher A. Faraone and Laura K. McClure (Madison: University of Wisconsin Press, 2006), pp. 77–92; and Budin, *The Myth of Sacred Prostitution in Antiquity* (New York: Cambridge University Press, 2008).

63. On definitions see Thomas McGinn, *The Economy of Prostitution in the Roman World: A Study of Social History and the Brothel* (Ann Arbor: University of Michigan Press, 2004), p. 7; and Edward E. Cohen, "Free and Unfree Sexual Work: An Economic Analysis of Athenian Prostitution," in Faraone and McClure, *Prostitutes and Courtesans*, p. 95.

64. Madeleine Henry, "Prostitution, Secular," in *The Oxford Classical Dictionary*, ed. Simon Hornblower and Anthony Spawforth (Oxford: Oxford University Press, 2003), p. 1264.

65. Under this definition even marriage was a form of prostitution, since it involved voluntary (as well as involuntary) sex in exchange for protection, security, and social standing. This was recognized by Hesiod, who considered marriage the exchange of a woman's sexual services for economic benefits (*Works and Days* 373–75, cited in Cohen, "Free and Unfree Sexual Work," p. 115n19).

66. For the cultural and linguistic complexities of these two terms, see Laura K. McClure, *Courtesans at Table: Gender and Greek Literary Culture in Athenaeus* (New York and London: Routledge, 2003), pp. 9–18; and Cohen, "Free and Unfree Sexual Work," pp. 95–99.

67. Plutarch, *Pericles* 24.3. On Epicurean *hetairai*-philosophers, see Snyder, *Woman and the Lyre*, pp. 101–5. For Athenian *hetairai* in general, see Marilyn B. Skinner, *Sexuality in Greek and Roman Culture* (Malden, MA: Blackwell, 2005), pp. 97–109.

68. Jane F. Gardner and Kelly Olson argue that the toga was *not* mandated dress for prostitutes or convicted adulteresses. See Gardner, *Women in Roman Law*, pp. 251–52; Olson, "*Matrona* and Whore: Clothing and Definition in Roman Antiquity," in Faraone and McClure, *Prostitutes and Courtesans*, pp. 186–204; and Olson, *Dress and the Roman Woman: Self-Presentation and Society* (New York: Routledge, 2008), pp. 47–51.

69. Thomas McGinn, "Zoning Shame in the Roman City," in Faraone and McClure, *Prostitutes and Courtesans*, pp. 161–76.

70. McGinn, *Economy of Prostitution*, p. 47.

71. Ibid., pp. 49–50.

72. Pomeroy, *Goddesses*, p. 92, alluding to the case of Neaera, a former slave prostitute who was living as the wife of a citizen (Demosthenes 59 [*Against Neaera*]). Male citizens who prostituted themselves lost the right to speak in the assembly, to hold public office, and to enter temples (Aeschines 1.21 [*Against Timarchus*], citing the laws of Solon).

73. Tacitus, *Annales* 2.85.

74. McGinn, *Economy of Prostitution*, pp. 134–57.

75. Justinian, *Novellae* 14.

76. Suetonius, *Gaius* 41. There are similar stories about Nero (Suetonius, *Nero* 11.2; Tacitus, *Annales* 14.14).

77. Catharine Edwards, "Unspeakable Professions: Public Performance and Prostitution in Ancient Rome," in *Roman Sexualities*, ed. Judith P. Hallett and Marilyn B. Skinner (Princeton, NJ: Princeton University Press, 1997), pp. 85–90.

78. Ibid., pp. 73, 75.

79. Gardner, *Women in Roman Law*, pp. 132–34.

80. Gruber, "Women of Greek Declamation," p. 119.

81. See the teachings of Paul, excerpted in Lefkowitz and Fant, *Women's Life*, pp. 307–9; and Clark, *Women in Late Antiquity*, p. 29.

82. Paul excluded prostitutes and their clients from the church (1 Cor. 6:15–16).

83. Augustine, *De Ordine* 2.12; and McGinn, "Zoning Shame," pp. 167–72.

84. *Codex Justinianus* 11.41.7; and Clark, *Women in Late Antiquity*, p. 30.

85. Justinian, *Novellae* 14.1.

86. Procopius, *Buildings* 1.9.2–9; and Clark, *Women in Late Antiquity*, pp. 30–31.

87. Michael Maas, ed., *Readings in Late Antiquity: A Sourcebook* (London and New York: Routledge, 2000), p. 223.
88. Ibid., pp. 223–25; Clark observes that these women do not marry but go on to lead monastic lives (*Women in Late Antiquity*, p. 31).
89. For examples, see Holt N. Parker, "Love's Body Anatomized: The Ancient Erotic Handbooks and the Rhetoric of Sexuality," in *Pornography and Representation in Greece and Rome*, ed. Amy Richlin (New York and Oxford: Oxford University Press, 1992), p. 106; and Hemelrijk, *Matrona Docta*, pp. 84–86.
90. Sempronia, for example (Sallust, *Bellum Catilinae* 25).
91. Hemelrijk, *Matrona Docta*, pp. 64–71.
92. Edwards, "Unspeakable Professions."
93. Laura K. McClure, "Introduction," in Faraone and McClure, *Prostitutes and Courtesans*, p. 8.

Chapter 7

1. See W.K. Lacey, "Thucydides II, 45, 2," *Proceedings of the Cambridge Philological Society* 10 (1964): 47–49; O. Andersen, "The Widows, the City and Thucydides (II.45.2)," *Symbolae Osloenses* 62 (1987): 33–49; and Paul Cartledge, "The Silent Women of Thucydides: 2.45.2 Re-Viewed," in *Nomodeiktes*, ed. R.M. Roden and J. Farrell (Ann Arbor: University of Michigan Press, 1993), pp. 125–32.
2. For Sparta: Paul Cartledge, "Spartan Wives: Liberation or License?" *Classical Quarterly* 31 (1981): 84–105; Elaine Fantham, Helene Peet Foley, Natalie Boymel Kampen, Sarah B. Pomeroy, and H. Alan Shapiro, "Spartan Women: Women in a Warrior Society," in *Women in the Classical World: Image and Text* (New York and Oxford: Oxford University Press, 1994), pp. 56–67; and Sarah B. Pomeroy, *Families in Classical and Hellenistic Greece: Representations and Realities* (Oxford: Oxford University Press, 1997), pp. 39–66. For Gortyn: R.F. Willetts, *The Civilization of Ancient Crete* (London: Orion, 1977); see also W.K. Lacey, *The Family in Classical Greece* (London: Thames and Hudson, 1968), pp. 208–16.
3. Matthew P.J. Dillon, *Girls and Women in Classical Greek Religion* (London and New York: Routledge, 2002), pp. 84–90.
4. Ibid., pp. 98–100.
5. Hesiod, *Works and Days* 57–82, *Theogony* 570–89; see also Froma I. Zeitlin, "Signifying Difference: The Myth of Pandora," in *Women in Antiquity: New Assessments*, ed. Richard Hawley and Barbara Levick (London and New York: Routledge, 1995), pp. 58–74.
6. Euripides, *Medea* 465–95; M. Shaw, "The Female Intruder: Women in Fifth Century Drama," *Classical Philology* 70 (1975): 255–68; and M. Katz, "The Character of Tragedy: Women and the Greek Imagination," *Arethusa* 27 (1994): 96–100.
7. Aeschylus, *Agamemnon* 1377–98; and Froma I. Zeitlin, *Playing the Other: Gender and Society in Classical Greek Literature* (Chicago: University of Chicago Press, 1996), pp. 89–92.

8. Sappho, *Fragments* 16, 132; J. Winkler, "Gardens of Nymphs: Public and Private in Sappho's Lyrics," in *Reflections of Women in Antiquity*, ed. Helene P. Foley (New York: Gordon and Breach, 1981), pp. 63–89; J. M. Snyder, "Public Occasion and Private Passion in the Lyrics of Sappho of Lesbos," in *Women's History and Ancient History*, ed. Sarah B. Pomeroy (Chapel Hill: University of North Carolina Press, 1991), pp. 1–19; and M. S. Cyrino, *In Pandora's Jar: Lovesickness in Early Greek Poetry* (Lanham, MD: University Press of America, 1995), pp. 133–64.

9. Herodotus, *Histories* 7.99, 7.103, 8.87.1–88.3; C. Dewald, "Women and Culture in Herodotos' Histories," in Foley, *Reflections of Women*, pp. 91–125; and R. V. Munson, "Artemisia in Herodotos," *Classical Antiquity* 7 (1988): 91–106.

10. Plutarch, *Pericles* 24.2–9; Aristophanes, *Acharnians* 524–29; Madeleine M. Henry, *Prisoner of History: Aspasia of Miletos and Her Biographical Tradition* (Oxford: Oxford University Press, 1995); and Anthony J. Podlecki, *Perikles and His Circle* (London and New York: Routledge, 1998), pp. 109–17.

11. Aristophanes, *Lysistrata* 507–20, 565–97; Shaw, "Female Intruder," 264–65; and Jeffrey Henderson, "Lysistrate: The Play and Its Themes," in *Aristophanes: Essays in Interpretation*, ed. J. Henderson (Cambridge: Cambridge University Press, 1980), pp. 153–218.

12. Aristotle, *Politics* 1269b39–1270a3.

13. Pausanias, *Description of Greece* 3.8.1; Plutarch, *Life of Agis* 4.1–2; J. Redfield, "The Women of Sparta," *Classical Journal* 73 (1978): 146–61; Cartledge, "Spartan Wives"; and Sarah B. Pomeroy, *Spartan Women* (Oxford: Oxford University Press, 2002).

14. Herodotus, *Histories* 5.51.1–3, 7.239; Plutarch, *Life of Lycurgus* 14.1–8, *Moralia* 225a and S. Hodkinson, "Land Tenure and Inheritance in Classical Sparta," *Classical Quarterly* 36 (1980): 378–406.

15. Paul Cartledge and Antony Spawforth, *Hellenistic and Roman Sparta* (London and New York: Routledge, 1989), pp. 38–47.

16. Simonides, *Fragment* 36; and Herodotus, *Histories* 5.92f.1–92g.1.

17. Thucydides, *Peloponnesian War* 6.59.3; and D. Harvey, "Women in Thucydides," *Arethusa* 18 (1985): pp. 67–90.

18. Athenaeus, *Deipnosophists* 13.557b–e; Diodorus Siculus, *Library of History* 19.11; Elizabeth D. Carney, *Olympias: Mother of Alexander the Great* (London and New York: Routledge, 2006), pp. 60–87; and Carney, *Women and Monarchy in Macedonia* (Norman: University of Oklahoma Press, 2000), pp. 62–67, 85–88, 119–23, 146–48.

19. Carney, *Women and Monarchy*, pp. 182–83.

20. Diodorus Siculus, *Library of History* 20.37.

21. Diodorus Siculus, *Library of History* 16.36; and Demosthenes, *Orations* 15.11.

22. Strabo, *Geographical Description* 14.2.17; Simon Hornblower, *Mausolus* (Oxford: Oxford University Press, 1982); and S. Ruzicka, *Politics of a Persian Dynasty: The Hecatomnids in the Fourth Century BC* (Norman: University of Oklahoma Press, 1992).

23. John E. G. Whitehorne, *Cleopatras* (London and New York: Routledge, 1994), pp. 87, 91; Sarah B. Pomeroy, *Women in Hellenistic Egypt: From Alexander to*

Cleopatra. (New York: Schocken Books, 1984), pp. 11–28; and S. M. Burstein, "Arsinoe II. Philadelphos: A Revisionist View," in *Philip II, Alexander the Great and the Macedonian Heritage*, ed. W. Adams and E. Borza (Lanham, MD: University Press of America, 1982), pp. 197–212.

24. Elizabeth D. Carney, "The Reappearance of Royal Sibling Marriages in Ptolemaic Egypt," *Past and Present* 237 (1987): 420–39; and G. Hölbl, *A History of the Ptolemaic Empire* (London and New York: Routledge, 2000), pp. 127–33.

25. Whitehorne, *Cleopatras*, pp. 80–88; and Hölbl, *History of the Ptolemaic Empire*, pp. 134–93.

26. L. Mooren, "The Wives and Children of Ptolemy VIII Euergetes II," *Proceedings of the XVIII Congress of Papyrology* 2 (1988): 435–44; Whitehorne, *Cleopatras*, pp. 89–131; and Hölbl, *History of the Ptolemaic Empire*, pp. 194–203.

27. Whitehorne, *Cleopatras*, pp. 132–48, 174–77; and Hölbl, *History of the Ptolemaic Empire*, pp. 204–21.

28. Whitehorne, *Cleopatras*, pp. 177–85; Hölbl, *History of the Ptolemaic Empire*, pp. 222–30; and M. Siani-Davies, "Ptolemy XII. Auletes and the Romans," *Historia* 46 (1997): 306–40.

29. Duane W. Roller, *Cleopatra: A Biography* (Oxford: Oxford University Press, 2010); Whitehorne, *Cleopatras*, pp. 186–96; and Hölbl, *History of the Ptolemaic Empire*, pp. 231–56, 289–303.

30. Whitehorne, *Cleopatras*, pp. 197–202.

31. Sallust, *Bellum Catilinae* 24.3–25.5; and Fantham, "Excursus: The 'New' Woman: Representation and Reality," in *Women in the Classical World*, pp. 280–85.

32. Cicero, *Philippics* 5.8.22; Plutarch, *Life of Antony* 10; C. L. Babcock, "The Early Career of Fulvia," *American Journal of Philology* 86 (1965): 1–32; R. A. Bauman, *Women and Politics in Ancient Rome* (London and New York: Routledge, 1992), pp. 78–90; and D. Delia, "Fulvia Reconsidered," in Pomeroy, *Women's History and Ancient History*, pp. 97–217.

33. Plutarch, *Life of Lucullus* 6.2–5.

34. Mary Beard, "The Sexual Status of Vestal Virgins," *Journal of Roman Studies* 70 (1980): 12–27; and Beard, "Re-reading (Vestal) Virginity," in Hawley and Levick, *Women in Antiquity*, pp. 166–77.

35. A. A. Barrett, *Livia: First Lady of Imperial Rome* (New Haven, CT: Yale University Press, 2000).

36. Ibid., pp. 115–73; P. A. Watson, *Ancient Stepmothers: Myth, Misogyny and Reality* (Leiden: Brill, 1995); Barbara Levick, "Julii and Claudii?" *Greece and Rome* 22 (1972): 29–38; and M. B. Flory, "Livia and the History of Public Honorific Statues for Women in Rome," *Transactions of the American Philological Association* 123 (1993): 287–308.

37. Tacitus, *Annales* 1.33, 2.71–72, 3.1–4.

38. A. Barrett, *Agrippina: Sex, Power and Politics in the Early Roman Empire* (New Haven, CT: Yale University Press, 1996), pp. 1–39; M. Kaplan, "*Agrippina semper atrox*: A Study in Tacitus' Characterization of Women," in *Studies in Latin Literature and Roman History*, vol. 1, ed. C. Deroux (Brussels: Collection Latomus 164, 1978), pp. 410–17; and D. C. A. Shotter, "Agrippina the Elder—a Woman in a Man's World," *Historia* 49 (2000): 341–57.

39. Suetonius, *Nero* 33, *Claudius* 44; C. Ehrhardt, "Messalina and the Succession to Claudius," *Antichthon* 12 (1978): 51–71; and Barbara Levick, *Claudius* (New Haven, CT, and London: Yale University Press, 1993), pp. 55–69.

40. Barrett, *Agrippina*, pp. 95–195; Miriam T. Griffin, *Nero: The End of a Dynasty* (New Haven, CT, and London: Yale University Press, 1985); and Levick, *Claudius*, pp. 65–78.

41. Suetonius, *Nero* 34.1, 37.3.

42. Barbara Levick, *Julia Domna* (London and New York: Routledge, 2007); G. W. Bowersock, "The Circle of Julia Domna," in *Greek Sophists in the Roman Empire* (Oxford: Clarendon, 1969), pp. 101–9; M. G. Williams, "Studies in the Lives of Roman Empresses: I. Julia Domna," *American Journal of Archaeology* 6 (1902): 259–305; and Anthony R. Birley, *Septimius Severus* (London and New York: Routledge, 1999), pp. 68–81; see also G. Turton, *The Syrian Princesses: The Women Who Ruled Rome, AD 193–235* (ACLS Humanities E-Book; London: Cassell, 2009).

43. Leonardo de Arrizabalaga y Prado, *The Emperor Elagabalus—Fact or Fiction?* (Cambridge: Cambridge University Press, 2010), esp. pp. 183–204; and Ronald Syme, "The Reign of Severus Alexander," in *Emperors and Biography: Studies in the Historia Augusta*, ed. R. Syme (Oxford: Oxford University Press, 1971), pp. 146–62.

44. Warwick Ball, *Rome in the East: The Transformation of an Empire* (London and New York: Routledge, 2001), pp. 74–86; and Richard Stoneman, *Palmyra and Its Empire: Zenobia's Revolt against Rome* (Ann Arbor: University of Michigan Press, 1995).

45. J. W. Drijvers, *Helena Augusta* (Leiden: Brill, 1997); and Hans A. Pohlsander, *The Emperor Constantine* (London and New York: Routledge, 2004), esp. pp. 57–62.

46. Kenneth G. Holum, *Theodosian Empresses: Women and Imperial Domination in Late Antiquity* (Berkeley: University of California Press, 1982), pp. 48–78; and Alan Cameron and Jacqueline Long, *Barbarians and Politics at the Court of Arcadius* (Berkeley: University of California Press, 1993).

47. Holum, *Theodosian Empresses*, pp. 79–111, 147–228.

48. Lynda Garland, *Byzantine Empresses: Women and Power in Byzantium AD 527–1204* (London and New York: Routledge, 1999), pp. 49–57, 136–57.

49. Ibid., pp. 73–94, 122–25.

50. Theophanes, *Chronographia* AM 6134; Judith Herrin, *Women in Purple: Rulers of Medieval Byzantium* (London: Weidenfeld, 2001); and Garland, *Byzantine Empresses*, pp. 66–72.

51. Procopius, *Wars* 1.24, *Secret History* 10.13; J.A.S. Evans, *Empress Theodora, Partner of Justinian* (Austin: University of Texas Press, 2002); and Garland, *Byzantine Empresses*, pp. 11–39.

52. Malalas, *Chronicle* 441; and Theophanes, *Chronographia* AM 6025.

53. Theophanes Continuatus, *Chronographia* 227–28, 318; and Skylitzes, *Synopsis of History* 122–23.

54. Thietmar, *Chronicon*, ed. W. Trillmich (Darmstadt, Germany: Wissenschaftliche Buchgesellschaft, 1957), pp. 114–15; and K. Ciggaar, "Theophano: An Empress

Reconsidered," in *The Empress Theophano: Byzantium and the West at the Turn of the First Millennium*, ed. Adelbert Davids (Cambridge: Cambridge University Press, 1995), pp. 49–63.

Chapter 8

1. Having been asked quite late to contribute to this publication, I needed to include images that were readily accessible; this explains why the collection of the British Museum is overused here. I would like to thank Christopher Sutherns, the picture library account manager of British Museum Images, for his prompt and effective service. Time constraints also explain the sometimes idiosyncratic bibliographic references. Generally I refer in notes, without much discussion, to publications that can be found relatively easily by a nonspecialist reader. I am grateful to the editor for her patience and to her and Amy Richlin for their helpful bibliographic advice.

2. The following is a selection of sources useful for the variety of their illustrations or their overviews of time periods and evidence: Lucilla Burn, *Hellenistic Art from Alexander the Great to Augustus* (Los Angeles: Getty Publications, 2005), who provides a thematic overview of Hellenistic art; John R. Clarke, *Art in the Lives of Ordinary Romans: Visual Representation and Non-Elite Viewers in Italy, 100 B.C.–A.D. 315* (Berkeley: University of California Press, 2003); John R. Clarke, *Looking at Lovemaking: Constructions of Sexuality in Roman Art 100 B.C.–A.D. 250* (Berkeley: University of California Press, 1998); John R. Clarke, *Roman Sex 100 B.C.–A.D. 250* (New York: Harry H. Abrams, 2003); Jonathan Edmonson and Alison Keith (eds.), *Roman Dress and the Fabrics of Roman Culture* (Toronto: University of Toronto Press, 2008); Ian Jenkins and Victoria Turner, *The Greek Body* (Los Angeles: J. Paul Getty Museum, 2010); Nicolaos Kaltsas and Alan Shapiro, eds., *Worshipping Women: Ritual and Reality in Classical Athens* (New York: Alexander S. Onassis Public Benefit Foundation, 2008); Diana E. E. Kleiner and Susan B. Matheson, eds., *I Claudia: Women in Ancient Rome* (Austin: University of Texas Press, 1996); Diana E. E. Kleiner and Susan B. Matheson, eds., *I Claudia II: Women in Roman Art and Society* (Austin: University of Texas Press, 2000); Fred S. Kleiner, *Gardner's Art through the Ages: The Western Perspective*, 13th ed. (Boston: Wadsworth, 2010); François Lissarrague, *Greek Vases: The Athenians and Their Images*, trans. K. Allen (New York: Riverside, 2001); Mary R. Lefkowitz and Maureen B. Fant, *Women's Life in Greece and Rome: A Source Book in Translation* (Baltimore: Johns Hopkins University Press, 2005); Sybille Haynes, *Etruscan Civilization: A Cultural History* (Los Angeles: J. Paul Getty Trust, 2000); Sian Lewis, *The Athenian Woman: An Iconographic Handbook* (London: Routledge, 2002); Mary T. Malone, *Women and Christianity: The First Thousand Years* (Maryknoll, NY: Orbis Books, 2001), pp. 2–11 (useful timeline); Jenifer Neils and John H. Oakley, *Coming of Age in Ancient Greece: Images of Childhood from the Classical Past* (New Haven, CT: Yale University Press, 2003); John H. Oakley and Rebecca H. Sinos, *The Wedding in Ancient Athens* (Madison: University of Wisconsin Press, 1993); Roberta Pazanelli, Eike Schmidt, and Kenneth Lapatin, eds., *The Color of Life: Polychromy in Sculpture from Antiquity to the Present* (Los

Angeles: Getty Research Institute, 2008); Nancy H. Ramage and Andrew Ramage, *Roman Art* (Upper Saddle River, NJ: Pearson Prentice Hall, 2005), which provides a general overview of Etruscan to late Roman art and historical periods with illustrations; Ellen D. Reeder, *Pandora: Women in Classical Greece* (Princeton, NJ: Princeton University Press, 1995); Brunilde Sismodo Ridgway, *Hellenistic Sculpture III: The Styles of ca. 100–31 B.C.* (Madison: University of Wisconsin Press, 2002); Martin Robertson, *The Art of Vase-Painting in Classical Athens* (Cambridge: Cambridge University Press, 1992); Marilyn B. Skinner, *Sexuality in Greek and Roman Culture* (Malden, MA: Blackwell, 2005); Andrew Stewart, *Art, Desire, and the Body in Ancient Greece* (Cambridge: Cambridge University Press, 1997); Andrew Stewart, *Classical Greece and the Birth of Western Art* (Cambridge, Cambridge University Press, 2008); Janet H. Tulloch, "Women Leaders in Family Funerary Banquets," in *A Woman's Place: House Churches in Earliest Christianity*, ed. Carolyn Osiek and Margaret Y. Macdonald (Minneapolis: Fortress, 2006); Christiane Vorster, "The Large and Small Herculaneum Women Sculptures," in *The Herculaneum Women: History, Context, Identities*, ed. Jens Daehner (Los Angeles: J. Paul Getty Museum, 2007).

3. For a look at the difficulties of juggling written, visual, and archaeological evidence in interpreting women's lives, see Joan Breton Connelly, *Portrait of a Priestess: Women and Ritual in Ancient Greece* (Princeton, NJ: Princeton University Press, 2007), chap. 1. Overviews of research on women in the past twenty years include Shelby Brown, "Feminist Research in Archaeology: What Does It Mean? Why Is It Taking So Long?" in *Feminist Theory and the Classics*, ed. Nancy S. Rabinowitz and Amy Richlin (New York: Routledge, 1993); Shelby Brown, "Ways of Seeing Women in Antiquity: An Introduction to Feminism in Classical Archaeology and Ancient Art History," in *Naked Truths: Women, Sexuality, and Gender in Classical Art and Archaeology*, ed. Ann Olga Koloski-Ostrow and Claire L. Lyons (London: Routledge, 1997); Anthony Corbeill, "Gender Studies," in *The Oxford Handbook of Roman Studies*, ed. Alessandro Barchiesi and Walter Scheidel (Oxford: Oxford University Press, 2010), pp. 221–22; Koloski-Ostrow and Lyons, *Naked Truths*; and Suzanne M. Spencer-Wood, "Feminist Gender Research in Classical Archaeology," in *Handbook of Gender in Archaeology*, ed. Sarah Milledge Nelson (Lanham, MD: AltaMira, 2006). Laura K. McClure, "Sexuality and Gender," in *The Oxford Handbook of Hellenic Studies*, ed. George Boys-Stones, Barbara Graziosi, and Phiroze Vasunia (Oxford: Oxford University Press, 2009), pp. 307ff., offers a good overview of the history of and approaches to studying "women in antiquity." Amelia Jones, ed., *The Feminism and Visual Culture Reader* (New York: Routledge, 2003), usefully collects classic texts with new ones on feminism and visual culture, although publication dates are too hard to find. Lisa Nevett, "Housing and Households: The Greek World," and Bettina Bergmann, "Housing and Households: The Roman World," both in *Classical Archaeology*, ed. Susan E. Alcock and Robin Osborne (Oxford: Blackwell, 2007), address the archaeology of the house and women's place within it.

4. Barbara E. Goff, *Citizen Bacchae: Women's Ritual Practice in Ancient Greece* (Los Angeles: University of California Los Angeles Press, 2004), p. 248; and Mark D.

Stansbury-O'Donnell, *Looking at Greek Art* (Cambridge: Cambridge University Press, 2011), pp. 96–98.

5. Sue Thornham, *Passionate Detachments: An Introduction to Feminist Film Theory* (London: Arnold, 1997), pp. 20–21.

6. Anne D'Alleva, *Methods and Theories of Art History* (London: Laurence King, 2005) and Stansbury-O'Donnell, *Looking at Greek Art*, offer a broad look at various theoretical approaches to interpreting art that have evolved from the early feminist and other approaches of the 1970s. For approaches today and areas into which feminism has spread or evolved, especially gender studies, see Corbeill, "Gender Studies," pp. 221–22; McClure, "Sexuality and Gender"; Kristina Milnor, "Women," in Barchiesi and Scheidel, *Oxford Handbook of Roman Studies*, pp. 824–25; Jacqueline Murray, "One Flesh, Two Sexes, Three Genders?" in *Gender and Christianity in Medieval Europe: New Perspectives*, ed. Lisa M. Bitel and Felice Lifshitz (Philadelphia: University of Pennsylvania Press, 2008); Giulia Sissa, *Sex and Sexuality in the Ancient World* (New Haven, CT: Yale University Press, 2008); Marilyn B. Skinner, "Gender Studies," in Boys-Stones, Graziosi, and Vasunia, *Oxford Handbook of Hellenic Studies*; and Thornham, *Passionate Detachments*, pp. 1–21.

7. Donald Preziosi and Louise Hitchcock, *Aegean Art and Architecture* (Oxford: Oxford University Press 1999), figs. 47, 54; and Jeremy Rutter, "Children in Aegean Prehistory," in *Coming of Age in Ancient Greece: Images of Childhood from the Classical Past*, ed. Jenifer Neils and John H. Oakley (New Haven, CT: Yale University Press, 2003), fig. 20.

8. Split skirt: Preziosi and Hitchcock, *Aegean Art and Architecture*, figs. 81, 83; Louise Schofield, *The Mycenaeans* (London: British Museum Press, 2007), figs. 55 and 106, 107; Spyridon Marinatos, *Excavations at Thera V* (Athens: Archaeological Society of Athens, 1972), plates G, H. Bare breasts: Preziosi and Hitchcock, *Aegean Art and Architecture*, fig. 86; Stewart, *Art, Desire, and the Body*, fig. 21. Hairstyles at different female ages: Rutter, "Children in Aegean Prehistory," fig. 22.

9. Schofield, *Mycenaeans*, figs. 79, 106, 107; Rodney Castleden, *Mycenaeans* (New York: Routledge, 2005), figs. 3.5, 6.2, 6.8, 6.9; and Preziosi and Hitchcock, *Aegean Art and Architecture*, fig. 104.

10. Goff, *Citizen Bacchae*, p. 247; Alan Johnston, "Greek Vases in the Marketplace," in *Looking at Greek Vases*, ed. Tom Rasmussen and Nigel Spivey (Cambridge: Cambridge University Press, 1991); and Stansbury-O'Donnell, *Looking at Greek Art*, pp. 125–28.

11. Jenifer Neils, *Goddess and Polis: The Panathenaic Festival in Ancient Athens* (Princeton, NJ: Princeton University Press, 1992).

12. Sue Blundell, *Women in Ancient Greece* (Cambridge, MA: Harvard University Press, 1995), pp. 92–93, 188.

13. Reeder, *Pandora*, figs. 12–14. The distinction between the skin of women and men is emphasized in Egyptian, Etruscan, Greek, and Roman art, and the convention continued into late antiquity and beyond. See Ramage and Ramage, *Roman Art*, p. 53.

14. John Griffiths Pedley, *Greek Art and Archaeology*, rev. ed. (New York: Prentice Hall, 2007), fig. 8.14.

15. Stewart, *Classical Greece*, fig. 4.5.

16. Lissarrague, *Greek Vases*, figs. 38, 213; and Reeder, *Pandora*, figs. 5, 6, 13.

17. Lloyd Llewellyn-Jones, *Aphrodite's Tortoise: The Veiled Woman of Ancient Greece* (Swansea: Classical Press of Wales, 2003), chap. 3, suggests that a veiling gesture can substitute for the veil and notes that young male *erastes* who are being wooed by older *eromenoi* in vase paintings wrap themselves thoroughly in their cloaks and cover their heads, like women, to show modesty or disinterest (p. 104). See Andrew Lear and Eve Cantarella, *Images of Ancient Greek Pederasty: Boys Were Their Gods* (New York: Routledge, 2008), fig. 3.1, pp. 108, 129–38; and Stewart, *Art, Desire, and the Body*, on desirable boys equated in art with women. John Younger's "Gender and Sexuality in the Parthenon Frieze," in Koloski-Ostrow and Lyons, *Naked Truths*, even concludes that sexually accessible youths replace (and are thus equated with) sexually accessible noncitizen women on the Parthenon frieze.

18. Pursuit and attack: Reeder, *Pandora*, pp. 398–402; Beth Cohen, "Divesting the Female Breast of Clothes in Classical Sculpture," in Koloski-Ostrow and Lyons, *Naked Truths*. Lapith maiden on the temple of Zeus at Olympia: Stewart, *Art, Desire, and the Body*, fig. 9. Cassandra being attacked at the statue of Athena: Stewart, *Art, Desire, and the Body*, fig. 12; Mark D. Fullerton, *Greek Art* (Cambridge: Cambridge University Press, 1999): fig. 66, far left. Eos: Stewart, *Art, Desire, and the Body*, fig. 108. Cassandra pursuing Ajax: Connelly, *Portrait of a Priestess*, fig. 4.12.

19. Gorgons: Reeder, *Pandora*, pp. 410–15 (note Medusa's more normal fifth-century face in fig. 135 and her attractive face and pose in fig. 136); Stewart, *Art, Desire, and the Body*, pp. 182–87; and Stephen R. Wilk, *Medusa: Solving the Mystery of the Gorgon* (Oxford: Oxford University Press, 2000), pp. 31–62.

20. Lissarrague, *Greek Vases*, fig. 91; and Robertson, *Art of Vase-Painting*, fig. 21.2. While mourning was women's business, female excess during mourning was a strong male concern: Matthew Dillon, *Girls and Women in Classical Greek Religion* (London: Routledge, 2002), p. 292.

21. Goff, *Citizen Bacchae*, p. 266ff.; and Jenifer Neils, "Others within the Other: An Intimate Look at Hetairai and Maenads," in *Not the Classical Ideal: Athens and the Construction of the Other in Greek Art*, ed. Beth Cohen (Leiden: Brill, 2000).

22. Thomas F. Scanlon, *Eros and Greek Athletics* (Oxford: Oxford University Press, 2002).

23. Old men and women were shown in art, often in humorous contexts. Stooped posture, disheveled hair, a walking stick, baldness, and gray hair signified old age. A fat-bellied youth in a scene of otherwise fit male athletes was probably an amusing riff on the standard beautiful male: Stephen G. Miller, *Ancient Greek Athletics* (New Haven, CT: Yale University Press, 2004), p. 271. Heavy athletes sometimes had particularly big bellies or posteriors, and their bodies showed physical damage logical for their combat style: ibid., fig. 80.

24. See Lewis, *Athenian Woman*, pp. 142–50, on bathing women. Robert F. Sutton, "Pornography and Persuasion on Attic Pottery," in *Pornography and Representation in Greece and Rome*, ed. Amy Richlin (Oxford: Oxford University Press,

1992), pp. 22–24, believes that certain types of scenes on pottery may reflect women's interests and that potters were influenced by female patronage; see also Goff, *Citizen Bacchae*, p. 250.

25. Reeder, *Pandora*, figs. 39, 40, 41; see Stewart, *Art, Desire, and the Body*, pp. 156–81, on sexual scenes in general; for prostitution terminology see McClure, "Sexuality and Gender," p. 313.

26. Clarke, *Art in the Lives of Ordinary Romans*, fig. 15; Stewart, *Art, Desire, and the Body*, pp. 164–65; and Robert F. Sutton, "The Good, the Base, and the Ugly: The Drunken Orgy in Attic Vase Painting and the Athenian Self," in Cohen, *Not the Classical Ideal*, pp. 190–91.

27. Oakley and Sinos, *Wedding in Ancient Athens*, figs. 113–14 and p. 37: discussion of Theseus-Ariadne wedding imagery. The *eros* between Greek men and available women was not assumed to exist between them and their wives: Eve Cantarella, "Friendship, Love, and Marriage," in Boys-Stones, Graziosi, and Vasunia, *Oxford Handbook of Hellenic Studies*, pp. 299–300.

28. Haynes, *Etruscan Civilization*, fig. 191: early fifth-century spectators of both genders in stands watch and discuss an event; below them is another world that includes sexual activity. The half-nude couple embraces on a sarcophagus in fig. 233; he wears a bracelet, she earrings, and both have elaborate coiffed hair. The more sedate couple is in fig. 232a.

29. The sarcophagus portrait is from Poggio Cantarello near Chiusi: ibid., fig. 266a, pp. 336–39.

30. Burn, *Hellenistic Art*, pp. 16–18, summarizes key aspects of Hellenistic art identified in major scholarly works of art history.

31. This pose has been named the *pudicitia* pose; see R.R.R. Smith, *Hellenistic Sculpture: A Handbook* (London: Thames and Hudson, 1991), figs. 111, 112, 113, 114, 116, 1–2; and Sheila Dillon, *The Female Portrait Statue in the Greek World* (Cambridge: Cambridge University Press, 2010), pp. 97ff.

32. Pazanelli, Schmidt, and Lapatin, *Color of Life*.

33. Christine Mitchell Havelock, *The Aphrodite of Knidos and Her Successors: A Historical Review of the Female Nude in Greek Art* (Ann Arbor: University of Michigan Press, 2008), chap. 5 (Aphrodite types and their context); Nanette Salomon, "Making a World of Difference: Gender, Asymmetry, and the Greek Nude," in Koloski-Ostrow and Lyons, *Naked Truths*, pp. 79–83; and Stewart, *Art, Desire, and the Body*, figs. 152–53.

34. Smith, *Hellenistic Sculpture*, fig. 196.5; see Athena's agonized opponent in fig. 196.3.

35. The meaning and context of such figures are debated; some may have been votives that reflected Dionysos's powers over the vine or the gods' ability to give wealth or poverty to mortals; others may have been privately owned as reminders of the vagaries of fate. See Smith, *Hellenistic Sculpture*, pp. 136–40, figs. 174–76; Jerome Jordan Pollitt, *Art in the Hellenistic Age* (Cambridge: Cambridge University Press, 1986), pp. 141–46, figs. 152, 153. Old, wretched males were also depicted in an inversion of the beautiful nude athlete: Smith, *Hellenistic Sculpture*, figs. 178, 179 (and 161: an old centaur tormented by Eros).

36. Metropolitan Museum accession no. 89.2.2141.
37. Pollitt, *Art in the Hellenistic Age*, fig. 152; and Smith, *Hellenistic Sculpture*, fig. 175.
38. R.M. Kousser, *Hellenistic and Roman Ideal Sculpture: The Allure of the Classical* (Cambridge: Cambridge University Press, 2008).
39. Jens Daehner, "The Statue Types in the Roman World," in Daehner, *Herculaneum Women*, pp. 87–92, 110–11; and Vorster, "Large and Small Herculaneum Women Sculptures," pp. 115–21. Faustina "wears" a Large Herculaneum Woman body in the Getty Villa in Malibu, California.
40. Eve D'Ambra, "Nudity and Adornment in Female Portrait Sculpture of the Second Century AD," in Kleiner and Matheson, *I Claudia II*, pp. 101–10; Guy P.R. Metraux, "Prudery and Chic in Late Antique Clothing," in Edmonson and Keith, *Roman Dress*, p. 275; and Peter Stewart, *Statues in Roman Society: Representation and Response* (Oxford: Oxford University Press, 2003), pp. 48–52.
41. On the difficulty of distinguishing prostitutes and respectable women by their clothing, see Kelly Olson, "Matrona and Whore: Clothing and Definition in Roman Antiquity," in *Prostitutes and Courtesans in the Ancient World*, ed. Christopher A. Faraone and Laura K. McClure (Madison: University of Wisconsin Press, 2006). On sexual terminology and the significance of penetration: Holt N. Parker, "The Teratogenic Grid," in *Roman Sexualities*, ed. Judith P. Hallett and Marilyn B. Skinner (Princeton, NJ: Princeton University Press, 1997); and Craig Williams, *Roman Homosexuality* (Oxford: Oxford University Press, 1999 [2010]), chap. 4. On the wall painting depicting the possible sexual encounter of a bride: Clarke, *Roman Sex*, pp. 28–33, figs. 9–11.
42. Apuleius describes punishment via sex with a donkey in *Metamorphoses* 10.29–34. Kelly Olson, *Dress and the Roman Woman: Self-Presentation and Society* (New York: Routledge, 2008), p. 50. Examples of lamps are found in K. Welch, *The Roman Amphitheatre: From Its Origins to the Colosseum* (Cambridge: Cambridge University Press, 2007), fig. 93.
43. See Elizabeth Castelli, *Martyrdom and Memory: Early Christian Culture Making* (New York: Columbia University Press, 2005), chap. 5, and especially p. 162 on the idealized femininity of Thecla's imagery in comparison with her behavior and resistance of cultural norms; Carolyn L. Connor, *Women of Byzantium* (New Haven, CT: Yale University Press, 2004), pp. 1–12; Stephen J. Davis, *The Cult of Saint Thecla: A Tradition of Women's Piety in Late Antiquity* (Oxford: Oxford University Press, 2008), pp. 117–18; and Shelby Brown, "Death as Decoration: Scenes of the Arena on Roman Domestic Mosaics," in Richlin, *Pornography and Representation*, on arena imagery and behavior.
44. Metraux, "Prudery and Chic," p. 273.
45. Tulloch, "Women Leaders." Images of women at funeral banquets in frescoes from the Catacomb of Saints Marcellino and Pietro offer a rare glimpse of female leadership in a private setting of the late third or early fourth century C.E.
46. Jas Elsner, "The Changing Nature of Roman Art and the Art-Historical Problem of Style," in *Late Antique and Medieval Art of the Mediterranean World*, ed. Eva Rose Hoffman, Blackwell Anthologies in Art History (Malden, MA: Blackwell, 2007 [1998]), p. 15.

47. Thomas F. Mathews, *The Clash of Gods: A Reinterpretation of Early Christian Art*, rev. exp. ed. (Princeton, NJ: Princeton University Press), p. 13.

48. Elsner, "Changing Nature," p. 18, fig. 1.3.

49. The casket is inscribed to Projecta and Secunda with the wish "Vivatis in Christo" ("May you live in Christ"). Averil Cameron, *The Later Roman Empire* (Cambridge, MA: Harvard University Press, 1993), front cover, pp. 160–63.

50. Ibid., p. 160. See Alan Cameron, *The Last Pagans of Rome* (Oxford: Oxford University Press, 2011), p. 737, on the images as unreal mementos; Erika Simon, "The Diptych of the Symmachi and Nicomachi: An Interpretation. In Memoriam Wolfgang F. Volbach 1892–1988," *Greece and Rome*, 2nd ser., 39 (1992): 56–65, on a wedding context; and Dale Kinney and Anthony Cutler, "A Late Ivory Plaque and Modern Response," *American Journal of Archaeology* 98 (3) (1994): 457–80, on the authenticity of the ivory plaques.

51. Kleiner, *Gardner's Art*, fig. 9.17.

52. Ibid., fig. 9.18.

53. Connor, *Women of Byzantium*, pl. 1; p. 189: Mary seemed lifelike to the patriarch Photius, who praised the color of the virgin's lips, noting that they seemed capable of speech; Kleiner, *Gardner's Art*, fig. 9.19.

54. David I. Perrett, D. Michael Burt, Ian S. Penton-Voak, Kieran J. Lee, Duncan A. Rowland, and Rachel Edwards, "Symmetry and Human Facial Attractiveness," *Evolution and Human Behavior* 20 (5) (1999): 295–307; and Daniel Hamermesh and Jeff Biddle, "Beauty and the Labor Market," *American Economic Review* 84 (5) (1993): 1174–95.

BIBLIOGRAPHY

Adams, J. N. 1982. *The Latin Sexual Vocabulary*. London: Duckworth.

Allison, Francis G. 1964. *Menander, the Principal Fragments*. Cambridge, MA: Harvard University Press.

Andersen, O. 1987. "The Widows, the City and Thucydides (II.45.2)." *Symbolae Osloenses* 62: 33–49.

Anson, John. 1974. "The Female Transvestite in Early Monasticism: The Origin and Development of a Motif." *Viator* 5: 1–32.

Appian. *Bellum Civile*.

Apuleius. *Apologia*.

Archard, David. 1993. *Children: Rights and Childhood*. London: Routledge.

Arnobius. *Adversus Gentes*.

Arrizabalaga y Prado, Leonardo de. 2010. *The Emperor Elagabalus—Fact or Fiction?* Cambridge: Cambridge University Press.

Arthur, Marilyn. 1981. "The Divided World of Iliad VI." In *Reflections of Women in Antiquity*, ed. Helene P. Foley. New York: Gordon and Breach.

Asconius. *Commentary on pro Milone*.

Ausonius. *Parentalia*.

Avagianou, Aphrodite. 1991. *Sacred Marriage in the Rituals of Greek Religion*. Bern: Peter Lang.

Babcock, C. L. 1965. "The Early Career of Fulvia." *American Journal of Philology* 86: 1–32.

Bagnall, Roger S., and Raffaella Cribiore, eds. 2006. *Women's Letters from Ancient Egypt: 300 B.C.–A.D. 800*. Ann Arbor: University of Michigan Press.

Bain, David. 1997. "Salpe's ΠΑΙΓΝΙΑ: Athenaeus 322A and Plin. *H.N.* 23.38." *Classical Quarterly* 48: 262–68.

Ball, Warwick. 2001. *Rome in the East: The Transformation of an Empire*. London and New York: Routledge.

Barber, Elizabeth Wayland. 1994. *Women's Work: The First 20 000 Years*. New York and London: W. W. Norton.

Barrett, A. A. 1996. *Agrippina: Sex, Power and Politics in the Early Roman Empire*. New Haven, CT: Yale University Press.

Barrett, A. A. 2000. *Livia: First Lady of Imperial Rome*. New Haven, CT: Yale University Press.

Barrett-Lennard, R.J.S. 1994. *Christian Healing after the New Testament: Some Approaches to Illness in the Second, Third, and Fourth Centuries*. Lanham, MD: University Press of America.

Bartsch, Shadi. 2006. *The Mirror of the Self: Sexuality, Self-Knowledge, and the Gaze in the Early Roman Empire*. Chicago: University of Chicago Press.

Bauman, R. A. 1992. *Women and Politics in Ancient Rome*. London and New York: Routledge.

Beard, Mary. 1995. "Re-reading (Vestal) Virginity." In *Women in Antiquity: New Assessments*, ed. Richard Hawley and Barbara Levick. London and New York: Routledge.

Beard, Mary. 1980. "The Sexual Status of Vestal Virgins." *Journal of Roman Studies* 70: 12–27.

Beard, Mary, John North, and Simon Price. 1998. *Religions of Rome*. Vols. 1–2. Cambridge: Cambridge University Press, 1998.

Beard, M., Alan K. Bowman, Mireille Corbier, Tim Cornell, James L. Franklin Jr., Ann Hanson, Keith Hopkins, and Nicholas Horsfall. 1991. *Literacy in the Roman World. Journal of Roman Archaeology* suppl. 3.

Bede. 1996. *The Ecclesiastical History of the English Church and People*. Oxford: Oxford University Press.

Bendlin, Andreas. 2007. "Purity and Pollution." In *A Companion to Greek Religion*, ed. Daniel Ogden. Oxford: Blackwell.

Benko, Stephen. 1984. *Pagan Rome and the Early Christians*. Bloomington: Indiana University Press.

Berg, Ria. 2010. "Il mundus muliebrus nelle fonti latine e nei contesti pompeiani." PhD diss., University of Helsinki, Faculty of Humanities.

Bergmann, Bettina. 2007. "Housing and Households: The Roman World." In *Classical Archaeology*, ed. Susan E. Alcock and Robin Osborne. Oxford: Blackwell.

Betz, Hans Dieter. [1986] 1992. *The Greek Magical Papryi in Translation*. Chicago: University of Chicago Press.

Bickersteth, J. E. 1980. "Unedited Greek Homilies (Acephalous, Anonymous or Attributed to John Chrysostom) for Festivals of the Virgin Mary." *Orientalia Christiana Periodica* 46 (2): 474–80.

Billigmeier, Jon-Christian, and Judy A. Turner. 1981. "The Socio-Economic Roles of Women in Mycenaean Greece: A Brief Survey from Evidence of the Linear B Tablets." In *Reflections of Women in Antiquity*, ed. Helene P. Foley. New York: Gordon and Breach.

Birley, Anthony R. 1999. *Septimius Severus*. London and New York: Routledge.

Blundell, M. W. 1998. *Sophocles' Antigone*. Newburyport, MA: Focus Classical Library.

Blundell, Sue. 1995. *Women in Ancient Greece*. Cambridge, MA: Harvard University Press.

Bodel, John. 2001. *Epigraphic Evidence: Ancient History from Inscriptions*. London: Routledge.

Bowersock, G. W. 1969. "The Circle of Julia Domna." In *Greek Sophists in the Roman Empire*. Oxford: Clarendon.

Bowman, Alan K. 2003. *Life and Letters on the Roman Frontier: Vindolanda and Its People*. London: British Museum Press.

Boyarin, Daniel. 1998. "Gender." In *Critical Terms for Religious Studies*, ed. Mark C. Taylor. Chicago: University of Chicago Press.

Boyd, Barbara W. 1987. "*Virtus Effeminata* and Sallust's Sempronia." *Transactions of the American Philological Association* 117: 183–201.

Bradley, Keith R. 1991. *Discovering the Roman Family: Studies in Roman Social History*. New York: Oxford University Press.

Bradley, Keith R. 1994. *Slavery and Society at Rome*. Cambridge: Cambridge University Press.

Bradley, Keith R. 1986. "Wet-Nursing at Rome: A Study of Social Relations." In *The Family in Ancient Rome: New Perspectives*, ed. Beryl Rawson. New York: Cornell University Press.

Bradshaw, Paul F., Maxwell E Johnson, L Edward Phillips, and Harold W Attridge. 2002. *The Apostolic Tradition: A Commentary*. Minneapolis: Fortress.

Branham, Joan R. 1997. "Blood in Flux, Sanctity at Issue." *RES: Anthropology and Aesthetics* 31: 53–70.

Branham, Joan R. 2002. "Bloody Women and Bloody Spaces: Menses and the Eucharist in Late Antiquity and the Early Middle Ages." *Harvard Divinity Bulletin* 30 (4) Available at: http://www.hds.harvard.edu/news/bulletin/articles/branham.html (accessed January 17, 2011).

Brodie, Neil. 2008. "Aramaic Incantation Bowls." In *Cultural Heritage Resource*. Palo Alto: Stanford Archaeological Center. Available at: http://www.stanford.edu/group/chr/drupal/ref/aramaic-incantation-bowls (accessed March 11, 2011).

Brooten, Bernadette J. 1996. *Love between Women: Early Christian Responses to Female Homoeroticism*. Chicago: University of Chicago Press.

Brooten, Bernadette J. 1985. "Early Christian Women and Their Cultural Context: Issues of Method in Historical Reconstruction." In *Feminist Perspectives on Biblical Scholarship*, ed. Adela Yarbo Collins, 65–91. Chico, CA: Scholars Press.

Brown, Peter. 1988. *The Body and Society: Men, Women, and Sexual Renunciation in Early Christianity*. New York: Columbia University Press.

Brown Peter. 1981. *The Cult of Saints*. Chicago: University of Chicago Press.

Brown, Shelby. 1992. "Death as Decoration: Scenes of the Arena on Roman Domestic Mosaics." In *Pornography and Representation in Greece and Rome*, ed. Amy Richlin. New York: Oxford University Press.

Brown, Shelby. 1993. "Feminist Research in Archaeology: What Does It Mean? Why Is It Taking So Long?" In *Feminist Theory and the Classics*, ed. Nancy S. Rabinowitz and Amy Richlin. New York: Routledge.

Brown, Shelby. 1997. "Ways of Seeing Women in Antiquity: An Introduction to Feminism in Classical Archaeology and Ancient Art History." In *Naked Truths: Women, Sexuality, and Gender in Classical Art and Archaeology*, ed. Ann Olga Koloski-Ostrow and Claire L. Lyons. London: Routledge.

Budin, Stephanie L. 2008. *The Myth of Sacred Prostitution in Antiquity*. New York: Cambridge University Press.

Budin, Stephanie L. 2006. "Sacred Prostitution in the First Person." In *Prostitutes and Courtesans in the Ancient World*, ed. Christopher A. Faraone and Laura K. McClure. Madison: University of Wisconsin Press.

Burke, Peter. 2008. *What Is Cultural History?* Malden, MA: Polity.

Burkert, Walter. 1985. *Greek Religion: Archaic and Classical*, trans. John Raffan. Oxford: Basil Blackwell.

Burn, Lucilla. 2005. *Hellenistic Art: From Alexander the Great to Augustus*. Los Angeles: Getty Publications.

Burstein, S.M. 1982. "Arsinoe II. Philadelphos: A Revisionist View." In *Philip II, Alexander the Great and the Macedonian Heritage*, ed. W. Adams and E. Borza. Lanham, MD: University Press of America.

Caesarius of Arles [Saint]. *Sermons*, vols. 1–2.

Calame, C. 1977. *Les Choeurs de jeunes filles in Grèce archad'que, I: Morphologie, fonction religieuse et sociale*. Rome: Edizioni dell' Ateneo and Bizzarri.

Cameron, Alan. 2011. *The Last Pagans of Rome*. Oxford: Oxford University Press.

Cameron, Alan, Jacqueline Long, and Lee Sherry. 1993. *Barbarians and Politics at the Court of Arcadius*. Berkeley: University of California Press.

Cameron, Averil, ed. 1989. *History as Text: The Writing of Ancient History*. London: Duckworth.

Cameron, Averil. 1993. *The Later Roman Empire*. Cambridge, MA: Harvard University Press.

Cameron, Averil, and Amélie Kuhrt, eds. 1983. *Images of Women in Antiquity*. London: Croom Helm.

Cantarella, Eva. 1992. *Bisexuality in the Ancient World*, trans. Cormac Ó Cuilleanáin. New Haven, CT: Yale University Press.

Cantarella, Eva. 2009. "Friendship, Love, and Marriage." In *The Oxford Handbook of Hellenic Studies*, ed. George Boys-Stones, Barbara Graziosi, and Phiroze Vasunia. Oxford: Oxford University Press.

Cantarella, Eva. 1991. "Homicides of Honor: The Development of Italian Adultery Law over Two Millennia." In *The Family in Italy: From Antiquity to the Present*, ed. David I. Kertzer and Richard P. Saller. New Haven, CT: Yale University Press.

Cantarella, Eva. 2002. *Itaca. Eroi, donne, potere tra vendetta e diritto*. Milan, Italy: Feltrinelli.

Cantarella, Eva. 2002. "Marriage and Sexuality in Republican Rome: A Roman Conjugal Love Story." In *The Sleep of Reason: Erotic Experience and Sexual Ethics in Ancient Greece and Rome*, ed. Martha C. Nussbaum and Juha Sihvola. Chicago: University of Chicago Press.

Cantarella, Eva. 1987. *Pandora's Daughters: The Role and Status of Women in Greek and Roman Antiquity*, trans. Maureen B. Fant. Baltimore: Johns Hopkins University Press.

Cantarella, Eva. 1996. *Passato prossimo. Donne romane da Tacita a Sulpicia*. Milan, Italy: Feltrinelli.

Cantarella, Eva. 2005. "Roman Marriage: Social, Economic and Legal Aspects." In *Hoping for Continuity: Childhood, Education and Death in Antiquity and the Middle Ages*, ed. Katariina Mustakallio et al. ACTA IRF 33. Rome: Institutum Romanum Finlandiae.

Cantarella, Eva. 1995. *Secondo natura. La bisessualità nel mondo antico*. Milan, Italy: Rizzoli.

Carney, Elizabeth D. 2006. *Olympias: Mother of Alexander the Great*. London and New York: Routledge.

Carney, Elizabeth D. 1987. "The Reappearance of Royal Sibling Marriages in Ptolemaic Egypt." *Past and Present* 237: 420–39.

Carney, Elizabeth D. 2000. *Women and Monarchy in Macedonia*. Norman: University of Oklahoma Press.

Carson, Anne. 1990. "Putting Her in Her Place: Woman, Dirt and Desire." In *Before Sexuality: The Construction of Erotic Experience in the Ancient Greek World*, ed. David M. Halperin, John J. Winkler, and Froma Zeitlin. Princeton, NJ: Princeton University Press.

Cartledge, Paul. 1993. *The Greeks: A Portrait of Self and Others*. Oxford: Oxford University Press.

Cartledge, Paul. 1993. "The Silent Women of Thucydides: 2.45.2 Re-Viewed." In *Nomodeiktes*, ed. R.M. Roden and J. Farrell. Ann Arbor: University of Michigan Press.

Cartledge, Paul. 1981. "Spartan Wives: Liberation or License?" *Classical Quarterly* 31: 84–105.

Cartledge, Paul, and Antony Spawforth. 1989. *Hellenistic and Roman Sparta*. London and New York: Routledge.

Cartlidge, David R., and J. Keith Elliot. 2001. *Art: The Christian Apocrypha*. London: Routledge.

Castelli, Elizabeth A. 2004. *Martyrdom and Memory: Early Christian Culture Making*. New York: Columbia University Press.

Castleden, Rodney. 2005. *Mycenaeans*. New York: Routledge.

Catullus. *Carmina*.

Cherubini, Laura. 2010. *Strix. La strega nella cultura romana*. Druento, Italy: UTET Libreria.

Ciggaar, K. 1995. "Theophano: An Empress Reconsidered." In *The Empress Theophano: Byzantium and the West at the Turn of the First Millennium*, ed. Adelbert Davids. Cambridge: Cambridge University Press.

Cicero. *Brutus*.

Cicero. *de Haruspicum Response*.

Cicero. *de Re Publica*.

Cicero. *Epistulae ad Atticum*.

Cicero. *Epistulae ad Brutum*.

Clark, Elizabeth A. 1986. *Ascetic Piety and Women's Faith: Essays on Late Ancient Christianity*. New York: Edwin Mellen.

Clark, Elizabeth A. 1977. "John Chrysostom and the 'Subintroductae'." *Church History* 46(2): 171–85.

Clark, Elizabeth A. 1983. *Women in the Early Church*. Wilmington, DE: Michael Glazier.

Clark, Gillian. 1993. *Women in Late Antiquity: Pagan and Christian Life-Styles*. Oxford: Oxford University Press.

Clarke, John R. 2003. *Art in the Lives of Ordinary Romans: Visual Representation and Non-Elite Viewers in Italy, 100 B.C.–A.D. 315*. Berkeley: University of California Press.

Clarke, John R. 1998. *Looking at Lovemaking: Constructions of Sexuality in Roman Art 100 B.C.–A.D. 250*. Berkeley: University of California Press.

Clarke, John R. 2003. *Roman Sex: 100 B.C.–A.D. 250*. New York: Harry H. Abrams.

Cloke, Gillian. 1995. *This Female Man of God: Women and Spiritual Power in the Patristic Age, A.D. 350–450*. London and New York: Routledge.

Cobb, L. Stephanie. 2009. "Real Women or Objects of Discourse? The Search for Early Christian Women." *Religion Compass* 3 (3): 379–94.

Codex Justinianus.

Cohen, Beth. 1997. "Divesting the Female Breast of Clothes in Classical Sculpture." In *Naked Truths: Women, Sexuality, and Gender in Classical Art and Archaeology*, ed. Ann Koloski-Ostrow and Claire L. Lyons. London: Routledge.

Cohen, David. 1991. *Law, Sexuality, and Society: The Enforcement of Morals in Classical Athens*. Cambridge: Cambridge University Press.

Cohen, David. 1996. "Seclusion, Separation, and the Status of Women in Classical Athens." In *Women in Antiquity*, ed. Ian McAuslan and Peter Walcot. Oxford and New York: Oxford University Press.

Cohen, Edward E. 2006. "Free and Unfree Sexual Work: An Economic Analysis of Athenian Prostitution." In *Prostitutes and Courtesans in the Ancient World*, ed. Christopher A. Faraone and Laura K. McClure. Madison: University of Wisconsin Press.

Cohen, Shaye J. D. 1991. "Menstruants and the Sacred in Judaism and Christianity." In *Women's History and Ancient History*, ed. Sarah B. Pomeroy. Chapel Hill: University of North Carolina Press.

Cokayne, K. 2003. *Experiencing Old Age in Ancient Rome*. London: Routledge.

Cole, Susan Guettel. 1992. "*Gynaiki ou Themis*: Gender Difference in the Greek *Leges Sacrae*." *Helios* 19: 104–22.

Cole, Susan Guettel. 1981. "Could Greek Women Read and Write?" In *Reflections of Women in Antiquity*, ed. Helene P. Foley. New York: Gordon and Breach.

Cole, Susan Guettel. 1984. "The Social Function of Rituals of Maturation: The Koureion and the Arkteia." *Zeitschrift für Papyrologie und Epigraphik* 55: 233–44.

Compton, M. 2002. "The Association of Hygieia with Asklepios in Graeco-Roman Asklepieion Medicine." *Journal of the History of Medicine* 57: 312–29.

Congourdeau, Marie-Hélène. 1993. " 'Metrodora' et son œuvre." In *Maladie et société à Byzance: Études présentées au 17e congrès international des sciences historiques (Madrid, 1990)*, ed. Evelyne Patlagean. Spoleto, Italy: Centro italiano di studi sull'Alto medioevo.

Connelly, Joan Breton. 2007. *Portrait of a Priestess: Women and Ritual in Ancient Greece*. Princeton, NJ: Princeton University Press.

Connolly, R. Hugh. 1929. *Didascalia Apostolorum: With Introduction and Notes*. Oxford: Clarendon.

Connor, Carolyn L. 2004. *Women of Byzantium*. New Haven, CT: Yale University Press.

Coon, Lynda L. 1997. *Sacred Fictions: Holy Women and Hagiography in Late Antiquity*. Philadelphia: University of Pennsylvania Press.

Cooper, Kate. 1996. *The Virgin and the Bride: Idealized Womanhood in Late Antiquity*. Cambridge, MA: Harvard University Press.

Corbeill, Anthony. 2010. "Gender Studies." In *The Oxford Handbook of Roman Studies*, ed. Alessandro Barchiesi and Walter Scheidel. Oxford: Oxford University Press.

Corbier, Mireille. 1995. "Male Power and Legitimacy through Women: The Domus Augusta under the Julio-Claudians." In *Women in Antiquity: New Assessments*, ed. Richard Hawley and Barbara Levick. London and New York: Routledge.

Corbier, Mireille. 1990. "La petite enfance à Rome. Lois, normes, pratiques individuelles et collectives." *Annales. Economies, Sociétés, Civilisations* 54: 1257–9.

Cornelius Nepos. *de Excellentibus Ducibus Exterarum Gentium*.

Cornelius Nepos. *de Viris Illustribus*.

Craik, E., trans. 1988. *Euripides: Phoenecian Women*. Warminster, UK: Aris and Phillips.

Cribiore, Raffaella. 2001. *Gymnastics of the Mind: Greek Education in Hellenistic and Roman Egypt*. Princeton, NJ, and Oxford: Princeton University Press.

Croom, A. T. 2002. *Roman Clothing and Fashion*. Stroud, UK: Tempus.

Crossan, John Dominic. 1992. *The Historical Jesus: The Life of a Mediterranean Jewish Peasant*. San Francisco: Harper Collins.

Cyrino, M. S. 1995. *In Pandora's Jar: Lovesickness in Early Greek Poetry*. Lanham, MD: University Press of America.

Daehner, Jens. 2007. "The Statue Types in the Roman World." In *The Herculaneum Women: History, Context, Identities*, ed. Jens Daehner. Los Angeles: J. Paul Getty Museum.

Dalby, Andrew. 2002. "Levels of Concealment: The Dress of Hetairai and Pornai in Greek Texts." In *Women's Dress in the Ancient Greek World*, ed. Lloyd Llewellyn-Jones. London: Classical Press of Wales.

Daley, Brian E. 2006. *Gregory of Nazianzus*. London: Routledge.

D'Alleva, Anne. 2005. *Methods and Theories of Art History*. London: Laurence King.

Daly, Mary. 1973. *Beyond God the Father: Toward a Philosophy of Women's Liberation*. Boston: Beacon.

D'Ambra, Eve. 2000. "Nudity and Adornment in Female Portrait Sculpture of the Second Century AD." In *I Claudia II: Women in Roman Art and Society*, ed. Diana E. E. Kleiner and Susan B. Matheson. New Haven, CT: Yale University Art Gallery.

D'Ambra, Eve. 2007. "Racing with Death: Circus Sarcophagi and the Commemoration of Children in Roman Italy." In *Constructions of Childhood in Ancient Greece and Italy*, ed. Ada Cohen and Jeremy B. Rutter. Princeton, NJ: American School of Classical Studies at Athens.

D'Ambra, Eve. 2007. *Roman Women*. New York: Cambridge University Press.

Daniélou, Jean. 1974. *The Ministry of Women in the Early Church*, trans. G. Simon. Westminster, MD: Faith Press.

Dasen, Véronique. 2005. "Blessing or Portent: Multiple Births in Ancient Rome." In *Hoping for Continuity: Childhood, Education and Death in Antiquity and the Middle Ages*, ed. Katariina Mustakallio et al. ACTA IRF 33. Rome: Institutum Romanum Finlandiae.

Dasen, Véronique, ed. 2004. *Naissance et petite enfance dans l'Antiquité. Actes du colloque de Fribourg, 28 novembre–1er décembre 2001*. Orbis Biblicus et Orientalis 203. Fribourg: Academie Press.

Davidson, James N. 1997. *Courtesans and Fishcakes: The Consuming Passions of Classical Athens*. New York: St. Martin's.

Davidson, James N. 1995. "Don't Try This at Home: Pliny's Salpe, Salpe's *Paignia* and Magic." *Classical Quarterly* 45: 590–92.

Davies, J.G. 1993. "Deacons, Deaconesses and the Minor Orders in the Patristic Period." In *Church, Ministry and Organization in the Early Church Era*, ed. Everett Ferguson. New York: Garland.

Davis, Stephen J. 2008. *The Cult of Saint Thecla: A Tradition of Women's Piety in Late Antiquity*. Oxford: Oxford University Press.

Dean-Jones, Lesley A. 1992. "The Politics of Pleasure: Female Sexual Appetite in the Hippocratic Corpus." *Helios* 19: 72–81.

Dean-Jones, Lesley A. 1994. *Women's Bodies in Classical Greek Science*. Oxford: Oxford University Press.

Delia, D. 1991. "Fulvia Reconsidered." In *Women's History and Ancient History*, ed. Sarah B. Pomeroy. Chapel Hill: University of North Carolina Press.

"Delphic Oracle." In *The Concise Oxford Companion to Classical Literature*, ed. M.C. Howatson and Ian Chilvers. New York: Oxford University Press, 1996. Oxford Reference Online. Available at: http://www.oxfordreference.com/views/ENTRY. html?subview=Mainandentry=t9.e887 (accessed June 10, 2010).

Demand, Nancy. 1994. *Birth, Death, and Motherhood in Classical Greece*. Baltimore and London: Johns Hopkins University Press.

Demand, Nancy. 1995. "Monuments, Midwives and Gynecology." In *Ancient Medicine in Its Socio-Cultural Context*, ed. Philip J. van der Eijk, H.F.J. Horstmanshoff, and P.H. Schrijvers. Amsterdam: Rodopi.

De Nie, Gieselle. 2003. "Fatherly and Motherly Curing in Sixth-Century Gaul: Saint Radegund's Mysterium." In *Women and Miracle Stories: A Multidisciplinary Exploration*, ed. Anne-Marie Korte. Leiden: Brill.

Dewald, C. 1981. "Women and Culture in Herodotos' Histories." In *Reflections of Women in Antiquity*, ed. Helene P. Foley. New York: Gordon and Breach.

Digest of Roman Law.

Dillon, Matthew. 2002. *Girls and Women in Classical Greek Religion*. London: Routledge.

Dillon, Sheila. 2010. *The Female Portrait Statue in the Greek World*. Cambridge: Cambridge University Press.

Dillon, Matthew, and Lynda Garland. 2010. *Ancient Greece: Social and Historical Documents from Archaic Times to the Death of Alexander the Great*. London: Routledge.

Dionysius Halicarnasseus. *Antiquitates Romanae.*

Dix, Gregory. 1937. *The Treatise on the Apostolic Tradition of St Hippolytus of Rome, Bishop and Martyr.* London: Society for Promoting Christian Knowledge.

Dixon, Suzanne. 2006. *Cornelia, Mother of Gracchi.* London and New York: Routledge.

Dixon, Suzanne. 1983. "A Family Business: Women's Role in Patronage and Politics at Rome 80–44 BC." *Classica et Mediaevalia* 34: 91–112.

Dixon, Suzanne. 2001. *Reading Roman Women: Sources, Genres, and Real Life.* London: Duckworth.

Dixon, Suzanne. 1992. *The Roman Family.* Baltimore: John Hopkins University Press.

Dixon, Suzanne. 1988. *The Roman Mother.* London and Sydney, Australia: Croom Helm.

Drivjers, J. W. 1997. *Helena Augusta.* Leiden: Brill.

Dronke, Peter. 1984. *Women Writers of the Middle Ages.* Cambridge: Cambridge University Press.

Duby, Georges, Michelle Perrot, Christiane Klapisch-Zuber, and Pauline Schmitt Pantel. 1992. *A History of Women in the West.* Cambridge, MA: Belknap Press of Harvard University Press.

Duschesne, L. 1956. *Christian Worship: Its Origins and Evolution.* London: SPCK Edelstein.

Edelstein, Emma J., and Ludwig Edelstein. 1998 [1945]. *Asclepius: A Collection and Interpretation of the Testimonies.* Vols. 1–2. Baltimore: Johns Hopkins University Press.

Edmonds, J. M., ed. 1929. *The Characters of Theophrastus: Herodes, Cercidas and the Greek Choliambic Poets,* trans. A. D. Knox. London: William Heinemann.

Edmonson, Jonathan. 2008. "Public Dress and Social Control in Late Republican and Early Imperial Rome." In *Roman Dress and the Fabrics of Roman Culture,* ed. Jonathan Edmondson and Alison Keith. Toronto: University of Toronto Press.

Edmonson, Jonathan, and Alison Keith. 2008. *Roman Dress and the Fabrics of Roman Culture.* Toronto: University of Toronto Press.

Edwards, Catharine. 1997. "Unspeakable Professions: Public Performance and Prostitution in Ancient Rome." In *Roman Sexualities,* ed. Judith P. Hallett and Marilyn B. Skinner. Princeton, NJ: Princeton University Press.

Ehrhardt, C. 1978. "Messalina and the Succession to Claudius." *Antichthon* 12: 51–71.

Elsner, Jas. 2007 [1998]. "The Changing Nature of Roman Art and the Art-Historical Problem of Style." In *Late Antique and Medieval Art of the Mediterranean World,* ed. Eva Rose Hoffman. Blackwell Anthologies in Art History. Malden, MA: Blackwell.

Epictetus. *Enchiridion.*

Epiphanius of Salamis. *Medicine Box.*

Euripides. *Medea.*

Euripides. *Phoenecian Women.*

Eusebius. *Ecclesiastical History.*

Evans, J.A.S. 2002. *Empress Theodora, Partner of Justinian.* Austin: University of Texas Press.

Fantham, Elaine. 1995. "Aemilia Pudencilla: Or the Wealthy Widow's Choice." In *Women in Antiquity: New Assessments,* ed. Richard Hawley and Barbara Levick. London and New York: Routledge.

Fantham, Elaine. 2008. "Covering the Head at Rome: Ritual and Gender." In *Roman Dress and the Fabrics of Roman Culture*, ed. Jonathan Edmonson and Alison Keith. Toronto: University of Toronto Press.

Fantham, Elaine. 2006. *Julia Augusti: The Emperor's Daughter*. London and New York: Routledge.

Fantham, Elaine, Helene Peet Foley, Natalie Boymel Kampen, Sarah B. Pomeroy, and H. Alan Shapiro. 1994. *Women in the Classical World: Image and Text*. New York and Oxford: Oxford University Press.

Faraone, Christopher. 2003. "New Light on Ancient Greek Exorcisms of the Wandering Womb." *Zeitschrift für Papyrologie und Epigraphik* 144: 189–97.

Ferrari, Gloria. 1990. "Figures of Speech: The Picture of *Aidos*." *Metis* 5: 185–200.

Finucane, Ronald C. 1997. *The Rescue of the Innocents: Endangered Children in Medieval Miracles*. New York: St. Martin's.

Flemming, Rebecca. 2000. *Medicine and the Making of Roman Women: Gender, Nature, and Authority from Celsus to Galen*. Oxford: Oxford University Press.

Flemming, Rebecca. 2007. "Women, Writing, and Medicine in the Classical World." *Classical Quarterly* 57: 257–79.

Flory, M. B. 1993. "Livia and the History of Public Honorific Statues for Women in Rome." *Transactions of the American Philological Association* 123: 287–308.

Flory, M. B. 1984. "*Sic exempla parantur*: Livia's Shrine to Concordia and the Porticus Liviae." *Historia* 33: 309–30.

Foley, Helene P. 2001. *Female Acts in Greek Tragedy*. Princeton, NJ: Princeton University Press.

Foley, Helene P. 1981. *Reflections of Women in Antiquity*. New York: Gordon and Breach.

Foucault, Michel. 1984. *History of Sexuality*, trans. Robert Hurley. New York: Random House, Inc.

Fowler, W. Warde. 1908. *The Roman Festivals of the Period of the Republic*. London: Macmillan.

Foxall, Lin. 1995. "Women's Ritual and Men's Work in Ancient Athens." In *Women in Antiquity: New Assessments*, ed. Richard Hawley and Barbara Levick. London and New York: Routledge.

Friesen, Steven J. 1999. "Asiarchs." *Zeitschrift für Papyrologie und Epigraphik* 126: 275–90.

Friggeri, Rosanna. 2001. *The Epigraphic Collection of the Museo Nazionale of the Baths of Diocletian*. Rome: Electa.

Fronrobert, Charlotte. 1997. "The Woman with a Blood-Flow (Mark 5.24–34) Revisited: Menstrual Laws and Jewish Culture in Christian Feminist Hermeneutics." In *Early Christian Interpretation of the Scriptures of Israel: Investigations and Proposals*, ed. Craig E. Evans and James A. Sanders. Journal for the Study of the New Testament Supplement Series 148. Sheffield: Sheffield University Press.

Fullerton, Mark D. 1999. *Greek Art*. Cambridge: Cambridge University Press.

Gagé, J. 1963. *Matronalia, Essai sur les dévotions et les organisations cultuelles des femmes dans l'ancienne Rome*. Brussels: Latomus.

Gaius. *Institutiones*.

Galen. *On Prognosis*.

Gardner, Jane F. 1986. *Women in Roman Law and Society*. Bloomington: Indiana University Press and London: Croom Helm.

Garland, Lynda. 1999. *Byzantine Empresses: Women and Power in Byzantium AD 527–1204*. London and New York: Routledge.

Geffcken, Katherine A. 1973. *Comedy in the Pro Caelio, with an appendix on the* In Clodium et Curionem. Leiden: Brill.

Gellius. *Noctes Atticae*.

Ginsburg, J. 2006. *Representing Agrippina: Construction of Female Power in the Early Roman Empire*. Oxford: Oxford University Press.

Glazebrook, Allison. 2006. "The Bad Girls of Athens: The Image and Function of *Hetairai* in Judicial Oratory." In *Prostitutes and Courtesans in the Ancient World*, ed. Christopher A. Faraone and Laura K. McClure. Madison: University of Wisconsin Press.

Glazebrook, Allison. 2009. "Cosmetics and Sôphrosuynê: Ischomachos's Wife in Xenophon's *Oikonomikos*." *Classical World* 102 (3): 233–48.

Glazebrook, Allison. 2005. "Prostituting Female Kin (Plut. Sol. 23.1–2)." *Dike: Rivista Di Storia Del Diritto Greco Ed Ellenistico* 8: 33–53.

Goff, Barbara E. 2004. *Citizen Bacchae: Women's Ritual Practice in Ancient Greece*. Los Angeles: University of California Los Angeles Press.

Gold, Barbara K. 1997. "Hrotswitha Writes Herself: *Clamor Validus Gandeshemensis*." In *Sex and Gender in Medieval and Renaissance Texts: The Latin Tradition*, ed. Barbara K. Gold, Paul Allen Miller, and Charles Platter. Albany: State University of New York Press.

Golden, Mark. 1990. *Children and Childhood in Classical Athens*. Baltimore: Johns Hopkins University Press.

Grant, Ian Michael, ed. 2004. *Women Writers of Ancient Greece and Rome: An Anthology*. Norman: University of Oklahoma Press.

Green, Anna. 2008. *Cultural History*. New York: Palgrave Macmillan.

Green, C.M.C. 2007. *Roman Religions and the Cult of Diana at Aricia*. New York: Cambridge University Press.

Green, Monica. 2000. "Medieval Gynaecological Texts: A Handlist." In *Women's Healthcare in the Medieval West: Texts and Contexts*, ed. Monica Green. Aldershot, UK: Ashgate.

Greene, Ellen. 1996. "Apostrophe and Women's Erotics in the Poetry of Sappho." In *Reading Sappho: Contemporary Approaches*, ed. Ellen Greene. Berkeley: University of California Press.

Greene, Ellen, ed. 2005. *Women Poets in Ancient Greece and Rome*. Norman: University of Oklahoma Press.

Gregory of Nyssa. *Life of Macrina*.

Gregory of Tours [Saint]. 1988. *Vita Patrum: The Life of the Fathers*, ed. and trans. Fr. Seraphim Rose. Platina, CA: St. Herman of Alaska Brotherhood.

Griffin, Miriam T. 1985. *Nero: The End of a Dynasty*. New Haven, CT, and London: Yale University Press.

Grillet, Bernard. 1975. *Les femmes et les fards dans l'antiquité grecque*. Lyon, France: Centre national de la recherche scientifique.

Grimal, Pierre. 1986. *Love in Ancient Rome*, trans. Arthur Train Jr. Norman: University of Oklahoma Press.

Grubbs, Judith Evans. 2005. "Children and Divorce in Roman Law." In *Hoping for Continuity: Childhood, Education and Death in Antiquity and the Middle Ages*, ed. Katariina Mustakallio et al. ACTA IRF 33. Rome: Institutum Romanum Finlandiae.

Grubbs, Judith Evans. 2011. "The Dynamics of Infant Abandonment: Motives, Attitudes and (Unintended) Consequences." In *Dark Side of Childhood in Late Antiquity and the Middle Ages*, ed. Katariina Mustakallio and Christian Laes. Oxford: Oxbow.

Gruber, Heather I. Waddell. 2008. "The Women of Greek Declamation and the Reception of Comic Stereotypes." PhD diss., University of Iowa.

Gryson, Roger. 1976. *The Ministry of Women in the Early Church*, trans. Jean Laporte and Mary Louise Hall. Collegeville, MN: Liturgical Press.

Guardasole, Alessia. 1998. *Eraclide di Taranto: Frammenti*. Naples, Italy: M. D'Auria.

Hägg, Tomas. 2006. "Playing with Expectations: Gregory's Funeral Orations on His Brother, Sister and Father." In *Gregory of Nazianzus: Images and Reflections*, ed. Jostein Børtnes and Tomas Hägg. Copenhagen: University Press.

Hallett, Judith. 1984. *Fathers and Daughters in Roman Society: Women and the Elite Family*. Princeton, NJ: Princeton University Press.

Hallett, Judith P. 1997. "Female Homoeroticism and the Denial of Roman Reality in Latin Literature." In *Roman Sexualities*, ed. Judith P. Hallett and Marilyn B. Skinner. Princeton, NJ: Princeton University Press.

Hallett, Judith. 2002. "The Vindolanda Letters from Claudia Severa." In *Women Writing Latin in Roman Antiquity, Late Antiquity, and the Early Christian Era*, ed. Laurie J. Churchill, Phyllis R. Brown, and Jane E. Jeffrey. New York and London: Routledge.

Hamel, Debra. 2003. *Trying Neaira: The True Story of a Courtesan's Scandalous Life in Ancient Greece*. New Haven, CT: Yale University Press.

Hamermesh, Daniel, and Jeff Biddle. 1993. "Beauty and the Labor Market." *American Economic Review* 84 (5): 1174–95.

Hänninen, Marja-Leena. 2005. "From Womb to Family: Rituals and Social Conventions Connected to Roman Birth." In *Hoping for Continuity: Childhood, Education and Death in Antiquity and the Middle Ages*, ed. Katariina Mustakallio, Jussi Hanska, Hanna-Leena Sainio, and Ville Vuolanto. ACTA IRF 33. Rome: Institutum Romanum Finlandiae.

Hanska, J. 2005. "Education as Investment: The Childhood of Pietro del Morrone in the Thirteenth Century Abbruzzi." In *Hoping for Continuity: Childhood, Education and Death in Antiquity and the Middle Ages*, ed. Katariina Mustakallio et al. ACTA IRF 33. Rome: Institutum Romanum Finlandiae.

Hanson, Ann Ellis. 1994. "A Division of Labor: Roles for Men in Greek and Roman Births." *Thamyris* 1: 157–202.

Hanson, Ann Ellis. 2004. "A Long-Lived 'Quick-Birther' (*Okytokion*)." In *Naissance et petite enfance dans l'Antiquité*, ed. Véronique Dasen. Fribourg: Academie Press.

Hanson, Ann Ellis. 1990. "The Medical Writers' Woman." In *Before Sexuality: The Construction of Erotic Experience in the Ancient Greek World*, ed. David M. Halperin, John J. Winkler, and Froma I. Zeitlin. Princeton, NJ: Princeton University Press.

Hanson, Ann Ellis. 1996. "Phaenarete: Mother and *Maia*." In *Hippokratische Medizin und antike Philosophie*, ed. Renate Wittern and Pierre Pellegrin. Hildesheim, Germany: Olms.

Hanson, Ann Ellis. 1995. "Uterine Amulets and Greek Uterine Medicine." *Medicina nei Secoli* 7: 281–99.

Hanson, Ann Ellis., and Monica H. Green. 1994. "Soranus of Ephesus: *Methodicorum Princeps*." In *Aufstieg und Niedergang der römischen Welt. Geschichte und Kultur Roms im Spiegel der neueren Forschung. Teil II. Principat. Band 37: Philosophie, Wissenschaften, Technik. 2 Teilband: Wissenschaften (Medizin und Biologie)*, ed. Wolfgang Hasse. Berlin and New York: Walter de Gruyter.

Harland, Philip A. 2003. *Associations, Synagogues and Congregations: Claiming a Place in Ancient Mediterranean Society*. Minneapolis: Fortress.

Harlow, Mary, and Ray Laurence. 2010. "Betrothal, Mid-Late Childhood and the Life Course." In *Ancient Marriage in Myth and Reality*, ed. Lena Larsson Lovén and Agneta Strömberg. Cambridge: Cambridge Scholars Publishing.

Harlow, Mary, and Ray Laurence. 2002. *Growing Up and Growing Old in Ancient Rome: A Life Course Approach*. New York and London: Routledge.

Harris, Charles. 1932. "Visitation of the Sick." In *Liturgy and Worship*, ed. W.K. Lowther Clarke and Charles Harris. London: SPCK, 1932.

Harris, William V. 1989. *Ancient Literacy*. Cambridge, MA: Harvard University Press.

Hart, Gerald D. 2002. *Asclepius, the God of Medicine*. London: Royal Society of Medicine Press.

Harvey, D. 1985. "Women in Thucydides." *Arethusa* 18: 67–90.

Havelock, Christine Mitchell. 2008. *The Aphrodite of Knidos and Her Successors: A Historical Review of the Female Nude in Greek Art*. Ann Arbor: University of Michigan Press.

Havice, Christine. 1999. "Approaching Medieval Women through Medieval Art." In *Women in Medieval Western European Culture*, ed. Linda E. Mitchell. New York: Garland.

Hawley, Richard. 1998. "The Dynamics of Beauty in Classical Greece." In *Changing Bodies, Changing Meanings: Studies on the Human Body in Antiquity*, ed. Dominic Montserrat. New York: Routledge.

Haynes, Sybille. 2000. *Etruscan Civilization: A Cultural History*. Los Angeles: J. Paul Getty Trust.

Helmreich, George. 1968. *Galeni De usu partium libri XVII. Editionem codicum fidem recensuit Georgius Helmreich*. Amsterdam: Adolf M. Hakkert.

Hemelrijk, Emily A. 1999. *Matrona Docta: Educated Women in the Roman Élite from Cornelia to Julia Domna*. New York and London: Routledge.

Hemelrijk, Emily A. 2010. "Women's Participation in Civic Life: Patronage and 'Motherhood' of Roman Associations." In *De Amicitia: Friendship and Social Networks in Antiquity and the Middle Ages*, ed. Katariina Mustakallio and Christian Krötzl. ACTA IRF 36. Rome: Edizione Quasar.

Henderson, Jeffrey. 1980. "Lysistrate: The Play and Its Themes." In *Aristophanes: Essays in Interpretation*, ed. J. Henderson. Cambridge: Cambridge University Press.

Henrichs, A., trans. 2004. "Epitaph of Alcmeonis, a Priestess of Dionysos." In *Women's Religions in the Greco-Roman World: A Sourcebook*, ed. Ross Shepard Kraemer. New York: Oxford University Press.

Henrichs, A., trans. 2005. "Rules of Ritual," Miletus, 276/5 B.C.E. In *Women's Life in Greece and Rome: A Sourcebook in Translation*, ed. Mary R. Lefkowitz and Maureen B. Fant. Baltimore: Johns Hopkins University Press.

Henry, Madeleine M. 1995. *Prisoner of History: Aspasia of Miletos and Her Biographical Tradition*. Oxford: Oxford University Press.

Henry, Madeleine M. 2003. "Prostitution, Secular." In *The Oxford Classical Dictionary*, ed. Simon Hornblower and Anthony Spawforth. Oxford: Oxford University Press.

Henry, Madeleine M., and Allison Glazebrook. 2011. *Prostitutes in the Ancient Mediterranean, 800 BCE–200 CE* Madison, Wis.: University of Wisconsin Press.

Herodotus. *Histories*.

Herrin, Judith. 2001. *Women in Purple: Rulers of Medieval Byzantium*. London: Weidenfeld.

Herter, Hans. 2003. "The Sociology of Prostitution in Antiquity in the Context of Pagan and Christian Writings," trans. Linwood DeLong. In *Sex and Difference in Ancient Greece and Rome*, ed. Mark Golden and Peter Toohey. Edinburgh: Edinburgh University Press.

Heschel, Susannah. 2004. "Gender and Agency in the Feminist Historiography of Jewish Identity." *Journal of Religion* 84 (4): 580–91.

Hillard, Tom. 1992. "On the Stage, behind the Curtain: Images of Politically Active Women in the Late Roman Republic." In *Stereotypes of Women in Power: Historical Perspectives and Revisionist Views*, ed. Barbara Garlick, Suzanne Dixon, and Pauline Allen. London: Greenwood.

Hodkinson, S. 1980. "Land Tenure and Inheritance in Classical Sparta." *Classical Quarterly* 36: 378–406.

Hölbl, G. 2000. *A History of the Ptolemaic Empire*. London and New York: Routledge.

Holum, Kenneth G. 1982. *Theodosian Empresses: Women and Imperial Domination in Late Antiquity*. Berkeley: University of California Press.

Horace. *Epistulae*.

Horace. *Satire*.

Horace. *Epode*.

Hornblower, Simon. 1982. *Mausolus*. Oxford: Oxford University Press.

Horne, Cornelia B. 2009. *"Let the Little Children Come to Me"*: *Childhood and Children in Early Christianity*. Washington, DC: Catholic University Press.

Hunter, David. 2007. *Marriage, Celibacy, and Heresy in Ancient Christianity*. Oxford: Oxford University Press.

Hunter, Erica C. D. 2002. "Manipulating Incantation Texts: Excursions in Refrain 'A'." *Iraq* 64: 259–73.

Hunter, Virginia J. 1994. *Policing Athens: Social Control in the Attic Lawsuits, 420–320 B.C.* Princeton, NJ: Princeton University Press.

Huskinson, Janet. 1996. *Roman Children's Sarcophagi: Their Decoration and Its Social Significance*. Oxford Monographs on Classical Archaeology. Oxford: Oxford University Press.

Irenaeus. [1957]. *Against Heresies*. In *The Ante-Nicene Fathers 1*, ed. and trans. Alexander Roberts and James Donaldson. Grand Rapids, MI: Wm. B. Eerdmans.

Jaekel, Siegfried, ed. 1964. *Menandri Sententiae*. Leipzig, Germany: Teubner.

Jameson, Michael H. 1990. "Domestic Space in the Greek City-State." In *Domestic Architecture and the Use of Space*, ed. Susan Kent. Cambridge and New York: Cambridge University Press.

Janowitz, Naomi. 2001. *Magic in the Roman World: Pagans, Jews and Christians*. London: Routledge.

Jenkins, Ian, and Victoria Turner. 2010. *The Greek Body*. Los Angeles: J. Paul Getty Museum.

Jerome. *Letters*.

John Chrysostom. *Homily 17*.

Johnson, Marguerite, and Terry Ryan, eds. 2005. *Sexuality in Greek and Roman Society and Literature: A Sourcebook*. London and New York: Routledge.

Johnston, Alan. 1991. "Greek Vases in the Marketplace." In *Looking at Greek Vases*, ed. Tom Rasmussen and Nigel Spivey. Cambridge: Cambridge University Press.

Jones, Amelia, ed. 2003. *The Feminism and Visual Culture Reader*. New York: Routledge.

Joshel, Sandra R. 1986. "Nurturing the Master's Child: Slavery and the Roman Child Nurse." *Signs* 12: 3–22.

Joshel, Sandra R. 1992. *Work, Identity, and Legal Status at Rome: A Study of Occupational Inscriptions*. Norman: University of Oklahoma Press.

Joshel, Sandra R., and Sheila Murnaghan, eds. 2001. *Women and Slaves in Greco-Roman Culture: Differential Equations*. London and New York: Routledge.

Joyal, Mark, Iain McDougall, and J. C. Yardley, eds. 2008. *Greek and Roman Education: A Sourcebook*. London and New York: Routledge.

Just, Roger. 1989. *Women in Athenian Law and Life*. London and New York: Routledge.

Justin Martyr. [1957]. *Dialogue with Trypho*. In *The Ante-Nicene Fathers 1*, ed. and trans. Alexander Roberts and James Donaldson. Grand Rapids, MI: Wm. B. Eerdmans.

Justinianus. *Codex*.

Kajava, Mika. 2004. "Hestia: Hearth, Goddess, and Cult." *Harvard Studies in Classical Philology* 102: 1–20.

Kajava, Mika. 1994. *Roman Female Praenomina: Studies in the Nomenclatura of Roman Women*. ACTA IRF 14. Rome: Institutum Romanum Finlandiae.

Kalavrezou, Iole. 2008. "The Cup of San Marco and the 'Classical' in Byzantium." In *Worshipping Women: Ritual and Reality in Classical Athens*, ed. Nikolaos Kaltsas and Alan Shapiro. New York: Alexander S. Onassis Public Benefit Foundation.

Kaltsas, Nikolaos, and Alan Shapiro, eds. 2008. *Worshipping Women: Ritual and Reality in Classical Athens*. New York: Alexander S. Onassis Public Benefit Foundation.

Kampen, Natalie B. 1981. *Image and Status: Roman Working Women in Ostia*. Berlin: Mann.

Kampen, Natalie B. 1996. *Sexuality in Ancient Art*. Cambridge: Cambridge University Press.

Kampen, Natalie B. 1982. "Social Status and Gender in Roman Art: The Case of the Saleswoman." In *Feminism and Art History*, ed. Norma Broude and Mary D. Garrard. New York: Harper and Row.

Kaplan, M. 1978. "*Agrippina semper atrox*: A Study in Tacitus' Characterization of Women." In *Studies in Latin Literature and Roman History*, vol. 1, ed. C. Deroux. Brussels: Latomus.

Katz, M. 1994. "The Character of Tragedy: Women and the Greek Imagination." *Arethusa* 27: 96–100.

Kearns, Emily. 2010. *Ancient Greek Religion: A Sourcebook*. Malden, MA: Wiley-Blackwell.

Keith, Alison. 1997. "*Tandem venit amor*: A Roman Woman Speaks of Love." In *Roman Sexualities*, ed. Judith P. Hallett and Marilyn B. Skinner. Princeton, NJ: Princeton University Press.

Kelly-Gadol, Joan. 1977. "Did Women Have a Renaissance?" In *Becoming Visible: Women in European History*, ed. Renate Bridenthal and Claudia Koonz. Boston: Houghton-Mifflin Boston.

Kennedy, George. 1987. "The History of Latin Education." In "Latinitas: The Tradition and Teaching of Latin," ed. M. Santirocco. *Helios*, special issue, 14 (2): 7–16.

Kerényi, Karl. 1959. *Asklepios: Archetypal Image of the Physician's Existence*, trans. Ralph Manheim. New York: Bolligen/Pantheon Books.

Keyser, Paul T., and Georgia L. Irby-Massie, eds. 2008. *The Encyclopedia of Ancient Natural Scientists: The Greek Tradition and Its Many Heirs*. London: Routledge.

King, Helen. 1986. "Agnodike and the Profession of Medicine." *Proceedings of the Cambridge Philological Society* 32: 53–77.

King, Helen. 1998. *Hippocrates' Woman: Reading the Female Body in Ancient Greece*. London and New York: Routledge.

Kinney, Dale, and Anthony Cutler. 1994. "A Late Antique Ivory Plaque and Modern Response." *American Journal of Archaeology* 98 (3): 457–80.

Kleiner, Diana E. E., and Susan B. Matheson, eds. 1996. *I Claudia: Women in Ancient Rome*. Austin: University of Texas Press.

Kleiner, Diana E. E., and Susan B. Matheson, eds. 2000. *I Claudia II: Women in Roman Art and Society*. Austin: University of Texas Press.

Kleiner, Fred S. 2010. *Gardner's Art through the Ages: The Western Perspective*. 13th ed. Boston: Wadsworth.

Klingshirn, William E. 1994. *Caesarius of Arles: The Making of a Christian Community in Late Antique Gaul*. Cambridge: Cambridge University Press.

Klingshirn, William E. 1994. *Caesarius of Arles: Life, Testament, Letters*. Liverpool: Liverpool University Press.

Koloski-Ostrow, Ann, and Claire Lyons, eds. 1997. *Naked Truths: Women, Sexuality, and Gender in Classical Art and Archaeology*. London: Routledge.

Kousis, A. P. 1945. "Metrodora's Work 'On the Feminine Diseases of the Womb' according to the Greek codex 75,3 of the Laurentian Library." *Praktikaēs Akadēmias Athēnōn* 20: 46–69.

Kousser, R. M. 2008. *Hellenistic and Roman Ideal Sculpture: The Allure of the Classical*. Cambridge: Cambridge University Press.

Köves-Zulauf, T. 1990. *Römische Geburtsriten*. Zetemata 87. Munich, Germany: Beck.

Kraemer, Ross Shepard. 1992. *Her Share of the Blessings: Women's Religions among Pagans, Jews and Christians in the Greco-Roman World*. New York: Oxford University Press.

Kraemer, Ross Shepard. 1985. "A New Inscription from Malta and the Question of Women Elders in Diaspora Jewish Communities." *Harvard Theological Review* 78 (3–4): 431–38.

Kraemer, Ross Shepard, trans. 2004. "Ten Inscriptions from a Synagogue Commemorating Contributions from Women for the Paving of a Mosaic Floor." In *Women's Religions in the Greco-Roman World: A Sourcebook*, ed. Ross Shepard Kraemer. New York: Oxford University Press.

Kraemer, Ross Shepard. 2011. *Unreliable Witnesses: Religion, Gender, and History in the Greco-Roman Mediterranean*. Oxford and New York: Oxford University Press.

Kraemer, Ross Shepard, ed. 2004. *Women's Religions in the Greco-Roman World: A Sourcebook*. New York: Oxford University Press.

Kraemer, Ross Shepard, and Mary Rose D'Angelo, eds. 1999. *Women and Christian Origins*. New York: Oxford University Press.

Krötzl, Christian, and Katariina Mustakallio. 2012. *On Old Age: Approaching Death in Antiquity and the Middle Ages*. Turnhout, Belgium: Brepols.

Kuefler, Matthew. 2001. *The Manly Eunuch: Masculinity, Gender Ambiguity, and Christian Theology in Late Antiquity*. Chicago: University of Chicago Press.

Kühn, Karl Gottlob. 1821–1833. *Claudii Galeni Opera Omnia. Editionem curavit D. Carolus Gottlob Kühn*. 20 vols. Leipzig.

Kydd, Ronald A. N. 1993. "Jesus, Saints and Relics: Approaching the Early Church through Healing." *Journal of Pentecostal Theology* 2: 91–104.

Lacey, W. K. 1968. *The Family in Classical Greece*. London: Thames and Hudson.

Lacey, W. K. 1964. "Thucydides II, 45, 2." *Proceedings of the Cambridge Philological Society* 10: 47–49.

Laes, Christian. 2005. "Childbeating in Roman Antiquity: Some Reconsiderations." In *Hoping for Continuity: Childhood, Education and Death in Antiquity and the Middle Ages*, ed. Katariina Mustakallio et al. ACTA IRF 33. Rome: Institutum Romanum Finlandiae.

Laes, Christian. 2010. "Schooling and Education." In *A Cultural History of Childhood and Family in Antiquity*, vol. 1, ed. R. Laurence and M. Harlow. London: Berg.

Lange, Lynda. 1979. "The Function of Equal Education in Plato's Laws." In *The Sexism of Social and Political Theory: Women and Reproduction from Plato to Nietzsche*, ed. Lorenne M. G. Clark and Lynda Lange. Toronto and Buffalo, NY: University of Toronto Press.

Langlands, Rebecca. 2006. *Sexual Morality in Ancient Rome*. Cambridge: Cambridge University Press.

Laqueur, Thomas W. 1990. *Making Sex: Body and Gender from the Greeks to Freud*. Cambridge, MA: Harvard University Press.

Larson, Jennifer. 1995. *Greek Heroine Cults*. Madison: University of Wisconsin Press.

Larsson Lovèn, Lena, and Agneta Strömberg. 2010. "Economy." In *A Cultural History of Childhood and Family in Antiquity*, vol. 1, ed. R. Laurence and M. Harlow. London: Berg.

Laurence, Ray. 2010. "Community." In *A Cultural History of Childhood and Family in Antiquity*, vol. 1, ed. R. Laurence and M. Harlow. London: Berg.

Laurence, Ray. 2010. "Lifecycle." In *A Cultural History of Childhood and Family in Antiquity*, vol. 1, ed. R. Laurence and M. Harlow. London: Berg.

Laurence, Ray. 1994. *Roman Pompeii: Space and Society*. London: Routledge.

Laurin, Joseph R. 2005. *Women of Ancient Athens*. London: Trafford.

Lear, Andrew, and Eva Cantarella. 2008. *Images of Ancient Greek Pederasty: Boys Were Their Gods*. New York: Routledge.

Lefkowitz, Mary R., and Maureen B. Fant, ed. 1992. *Women's Life in Greece and Rome: A Source Book in Translation*. 2nd ed. Baltimore: Johns Hopkins University Press.

Lesko, Barbara S., ed. 1989. *Women's Earliest Records from Ancient Egypt and Western Asia*. Atlanta, GA: Scholars Press.

Levick, Barbara. 1993. *Claudius*. New Haven, CT, and London: Yale University Press.

Levick, Barbara. 2007. *Julia Domna*. London and New York: Routledge.

Levick, Barbara. 1972. "Julii and Claudii?" *Greece and Rome* 22: 29–38.

Levine, Lee I. 2005. *The Ancient Synagogue: The First Thousand Years*. 2nd ed. New Haven, CT: Yale University Press.

Lewis, Sian. 2002. *The Athenian Woman: An Iconographic Handbook*. London: Routledge.

LiDonnici, Lynn R. 1995. *The Epidaurian Miracle Inscriptions: Text, Translation, and Commentary*. Atlanta, GA: Scholars Press.

Lightstone, Jack N. 2007. "Roman Diaspora Judaism." In *A Companion to Roman Religion*, ed. Jörg Rüpke. Oxford: Blackwell.

Lissarrague, François. 2001. *Greek Vases: The Athenians and Their Images*, trans. K. Allen. New York: Riverside.

Littré, Émile. 1839–1861. *Oeuvres complètes d'Hipocrate. Traduction nouvelle avec le texte grec en regard, collationné sur tous les manuscrits et toutes les éditions: accompagnée d'une introduction, de commentaires médicaux, de variantes et de notes philologiques*. 10 vols. Paris: J.B. Baillière.

Livy. *Ab Urbe Condita*.

Llewellyn-Jones, Lloyd. 2003. *Aphrodite's Tortoise: The Veiled Woman of Ancient Greece*. Swansea: Classical Press of Wales.

Lloyd, Geoffrey E.R. 1996. *Adversaries and Authorities: Investigations into Ancient Greek and Chinese Science*. Cambridge: Cambridge University Press.

Lloyd, Geoffrey E.R. 2003. *In the Grip of Disease: Studies in the Greek Imagination*. Oxford: Oxford University Press.

Lloyd, Geoffrey E.R. 1983. *Science, Folklore and Ideology: Studies in the Life Sciences in Ancient Greece*. Cambridge: Cambridge University Press.

Luck, G. 1985. *Arcana Mundi: Magic and the Occult in the Greek and Roman World*. Baltimore: Johns Hopkins University Press.

Lyons, Deborah. 2007. "The Scandal of Women's Ritual." In *Finding Persephone: Women's Rituals in the Ancient Mediterranean*, ed. Maryline Parca and Angeliki Tzanetou. Bloomington: Indiana University Press.

Lysias. *Against Eratosthenes*.

Maas, Michael, ed. 2000. *Readings in Late Antiquity: A Sourcebook*. London and New York: Routledge.

MacDonald, Margaret Y. 1996. *Early Christian Women and Pagan Opinion: The Power of the Hysterical Woman*. Cambridge: Cambridge University Press.

MacMullen, Ramsay. 1980. "Women in Public in the Roman Empire." *Historia: Zeitschrift für Alte Geschichte* 29 (2): 208–18.

Macrobius. *Saturnalia*.

Madigan, Kevin, and Carolyn Osiek, eds. 2005. *Ordained Women in the Early Church: A Documentary History*. Baltimore: Johns Hopkins University Press.

Malina, Bruce J., and Jerome H. Neyrey. 1996. *Portraits of Paul: An Archaeology of Ancient Personality*. Louisville, KY: Westminster John Knox.

Malone, Mary T. 2001. *Women and Christianity: The First Thousand Years*. Maryknoll, NY: Orbis Books.

Mantle, I. C. 2002. "The Roles of Children in Roman Religion." *Greece and Rome*, 2nd ser., 49: 85–106.

Manuli, Paula. 1980. "Fisiologia e patologia del femminile negli scritti ippocratici dell' antica ginecologia greca." In *Hippocratica: actes du Colloque hippocratique de Paris, 4–9 septembre 1978*, ed. Mirko D. Grmek and F. Robert. Paris: Éditions du Centre national de la recherche scientifique.

Marinatos, Spyridon. 1972. *Excavations at Thera V*. Athens: Archaeological Society of Athens.

Marrou, H. I. 1956. *A History of Education in Antiquity*, trans. George Lamb. Madison: University of Wisconsin Press.

Marshall, A. J. 1989. "Ladies at Law: The Role of Women in the Roman Civil Law Courts." In *Studies in Latin Literature and Roman History*, vol. 5, ed. Carl Deroux. Brussels: Latomus.

Martimort, Aime Georges. 1986. *Deaconesses: An Historical Study*. San Francisco: Ignatius Press.

Mattern, Susan P. 2008. *Galen and the Rhetoric of Healing*. Baltimore: Johns Hopkins University Press.

Mathews, Thomas F. 1999. *The Clash of Gods: A Reinterpretation of Early Christian Art*. Rev. exp. ed. Princeton, NJ: Princeton University Press.

Mayhew, Robert. 2004. *The Female in Aristotle's Biology: Reason or Rationalization*. Chicago and London: University of Chicago Press.

McCauley, Leo P., John J. Sullivan, Martin R. P. McGuire, and Roy J. Deferrari. 1953. *Funeral Orations by Saint Gregory Nazianzen and Saint Ambrose*. Washington, DC: Catholic University of America Press.

McClure, Laura K. 2003. *Courtesans at Table: Gender and Greek Literary Culture in Athenaeus*. New York and London: Routledge.

McClure, Laura K. 2006. "Introduction." In *Prostitutes and Courtesans in the Ancient World*, ed. Christopher A. Faraone and Laura K. McClure. Madison: University of Wisconsin Press.

McClure, Laura K. 2009. "Sexuality and Gender." In *The Oxford Handbook of Hellenic Studies*, ed. George Boys-Stones, Barbara Graziosi, and Phiroze Vasunia. Oxford: Oxford University Press.

McClure, Laura K., ed. 2002. *Sexuality and Gender in the Classical World*. Oxford and Malden, MA: Blackwell.

McGinn, Thomas A. 2004. *The Economy of Prostitution in the Roman World: A Study of Social History and the Brothel*. Ann Arbor: University of Michigan Press.

McGinn, Thomas A. J. 2002. "Pompeian Brothels and Social History." *Journal of Roman Archaeology* 47: S7–S46.

McGinn, Thomas A. J. 1998. *Prostitution, Sexuality, and the Law in Ancient Rome*. New York: Oxford University Press.

McGinn, Thomas A. 2006. "Zoning Shame in the Roman City." In *Prostitutes and Courtesans in the Ancient World*, ed. Christopher A. Faraone and Laura K. McClure. Madison: University of Wisconsin Press.

McGuckin, John A. 2001. *St. Gregory of Nazianzus: An Intellectual Biography*. Crestwood, NY: St. Vladimir's Seminary Press.

McKeown, Niall. 2007. "Had They No Shame? Martial, Statius and Roman Sexual Attitudes towards Slave Children." In *Children, Childhood and Society*, ed. Sally Crawford and Gillian Shepherd. BAR International Series 1696. Oxford: Hadrian Books.

Meeks, Wayne A., and Robert L Wilken. 1978. *Jews and Christians in Antioch in the First Four Centuries of the Common Era*. Missoula, MT: Scholars Press.

Metraux, Guy P. R. 2008. "Prudery and Chic in Late Antique Clothing." In *Roman Dress and the Fabrics of Roman Culture*, ed. Jonathan Edmonson and Alison Keith. Toronto: University of Toronto Press.

Metz, René. 1959. *La consecration des vierges dans l'Église romaine*. Paris: Presses universitaires de France.

Meyer, M., and P. Mirecki, eds. 1995. *Ancient Magic and Ritual Power*. Leiden: Brill.

Miles, Gary B. 1995. *Livy: Reconstructing Early Rome*. Ithaca, NY: Cornell University Press.

Miller, Patricia Cox. 1993. "The Blazing Body: Ascetic Desire in Jerome's Letter to Eustochium." *Journal of Early Christian Studies* 1 (1): 21–45.

Miller, Patricia Cox. 2005. *Women in Early Christianity: Translations from Greek Texts*. Washington, DC: Catholic University of America Press.

Miller, Stephen G. 2004. *Ancient Greek Athletics*. New Haven, CT: Yale University Press.

Milnor, Kristina. 2005. *Gender, Domesticity, and the Age of Augustus: Inventing Private Life*. New York: Oxford University Press.

Milnor, Kristina. 2010. "Women." In *The Oxford Handbook of Roman Studies*, ed. Alessandro Barchiesi and Walter Scheidel. Oxford: Oxford University Press.

Mooren, L. 1988. "The Wives and Children of Ptolemy VIII Euergetes II." *Proceedings of the XVIII Congress of Papyrology* 2: 435–44.

Morgan, Janett. 2007. "Women, Religion, and the Home." In *A Companion to Greek Religion*, ed. Daniel Ogden. Oxford: Blackwell.

Morgan, Teresa. 1998. *Literate Education in the Hellenistic and Roman Worlds*. Cambridge: Cambridge University Press.

Munson, R. V. 1988. "Artemisia in Herodotos." *Classical Antiquity* 7: 91–106.

Murray, Jacqueline. 2008. "One Flesh, Two Sexes, Three Genders?" In *Gender and Christianity in Medieval Europe: New Perspectives*, ed. Lisa M. Bitel and Felice Lifshitz. Philadelphia: University of Pennsylvania Press.

Mustakallio, Katariina. 2010. "Creating Roman Identity: Exemplary Marriages." In *Ancient Marriage in Myth and Reality*, ed. Lena Larsson Lovén and Agneta Strömberg. Cambridge: Cambridge Scholars Publishing.

Mustakallio, Katariina. 1999. "Legendary Women and Female Groups in Livy." In *Female Networks and Public Sphere in Roman Society*, ed. Päivi Setälä and Liisa Savunen. ACTA IRF 22. Rome: Institutum Romanum Finlandiae.

Mustakallio, Katariina. 2012. "Representing Older Women: Hersilia, Veturia, *Virgo Vestalis Maxima*." In *On Old Age: Approaching Death in Antiquity and the Middle Ages*, ed. Christian Krötzl and Katariina Mustakallio. Turnhout, Belgium: Brepols.

Mustakallio, Katariina. 2005. "Roman Funerals: Identity, Gender and Participation." In *Hoping for Continuity: Childhood, Education and Death in Antiquity and the Middle Ages*, ed. Katariina Mustakallio et al. ACTA IRF 33. Rome: Institutum Romanum Finlandiae.

Mustakallio, Katariina. 2003. "Women and Mourning in Ancient Rome." In *Gender, Cult, and Culture in the Ancient World*, ed. Lena Larsson Lovén and Agneta Strömberg. Sävedalen, Sweden: Paul Åströms.

Mustakallio, Katariina, Jussi Hanska, Hanna-Leena Sainio, and Ville Vuolanto, eds. 2005. *Hoping for Continuity: Childhood, Education and Death in Antiquity and the Middle Ages*. ACTA IRF 33. Rome: Institutum Romanum Finlandiae.

Neils, Jenifer. 2000. "Others within the Other: An Intimate Look at Hetairai and Maenads." In *Not the Classical Ideal: Athens and the Construction of the Other in Greek Art*, ed. Beth Cohen. Leiden: Brill.

Neils, Jenifer. 1992. *Goddess and Polis: The Panathenaic Festival in Ancient Athens*. Princeton, NJ: Princeton University Press.

Neils, Jenifer, and John H. Oakley. 2003. *Coming of Age in Ancient Greece: Images of Childhood from the Classical Past*. New Haven, CT: Yale University Press.

Nelson, J. 1994. "Parents, Children, Church." In *The Church and Childhood. Papers Read at the 1993 Summer Meeting and the 1994 Winter Meeting of the Ecclesiastical History Society*, ed. Diana Wood. Oxford and Malden, MA: Blackwell.

Nevett, Lisa C. 1999. *House and Society in the Ancient Greek World*. Cambridge and New York: Cambridge University Press.

Nevett, Lisa. 2007. "Housing and Households: The Greek World." In *Classical Archaeology*, ed. Susan E. Alcock and Robin Osborne. Oxford: Blackwell.

Nevett, Lisa C. 1995. "Gender Relations in the Classical Greek Household." *Annual of the British School at Athens* 90: 363–81.

Nickel, Dietrich. 1971. *Galenus, De uteri dissectione*. Berlin: Akademie Verlag.

Nielsen, Marjatta. 2003. "Fit for Fight, Fit for Marriage: Fighting Couples in Nuptial and Funerary Iconography in Late Classical and Early Hellenistic Periods." In

Gender, Cult, and Culture in the Ancient World from Mycenae to Byzantium, ed. Lena Larsson Lovén and Agneta Strömberg. Sävedalen, Sweden: Paul Åströms.

Nitzsche, Jane Chance. 1975. *The Genius Figure in Antiquity and the Middle Ages.* New York: Columbia University Press.

Nixon, Lucia. 1995. "The Cults of Demeter and Kore." In *Women in Antiquity: New Assessments*, ed. Richard Hawley and Barbara Levick. London and New York: Routledge.

North, Helen F. 1977. "The Mare, the Vixen and the Bee: Sophrosyne as the Virtue of Women in Antiquity." *Illinois Classical Studies* 2: 35–48.

North, Helen F. 1966. *Sophrosyne: Self-Knowledge and Self-Restraint in Greek Literature.* Cornell Studies in Classical Philology 35. Ithaca, NY: Cornell University Press.

Nutton, Vivian. 2004. *Ancient Medicine.* London and New York: Routledge.

Nutton, Vivian. 1979. *Galen, On Prognosis. Text, Translation, Commentary.* Berlin: Akademie Verlag.

Nutton, Vivian. 1992. "Healers in the Medical Market Place: Towards a Social History of Graeco-Roman Medicine." In *Medicine in Society: Historical Essays*, ed. Andrew Wear. Cambridge: Cambridge University Press.

Oakley, John H., and Rebecca H. Sinos. 1993. *The Wedding in Ancient Athens.* Madison: University of Wisconsin Press.

Oden, Thomas C., and Christopher A. Hall, eds. 1998. *Ancient Christian Commentary on Scripture, New Testament 2 (Mark).* Downers Grove, IL: Intervarsity Press.

Ogilvie, R. M. 1986 [1968]. *The Romans and Their Gods.* London: Hogarth.

Olender, Maurice. 2005. "Baubo." In *Encyclopedia of Religion*, vol. 2, ed. Lindsay Jones. 2nd ed. Detroit: Macmillan Reference USA.

Olson, Kelly. 2008. *Dress and the Roman Woman: Self-Presentation and Society.* New York: Routledge.

Olson, Kelly. 2006. "*Matrona* and Whore: Clothing and Definition in Roman Antiquity." In *Prostitutes and Courtesans in the Ancient World*, ed. Christopher A. Faraone and Laura K. McClure. Madison: University of Wisconsin Press.

Osborne, Robin. 2004. "Hoards, Votives, Offerings: The Archaeology of the Dedicated Object." *World Archaeology* 36: 1–10.

Osiek, Carolyn. 2003. "Female Slaves, Porneia, and the Limits of Obedience." In *Early Christian Families in Context: An Interdisciplinary Dialogue*, ed. David L. Balch and Carolyn Osiek. Grand Rapids, MI: Eerdmans.

Osiek, Carolyn, and Margaret Y. Macdonald, with Janet H. Tulloch. 2006. *A Woman's Place: House Churches in Earliest Christianity.* Minneapolis: Fortress.

Palladius. 1965. *The Lausiac History*, trans. Robert Meyer. New York: Newman Press.

Panciera, M. 2004. "Livy, Conubium and Plebeians' Access to the Consulship." In *Augusta Augurio, Rerum humanarum et Livinarum commentationes in honorem Jerzy Linderski*, ed. C. F. Kondrad. Wiesbaden, Germany: Franz Steiner.

Parca, Maryline, and Angeliki Tzanetou, eds. 2007. *Finding Persephone: Women's Rituals in the Ancient Mediterranean.* Bloomington: Indiana University Press.

Parker, Holt N. 1992. "Love's Body Anatomized: The Ancient Erotic Handbooks and the Rhetoric of Sexuality." In *Pornography and Representation in Greece and Rome*, ed. Amy Richlin. New York: Oxford University Press.

Parker, Holt N. 1993. "Sappho Schoolmistress." *Transactions of the American Philological Association* 123: 309-51.

Parker, Holt N. 1997. "The Teratogenic Grid." In *Roman Sexualities*, ed. Judith P. Hallett and Marilyn B. Skinner. Princeton, NJ: Princeton University Press.

Parker, Holt N. 1997. "Women Doctors in Greece, Rome, and the Byzantine Empire." In *Women Healers and Physicians: Climbing a Long Hill*, ed. Lilian R. Furst. Lexington: University Press of Kentucky.

Parker, Robert. 1983. *Miasma: Pollution and Purification in Early Greek Religion.* Oxford: Clarendon.

Parkin, Tim G. 2003. *Old Age in the Roman World.* Baltimore: Johns Hopkins University Press.

The Passion of Saints Perpetua and Felicitas. n.d. Trans. R. E. Wallis. Available at: http://www.ccel.org/ccel/schaff/anf03.vi.vi.i.html (accessed March 2010).

Patterson, Cynthia B. 1998. *The Family in Greek History.* Cambridge, MA: Harvard University Press.

Pazanelli, Roberta, Eike Schmidt, and Kenneth Lapatin, eds. 2008. *The Color of Life: Polychromy in Sculpture from Antiquity to the Present.* Los Angeles: Getty Research Institute.

Pedley, John Griffiths. 2007. *Greek Art and Archaeology.* Rev. ed. New York: Prentice Hall.

Peradotto, John, and J. P Sullivan, eds. 1984. *Women in the Ancient World: The Arethusa Papers.* Albany: State University of New York Press.

Perrett, David I., D. Michael Burt, Ian S. Penton-Voak, Kieran J. Lee, Duncan A. Rowland, and Rachel Edwards. 1999. "Symmetry and Human Facial Attractiveness." *Evolution and Human Behavior* 20 (5): 295–307.

Philostorgius. *Church History.*

Philostratus. *The Life of Apollonius of Tyana.*

Plant, I. M., ed. 2004. *Women Writers of Ancient Greece and Rome: An Anthology.* London: Equinox.

Plato. *Laws.*

Plato. *Republic.*

Pliny the Younger. *Epistulae.*

Plutarch. *Moralia.*

Plutarch. *Roman Questions.*

Plutarch. *Vita Romuli.*

Podlecki, Anthony J. 1998. *Perikles and His Circle.* London and New York: Routledge.

Pohlsander, Hans A. 2004. *The Emperor Constantine.* London and New York: Routledge.

Pollitt, Jerome Jordan. 1986. *Art in the Hellenistic Age.* Cambridge: Cambridge University Press.

Pomeroy, Sarah B. 1997. *Families in Classical and Hellenistic Greece: Representations and Realities.* Oxford: Oxford University Press.

Pomeroy, Sarah B. 1975. *Goddesses, Whores, Wives, and Slaves: Women in Classical Antiquity.* New York: Schocken Books.

Pomeroy, Sarah B. 2002. *Spartan Women.* Oxford: Oxford University Press.

Pomeroy, Sarah B. 1977. "*Technikai kai Mousikai*: The Education of Women in the Fourth Century and in the Hellenistic Age." *American Journal of Ancient History* 2: 51–68.

Pomeroy, Sarah B. 1984. *Women in Hellenistic Egypt: From Alexander to Cleopatra*. New York: Schocken Books.

Pomeroy, Sarah B. 1991. *Women's History and Ancient History*. Chapel Hill: University of North Carolina Press.

Porterfield, Amanda. 2005. *Healing in the History of Christianity*. Oxford: Oxford University Press.

Powell, Jim, trans. 2007. *The Poetry of Sappho*. Oxford and New York: Oxford University Press.

Preziosi, Donald, and Louise Hitchcock. 1999. *Aegean Art and Architecture*. Oxford: Oxford University Press.

Prudentius. 1953. *Peristephanon*, trans. H. J. Thomson. London: Heinemann, 1953.

Purcell, Nicholas. 1986. "Livia and the Womanhood of Rome." *Proceedings of the Cambridge Philological Society* 32: 78–105.

Quintilian. *Institutiones*.

Ramage, Nancy H., and Andrew Ramage. 2005. *Roman Art*. Upper Saddle River, NJ: Pearson Prentice Hall.

Rawson, Beryl. 2003. *Children and Childhood in Roman Italy*. Oxford: Oxford University Press.

Redfield, J. 1978. "The Women of Sparta." *Classical Journal* 73: 146–61.

Reeder, Ellen D. 1995. *Pandora: Women in Classical Greece*. Baltimore: Trustees of the Walters Art Gallery.

Reeder, Ellen D. 1995. "Representing Women." In *Pandora: Women in Classical Greece*, ed. Ellen D. Reeder. Baltimore: Trustees of the Walters Art Gallery.

Reynolds, L. D., and N. G. Wilson. 1991. *Scribes and Scholars: A Guide to the Transmission of Greek and Latin Literature*. 3rd ed. Oxford: Clarendon.

Richlin, Amy. 1997. "Pliny's Brassiere." In *Roman Sexualities*, ed. Judith P. Hallett and Marilyn B. Skinner. Princeton, NJ: Princeton University Press.

Richlin, Amy, ed. 1992. *Pornography and Representation in Greece and Rome*. New York: Oxford University Press.

Ridgway, Brunilde Sismodo. 2002. *Hellenistic Sculpture III: The Styles of ca. 100–31 B.C.* Madison: University of Wisconsin Press.

Robertson, Martin. 1992. *The Art of Vase-Painting in Classical Athens*. Cambridge: Cambridge University Press.

Roller, Duane W. 2010. *Cleopatra: A Biography*. Oxford: Oxford University Press.

Rousselle, Aline. 1980. "Images médicales du corps: observation féminine et idéologie masculine. Le corps de la femme d'après les médecins grecs." *Annales: Economies, Sociétés, Civilisations* 35: 1089–115.

Rowlandson, Jane, ed. 1998. *Women and Society in Greek and Roman Egypt: A Sourcebook*. Cambridge: Cambridge University Press.

Rutter, Jeremy. 2003. "Children in Aegean Prehistory." In *Coming of Age in Ancient Greece: Images of Childhood from the Classical Past*. New Haven, CT: Yale University Press.

Ruzicka, S. 1992. *Politics of a Persian Dynasty: The Hecatomnids in the Fourth Century BC*. Norman: University of Oklahoma Press.

Said, Edward W. 1993. *Culture and Imperialism*. New York: Knopf.

Said, Edward W. 1978. *Orientalism*. New York: Vintage Books.

Salisbury, Joyce E. 1992. *Church Fathers, Independent Virgins*. London and New York: Verso.

Salisbury, Joyce E. 1997. *Perpetua's Passion: The Death and Memory of a Young Roman Woman*. New York: Routledge.

Saller, Richard. 2007. "Household and Gender." In *The Cambridge Economic History of the Greco-Roman World*, vol. 1, ed. Walter Scheidel, Ian Morris, and Richard Saller. Cambridge Histories Online. Cambridge: Cambridge University Press. Available at: http://dx.doi.org/10.1017/CHOL9780521780537.005 (accessed August 13, 2010).

Sallust. *Bellum Catilinae*.

Salomon, Nanette. 1997. "Making a World of Difference: Gender, Asymmetry, and the Greek Nude." In *Naked Truths: Women, Sexuality, and Gender in Classical Art and Archaeology*, ed. Ann Koloski-Ostrow and Claire L. Lyons. New York: Routledge.

Salzman, Michele Renee. 1990. *On Roman Time: The Codex-Calendar of 354 and the Rhythms of Urban Life in Late Antiquity*. Berkeley: University of California Press.

Samama, Évelyne. 2003. *Les médecins dans le monde grec: sources épigraphiques sur la naissance d'un corpus médical*. Geneva: Librairie Droz.

Saxonhouse, Arlene. 2005. "Another Antigone: The Emergence of the Female Political Actor in Eurpides' *Phoenician Women*." *Political Theory* 33 (4): 472–94.

Scanlon, Thomas F. 2002. *Eros and Greek Athletics*. Oxford: Oxford University Press.

Schaps, D. 1977. "The Woman Least Mentioned: Etiquette and Women's Names." *Classical Quarterly* 27: 323–30.

Schultz, Celia E. 2007. "Sanctissima Femina: Social Categorization and Women's Religious Experience in the Roman Republic." In *Finding Persephone: Women's Rituals in the Ancient Mediterranean*, ed. Maryline Parca and Angeliki Tzanetou. Bloomington: Indiana University Press.

Schmitt, Pauline. 1977. "Athena Apatouria et la ceinture: les aspects féminins des Apatouries à Athénes." *Annales: Economies, Sociétés, Civilizations* 32 (1977): 1059–73.

Schofield, Louise. 2007. *The Mycenaeans*. London: British Museum Press.

Sebesta, J. L. 1994. "Symbolism in the Costume of the Roman Woman." In *The World of Roman Costume*, ed. J. L. Sebesta and L. Bonafonte. Madison: University of Wisconsin Press.

Sebesta, J. L. 1998. "Women's Costume and Feminine Civic Morality in Augustan Rome." In *Gender and the Body in the Ancient Mediterranean*, ed. Maria Wyke. Oxford: Blackwell.

Segal, J. B. 2000. *Catalogue of Aramaic and Mandaic Incantation Bowls in the British Museum*. London: Trustees of the British Museum.

Selvidge, Mary Jean. 1990. *Woman, Cult and Miracle Recital: A Redactional Critical Investigation on Mark 5:24–34*. London: Associated University Presses.

Shaw, B. 2001. "Raising and Killing Children: Two Roman Myths." *Mnemosyne* 54: 31–77.

Shaw, M. 1975. "The Female Intruder: Women in Fifth Century Drama." *Classical Philology* 70: 255–68.

Shelton, Jo-Ann, ed. 1998. *As the Romans Did: A Sourcebook in Roman Social History*. 2nd ed. New York and Oxford: Oxford University Press.

Shopkorn, Jana. n.d. *"Til Death Do Us Part": Marriage and Funeral Rites in Classical Athens*. Available at: http://perseus.mpiwg-berlin.mpg.de/classes/JSp.html (accessed July 9, 2012).

Shotter, D.C.A. 2000. "Agrippina the Elder—a Woman in a Man's World." *Historia* 49: 341–57.

Siani-Davies, M. 1997. "Ptolemy XII. Auletes and the Romans." *Historia* 46: 306–40.

Silvan, Hagith. 1993. "Anician Women, the Cento of Proba and Aristocratic Conversion in the Fourth Century." *Vigiliae Christianae* 47 (2): 140–57.

Silvan, Hagith. 1988. "Piety and Pilgrimage in the Age of Gratian." *Harvard Theological Review* 81 (1): 59–72.

Simon, Erika. 1992. "The Diptych of the Symmachi and Nicomachi: An Interpretation. In Memoriam Wolfgang F. Volbach 1892–1988." *Greece and Rome*, 2nd ser., 39: 56–65.

Sissa, Giulia. 1990. *Greek Virginity*, trans. Arthur Goldhammer. Cambridge, MA: Harvard University Press.

Sissa, Giulia. 1990. "Maidenhood without Maidenhead." In *Before Sexuality: The Construction of Erotic Experience in the Ancient Greek World*, ed. David M. Halperin, John J. Winkler, and Froma Zeitlin. Princeton, NJ: Princeton University Press.

Sissa, Giulia. 2008. *Sex and Sexuality in the Ancient World*. New Haven, CT: Yale University Press.

Skinner, Marilyn B. 1983. "Clodia Metelli." *Transactions of the American Philological Association* 113: 273–87.

Skinner, Marilyn B. 2009. "Gender Studies." In *The Oxford Handbook of Hellenic Studies*, ed. George Boys-Stones, Barbara Graziosi, and Phiroze Vasunia. Oxford: Oxford University Press.

Skinner, Marilyn B. 2005. *Sexuality in Greek and Roman Culture*. Malden, MA: Blackwell.

Smith, R.R.R. 1991. *Hellenistic Sculpture: A Handbook*. London: Thames and Hudson.

Smith, Wesley D., ed. and trans. 1994. *Hippocrates*. Vol. 7, *Epidemics 2, 4–7*. Cambridge, MA, and London: Loeb Classical Library.

Snyder, Jane McIntosh. 1991. "Public Occasion and Private Passion in the Lyrics of Sappho of Lesbos." In *Women's History and Ancient History*, ed. Sarah B. Pomeroy. Chapel Hill: University of North Carolina Press.

Snyder, Jane McIntosh. 1989. *The Woman and the Lyre: Women Writers in Classical Greece and Rome*. Carbondale: Southern Illinois University Press.

Solon. *Fragmenta*.

Sophocles. *Antigone*.

Spencer-Wood, Suzanne M. 2006. "Feminist Gender Research in Classical Archaeology." In *Handbook of Gender in Archaeology*, ed. Sarah Milledge Nelson. Lanham, MD: AltaMira.

Spivak, Gayatri Chakravorty. 1987. *In Other Worlds: Essays in Cultural Politics*. New York: Methuen.

Spivak, Gayatri Chakravorty. 1990. *The Post-Colonial Critic: Interviews, Strategies, Dialogues*. New York: Routledge.

Stansbury-O'Donnell, Mark D. 2011. *Looking at Greek Art*. Cambridge: Cambridge University Press.

Stark, Rodney. 1996. *The Rise of Christianity: A Sociologist Reconsiders History*. Princeton, NJ: Princeton University Press.

Starr, Raymond. 1987. "The Circulation of Literary Texts in the Roman World." *Classical Quarterly* 37: 213–23.

Stehle, E. 1997. *Performance and Gender in Ancient Greece: Nondramatic Poetry in Its Setting*. Princeton, NJ: Princeton University Press.

Stewart, Andrew. 1997. *Art, Desire, and the Body in Ancient Greece*. Cambridge: Cambridge University Press.

Stewart, Andrew. 2008. *Classical Greece and the Birth of Western Art*. Cambridge: Cambridge University Press.

Stewart, Peter. 2003. *Statues in Roman Society: Representation and Response*. Oxford: Oxford University Press.

Stewart-Sykes, Alistair. 2006. *The Apostolic Church Order*. Strathfield, Australia: St. Paul's Publications.

Stewart-Sykes, Alistair. 2009. *The Didascalia Apostolorum*. Turnhout, Belgium: Brepols.

Stoneman, Richard. 1995. *Palmyra and Its Empire: Zenobia's Revolt against Rome*. Ann Arbor: University of Michigan Press.

Stratton, Kimberly B. 2007. *Naming the Witch: Magic, Ideology, and Stereotype in the Ancient World*. New York: Columbia University Press.

Suetonius. *Caligula*.

Suetonius. *Claudius*.

Suetonius. *Divus Augustus*.

Sutton, Robert F. 2000. "The Good, the Base, and the Ugly: The Drunken Orgy in Attic Vase Painting and the Athenian Self." In *Not the Classical Ideal: Athens and the Construction of the Other in Greek Art*, ed. Beth Cohen. Leiden: Brill.

Sutton, Robert F. 1992. "Pornography and Persuasion on Attic Pottery." In *Pornography and Representation in Greece and Rome*, ed. Amy Richlin. New York: Oxford University Press.

Syme, Ronald. 1971. "The Reign of Severus Alexander." In *Emperors and Biography: Studies in the Historia Augusta*, ed. R. Syme. Oxford: Oxford University Press.

Tacitus. *Annales*.

Tacitus. *Historiae*.

Takács, Sarolta A. 2008. *Vestal Virgins, Sibyls, and Matrons: Women in Roman Religion*. Austin: University of Texas Press.

Tertullian. [1959]. *On Prescription against Heretics*. In *The Ante-Nicene Fathers 3*, ed. Alexander Roberts and James Donaldson, trans. Peter Holmes. Grand Rapids, MI: Wm. B. Eerdmans.

Theognis. *Poems*.

Thietmar. 1957. *Thietmari Merseburgensis Episcopi Chronicon*, ed. W. Trillmich. Darmstadt, Germany: Wissenschaftliche Buchgesellschaft.

Thomas, B. 2002. "Constraints and Contradictions: Whiteness and Femininity in Ancient Greece." In *Women's Dress in the Ancient Greek World*, ed. Lloyd Llewellyn-Jones. London: Classical Press of Wales.

Thornham, Sue. 1997. *Passionate Detachments: An Introduction to Feminist Film Theory*. London: Arnold.

Thucydides. *Peloponnesian War.*

Thurlkill, Mary F. 2007. *Chosen among Women: Mary and Fatima in Medieval Christianity and Shi'ite Islam*. Notre Dame, IN: University of Notre Dame Press.

Thurston, Bonnie. 1998. *Women in the New Testament: Questions and Commentary*. New York: Crossroad.

Thurston, Herbert. 1910. "The Early Cultus of the Reserved Eucharist." *Journal of Theological Studies* 11: 275–79.

Torelli, Mario. 1984. *Lavinio e Roma. Riti iniziatici e matrimonio tra archeologia e storia*. Rome: Quasar.

Totelin, Laurence M.V. 2009. *Hippocratic Recipes: Oral and Written Transmission of Pharmacological Knowledge in Fifth- and Fourth-Century Greece*. Leiden: Brill.

Treggiari, Susan. 1976. "Jobs for Women." *American Journal of Ancient History* 1: 76–104.

Treggiari, Susan. 1979. "Lower-Class Women in the Roman Economy." *Florilegium* 1: 65–86.

Treggiari, Susan. 1991. *Roman Marriage: Iusti Coniuges from the Time of Cicero to the Time of Ulpian*. Oxford: Clarendon.

Treggiari, Susan. 2007. *Terentia, Tullia and Publilia: The Women of Cicero's Family*. London and New York: Routledge.

Tulloch, Janet H. 2004. "Art and Archaeology as a Historical Resource for the Study of Women in Early Christianity: An Approach for Analyzing Visual Data." *Feminist Theology* 12 (3): 277–304.

Tulloch, Janet H. 2011. "Devotional Visuality in Family Funerary Monuments in the Roman World." In *A Companion to Families in the Greek and Roman Worlds*, ed. Beryl Rawson. Malden, MA: Wiley-Blackwell.

Tulloch, Janet H. 2006. "Women Leaders in Family Funerary Banquets." In *A Woman's Place: House Churches in Earliest Christianity*, by Carolyn Osiek and Margaret Y. Macdonald. Minneapolis: Fortress.

Turton, G. 1974. *The Syrian Princesses: The Women Who Ruled Rome, AD 193–235*. London: Cassell.

Ullmann, Manfred. 1970. *Die Medizin im Islam*. Leiden: Brill.

Valerius Maximus. *Memorable Words and Deeds.*

Van Bremen, Riet. 1996. *The Limits of Participation: Women and Civic Life in the Greek East in the Hellenistic and Roman Periods*. Amsterdam: J.C. Gieben.

Van Dam, Raymond. 1988. "Images of Saint Martin in Late Roman and Early Merovingian Gaul." *Viator* 19: 1–27.

Van Dam, Raymond. 1993. *Saints and Their Miracles in Late Antique Gaul*. Princeton, NJ: Princeton University Press.

Van de Paverd, Frans. 1976. "A Text of Gregory of Nazianzus Misinterpreted by F. E. Brightman." *Orientalia Christiana Periodica* 42 (1): 197–206.

Vindolanda Tablets. Available at: http://vindolanda.csad.ox.ac.uk/.

Vitruvius. *de Architectura*.

Vivante, Bella. 2007. *Daughters of Gaia: Women in the Ancient Mediterranean World*. Westport, CT: Praeger.

Von Staden, Heinrich. 1992. "Women and Dirt." *Helios* 19: 7–30.

Von Staden, Heinrich. 1989. *Herophilus: The Art of Medicine in Early Alexandria*. Cambridge: Cambridge University Press.

Vorster, Christiane. 2007. "The Large and Small Herculaneum Women Sculptures." In *The Herculaneum Women: History, Context, Identities*, ed. Jens Daehner. Los Angeles: J. Paul Getty Museum.

Vuolanto, Ville. 2010. "Children and Religion." In *A Cultural History of Childhood and Family in Antiquity,* vol. 1, ed. R. Laurence and M. Harlow. London: Berg.

Vuolanto, Ville. 2011. "Infant Abandonment and the Christianization of Europa." In *Dark Side of Childhood in Late Antiquity and the Middle Ages*, ed. Katariina Mustakallio and Christian Laes. Oxford: Oxbow.

Wainwright, Elaine E. 2006. *Women Healing/Healing Women: The Genderization of Healing in Early Christianity*. London: Equinox.

Walker, Susan. 1983. "Women and Housing in Classical Greece: The Archaeological Evidence." In *Images of Women in Antiquity*, ed. Averil Cameron and Amélie Kuhrt. London: Croom Helm.

Wallace-Hadrill, Andrew. 1994. *Houses and Society in Pompeii and Herculaneum*. Princeton, NJ: Princeton University Press.

Warrior, Valerie M. 2006. *Roman Religion*. Cambridge Introduction to Roman Civilization. New York: Cambridge University Press.

Watson, P. A. 1995. *Ancient Stepmothers: Myth, Misogyny and Reality*. Leiden: Brill.

Welch, K. 2007. *The Roman Amphitheatre: From Its Origins to the Colosseum*. Cambridge: Cambridge University Press.

Wemple, Suzanne F. 1981. *Women in Frankish Society: Marriage and the Cloister, 500 to 900*. Philadelphia: University of Pennsylvania Press.

Whitehorne, John E. G. 1994. *Cleopatras*. London and New York: Routledge.

Wiedemann, Thomas. 1989. *Adults and Children in the Roman Empire*. London and New York: Routledge.

Wiedemann, Thomas. 1981. *Greek and Roman Slavery: A Sourcebook*. London: Croom Helm.

Wilk, Stephen R. 2000. *Medusa: Solving the Mystery of the Gorgon*. Oxford: Oxford University Press.

Willetts, R. F. 1977. *The Civilization of Ancient Crete*. London: Orion.

Williams, Craig. 1999 [2010]. *Roman Homosexuality*. Oxford: Oxford University Press.

Williams, Frank, trans. 1994. *The Panarion of Epiphanius of Salamis*. Leiden: Brill.

Williams, M. G. 1902. "Studies in the Lives of Roman Empresses: I. Julia Domna." *American Journal of Archaeology* 6: 259–305.

Williamson, Beth. 2004. *Christian Art: A Very Short Introduction*. Oxford: Oxford University Press.

Wilson, Lyn Hatherly. 1996. *Sappho's Sweet Bitter Songs: Configurations of Male and Female in Ancient Greek Lyric*. New York: Routledge.

Wilson, Stephen, ed. 1983. *Saints and Their Cults: Studies in Religious Sociology, Folklore and History.* Cambridge: Cambridge University Press.

Wilson-Kastner, Patricia. 1981. *A Lost Tradition: Women Writers in the Early Church.* Washington, DC: University Press of America.

Winkler, J. 1981. "Gardens of Nymphs: Public and Private in Sappho's Lyrics." In *Reflections of Women in Antiquity*, ed. Helene P. Foley. New York: Gordon and Breach.

Wyke, M. 1994. "Taking the Woman's Part: Engendering Roman Love Elegy." *Hermes* 23: 110–28.

Wyke, M. 1994. "Woman in the Mirror: The Rhetoric of Adornment in the Roman World." In *Women in Ancient Societies: An Illusion of the Night*, ed. L. J. Archer, S. Fischer, and M. Wyke. London: Routledge.

Xenophon. *Constitution of the Lacedaemonians.*

Xenophon. *Oeconomicus.*

Younger, John. 1997. "Gender and Sexuality in the Parthenon Frieze." In *Naked Truths: Women, Sexuality, and Gender in Classical Art and Archaeology*, ed. Ann Koloski-Ostrow and Claire Lyons. London: Routledge.

Zaidman, Louise Bruit. 1992. "Pandora's Daughters and Rituals in Grecian Cities." In *History of Women I: From Ancient Goddesses to Christian Saints*, ed. Pauline Schmit Pantel. Cambridge, MA: Harvard University Press.

Zeitlin, Froma I. 1996. *Playing the Other: Gender and Society in Classical Greek Literature.* Chicago: University of Chicago Press.

Zeitlin, Froma I. 1995. "Signifying Difference: The Myth of Pandora." In *Women in Antiquity: New Assessments*, ed. Richard Hawley and Barbara Levick. London and New York: Routledge.

Zlotnick, Helena. 2002. *Dinah's Daughters: Gender and Judaism from the Hebrew Bible to Late Antiquity*. Philadelphia: University of Pennsylvania Press.

CONTRIBUTORS

Shelby Brown, specialist for academic and adult audiences at the J. Paul Getty Museum, Getty Villa, Malibu, California, is a classical archaeologist and classicist interested in the ways societies categorize people as "others." She has published on ancient institutionalized violence, gender bias, and feminist art history. Other interests include teaching people of all ages about classical culture, art, and archaeology.

Lynda Garland is professor and head of school in the Faculty of Arts and Sciences, School of Humanities, University of New England, New South Wales, Australia. Her research interests include Byzantine social and political history, the Crusades, ancient Greek and Roman history, and women and religion.

Allison Glazebrook is associate professor of classics at Brock University, St. Catharines, Ontario, Canada. Her research focuses on women and female sexuality, with a specific interest in the female prostitute. She has published on Greek oratory, Attic vase painting and Athenian law. She is co-editor (with M. M. Henry) of *Greek Prostitutes in the Ancient Mediterranean, 800 B.C.E–200 C.E* (2011).

Marcia Lindgren is a lecturer and director of the Latin program in the Department of Classics at the University of Iowa, where she received MA and PhD degrees in classics. Her teaching and research interests include pedagogy, Roman poetry, gender in antiquity, and the promotion of the study of classical languages.

Nicola Mellor completed her PhD at the University of Reading in 2008 on the subject of women as symbols in early Christian texts, particularly focusing on the letters of Jerome of Strido. She works for an educational charity in the United Kingdom.

Kristina Milnor is professor at Barnard College in the Department of Classics and Ancient Studies. Her research interests focus on Latin literature, feminist theory, and Roman social history in the late republic and early Roman Empire. She has published on gender studies and law in the age of Augustus. Her most recent book is *Graffiti and the Literary Landscape in Roman Pompeii* (2013).

Steven Muir is professor of religious studies at Concordia University College of Alberta, Canada. He has published articles on religious healing, charity, group conflict, and the interplay between religion and travel in the classical, Hellenistic, and Roman periods.

Katariina Mustakallio, currently director of Institutum Romanum Finlandiae and senior lecturer of history at the University of Tampere, Finland, has concentrated her studies on Roman religion, gender, and the life span. Some of her recent publications include *De Amicitia: Friendship and Social Networks in Antiquity and the Middle Ages* (Acta IRF 36, 2009), *The Dark Side of Childhood in Late Antiquity and the Middle Ages* (2011), and *On Old Age: Approaching Death in Antiquity and the Middle Ages* (2011).

Laurence Totelin is a lecturer in ancient history at the University of Cardiff, United Kingdom. She works on the history of ancient science and medicine, with a particular interest in gender issues. Her publications include *Hippocratic Recipes: Oral and Written Transmission of Pharmacological Knowledge in Fifth- and Fourth-Century Greece* (2009).

Janet H. Tulloch is a contract instructor in the College of Humanities, Carleton University, Ottawa, Canada. Her research interests focus on visual theory and symbolism in ancient religions with a particular emphasis on women. Her most recent publication is "Visual Representations of Children and Ritual in the Early Roman Empire," *Studies in Religion/Sciences Religieuses* 41 no. 3 (September 2012): 408–38.

INDEX